About this Series: General Editor, Abdullahi A. An-Na'im

The present book is the outcome of two related research projects led by Professor Abdullahi A. An-Na'im at the School of Law, Emory University, and funded by the Ford Foundation. Both projects deploy the notion of cultural transformation to promote human rights in African and Islamic societies. The first explores this notion in theoretical terms and then focuses on issues of women and land in Africa from customary, religious and statutory rights perspectives, with a view to linking research to advocacy, for securing the rights of women to own or control land as a vital economic resource. The second project is a global study of Islamic family law, including some country studies and thematic studies, from a human rights perspective. Four volumes are being published at this stage of these on-going projects:

VOLUME I *Cultural Transformation and Human Rights in Africa*, edited by Abdullahi A. An-Na'im

VOLUME II *Islamic Family Law in a Changing World: A Global Resource Book*, edited by Abdullahi A. An-Na'im

VOLUME III *Women and Land in Africa: Linking Research to Advocacy*, edited by L. Muthoni Wanyeki

VOLUME IV *Women's Rights and Islamic Family Law: Perspectives on Reform*, edited by Lynn Welchman

Women's Rights and Islamic Family Law: Perspectives on Reform

edited by
Lynn Welchman

Zed Books Ltd
LONDON • NEW YORK

Women's Rights and Islamic Family Law: Perspectives on Reform was first published by Zed Books Ltd, 7 Cynthia Street, London N1 9JF, UK and Room 400, 175 Fifth Avenue, New York, NY 10010, USA in 2004.

www.zedbooks.co.uk

Cover designed by Andrew Corbett
Set in Monotype Baskerville and Univers Black by Ewan Smith, London
Printed and bound in the EU by Biddles Ltd, www.biddles.co.uk

Distributed in the USA exclusively by Palgrave Macmillan, a division of St Martin's Press, LLC, 175 Fifth Avenue, New York, NY 10010.

A catalogue record for this book is available from the British Library
Library of Congress Cataloging-in-Publication Data: available

ISBN 1 84277 094 2 cased
ISBN 1 84277 095 0 limp

Contents

Tables

Part II

Acknowledgements

As editor of this volume, I would first like to thank Abdullahi an-Na'im for paying me the honour of asking me to undertake this function, and Robert Molteno, Editor at Zed Press. My particular thanks go to the authors: Essam Fawzy, Lisa Hajjar, Rema Hammami, Penny Johnson, Fadwa Labadi, Asifa Quraishi and Najeeba Syeed-Miller, for their efforts in their different pieces and for their generous and prompt responses to editorial comments and inquiries. The different papers also name and thank a number of other researchers, and I would add the names of Ivesa Luebban for her work on the Egyptian case study, and Ashraf Hesain, research assistant for the Egypt study. Also to be thanked are the hundreds of respondents and interviewees whose opinions and insights have informed different parts of the papers in this volume. I am also particularly grateful to Joyce Song and Fouzia Khan, for their intensive and cheerful assistance in final stages, and to Scott Newton for his constructive input. My thanks also go to my family (the Knights and the Smiths); my friends, especially Randa Alami, Laila Othman Asser and Sara Hossain; and to my husband, Akram Khatib, for everything.

Introduction

Lynn Welchman

§ THE papers presented in this volume were produced as part of the project Islamic Family Law: Possibilities of Reform through Internal Initiatives, directed by Professor Abdullahi An-Na'im at the Law and Religion Programme of Emory University. This is the second volume to have been produced from this research project, the first being *Islamic Family Law in the World Today: A Resource Book*, edited by Abdullahi An-Na'im (2002). The project, starting from an approach 'conditioned by a strong commitment to universal human rights norms, especially the human rights of women and children', explained in its mandate that:

> In many settings, Islamic family law is the contested ground between conservative and fundamentalist forces, on the one hand, and modernist and liberal trends, on the other. Unfortunately, the cause of genuine and legitimate reform is often lost in such rhetorical absolutist confrontation. [...] To be effective in practice, reform proposals must not only be conceived and framed in realistic terms, but should also be advocated in ways that motivate and empower actual or potential supporters working within their own communities.

The papers presented in this volume reflect these statements in different ways. The focus is not the 'compatibility' of '*shari'a*' with 'universal human rights norms' or vice versa, a debate much covered in the literature and given historical and political context in Lisa Hajjar's contribution. Rather, the authors examine the specifics of the 'contested ground' of Islamic family law: at what different levels, why, how and by whom this ground is contested in the particular contexts they examine. These examinations are presented with a view to considering and serving as a resource for internal initiatives aimed at expanding and protecting women's rights in the family as articulated in human rights norms. The papers accordingly consider the directions of other 'reform' initiatives and perceptions of women's rights in Islamic family law, including activist positions articulated by those associated with Islamist movements, as well as dominant interpretations articulated by establishment authorities (including states) of what those rights are. Many of the initiatives considered in the papers thus deal explicitly with contested understandings of what 'Islamic family law' (or what '*shari'a*') 'is' or 'is becoming' from the perspectives of a variety of actors. The papers were written by researchers from different disciplines of the social sciences engaged at different levels with the contexts and in some cases the movements and initiatives about which they write. Three of the papers (Egypt, Palestine, USA) were produced as case or country studies, the fourth (on domestic violence) as a thematic study.

Of the case studies, those on Egypt and Palestine include and analyse the results of opinion surveys on critical and contested points of family law, as well as more contextual social questions. In Egypt (Part I), Essam Fawzy provides three different sets of data, the first a public opinion survey eliciting expectations and understandings of different elements of marriage among male and female respondents (for example, what is the real point of dower? What is the ideal age of marriage?). The study then moves on to examine attitudes of the respondents to key issues in Law no. 1 of 2000, often referred to as 'the law of *khul*' in reference to its establishment of a woman's right to secure a *khul* divorce from the court (a 'judicial *khul*', in the event that her husband is refusing to agree to divorce her) by returning her dower and waiving any remaining financial rights. These data are complemented by a further survey of opinions on key provisions of Law no. 1 of 2000 using a sample selected from among more elite social sectors – opinion-makers, the judiciary, civil society activists and so on. The study closes with summaries of recommendations for reform made by civil society activists and members of the judiciary in regard to Muslim family law in Egypt.

The Palestine case study (Part II) examines the debates around Muslim family law in the West Bank and Gaza Strip in the 'transitional' period following the conclusion of the Oslo Accords and until the end of 2001. This study is presented as a series of papers by members of the research team from the Institute of Women's Studies at Birzeit University, including Rema Hammami, Penny Johnson and Fadwa Labadi, a team I was honoured to join. In its consideration of societal opinions on issues related to women's rights in the family, this paper compares the results of previous surveys of public opinion with the survey undertaken for this study, indicating the impact of public debates on these opinions and perceptions in the intervening years. The study situates the debates and issues into both 'the processes of state formation and social dynamics within Palestinian society'. It thus examines the workings of the Palestinian Authority and the role of civil society groups in Palestine (especially the women's movement) to determine factors of relevance for advocacy and strategies for reform, set out at the end. Annexed to the study is an examination of the ways in which bereaved families 'mobilized several legal systems and systems of rule to seek justice and compensation, utilizing both the public channels of law and government and the processes of customary law' revolving around the traditional (and '*shar'i*') institution of *diya*, following a tragic factory fire in Hebron in which fourteen female workers burned to death.

The third country study in this volume, by Asifa Quraishi and Najeeba Syeed-Miller (Part III), considers the role of Islamic family law for Muslims in the United States, identifying the actors who invoke or recognize the rules, and the processes by which they do so, and analysing the application of those rules with or without the intervention of the formal US legal system. The authors survey the sources of information on family law available to Muslims in the USA in a discussion of 'authority figures' and with reference also to a wealth of information available on dedicated websites. Practice is examined *inter alia* in the light of the authors' empirical knowledge of the field, and the positions taken by US courts on a variety of issues from marriage itself to dower and divorce are reviewed, with a view not only to establishing trends in different courts but to identifying the judicial understandings (or misunderstandings) of institutions such as the dower (or dowry). The study concludes with an examination of the 'significant trends of reform and activism addressing Islamic family law' among Muslim communities in the USA, the potential of these actors, and the challenges and opportunities of the particular context of the USA.

Part IV, by Lisa Hajjar, is a broader thematic consideration of family law and intra-family violence, which identifies the 'challenges of contesting and altering' inequalities and hierarchies within family roles and relations where the assertion of '*shari'a*' as the authority for these hierarchies may complicate advocacy efforts for changes to the regulatory framework (including issues of male 'guardianship' or 'authority' over women, women's divorce rights and other matters). Given that domestic violence is a truly global phenomenon, she seeks to provide resource tools for advocacy by reviewing the actions of states in specific contexts. She examines, *inter alia*, different interpretations of Sura 4: 34 of the Qur'an, ranging from views in 'classical' jurisprudence that permitted 'light physical discipline' of the wife by her husband in certain circumstances, to more recent interpretations (citing scholars in the USA and in Iran) disallowing any use of force and the juxtaposition of other Qur'anic verses enjoining good relations and mutual kindness between spouses. This examination is undertaken since 'although the problem of domestic violence and efforts to deter and combat it are global in scope, any possibility for success must involve strategies and analyses that resonate with cultural and religious norms and values'. Her main focus is on manifestations and implications of gender inequality, patriarchy in social relations, social (and judicial) dealings, and 'state patriarchy', or more specifically state failure to combat effectively the various manifestations of gender violence she considers. The paper is an attempt to consider a very complex set of issues complicated further by a general lack of adequate data on domestic violence whether in countries with Muslim majorities or anywhere else in the world.

A consideration of themes recurring in the four papers follows below. It remains to be noted that the papers were researched and written independently by the authors and vary in their approaches and analyses. Accordingly, no one paper necessarily reflects the views of the other authors, or indeed of myself as editor of this volume.

The case studies summarized above tell different stories about the ways in which

'Islamic family law' is understood, presented and applied by states, judiciaries, scholars, politicians, activists and lay Muslims in particular national and socio-economic contexts, and discuss the multiple and divergent implications for pro-tecting and strengthening women's rights in the family. The complex, multiple and shifting dynamics of the debates on family law are matched by a recognition of the varying needs and priorities of women positioned differently in the various contexts. The ground is contested not only at the ideological/political level: what Lila Abu-Lughod (1998: 243) calls 'that familiar dynamic of postcolonial politics in which "the woman question" animates political and ideological contests couched in the language of cultural authenticity versus foreign influence'. It is also contested at the pragmatic level of reform strategies. The relationship of 'Islamic family law' to identity – national, communal, cultural and individual – and thus to the politics of identity is a particular factor for consideration by those seeking change in existing regulatory regimes – as for that matter is the nature of the state or political authority, and the notion of 'citizenship' in relation to 'the family'. Moreover and concurrently, in all the contexts considered in this volume, 'authority' and/or 'voice' in the representation of 'Islamic family law' is contested.

In the Muslim countries considered in this volume, Muslim family law is governed by 'Islamic family law' as codified by the state. Suggestions for even an optional civil law for those wishing to marry outside a religious jurisdiction are currently resisted in Palestine, as discussed in the study, and a similar proposal in Lebanon was shelved. In the USA, the case study examines the practice of Muslims choosing to regulate their family life under principles of Islamic family law within the official civil legal system of the USA. Thus, the reform strategies considered here might often be understood as a contest of 'Islamic norms', provided one follows Dupret's distinction (1999: 32, following Lochack 1993: 393) of justificatory normativity or normality ('the usual condition, encountered in most cases') and prescriptive normativity ('the abstract formulation of what ought to be'). If the 'actors in the legal sphere' often tend 'to make justificatory norma-tivity and prescriptive normativity coincide' (Dupret 1999: 32), the approach of reform-minded activists is rather the opposite: just because that's how it *is*, it doesn't mean that's how it *has to be*. In many ways, the term 'reform' in this context might be substituted with 'reformulation'.

As brief background, particular areas of Islamic family law that preoccupied Muslim states issuing codifications of 'Islamic family law' as part of nation- and state-building projects in the twentieth century included polygyny and the hus-band's power of unilateral repudiation (*talaq*), both of which have been constrained to varying extents; child custody, where efforts have been made to extend the period of custody assigned to the mother following termination of a marriage; the age of marriage, and the constraint of the authority of the male guardian in the marriage of females; widening a wife's access to divorce; extending an ex-husband's financial obligations towards a wife 'unjustly' or 'arbitrarily' divorced;

constraining the wife's duty of 'obedience', particularly in regard to waged labour outside the home and an end to forcible implementation of court rulings requiring a 'disobedient' wife to return to the marital home. Many states have also legislated for the enforcement of stipulations that may be included in the marriage contract by the spouses, holding the potential to alter certain aspects of the otherwise 'standard' regulatory regime within the marriage. While the gender-specific inheritance portions of the 'classical' rules have largely been maintained, '[t]he special position of agnates in inheritance law has been restricted, and measures have been taken to favour the basic family unit at the expense of patrilineal heirs' (Moors 1999: 142).

As the articles in this volume show, many of these issues remain – again, to varying extents depending on the particular context – a focus for the efforts of those wishing to see further protection and expansion of women's rights in the family, including, in many countries and communities, women's movements, human rights movements and social reform movements. Individuals and groups engaged in these efforts work from a variety of perspectives and in complex and specific socio-economic and political contexts. The question of voice and authority in prescriptive normativity remains an issue in the US Muslim communities as well in Egypt and Palestine. The fact that 'Islamic family law' is asserted, expressed and lived at different levels, many beyond the reach of the state, is a feature of all the studies, and, if not a particularly surprising one in itself, invites specific consideration. Although the state (in all its heterogeneous make-up) is recognized as a (sometimes the) key actor, normative pluralism (or legal pluralism; Griffiths 1999: viii) that denies the state monopoly as the originator or legitimizer of 'law' has critical significance for the reform strategies discussed.

In his exposition of a three-level interacting structure of law consisting of official law, unofficial law and legal postulates, Masaji Chiba (1986: 5) includes Islamic law among his examples of religious laws that might be termed 'official law' although not entirely 'state law': 'religious law may be partially included in or accommodated by state law, but partially functioning out of the jurisdiction of the latter, thus forming its own system different from state law'. Arabi's (2001: 193) references to 'state Islamic law' in modern Muslim states may coincide with Berger's (1999: 113) description of 'formal *shari'a*' in Syria as being those parts of *shari'a* incorporated into the legislation of the state, while 'informal *shari'a*' is 'all *shari'a* which is being applied, but which is not promulgated as law by the legislator'. The reference to 'informal *shari'a*' serves to remind us of the reach of *shari'a* beyond subjects addressed in state law (Berger's examples are pilgrimage and alms giving). The 'voluntarism' that characterizes compliance with 'informal *shari'a*' in Muslim states applies also to the application of Islamic family law by Muslims in the United States, where Islamic law is best described in Chiba's scheme as unofficial law, underpinned by a basic legal postulate among those Muslims who choose to regulate their family relations in accordance therewith. Chiba's explanation of a legal postulate is a 'value principle or value system, specifically connected with a particular official or unofficial law, which acts to found, justify, and orient the latter' (Chiba 1986: 6). In Egypt and Palestine, 'state Islamic law' governs family law for Muslims; as Arabi (2001: 190) puts it: 'Islamic family law still occupies pride of place in the jurisdictional system of modern Muslim states as the only domain of *shari'a* to have successfully resisted westernisation.' Chiba's definition of official law may cover 'Islamic law' in general, given constitutional recognition of the *shari'a* (although with differences) in both. Nevertheless, the assertion of *'shar'i* norms' in opposition to the particular provisions of state Islamic law is described in both case studies, illustrating Dupret's (1999: 39) description of 'each actor's relationship with the norm' as 'highly strategic in nature' and constituting a significant factor in reform strategies on the ground.

Thus, to the 'outright normative pluralism' of pre-nineteenth-century *shari'a* (Arabi 2001: 194), with its diversity of rulings and norms, have been added the developing norms of 'positivized' state Islamic law. Arabi considers the developments as follows:

> This major reconstruction of Islamic law, both in substance and procedure, is issuing in what might be termed a new *shari'a* [...] Modern Islamic law is better viewed as what present-day Muslim jurists, legislators, judges and theologians take to be Islamic provisions and rulings in the altered, complex world of today, rather than an a priori-constituted corpus that is conserved, albeit in an astoundingly rich variety, in classical legal manuals. (ibid., p. 18)

In this vein, Arabi (ibid., p. 188) considers as a 'radical break with extant Islamic family law' the promulgation of the provision on judicial *khul'* in Egypt whereby a wife may obtain a divorce from the court if she returns the dower and waives her other *shar'i* financial rights. Under the 'classical' rulings, this type of divorce involved the consent of the husband, since it was he, not a court, who issued the divorce. Arabi considers this to have given effect to the original intention of the source texts considered, and draws conclusions from this about the mechanisms through which the state is able to approach its 'reconstruction' of Islamic law. The idea of a (in this case) state law-led 'new *shari'a*' may take some support from the fact that in Jordan, on the last day of 2001, King Abdullah II issued a temporary law in the absence of a sitting parliament amending the law of personal status (itself issued as a temporary law) including the establishment of judicial *khul'* in a provision very similar (though not identical) to the Egyptian precedent.

However, the manner of promulgation of the Jordanian law is also quite telling. In this volume, Fawzy points up the opposition voiced to the Egyptian provision on judicial *khul'* *inter alia* on the grounds of *qiwama*, the *shar'i* principle considered in dominant interpretations as according authority to males over females in family relations and frequently articulated in the manner of a basic value principle or postulate. From Fawzy's account, those defending the provision asserted their reading of the specific source texts in support of a provision that on a practical level fitted the needs of contemporary Egyptian society, rather than taking up directly the concept of *qiwama*. In the public opinion survey, while 60 per cent of the 'elite' sample questioned declared support for the provision (Table 1.22), slightly fewer of the respondents in the general public opinion sample were in favour than were opposed, with more women than men in support (Table 1.29). In Hammami's data from Palestine, around a third of respondents in the sample stated they would support the enactment of a similar law in Palestine, with slightly more women than men in support, but with many of those opposed, particularly women, expressing reservations not because of an opposition to women's right to divorce as such, but rather because 'women should not lose their property rights' in order to secure one (Table II.13). This can be seen as an articulation of a general sense of 'justice' that a considerable constituency might expect to see represented in state-issued Islamic family law, a subject discussed further below.

The above material shows something of the workings of the 'mechanisms of the Islamic reference' (Dupret 1999: 40). The fact that something is legislated by the state as Islamic family law does not necessarily make it so to those outside the process. In the context of the 1979 personal status legislation in Egypt, Fawzy notes particular opposition to the law's presumption of injury in the case of a man's polygynous marriage, entitling the existing wife to a divorce; he cites Shmais (1994) on one judge stating that he had 'refused to implement the law and had postponed all such cases referred to him'. Since the relevant Qur'anic verses are generally understood as permitting polygyny, albeit under certain constraints, the difficulty lay in the state law presuming an injury in situations contemplated as legitimate under dominant interpretations of the source texts. In this instance, the 'radical break' with the 'classical' rules was reversed by the state in deference to the opposition when the 1979 law was repealed and replacement legislation issued in 1985 required the wife to establish such injury should she wish to seek a divorce as a result of her husband's marriage.

On the other hand, the Egyptian law maintained its notification requirements, requiring that the existing wife and the new wife both be made aware of the husband's polygynous status. These requirements have been adopted in many Muslim states, with the stated objective of protecting the rights of the women involved. As well as the protection objective, such state law requirements open the space for intervention by other potential sources of constraint upon the husband's conduct: the women, particularly perhaps the first wife, and their families. In his consideration of 'ambulant marriage' in Saudi Arabia, Arabi (2001: 160) notes that secrecy is a 'frequent concomitant of polygamous marriage in general', and considers as follows the objections to ambulant marriage on grounds of its secret character: 'the proclamation of the second marriage and thus its disclosure to the first wife is a tactical move aimed to implicate the husband in the inevitable unhappy conflict with his first wife, *umm al-'iyal*, the mother of the children, consequent upon her knowledge of his second marriage' (p. 161).

In Egypt, Fawzy notes that one of the motivating factors for men to conclude

'urfi marriages ('customary' marriage, discussed further below) is to conceal the
fact of the second marriage from the first wife, who would be notified of it if he
complied with the registration requirements of state law. In the public opinion
survey, Fawzy reports that a large number of male respondents objected to the
requirements that their marital status be disclosed, while all the women respondents approved; surely a validation of the expectation that such procedures effect
a change in the balance of power through the likely mobilization of effective
intervention by non-state actors.

The diverse attitudes of Muslims in the USA towards polygyny are discussed
by Quraishi and Syeed-Miller in this volume. Here, those Muslim men not only
asserting but acting on what they consider to be a right under Islamic law to marry
polygynously illustrate the 'relation of conflict' described by Woodman (1999: 17)
in a situation of normative pluralism. On the other hand, some of the arguments
being made from within the Islamic law framework for the acceptance of the
secular prohibition are indicative of attempts at 'integration' of norms: thus, for
example, the argument that 'because the subsequent wives are not legally married
under the laws [of the USA] then by definition they are not treated equally, a
requirement of Islamic law in polygynous marriages'. Another example given by
Quraishi and Syeed-Miller is 'the simple jurisprudential principle that one must
obey the laws of the land where one chooses to live, as long as they do not prevent
one from performing one's religious obligations'. Polygyny being by no means an
obligation, the argument is made that the US law should be respected.

In Palestine, the Jordanian and Egyptian legislation governing Muslim personal
status in the West Bank and Gaza Strip respectively does not contain the notification requirements legislated in more recent years by Jordan and Egypt, nor yet
specific provision for the wife to seek to establish injury in pursuit of a judicial
divorce in the event that her husband marries another wife. In light of this,
Hammami notes that 20 per cent of respondents in the sample cited a polygynous
marriage as an acceptable reason for divorce: 'it is significant that there is even
this amount of support for divorce on grounds not recognized as such by prevailing personal status law'. Of equal significance is her finding that 'a "nationalist"
justification, the husband being a "political collaborator", came out as the 'number
one acceptable reason' for women to seek divorce (Table 11.10). Nationalist postulates born of a specific political experience and community response thus produce
the specifics of a vision of a Palestinian personal status law that the significant
majority of respondents in the sample consider should be governed 'by *shari'a*'.
As Dupret observes:

> [T]he invocation of 'Islam' or '*shari'a*' as a legal repertoire does not mean that
> we are dealing with Islamic law in its classical and technical sense. From a
> sociological perspective, 'Islam' is what Muslims claim that Islam is and
> 'Islamic law' is what Muslim people characterize as Islamic law. The fact that
> people utter the word '*fiqh*' or '*shari'a*,' or use a lexicon which I call the 'Islamic

repertoire' [...] does not mean that there is a necessary connection between present and past uses of the terms of this lexicon. (Dupret 2001: 44)

Nor should it be assumed that those invoking '*shari'a*' themselves assume such a connection, at least on the level of detailed rules; the strategic articulation of such a connection by politically engaged advocates or opponents of change (state law reform being an inescapably political process) is to be differentiated from the 'legal postulate' or, as discussed further below, the 'doxa' of *shari'a* and its connection with Muslim personal status law.

One area of the relationship between state authority and the normative authority assigned to 'the *shari'a*' that arises in the three country studies in this volume is the bureaucratic requirements imposed by states on matters of marriage and divorce. Registration with some 'official' or 'central' authority serves a number of purposes, including information on and a degree of control over the 'private' affairs of citizens, and the possibility of levying fees or taxes, but also the potential for ensuring that other laws laid down by the state are in fact being observed and upheld: those on the minimum age of marriage, and the consent of parties to the contract, for example. The 'classical' rules of Islamic law did not make the validity of a marriage or a divorce conditional upon any form of written documentation, let alone registration with a central authority. Formal procedures of registration have generally been legislated in Muslim states, but do not necessarily affect the validity of a marriage or divorce not so registered, in deference to the continuing currency of the 'classical' rules. In Egypt, the debate over '*urfi* marriage described by Fawzy in this volume illustrates the resulting tension. He describes '*urfi* marriage as 'the most popular means of getting around the constraints imposed by law on marriage and divorce in Egypt'. Egyptian law requires registration and denies jurisdiction to the courts to hear claims arising from unregistered marriages in the event one of the parties denies the union. The new Egyptian Law no. 1 of 2000 includes a provision allowing a party possessing written evidence (such as the customary '*urfi* document) establishing an unregistered marriage to apply for a divorce from the court, although still not to realize any other rights from the marriage through the court process. Provided an unregistered marriage complied with the *shar'i* requirements, it is still valid, and the attempt to encourage registration through judicial non-enforcement of the *shar'i* rights and duties arising accordingly had, judging from Fawzy's discussion, in many cases badly disadvantaged the female party to such a marriage. In the event of a non-amicable breakdown or desertion, for example, she would not only be unable to seek to enforce maintenance and dower rights through the courts but also be unable to obtain a divorce, leaving her, in Fawzy's words, 'suspended'. As further background, Fawzy also notes some of the motivations for entering into an '*urfi* marriage, including as noted above keeping the fact of a polygynous union from an existing wife, but also 'a woman who does not want to lose her entitlement to her former husband's pension, or a widow seeking to keep her son exempted from military service as her only son and sole provider' – women who would not therefore wish their new marriage to come to the attention of the state authorities and whose desire to marry under the *shari'a* is satisfied by the *'urfi* institution. Of possibly more political significance, Fawzy also notes the support given to the institution of *'urfi* marriage by 'the religious tendency in the universities', an assertion of legitimacy beyond state control coinciding with the interests of those feeling burdened by the state-imposed rules.

In Palestine, the institution of *'urfi* marriage was referred to as harming the rights of wives in a *fatwa* from the Supreme Fatwa Council supporting existing registration requirements and an increase in the criminal sanction for failure to comply. Registration procedures were presented as legitimate requirements by the state in order to protect society and in particular the rights of the wife. Although a criminal offence, failure to register does not affect the validity of a marriage, nor is recourse denied at court if the marriage can be established to have been valid under *shar'i* rules. A few years later, however, the Council issued another *fatwa*, this time on the question of a minimum age for marriage, where the reference was to 'classical' rules without reference to the minimum ages of capacity (of fifteen and sixteen) under Jordanian law applied in the West Bank and below which marriage is a criminal offence and could not of course be registered under the terms of existing law. Johnson puts the later *fatwa* in the context of the extensive and heated public debates on family law, including considerable public and establishment support for the age of capacity for marriage to be raised (Table 11.9), which had occurred in the years following the *fatwa* in support of increased state intervention in the matter of registration requirements. At the same time, the head of the *shari'a* courts issued administrative directives to the court personnel tightening procedures of registration, having previously expressed concern at instances of parents trying to marry off underage daughters. The Council's reference only to 'classical' rules thus avoids the norms both of codified law and of a significant section of Palestinian society, while presumably finding a resonance with certain others.

In the USA, Quraishi and Syeed-Miller explore Muslim marriage practices ranging from concluding a Muslim marriage contract without complying with state licence and registration requirements, to having two separate events ('a Muslim ceremony as well as a civil ceremony through state channels'), to a Muslim marriage ceremony conducted by an officiant licensed by the state which ensures simultaneous validity under US law. An interesting point of resonance with the Egyptian case study is provided by the authors' discussion of the increasing attention being given by US Muslims to the insertion of special stipulations in the marriage contract. The Egyptian case study examines the new marriage contract document issued after Law no. 1 of 2000 with space for such stipulations, and provides a list of conditions that respondents in the sample held to be of priority. Fawzy sees great potential value for the protection and expansion of women's rights in the family in this development, and on asking female respondents in the public opinion survey to rank in order of priority stipulations that might be included in a marriage contract finds that top of the list was the wife's power of delegated *talaq*, followed (with urban/rural differences) by the wife's right to go out to work, and then the completion of her education. It remains to be seen whether these opinions translate into practice; of all possible stipulations, it is perhaps delegated divorce that has the potential to affect most fundamentally the 'power balance' within the marital relationship, and accordingly may prove difficult to negotiate. Examinations of marriage contracts in the Palestinian West Bank have variously found the most common stipulation to concern the location of the marital home or the fact that it should be in 'independent accommodation' (Welchman 1999: 72; 2000: 166), with fewer rather than more contracts including a general delegation of *talaq* to the wife in the later years.

Behind the Egyptian marriage document lies a project initiated in the non-governmental sector with the idea of including in the state-issued marriage contract document a list of stipulations which would form part of the agreed rules governing the marriage unless the parties struck them out. The effect would have been to address the general lack of awareness of the possibility of such protective stipulations and problems in phrasing them in such a way as to give them legal value should it be needed. Crucially, it would reverse the burden during the negotiating process, away from the party seeking to have stipulations inserted and on to the party resisting their terms; the proposed list included, for example, the wife's right to delegated divorce, to continue her education, to go out to work and to travel abroad, as well as an agreement that the spouses would cooperate in work, looking after the family and the house and bringing up children, and a limit on the amount of time that either spouse might work outside the country.

Commenting on these proposals, Zulfikar and al-Sadda (1996: 251) presented the project as an effort 'to encourage frankness, mutual understanding and dialogue' between the spouses, reduce the need to have recourse to the courts in difficult and bitter litigation procedures, and 'raise awareness of legal and *shar'i* rights and encourage people to exercise them'. In Part III of this volume, Quraishi and Syeed-Miller report that Muslim women's organizations and activists in the USA 'see the use of additional stipulations as a tool for women's empowerment' but also that 'far from considering it a new, reformist tool many see the proactive use of the Islamic marriage contract as a way of protecting their basic Islamic rights' in the sense of a means 'for both spouses to proactively express partnership in their new, unique union'. These and other motivations are discussed by the authors as underlying the insertion of different stipulations, 'despite a realization by the couple that a US court will likely not enforce such terms'.

Whether or not such stipulations are enforceable in court, their assertion as norms governing a particular marriage is, in these contexts, voluntary. The choice of stipulations, and the ability to insert them, depends on the particular circumstances and aspirations of the parties involved. The 'normalization' of stipulations somewhat different to the examples given above is described by Arabi (2001: 147–

67) as 'grass roots law-making' – the development in Saudi Arabia of 'ambulant marriage' as a 'highly specific legal structure possessing features of religiously lawful marriage [...] in a strikingly novel configuration'. This reformulation includes the wife's consent to stay at her parents' house and therefore the lapsing of the obligation of the husband to provide her with accommodation, and the lack of cohabitation, with the husband 'visiting [...] his wife's residence during certain hours'. Under 'classical' rules, stipulations that a husband would not pay maintenance or cohabit with his wife would not have been valid, impacting as they do on rights arising directly from the contract. Arabi observes that such stipulations would impact on the 'gender power structure at the base of Muslim marriage', since the Qur'anic norm of *qiwama* linking male material support of women with their authority over them is in the dominant interpretations treated as prescriptive, not justificatory. Arabi emphasizes the 'expansive use of the principle of mutual consent [...] as a cornerstone for the validity of the contract' and that, for those arranging such marriages, 'what carried weight was the future partners' mutual consent to the specific financial, cohabitation and secrecy stipulations of their contract'. Opposition to the practice on the grounds of the rights of an existing wife has already been noted, and the Grand Mufti's eventual endorsement of such contracts was conditioned on the requirement that the marriage be made public, rather than kept secret.

Arabi's analysis is focused on the development of norms among non-state and non-establishment lay actors, culminating in their formal endorsement as *shar'i* by authority figures, an endorsement apparently not critical before the fact to the participants' own perception of their arrangements as *shar'i*. Where the use of special stipulations is included in strategies of reform (or reformulation), proactive and conscious efforts are made to emphasize the *shar'i* validity of consensual arrangements expressing the nature of the partnership, as described in the USA and in Egypt. Similarly, considerable effort is invested in articulating and seeking to normalize interpretations of the source texts that challenge dominant interpretations which, it is argued, owe more to an underlying postulate of patriarchy than to inherent 'meanings' of the texts. Thus Quraishi and Syeed-Miller describe the work of al-Hibri in the USA as 'emphasizing the ways that Islamic principles promote women's liberty in a way contrary to how these principles were applied and interpreted in patriarchal Muslim societies, ultimately leading to biases in the law itself'. Particular attention is paid to the interpretations of the texts on male superiority/authority/guardianship, challenging understandings of a prescriptive norm underlying specific rules on, for example, male guardianship at marriage, the wife's duty of obedience, divorce, child custody and polygyny. They also include the issue of domestic violence: Quraishi and Syeed-Miller report that 'the idea of male superiority sometimes is used to justify physical and mental abuse of other family members, especially women and children, presented as somehow endorsed by the *shari'a*' and describe current moves in the US Muslim communities to 'take proactive steps inspired by Islamic principles to respond to the situation'.

Hajjar similarly reviews interpretative work on the source texts by scholars based in the USA and in Iran, as part of the challenge 'to cultivate a persuasive distinction between "culture" and violence against women'. With an eye on the state as key to the protection of women from domestic violence, she examines how various failings on the state level inflate 'the importance of family and kinship relations for social survival'. This in turn complicates demands for the empowerment of women as a 'threat' to family stability, a theme reported by Fawzy in the Egyptian debates over expanding women's divorce rights and by Johnson in regard to the debates provoked by the model parliament. The challenges faced by activists fighting domestic violence are, as Hajjar explains, critically compounded by the choices made by states in their regulation of family relations, and a state may endorse conservative interpretations of Islamic family law 'as a means of shifting critical attention from its own failings on to the putative dangers posed by advocates of women's rights'.

While recognizing different understandings, expectations and applications of 'Islamic family law', it is official law, in the sense of state-issued 'Islamic family law', that was the focus of the particular reform initiatives considered in the Egyptian and Palestinian case studies in this volume. Fawzy's conclusion, having analysed the substance and context of the new Egyptian Law no. 1 of 2000, is that perhaps more important than the particular provisions of the law was the fact that 'the new law was a product of battles and balances between dynamic groups in society'. He continues: 'This was the first time that this principle became clear for all to see [...] The widespread understanding – through direct experience – that it is possible to change the law through such pressure, and that the law itself is neither sacrosanct nor impossible to change opens the possibility for women to organize themselves for advocacy towards new gains.'

The legal postulate of *shari'a* is thus accompanied by intensely political debates over the way in which that postulate is expressed in legislation. In Palestine, Hammami finds the relationship between personal status law for Muslims and *shari'a* to be a 'doxa', where (following Bourdieu 1979) 'doxa stands for aspects of tradition and culture which are so internalized that they exist as unquestionable common sense beliefs and dispositions'. This is based on the results of the public opinion survey carried out for the purposes of this study, which revealed a 'profound commitment to *shari'a* as the basis for family law by both [men and women] but especially by women'. Probing further at the practical implications of the 'doxa of *shari'a*', however, the survey showed, *inter alia*, a gender gap in the level of satisfaction with the day-to-day operation of the courts, for example with the premise that as implemented the law supported men's rights over those of women, being the opinion of more women than men (Table II.7). Comparing the results of this survey with earlier polls, Hammami finds a growth in support for the principle of reform of *shari'a*-based personal status law, suggesting the impact of the model parliament campaign discussed in the case study. Here again, the survey showed (Table II.12.) that some 20 per cent more women than men wanted more rights to be given to women in family law as and when reformed by a Palestinian legislature. For those respondents desiring change, it is not the legal postulate but the official law that is at issue. At the same time, the contents of the official law, and therefore particular legislative expression of the legal postulate, is subject to other underlying value systems as well as contending political constituencies: when considering the results of the survey as to who should be responsible for the reform of personal status law, Hammami finds that 'democratic and inclusive decision-making is an orthodoxy within Palestinian society' and thus sees 'an opportunity for the development of a unified Palestinian personal status law through a process which is based on public debate and inclusion'.

In the USA, with 'Islamic family law' in the status of an unofficial law in interaction with other legal postulates in US official law, Quraishi and Syeed-Miller emphasize the diversity of the Muslim community and individual Muslim practice, and the activism-focused efforts of many US Muslims who 'find the impetus to form social change movements inherent in the fact that they are Muslim, and hope to find a space that exists between the realm of an Islamic belief system and their US cultural milieu'. Among the challenges to 'significant trends of reform and activism in addressing Islamic family law' they note 'on-going internal debates in the United States Muslim community as to who should be in charge or involved in formulation of community-wide agendas'. The issue of voice in articulating the norms is contested in 'unofficial law' as it is in the Muslim states considered in this volume where *shari'a* is 'official law'.

The papers in this volume provide insights into the interaction of coexisting legal postulates and norms, including the equality paradigm, and the manner in which specific political and socio-economic contexts affect not only what is presented by establishment authorities as 'Islamic family law' but also how it is understood by different non-establishment actors. Addressing the contest over this ground in the specific contexts addressed, the papers in the volume shed light on the diversities and complexities of reform strategies aimed at protecting and expanding women's rights in the family.

Part I

Muslim Personal Status Law in Egypt: the Current Situation and Possibilities of Reform through Internal Initiatives

Essam Fawzy

Introduction

§ THIS case study was carried out in accordance with the goals, theoretical hypotheses and methodologies of the research project entitled *Islamic Family Law – Possibilities of Reform Through Internal Initiatives* coordinated by Professor Abdullahi An-Na'im of Emory School of Law, Atlanta. The study focuses in particular on the different approaches to and the outcomes of implementing personal status laws in Egypt, contributing to the principal questions posed by the research project as a whole, and adding different levels to the suggested model. The full Arabic text of the study is held on file with the project director and with the author; the English translation has been edited for the purposes of publication in the current volume.

Personal status law (or Islamic family law) plays a particularly significant role in defining social relations in Arab and Muslim countries, remaining very close to people's daily lives as it governs family affairs and defines the rights and the duties of all parties to family relationships, regulating marriage, divorce, childcare and the social, psychological and financial consequences of divorce. As Nasser Hamed Abu Zeid has observed (1999: 283), the position of women in the social hierarchy is particularly sensitive, and by reflecting directions of social momentum, personal status laws reveal and mirror women's status and position, and indicate to what extent relevant human rights principles are implemented in the legislation of a given society.

As Professor An-Na'im has pointed out, despite the fact that Arab and Islamic countries have taken similar approaches in adopting family and personal status laws derived from Islamic *fiqh* (jurisprudence), each Muslim and Arab society has its own characteristics, leading to significant differences between the specific *fiqh*-based rules, juristic opinions and textual interpretations implemented in the personal status codes adopted in different countries. In Egypt as elsewhere, legislators present Egyptian personal status law for Muslims as *fiqh* rules extracted from the *shari`a*. Personal status law is the only jurisdiction to have resisted consecutive attempts at secularization, both during the colonial period and subsequently under the national state. It is not the remit of this study to examine the reasons for such resistance, but it should be noted that, as discussed in detail later, governments in Egypt have been cautious in their attempts to amend Muslim personal status law, seeking to avoid provocation of the prevailing religious, male hierarchical and ideological movements within the middle class.

Although the legal and jurisprudential aspects of the law are equally significant, the research team undertaking this case study chose to focus on the social aspects of the law, aiming to answer three major questions:

1. What are the sources of discrimination against women that still exist in the law and that should be removed?
2. Is it enough to secure women's rights legally for them to be implemented in practice?
3. What are the means that enable women to exercise those rights that already exist in the legal system?

The process of collecting material on the law, selecting samples for field studies and collecting data for the questionnaire for the purpose of this case study was already in progress when at the end of 1999 the Egyptian parliament was suddenly presented with a proposed draft to amend the existing personal status law. The draft provoked a prolonged debate, which spread to involve local media and the legal and executive institutions. The research team monitored the debate closely with a view to examining the points of controversy and the behind-the-scenes decision-making processes. A new questionnaire was prepared and put to the existing respondents, and the team also designed a questionnaire for a sample of the Egyptian elite taking part in the drafting process, as detailed below. This new survey was undertaken while work continued with the sample of men and women in four urban and rural governorates selected by the project. As work continued, the team was obliged to return twice more with fresh questions to the original respondents, in the light of two further developments in the debates and amendments to the draft legislation, detailed below in this case study: the issue of the wife's right to travel abroad without her husband's consent, and the power finally granted to the courts to order imprisonment of the husband for failure to pay maintenance. Finally, when the research was about to be finalized at the end of May 2000, the new marriage contract document was published, permitting the wife to insert certain stipulations into her marriage contract. This was seen as quite progressive in regard to the potential protection of women's rights, and the field researchers thus returned to respondents for a fourth time with questions about this issue.

Our persistence in returning to the sample to identify their opinions on certain issues or on a development in the law stems from the fact that any law is the cumulative outcome of the will of the individuals and of groups, who might agree or disagree with some parts of the legislation. It was our view that research dealing only with the jurisprudence and the theoretical discussions on such issues, though of considerable significance, would be incomplete, since it would lack an exploration of the views of those who would be subject to the implementation of the law. Neither jurisprudence nor legal developments are self-sufficient processes, but rather social reactions based on the nature, influence and power of social groups, which might demand or resist changes or developments in the law. On a practical level, this means that any legal or juridical development in a given society is a direct response to and necessarily a reflection of a trend among the main social groups and sectors representing conflicting interests within the social structure. The focus of the research team was thus not so much the legal texts but rather the social and political alliances, conflicts and interactions that directed the wording, approval and execution of the law. The fieldwork thus found particular significance in indicating the extent to which people were aware of the amendments and the circumstances that surrounded the process.

Methodology

The methodologies used in the field study were chosen in the light of the goals set by the general project, and revolved round a set of defining questions, as follows:

1. To what extent were men and women aware of the content and the provisions of personal status law and how far had they been involved in following up the proposed amendments and the arguments that were raised?
2. What did people think about the religious and the secular references in the law?
3. What were the areas of controversy in the law?
4. What approaches were used by those holding rival views, and to what extent were they successful?
5. Which official and non-official institutions were involved in the formulation and implementation of the law?
6. How do people try to manoeuvre around the implementation of the law?
7. What impact do social and economic conditions have on women's awareness of the law and to what extent can women challenge the law when it is in contradiction to their interests?
8. Which proposed reforms of the law respond to the different needs of family members, especially women and children as the most vulnerable family members?

In seeking to answer these questions, this study employed anthropological and sociological analysis to understand and document the practical implementation of the law and its impact on society as a whole (men, women and children) in order to identify the theoretical and practical dynamics of the law within certain contexts (social, cultural, economic and political). The study highlights the role of activists, official institutions, legal experts and jurists and non-official institutions in relation to women's rights and social justice. Anthropological methods were employed in particular to study the non-official aspects of social relationships, while social-historical methodology was used to examine the economic and social contexts of the formulation and promulgation of Egyptian personal status law.

Three sources of data were used for the study. First, the relevant legal drafts and texts, court records and personal status cases, as well as minutes of out-of-court settlements. Second, empirical data collected through interviews and group discussions conducted by the researchers. Third, press archives documenting the position of various political groupings and the various objections made to and questions raised by the public about the law and its implementation. The specific sources are detailed below.

Questionnaire and purposive sample The questionnaire was administered to a sample of 200 persons (men and women) in four cities: Minya and Qena in southern Egypt, Al Sharqia in the north, and Cairo. The sample was selected on the basis of marital status, age, level of education, occupation and professional status, economic status, urban/rural residence and dependants. The responses were computerized and subjected to qualitative and quantitative analysis. Details on the sample and the results of the questionnaire are set out in Chapter 3 below.

Interviews Extended and in-depth interviews were conducted with a small sample of men and women (twenty individuals) from urban and rural areas. We employed speech analysis methodology to place the individual's answers within his or her economic and social environment, by identifying his/her social position, ideological and class identity, and his/her interests, in an attempt to identify factors influencing the attitude of respondents towards the law. An 'interview guide' was employed during these interviews. In-depth interviews were also conducted with some members of the judiciary and leaders of civil society working in areas related to women and children.

Press archives In order to analyse the positions of different political parties, we applied qualitative methods to comments on the law published in the newspapers of the main opposition groups (*al-Sha`ab, al-Ahali, al-Ahrar* and *al-Wafd*).

Case observation Researchers observed personal status cases before the courts and also out-of-court reconciliation meetings dealing with marital disputes. This was in order to help us identify the attitudes and approaches of women and men, how they presented their cases, the defences they raised and the ways in which they sought to defeat the other party's position, as well as the attitudes of lawyers, the judge, family and friends.

Group discussions Group discussions were held with three groups: women adversely affected by the implementation of specific provisions of personal status law; men; and mixed groups of men and women.

Elite opinion survey As noted above, the opinion survey focusing on the Egyptian elite was added to the existing tools of the research after the presentation of the draft amendments to the People's Assembly (parliament) and the arousal of wide media interest and public debate around the issues. Since the questionnaire already sought to investigate the attitudes of the sample in relation to the law, the opinion survey of the elite served to include the views of those defining the trends in attitudes among decision-makers at this particularly critical time in the development of personal status law. We identified a selective group of specialists and politicians working in the personal status field, and other representatives, such as religious clerks, judges, politicians, civil society workers, journalists and women leaders, whose opinions were to be explored. The survey sought to explore the reasons given for approval or disapproval of the amendments applied in the new law and, in the case of disagreement, alternative and proposed views, amendments or changes. The associated environment was monitored through press reports and articles and transcripts of parliamentary discussions on the law.

For the purposes of the questionnaire designed for the elite opinion survey, a sample of 300 people was selected, including twenty-five members of judicial institutions charged with practical implementation of the law; thirty-five lawyers; sixty-seven political party functionaries, including political party leaders, leaders of general committees, general secretariats and district committee members, from six political parties and in proportion to the role and impact of the party in the political arena; forty-five journalists[1] from nine national and opposition newspapers:[2] sixty civil society activists, some from organizations and associations not aligned with any particular political tendency or ideology, some from those with 'Islamist' characteristics, working with families and children, and in areas of human rights; and eighteen activist women leaders, including eight known to represent the 'Islamist' trend.

ONE
Social context

§ DURING the past few decades, there has been a wealth of publications and writings on personal status problems and the relevant laws implemented in Egypt, coinciding with an increasing interest on the part of local NGOs in the problems experienced by women and children as the most vulnerable sectors of society. However, most of these studies have tended to concentrate on the legal aspects and have not examined in any depth the social background of the problems. Two aspects of the position of women merit particular attention to provide adequate context for a study of the impact of personal status law: women's de facto status in society, which renders them the vulnerable party in society and social encounters; and women's social image, which promotes the idea of a weaker and second-grade sex. Many women have themselves accepted and promoted this suppressed set of values.

The social role of women has been defined by the economic, social and cultural values of this society. Of the many social and economic factors that interact in this complicated picture underlying the drafting and implementation of the law, economic factors and the issue of illiteracy are arguably the most critical. In the context of the family structure, women tend to suffer a double social and political suppression. Moreover, men have the advantage of being more involved in social life and are therefore generally more experienced than women, apart from the few women who manage to overcome the restricted boundaries of the family.

Education

The contradiction between legal texts and the lived reality of Egyptian women is strikingly manifest in the realm of education. Article 18 of Egypt's Constitution states that education is a right guaranteed by the state and is compulsory at the primary level. There is no discrimination between males and females in this text. However, in reality, although women make up half of the population, according to the last census they do not match this percentage in the education system.[3]

The low rate of females in all educational levels is reflected in the gender structure of literacy in Egypt.[4] The picture is more gloomy in the countryside, particularly in Upper Egypt (the south), where illiteracy is more common among females because of conservative cultural and social structures which underpin discrimination against women in education at a higher level in rural than in urban areas. Recent studies reveal that the drop-out rate of girls at the preparatory and secondary school stages is especially high in rural areas, where families may prefer to keep girl children at home after the compulsory primary stage of education, to work in the house and help with agricultural work.[5] Early marriage is another obstacle that hampers a female's educational process. Empirical studies on women in Egypt show a number of pertinent facts that may be summarized as follows (Abdul Rahman 1999):

1. The imbalance in quality, quantity and geography in Egypt's educational map varies significantly, with a negative impact on the size and quality of female participation throughout the different educational levels.
2. There is a large number of illiterate females in rural areas and in poor and slum areas of the cities, by reason of the sway of inherited cultural values and traditions, which give males priority over females when it comes to education, in addition to high levels of poverty.
3. There are shortcomings in educational curricula in regard to women's position and rights; these curricula are dominated by a male vision that reproduces a traditional view of women, their roles and responsibilities, and does not seek to correct conceptions that contradict women's real status and their historical and contemporary role in constructing civilization.
4. The local media also have failed to play a positive role in eradicating female illiteracy and contributing to raising and developing women's awareness of their rights, especially rural women.
5. Although women's participation in the educational process has increased over the past four decades, their contribution to the workforce and to political activities has not witnessed a similar increase. This removes the social content from the educational process with regard to women, making it more of a tool that shows some degree of progress on the surface but that in essence aims to maintain the traditional situation for educated women.

Workforce participation

Under the Constitution and the law, Egyptian women are entitled to full equality in the field of work. However, in reality, women's participation in economic activities differs drastically from the texts of the Constitution, the law and international treaties, and both rural and urban women fare badly in the labour market. According to official statistics, in 1986, women's participation in the labour force on the national level was not more than 10 per cent; this rate increased to 21 per cent according to 1991 employment statistics at that time, which redefined employment to include women working in the informal sector, especially those involved in agriculture and animal husbandry. This new definition was based on the 1995 Human Development Report, which introduced a gender-related guide to human development, and which classified Egypt among states with a low rate of human development due to the increasing male–female inequality in the distribution of human capacities (Abdul Rahman 1999: 14).

Under the impact of the side effects of economic reform and privatization policies, women have suffered more than men from increased unemployment rates, with female unemployment rates starting to increase in the mid-1980s and overtaking those of men. At the same time, the number of women living below the poverty level has increased, which in turn has led to an increasing number of females dropping out of school, leading to enhanced rates of female illiteracy as against those of males, in addition to their early entry into the labour market and deprivation of education and training, constraining their competitive capabilities in the labour market. The past few years have also witnessed a retreat from the principle of women's equality in work, as shown by certain practices in violation of the law and the Constitution such as notices in the daily newspapers advertising vacant posts for male applicants. There have been calls for women to stop going out to work. The numbers of women working for a cash wage increased relatively from 58 per cent in 1976 to 76 per cent in 1986; but the same period (1976–86) also witnessed a relative increase in the number of unemployed women, especially with a new wave of unemployed females, with an unemployment rate of 23.8 per cent out of the total number of women in the workforce being reached (CBNSS, *Census 1976–1986*).

Women's image

The situation of women is tough indeed, but it may be that even more dangerous is the image formulated by society of women's roles and character. The danger here may lie in that fact that women themselves are not unaffected by this image, and may indeed themselves adopt it. We consider this to be the basic obstacle to attempts to develop the position of women in Egypt because resistance, in such cases, comes from the women themselves. Significant efforts are needed to change this negative image.

The image of women in religious thought Some conservative religious thought presents an image of women as inferior, at worst devils, at best a tool for the sexual gratification of their husbands. Ibn al-Gouzi's book *Rulings on Women* (n.d.: 62–95), for example, has an entire section dedicated to 'Deterring women from wrong-doing and letting them know that they are more likely to go to hell'. Al-Buti (n.d.: 43–4) also articulates a conservative understanding of marriage, to the effect that it is not in a woman's nature to look for a husband herself, and since God has created her psychologically and physically in a way that makes her appealing and desirable to men, her own joy is to be found in the feeling that she is desirable. For this to remain the case, the man should be the breadwinner and the maintainer, and women should not go out to work for an income, except in the most straitened of circumstances and in cases of necessity (ibid.: 48). In such views, marriage is a framework in which women are a means of reproduction and of entertainment for men. Certain views from jurists are cited to the same effect (Hatab 1976: 45).

Al-Maududi (n.d.: 132–3) takes these sex-related views further, and provides a basis for positions taken on women's affairs by some contemporary political Islam groups, particularly since the rise of radical political Islam groups in Egypt around the mid-1970s. Differences in political and *fiqh* positions notwithstanding, these groups tend to concur on certain matters related to women: the wearing of the *hijab* (head covering), or sometimes even the *niqab* (full black head, face and body cover) and for unveiling to be forbidden; for women to be confined to their homes and not go out to work; segregation between men and women in public places; and for women not to be allowed to hold leadership positions, especially in the judiciary, as they lack the necessary rational and religious capabilities. The focus of certain political Islam groups on women and the attempt to prevent women being active members of society on an equal footing with men have had a destructive impact both on women and on society.

The promotion of these views has led to their becoming part and parcel of the educated middle classes' convictions, emphasizing men's role and social power while promoting an image of women as silent followers. These concepts are legitimized *inter alia* through the prevailing culture, popular and religious heritage, the law and the media.

The only roles for women recognized by the dominant culture among members of the middle classes are those of wife and homemaker. A woman is allowed to get an education and go to work in order to enhance her chances of a better marriage, provided that her career and education do not clash with her role of serving her husband and bringing up the children. Regardless of what she may have achieved by way of university degrees or professional status, a woman without a husband or male children is seen as an object of pity in society. Families bring up their girl children to play the role of wife and homemaker, encouraging them to show off their femininity while simultaneously prohibiting them from mixing with their male counterparts. This contradiction, which sets the exaggerated sexual aspect in a woman's character (woman as a tool for sex, for entertainment and for reproduction) against suppressive social, cultural and religious values, has added to a disempowerment of women even more severe than their economic disempowerment, though closely connected.

The image of women in popular culture At first glance it appears that popular discourse is in line with the limits set by dominant culture and religious thought, but a closer examination of this discourse reveals that it is not totally subordinate to these ideologies. Public discourse reflects a variety of positions, differing from class to class and sector to sector, with significant differences between rural and urban areas, as sub-sectors of the overall social set-up. On the one side, the urban middle class, whether in the capital or other cities, tends to be closely linked to the central governing institutions, and has been exposed to pervasive and highly intensive ideological input from institutions such as schools, local media and prominent mosques, presenting women as taboo and adding to women's alienation in the collective and popular psychology of the urban petite bourgeoisie. On the other side, people in rural areas and the poor districts in the cities seem to be less controlled by the input of ideological institutions and not seriously committed to the religious rhetoric of the local media. Their discourse is in a process of interaction with the others, but is nevertheless different from that of the urban middle class and of radical Islamists. In the rural areas women represent a major sector of the workforce, and the children they bear and raise are, for the farmer, his major source of well-being. Talk of sex is more straight-forward – the taboo of the urban middle class does not apply – and is enhanced by the educative role of the extended family. Nevertheless, we cannot claim that the popular and rural image of women is essentially different from that of the middle class; naturally, the latter view has found its way also through to other classes and sections of society, and the economic deprivation of the popular classes has led them in turn to suppress women.

Due to its above-mentioned contradictory nature, popular heritage includes a number of concepts that entrench and legitimize systems and values that advocate the suppression of women and reduce their role to a minimum within the family and the societal framework. Families tend to prefer boy children to girl children, a position backed up by popular sayings for the occasion of the birth of a boy or a girl. Other sayings attest to the identification of girls as sources of worry and potential shame, and a subsequent desire to be rid of them.[6] Marriage itself echoes the contradictions shown in popular opinion; many proverbs suggest that whatever her own opinion or aspirations, and whatever the status of the proposed husband, the girl should always opt for marriage, as and when proposed by her family, while an alternative saying encourages aiming for the best: 'Sit [alone] in sadness rather than marry and regret.' As for decision-making in the family, any participation of the wife should be covert, since it might suggest an 'unmanly' attitude.

There is also evidence among the popular classes of practices that may not accord with the constraints of the *shar'i* rulings. By way of example, among the poor, it is reported to be commonplace for a man to employ the phrases of *ila'* or *zihar*,[7] or to pronounce an oath of *talaq*, but being unable financially to make the required expiation that would remove the effect of the pronouncement, returns to marital intimacy with his wife anyway, in violation of the *shar'i* rules. Hence the externalities of awareness of the law, of what is permitted (*halal*) and what is prohibited (*haram*), become confused (Abdul Fattah 1991: 252–63, as cited in Shukri et al. 1995: 126).[8]

There are also several ways of circumventing the text of personal status law applied in the courts. 'Ashmawi (1996: 50) notes one particularly well-known form of circumvention of the rules of the marriage contract in Egypt, the *muhallal*, a person who marries a woman who has been divorced in the 'greater finality' (*baynuna kubra*, the third of three divorces) and is thus no longer lawful to the man who has divorced her, until she has undergone marriage to another man. The marriage to the *muhallal* is a marriage of form only, and is accompanied by a divorce at the same time, enabling the original husband to remarry the woman. 'Ashmawi further notes that in the sphere of inheritance, many people circumvent the legal provisions by drawing up form contracts of gift or sale, or dispositions postponed till after death, with the intention of favouring one of the heirs or avoiding what they consider would be a hardship were they not to be so favoured. However, it is perhaps *'urfi* marriage (literally 'customary' marriage, discussed further below, that is the clearest popular means of getting around the constraints imposed by law on marriage and divorce in Egypt. At the same time, the religious tendency which has spread in the universities has taken up the idea of *'urfi* marriage and holds it to be *shar'i* and not involving any religious infraction.

The image of husband and wife The sexual relationship of a married couple in Egyptian society is not balanced. There is a common belief that men are more sexually motivated than women and thus take the lead. Unlike men, women's sexual activity usually starts with marriage; society approves a man's right to have sex before marriage but firmly rejects the same right for women. This stand reflects the social concept that virginity is closely related to family honour and to the woman's future fidelity to her husband. In this regard, social values are at odds with the religious rulings that approve sex only within the marriage framework for both sexes.

As for divorce, this is generally not considered a feasible option even by women wishing to end their marriage, particularly if they have children and are faced with the uncertain future of an unmarried woman and society's disapproval. These considerations tend to place women in the position of accepting their inferior status, and although education has a major role to play in empowering women to strike a balance here, even those who have had a good education tend to view marriage as a means of protection, as well as bringing mental and moral harmony. Having children is a large part of this, since society tends to value those who have children and to consider those who cannot as 'incomplete'. Finally, early marriage, especially in rural areas, accompanied by low levels of education and socialization, along with frequent pregnancy, malnutrition and a volatile social status, create and entrench the traditional position of women in society.

To close this consideration of the perceptions of the marital relationship we will summarize some of the findings of a 1973–74 study carried out by Dr Sayyed 'Awais (1977) among urban Egyptian youth. Unmarried young men and women were questioned on the choice of their future spouse wives and husbands, revealing the following positions:

1. Of the male respondents in this study, 71.4 per cent wanted their future bride to be younger than them, while 28.6 per cent wanted a wife of the same age; 68.5 per cent of the female respondents wanted their future husband to be older than them, while 28.5 per cent wanted him to be the same age.

2. That the future wife should be an Egyptian non-relative was the preference of 62.8 per cent of male respondents, while 28.6 per cent preferred an Egyptian relative; the female respondents' choices were 71.4 per cent and 22.9 per cent respectively.

3. When asked about the preferred educational level of a future wife, 68.6 per cent of male respondents wanted the wife to have an education equal to theirs, while 31.4 per cent preferred a wife educated to a lower standard than themselves. Among the female respondents, some 60 per cent wanted a husband educated to a higher standard than themselves, 34.4 per cent looked for the same educational standard, and 5.7 per cent expressed a preference for a husband with a lower educational level than themselves. There is a particularly significant difference here between males and females in regard to those expressing a preference for a future spouse of the same educational level.

4. All of the male respondents and 97.1 per cent of the females said that their ideal future spouse would not have been previously married.

5. Among both male and female respondents, 94.3 per cent aspired to their own private dwelling in their family life.

6. Almost 28.6 per cent of the male respondents agreed that divorce should take place in court, while 71.4 per cent disagreed; the female respondents were split evenly (50:50) in their response to this question.

Returning to reality

The conflicting views on marriage have undoubtedly been a significant factor behind many social ills and imbalances in the structure of the Egyptian family. By way of example, one study shows that 39 per cent of women marry men who are related to them, a practice that is closely related to early marriage, with a high rate of childbirth and increased risks of infant mortality and disability (el-Zanaty 1999). Early marriage remains widespread among Egyptian females; although the law specifies a minimum age of capacity for marriage, in many rural and poor urban areas girls still marry below that age as a result of poverty, ignorance or inadequate enforcement of the law. Documentation is forged so the rate of marriage of minors appears extremely low; doctors who produce 'age certificates'[9] and village heads who fill in the marriage forms may falsify the supporting documentation to enable families to marry off underage girls. In this regard the results of our field study reach the same conclusions as earlier studies on this subject in Egypt (Toubia 1994 : 25).

As for marital breakdown, in January 1998 the Central Bureau for National Service and Statistics issued a report showing an annual rate of thirty-three divorces for every 100 officially registered marriages. The rate was higher in urban areas, at 35 per cent (CBNSS 1998). During periods of economic stability, marital disputes are greatly reduced; one indication of this is the number of personal status cases brought to the first instance courts, particularly divorce and filiation suits, indicating family breakdown. Between 1965 and 1969 there was a decreasing number of such cases, 4,160 in 1965 and 3,735 cases in 1969; however, when Egyptian society entered the period of economic change known as the 'economic opening', the subsequent upheavals had an impact on the stability of the Egyptian family, and the number of divorce cases[10] increased, reaching 5,867 in 1975 and going up to 13,295 cases in 1979 (National Centre for Social and Criminal Studies 1985: 672–3).

Domestic violence against women

Although in some cases husbands complain of violence by their wives, in the vast majority of cases it is the wife who is exposed to violence, as the weaker partner in the marital relationship. The problem of violence in marital relationships is found in all social classes, but is more widespread among the poor and uneducated classes (Ramsis 1991: 283). In these classes, manifold economic and social problems may lead to violent behaviour.

Violence against women and children is a phenomenon with social, economic and psychological implications that substantively affects the coming generations, their social relationships and productive capacities. The degree of a man's violence is heavily dependent on his inability or reluctance to settle disputes or problems through discussion. Many men seek to justify their resort to violence on such baseless pretexts as disciplining the wife, correcting her conduct and deterring her from wrongdoing; sometimes they also feel that this is a right protected legally and supported religiously.

Statistics issued by different research centres and departments of sociology and anthropology in Egypt reveal that the breakdown of family life and destruction of the family is usually caused by the man; that domestic violence is usually carried out by the man; and that desertion, abandonment and divorce usually occur at the will of the man. Across all social classes it is common for women to put up with a lot from their husbands in order to preserve the family and keep it stable; moreover, the woman cannot resolve the problem of marital violence as she has nowhere to seek refuge. Thus many women put up with humiliation in their marriage for fear otherwise of having to leave their homes.

This brief overview has sought to describe the key factors of the social context within which the discussions on the personal status law were set, and where the opinions on and awareness of the law were formed. It is to those discussions that we now turn.

TWO

Personal status law in Egypt: an historical overview

Between heritage and modernization

§ THE situation of Egyptian women has attracted the attention of both conservative and progressive elements in Egyptian society since the beginning of its
modern history, and the area of family law was from early on a contested site
and a target for attention, criticism and calls for reform. Early reformist Muslim
scholars at the end of the nineteenth century included Rafa al-Tahtawi, who *inter
alia* argued for the legal age of marriage for women to be raised to twenty-five,
although this was not at the time a popular demand (Ghasoub 1991: 21–2). Like
many other Egyptian progressives at the time, Tahtawi argued that women's poor
situation had nothing to do with Islam, contrary to the claims of many Western
Orientalists (who focused in this regard particularly on the *hijab* and on polygyny),
but was rather related to reactionary customs and social traditions inherited from
antiquity. Imam Shaykh Mohammed Abdu furthered the progressive arguments,
including an insistence that women had the same right to choose their husband
as men did their wives ('Amara 1991: 70), and support for the abolition of polygyny (ibid., p. 92); his proposed remedy was that women should be educated
about their rights and build their self-esteem (ibid., p. 73).

Despite long-standing criticism of existing personal status law in Egypt, many
of the specific aspirations of such early reformists have yet to be realized. One of
the main obstacles to such reform is found in a general concept of male superiority over females, frequently traced by defenders of this principle to the concept
of *qiwama* in the Qur'an (Surat al-Nisa, 34). The term can be understood (and
translated) in various ways (guardianship/protection/control etc.) in the context
of the verse. Stowasser (1998: 32–3) gives the following English translation of
Sura 4: 34 as 'the pivotal Qur'anic verse on gender relations':

> Men are in charge of [are guardians of/are superior to/have authority over]
> women (*al-rijalu qawwamuna 'ala l-nisa'*) because God has endowed one with
> more [because God has preferred some of them over others] (*bi-ma faddala
> Allahu ba'dahum 'ala ba'din*) and because they spend of their means (*wa-bi-ma
> 'anfaqu min amwalihim*).

This verse is also considered in the context of other verses in the Qur'an understood as underlining the equality of males and females. Down the centuries, jurists have given it much attention, including a view that God has given men a general guardianship or leadership role over women.[11]

While this is not the place to review the various interpretations of the verse or the concept of *qiwama*, it is worth noting that Egyptian scholars have sought to understand the concept in the context of contemporary Egyptian society. During the 1960s, Shaykh Mohammed Shaltut argued that what was meant was men's responsibility towards women, rather than their leadership over them (Shaltut n.d.: 159–268). More recently, Nasr Abu Zeid has argued that the verse is not so much a legal prescription, but rather a description of the status of women before Islam, the idea of the 'preference' of men over women not so much an absolute rule as a situation that needs to be changed in order to achieve the original equality of women. Abu Zeid refers to another verse (Surat al-Baqarah, 228) ('and women shall have rights similar to the rights against them according to what is equitable') to argue that women's rights and responsibilities are defined according to the customs and traditions of a given society, not that customs and traditions themselves become absolute and abiding rules (Abu Zeid 1999: 214). Similarly, his understanding of *qiwama* is the idea of responsibility, rather than power and leadership, and he poses to those who link *qiwama* with men's financial maintenance of women the question whether in cases where a woman is the breadwinner for the family, and the man is unemployed, the man would grant the woman all the rights of *qiwama* understood as accruing to men in that situation (ibid., p. 215).

This might be seen to be a fair question in the light of the social and economic changes that have taken place in Egyptian society. With increasing male unemployment rates as a result of structural adjustment policies, and labour migration by a large number of Egyptian men to other Arab states, the Egyptian workforce has been described as having been 'feminized'. A 1993 study showed that 15 to 20 per cent of families depend solely on women's income (Badran 1994). The Egyptian government reported in 2000 that 'the proportion of women supporting families has grown to 22%'.[12]

Nevertheless, the more traditional understanding of *qiwama* as male 'superiority' supports the inferior position of Arab and Egyptian women at all levels. The concept reflects a social repression expressed through male–female discrimination in the family and in society, in opportunities for work, promotion, salary, education, choice in marriage, social and political participation, and decision-making in the family.

Personal status law: residual sources and jurisdiction

The requirement of adherence to the Hanafi school of jurisprudence was introduced by an Ottoman decree issued in the nineteenth century and, contrary to previous Egyptian practice, was taken up in subsequent regulations such as that of 26 December 1856, and the decree regulating *shari'a* courts in 1897. In subsequent legislation, due in particular to the intransigent Hanafi positions regarding women's right to divorce, the Egyptian legislator has been obliged to introduce rulings from other schools of law and other jurists, in a process of opening up to other doctrines that are better suited to social developments (al-Bishri 1996: 59). Regarding divorce, it is mostly rulings from the Maliki school that have been introduced to widen women's options. Nevertheless, it remains the case that the judge is required to apply the dominant opinion of the Hanafi school unless there is an explicit text in Egyptian legislation on the personal status matter under consideration.[13]

The term 'personal status' in the Islamic *shari'a* was not known to the Muslim jurists. The rulings of the *shari'a* are divided into two parts: one relates to articles of faith such as monotheism, and belief in God and his angels, his Book and his prophets, the other to the acts of humans, which in turn is divided into acts of worship or ritual (*'ibadat*), and transactions (*mu'amalat*). *'Ibadat* are acts that bring a person closer to God, such as praying and fasting, while *mu'amalat* regulate relationships between people, including contracts and dispositions, whether these concern family relationships, such as engagement and marriage, or property and acts of sale and hire.

In 1934, the Egyptian Court of Cassation established a definition for the term 'personal status':

All that which differentiates one person from another in terms of natural or family characteristics and which have a legal effect in his social life through being a male or a female, husband or widower or divorcée, a father or a son, of full legal capacity or not due to minor age, imbecility or insanity, or being of absolute capacity or limited capacity due to legal reasons.[14]

In a 1949 Egyptian law, the following were listed as personal status issues:

disputes and questions related to the status of persons and their legal capacity, or related to the regulation of the family, such as engagement, marriage, the mutual rights and responsibilities of the spouses, dower and dowry, financial arrangements between the spouses, *talaq*, judicial divorce and judicial dissolution, paternity and denial of paternity, the relations between ascendants and descendants, maintenance of relatives, in-laws, correction of filiation, adoption, guardianship, tutorship and trusteeship, interdiction and permission to administer; absence and considering a missing person dead, and similarly disputes and questions related to inheritance, bequests and other dispositions after death.[15]

Some of these issues, such as interdiction and permission to administer, have been regulated by unified civil legislation applicable to all Egyptians regardless of religion; however, marriage and divorce, and matters related to them, remain regulated by religious laws – the Islamic *shari'a* for Muslims and Christian and Jewish rules for the respective communities.

Regulating the Muslim family in Egypt: the development of personal status law

The first law including procedural rules for litigation in personal status disputes was issued on 27 May 1897 and applied only to Muslim Egyptians. Amendments were introduced by Decree no. 25 of 10 December 1909 and again by Decree no. 3 Organizing *Shari'a* Courts of 3 July 1910; these were replaced by the provisions of Law Decree no. 78/1931 which was applicable until the issuing of the new law (Law no. 1 of 2000).

As for substance, a year after Egypt became a British protectorate in 1914, a committee chaired by the Minister of Justice was formed to propose ways in which Islamic law might be reformed; after the war, Law no. 25/1920 was promulgated introducing certain new rulings in personal status matters. In 1926 another committee was formed to propose further reforms, and subsequently Law Decree no. 25/1929 was issued with further amendments to personal status law. At the same time, as noted above, where the state-issued legislation did not cover the matter in hand, the court was to rule according to the dominant opinion of the Hanafi school; this was explicitly stated in the 1931 law on *shari'a* courts (al-Bishri 1996: 67). The following paragraphs provide an overview of the contents of the relevant laws affecting personal status for Muslims in Egypt from 1920 until 1985, leaving consideration of the new law of 2000 to Chapter 4 below.[16]

Law no. 25 of 1920: concerning maintenance and certain matters of personal status This law codified rules governing the wife's maintenance, judicial separation at the wife's petition for the husband's non-payment of or inability to pay maintenance, and for the husband being afflicted by certain serious physical or psychological conditions (the examples given being 'insanity or the two kinds of leprosy').

With regard to the wife's maintenance, the law states that the wife's maintenance is the responsibility of her husband even if she is wealthy or of a different religion, nor is her entitlement affected if she is sick. Maintenance covers the costs of food, clothes, medical treatment and accommodation and other matters covered by the *shari'a*. The inclusion of medical treatment was in accordance with the positions of the Zaydis and Imam Malik rather than Hanafi doctrine. The conditions in which the wife loses her entitlement to maintenance are also set out: 'if she apostasizes or if she refrains by choice from submitting herself without justification or is forced so to refrain by circumstances which are not the fault of the husband, or if she leaves the matrimonial home without the permission of her husband'.

Law no. 25 of 1929: concerning certain matters of personal status This law included provisions on unilateral divorce (*talaq*), judicial divorce for injury, the maintenance of the wife and children, child custody and other matters. Article 6 sets out the basic principle of divorce for injury, based on Maliki and Hanbali principles:

> If the wife claims that the husband has caused her harm of a kind which would make living together impossible for a couple such as them she may ask the judge for judicial divorce (*tafriq*) and the judge shall then grant her an irrevocable divorce if the harm is proved and he is unable to bring about reconciliation between them.

These two early laws might be viewed as to some extent progressive, and represent the first attempt by the Egyptian legislators to have reference to the rulings of non-Hanafi schools and jurists. The Explanatory Memorandum to Law no. 25 of 1929 stated in this regard:

> The Ministry decided to restrict the scope of *talaq* in accordance with the sources and rules of religion and in accordance with the imams and the jurists, even if these [be taken from] other than the adherents of the four schools ... There is nothing that forbids this, particularly if adopting their views leads to improved knowledge or the removal of injury, in accordance with the true views of the scholars of jurisprudence ...

The Memorandum added that:

> It is *shari'a* policy (*siyasa shar'iyya*) that the door of mercy be opened for the people from the *shari'a* [meaning *fiqh*] itself, and to have recourse to the views of scholars in order to find a remedy for social ills when these ills become insidious, so that people feel that the *shari'a* [*fiqh*] is a way out of want and a relief from hardship.

Regulation on the organization of *shari'a* courts issued in accordance with Law Decree no. 78 of 1931 Article 5 of this regulation gave the *shari'a* primary courts final jurisdiction over marital and child maintenance claims, under a certain amount (not more than a few pounds), allowing the wife and the husband to take his/her case regarding maintenance of the wife and children to the Court of Cassation when the claim exceeded the limits. Similarly, limits were specified for dower and *jihaz* claims. These limits were set according to the economic and social conditions of the time, but as the value of the currency decreased, amendments had to be made. Also, Article 280 of this law provided that the dominant opinion of the Hanafi school was the residual reference for personal status issues.

In the following decades, social and economic development paved the way towards a more progressive view of marital relations, and led to a series of amendments, which were introduced to the law gradually and cautiously. In some cases these amendments were introduced to alleviate an element of bias against women within the law. For example, a ministerial decision issued in 1967 provided that a wife who was held to be disobedient stood to forfeit her right to maintenance, ending the forcible implementation of awards of obedience (requiring wives to return to the matrimonial home) provided for in Article 345 of Law Decree no. 78/1931.

During the 1950s and 1960s, the Arab world witnessed relative progress in the understanding and interpretation of *shari'a* and an effort to reconcile it with the needs of the time. These new approaches were also a reflection of the increasing calls for equality and gender liberation. In Egypt, the July Revolution of 1952 tried to change fundamentally the role of women through the introduction of legislation dealing with women's political, social and economic rights and responsibilities. By way of example, the 1956 Constitution granted women the right to vote, and equal pay and conditions for equal work. The government policy of free education also had a positive impact, as it granted equal opportunities to female Egyptians on a level with men at all stages of education. However, these rights remained restricted and incomplete so long as the law governing family relations remained as it was; it was not surprising that women could not benefit fully from the laws affirming their equality with men while they remained oppressed inside the family. The promulgation of legislation is thus not an indicator of the mobilization of positive participation by women or a comparator for their actual emancipation. Women continued to suffer from harsh traditions represented in the domination of the family and of the man, in retrogressive traditions and beliefs, and in low cultural, economic and political awareness among the majority of women.

Law no. 44 of 1979: an aborted effort The best-known attempt to amend personal status law took place in 1979, when a presidential decree was issued as Law 44/1979 to 'liberate' personal status law. The law was known as 'Jihan's law', after the then First Lady and wife of late President Anwar Sadat who was a major supporter of the amendments. Among the most significant provisions of the law were the following.

1. The wife's right to maintenance was not to be affected if she went out to work without her husband's consent, unless her work was against the interest of her family or she misused the right.
2. The polygynous marriage of the husband without the wife's consent was considered as injurious to the wife *per se*, even if she did not stipulate this in the marriage contract; similarly (for the new wife) the husband having hidden the fact that he was married to another woman. The wife then had a right to seek divorce from the court without having to establish injury; this right lapsed one year after she had been informed of her husband's action, provided she had not consented to it explicitly or implicitly.

3. The use of force to execute awards of obedience was prohibited; this had already been established by administrative measures mentioned above, and the law confirmed that a wife who refused to obey her husband without good reason would forfeit her right to maintenance.

4. The period that a mother was entitled to keep her children in her custody was extended. Previously, mothers were entitled to keep their sons in their care until the age of seven years and daughters until they reached ten, with the possibility of extension to nine and eleven respectively. Under the 1979 law, these ages were extended to ten for the boy and twelve for the girl, while after these ages the judge could allow the son up to age fifteen and the daughter until she married to remain in the custody of the mother without the fee for custody being due, if it appeared their interest so required.

5. The law gave a divorced woman with custody of children the exclusive right to the rented matrimonial home, so long as the divorcing husband had not prepared another suitable dwelling. When the custody period ended, or if the woman remarried, her former husband had the exclusive right to the dwelling if he was legally entitled to keep it.

These amendments met with broad disagreement and opposition, mostly from men. The most important amendment was that a woman had the right to seek divorce if her husband married another wife without her consent, and this provision in particular was among the reasons for opposition to the law among men and rejection by certain religious institutions and legal professionals. The striking thing is the significant role played by women in the campaign for repeal of the law; huge demonstrations gathered at Al-Azhar University (their mainstay being female students at the university) opposing the law, which they considered contrary to the Islamic *shari'a*. It is worth noting here that the fact that the law was popularly called 'Jihan's law' indicates the public's rejection of the intervention by the President's wife in the formulation of laws having a direct effect on their daily lives, even if these laws brought a certain benefit to women. This incident raises important questions as to the extent of women's awareness of their rights and how these might be realized in accordance with the *shari'a*. Moreover, the arguments against the law were constructed along masculine perspectives and conservative interpretations of the *shari'a*.

The law also provoked wide opposition among the judiciary. In a study on the position of judges towards petitions for divorce (Shmais 1994), when asked about their view of the article giving the custodian exclusive right to the rented matrimonial home after divorce, almost 60 per cent of the judges questioned expressed antipathy, holding it to be contrary to Islam and to the *shari'a*, according to which a divorced woman should return home to her family. The judges believed that in light of the ongoing housing crisis, this article would create a real problem for the husband, and the custodian should rather leave the matrimonial home and obtain a maintenance award for accommodation. They also feared the law would encourage the wife to lie and seek divorce in order to get the house to herself and marry another man. On a woman's right to divorce if the husband marries again, twenty out of twenty-seven judges said it was a explicit violation of the Qur'an, giving scope to women to seek divorce and constraining men's right to marry polygynously. Women, it was said, were created with the psychological make-up to accept polygyny, and the provision was immoral because it encouraged women to divorce when the natural thing would be for a wife eager for her husband's happiness to be happy herself if he took another wife, as this would protect him from immorality (Shmais 1994: 133–46). Others added that the law would en-courage immorality in wives, since it was against the Islamic *shari'a*, and if a wife divorced on these grounds and married another man, she would have committed adultery as her divorce was null and void. One of the judges went so far as to say that the law was a creation of Jihan Sadat, its aim to divert public attention from the economic problems besetting the country; he explained that he himself had refused to implement the law and had postponed all such cases referred to him (Shmais 1994: 144).

'Jihan's law' also faced much opposition from religious circles on the pretext that it restricted men's right to polygyny and divorce. In fact, the law rather restructured men's right to take another wife in a way that respected the humanity and dignity of both first and second wives. The law obliged the husband to state the name and address of the wife or wives to whom he was already married before concluding the new marriage contract; the notary was to give her or them notice of their husband's new marriage by registered mail. Should these pro-cedures not be implemented, the husband could be sentenced to up to six months in prison or receive a fine of 200 Egyptian pounds, while the notary could be imprisoned for up to six months and a fine of 50 pounds, plus he might be struck off or suspended from his job for up to a year.

The second issue that provoked particular opposition was the provision regard-ing the right of the divorced wife to stay in the marital home with children in her custody, unless the husband offered alternative suitable accommodation. Here, the law took the children's side regarding the economic interest, giving them the matrimonial home in the company of the custodian (male or female), but it failed to consider the circumstances of unemployed or older women made to leave their home when the period of child custody and their right to maintenance came to an end.

As for divorce, Law no. 44 of 1979 required the husband to register his divorce papers with the relevant authorized official. This obligation indicated a desire on the part of the legislator to regulate and protect the family. Close examination of divorce cases had shown that some husbands would resort to pronouncing *talaq* in the absence of their wives and hide the fact of the divorce from them, causing them injury; indeed, there were some cases where the husband actually registered the divorce officially but kept the document to himself and pretended that married life was going on as normal. A decision by the Minister of Justice in 1979[17] accordingly obliged the notary responsible for registering certificates of divorce to establish clearly in the document the residential address of the divorcée and whether she was present at the notarization; the 1979 law also required the notary to provide a copy of the divorce certificate to the divorced wife in person or to her representative. The *talaq* was to take effect from the date the wife was informed of it; she would be considered informed of the divorce if she was present when it was registered, or when the notary provided her or her representative with a copy of the document.

In May 1985, the Supreme Constitutional Court ruled to abolish Law no. 44/ 1979, a decision based on reasons of form rather than substance: the law had been promulgated by presidential decree during a period of vacation when the People's Assembly was not sitting, and had not thereafter been presented for approval when parliament reconvened, as required by the Constitution. This meant that the personal status laws issued in the 1920s under very different social and economic conditions once again came into force in Egypt (Zulfikar 1995: 135–6). This situation was rectified to some extent in July by the promulgation of Law no. 100/1985.

Law no. 100 of 1985: amending certain rulings on personal status Law no. 100/1985 comprised similar articles to the repealed Law no. 44/1979, but presented certain concessions in light of the opposition to the previous law. Most significantly, the new law required a wife whose husband had married another woman to establish the material or mental injury that had been caused her if she wished to obtain a divorce;[18] in the 1979 law, this injury had been a legal presumption. Under the 1985 law, the injury was not defined, but had to be of a kind that rendered it impossible for 'a couple such as them' to continue married life; this indicated a relative definition of injury that might vary according to cultural and contextual circumstances and the social status of the injured person (the wife).

As for the other particularly controversial article on the custodian's right to the matrimonial dwelling, the 1985 law changed the wording, stating that: 'A divorced husband shall be required to provide appropriate independent accommodation for his young children by his divorced wife and for their custodian. If he does not do so during the waiting period, they shall continue to occupy the matrimonial home if it is rented for the duration of the period of custody.'[19] An appeal to the Supreme Constitutional Court against this article was eventually rejected by the court for reasons of form.

In another change to the 1979 law, under the 1985 law 'the consequences of *talaq* shall be effective from the date it is made unless the husband conceals it from the wife, in which case its consequences in terms of inheritance and other financial rights shall only be effective from the date of her knowledge of it'.[20] Finally in this overview, the 1985 law reproduced with a few changes the 1979 provisions on the 'house of obedience', which are naturally of significance to a study of marital relations and the position of the wife. The first clause related to obedience comes as an addition to the original text or law no. 25/1920 cited above, to provide:

> It shall not be deemed grounds for forfeit of maintenance if the wife leaves the matrimonial home without the permission of her husband in circumstances in which this is permitted by a rule of the *shari'a* for which there is some text or prevailing custom or where this is required by necessity, nor if she goes out for lawful work provided that it does not appear that her use of this right is corrupted by abuse of the right, or that it is contrary to the interests of the family, and provided that her husband has not asked her to refrain from exercising her right.

This article appears to give the wife the right to go out to work and then takes it back again by allowing for 'abuse of the right' or a conflict with the interests of the family. If the husband is considered better placed to decide where the interests of the family lie, the law gives him the right to prohibit his wife from working, or from letting her leave the house. As for procedures that are to be followed in the event of the wife being held to have refused to obey her husband without a legitimate reason, the 1985 law sets these out in the section dealing with divorce for discord between the spouses and divorce on grounds of injury.[22]

Problems in practice

Many of the provisions of the personal status laws described above contradicted the basic rights of women, and the field study, the intensive interviews conducted with some of the respondents in the sample and the observations by researchers of personal status cases in court revealed particular problems as a result. Some of these clearly provide context for the reforms to the law introduced in new Law no. 1 of 2000, and are summarized below.

Divorce Divorce law is a striking example of the principle of *qiwama* informing Egyptian personal status law; *talaq* occurs at the wish of men, while women have to go to court to establish cause if they wish to obtain a divorce against the wishes of their husband. Furthermore, in practice, women going to court to seek a judicial divorce faced enormous difficulties. As noted above, laws of the 1920s introduced rulings from the non-Hanafi schools allowing women to seek divorce on such grounds as discord or injury, non-payment of maintenance, and certain chronic physical or psychological conditions (impotence, madness etc.), or the husband's absence for more than a year. In regard to injury, a woman generally has to prove that the harm inflicted on her by her husband is intolerable for 'women like her' (i.e. her peers from a similar social and cultural background). In practice, it appears to have been difficult for women to prove injury in general, and psychological injury in particular, as a basis for divorce, and such claims often led to very long court procedures, sometimes continuing for as long as five to seven years. Furthermore, the husband may use an obedience claim against the divorce petition to also deprive her of maintenance.

Another particularly acute problem observed by our researchers was faced by women who had finally managed to get a judicial divorce at the appeal court and then remarried, only for the Court of Cassation to refuse the divorce. Such cases placed women in the position of being married to two men, a dreadful social, humanitarian and particularly religious dilemma. If the Court of Cassation decided that a woman was to return to her first husband, she would not even have the right to keep her children from the second husband. The recurring incidence of such cases meant that the only solution was to speed up decisions on divorce cases at the Court of Cassation.

Maintenance A consideration of several maintenance cases in the courts revealed many problems of implementation. Among the most important of these perhaps were the lengthy procedures involved in settling maintenance cases through the courts and the issuing of rulings that cannot be enforced. Time-consuming investigations of the husband's income might be diverted to bring about misleading assessments, leading to the undermining of the rights of wife and children, especially where the husband worked freelance. If a prison order was made in accordance with Article 347 of the 1931 regulations on *shari'a* courts, allowing for a prison sentence of up to thirty days against a man able but refusing to pay a maintenance award made against him, enforcement was difficult because final investigations of the husband's ability to pay might not have reached the court. There were cases where the husband would pay a small amount of money towards the debt to undermine the wife's rights just as, after many sessions, the court prepared to make a final ruling that could be implemented.

Denial of paternity (*nasab*) The Egyptian courts see around twelve thousand cases of denial of paternity annually. Where the man and woman involved are married, the husband's denial of paternity might be based on adultery by the wife – she either having been caught in the act or having confessed to it. These claims are always rejected and the courts rule to establish paternity of the child to the husband, on the basis of the *hadith* 'the child belongs to the [marriage] bed and the adulterer shall be stoned'. This is understood to mean that the marriage of the spouses requires that the child's filiation is to the spouses, while the wife's punishment is to be stoned to death; so even if the wife had a child as a result of her adultery, that child's filiation will nevertheless be attributed to her husband, so that the child would not be condemned for being born of adultery.[23]

As for when the man and woman are not married, if a woman claims that she has had a child from an unlawful relationship with a man and wants to have his paternity of her child established, even if the man acknowledges this relationship, the court rules to reject the claim. This is because an acknowledgement must

either 'legitimize the lawful or prevent the prohibited', and adultery and fornication do not give rise to legitimate paternity; the latter is established by a *shar`i*
marriage documented either by official registration or by a customary document.
The increase in the number of cases of denial of paternity may be linked to
attempts to evade the prohibition on adoption; a married couple wanting to adopt
a child might have the wife raise a claim to establish paternity against her husband
so that they could get a court ruling recognizing them as the parents of the child
they want to adopt.

Denial of paternity cases may also arise through the procedure of *li'an* where
a husband suspects his wife of adultery and denies paternity of her child. This
is an ancient procedure established in Islamic jurisprudence and may arise for
example if he divorces her and she then raises a claim for maintenance for the
child, which he defends by denying paternity. The husband will then be asked by
the court to swear an oath four times to the effect that he is telling the truth in
his accusation of her, and in the fifth oath he calls down God's curse upon himself
if he is lying; the wife is then asked to swear the oath four times that he is lying
and in the fifth to call down God's wrath upon herself if he is telling the truth.
The majority of the jurists held that the *li'an* procedure, if completed, entailed
an irrevocable divorce of the couple by the 'greater finality' (*baynuna kubra*) and
filiation of the child to the mother. In traditional jurisprudence, if the man
retracted his oath he would be liable to the *hadd* penalty for *qadhf* (false accusation
of adultery or fornication [*zina*]) which was eighty lashes of the whip, while if the
woman retracted she would be liable to the *hadd* penalty for adultery (*zina* by a
married person), that is, stoning to death. If the procedure is completed and the
final separation of the spouses effected, the ex-husband is allowed subsequently
to attribute the child's filiation to himself whatever the age of the child, although
not after the child's death.

Although Egyptian personal status law does not deal with *li'an*, the courts
have considered such cases on the basis of Article 280 of Law Decree no. 78 of
1931 stipulating the dominant opinion of the Hanafi school as the residual source
of law for personal status cases. There are many texts not included in the laws
but which constitute a reference, including a position to the effect that *li'an* is
applicable to spouses only if the wife has a child less than six months after her
marriage, but anything after six months gives no scope for the procedure; thus,
if the spouses engage in the *li'an* procedure they must be divorced and the child's
filiation is ascribed to its mother if she gave birth less than six months after she
got married.

The 'virgin wife' Few women petition the courts for divorce on the grounds
that the marriage has not been consummated despite years of marriage; many
women face this problem but it is too shameful for most of them to seek divorce,
and the few who do have recourse to the courts confront further problems in the
form of the measures necessary to prove the husband's incapacity. In the case of

a 'virgin wife', both spouses have to undergo tests to identify the reason for the impotence and the potential for the marriage to be consummated following treatment; the court will usually rule for a 'trial period' of a year, after which another investigation of both spouses will be undertaken, to see whether or not the marriage has been consummated. These procedures take a very long time, and lawyers in such cases, particularly where the husband is mistreating his wife, often resort to changing the claim to divorce for injury, in the expectation of speedier resolution. A further complication in divorce for the husband's sexual incapacity, according to a newspaper report, is the lack of consensus among the jurists as to how often the husband was required to have intercourse with his wife to maintain the marriage – for example, once in his life (i.e. consummation), once every two months, or other views (*al-Wafd*, 6 December 1998).

'Urfi marriage *'Urfi* or 'customary' marriage is a valid *shar`i* marriage provided it meets the requirements of the pillars of the contract, the conditions of conclusion and the requirements of publicity, as set out, with differences between the schools, by the scholars of *fiqh*. The rules of the Islamic *shari'a* do not require an official document or a state notary for the contract to be valid. However, the 1931 law provided that 'in the event of denial, claims of marriage or confirmation (*iqrar*) of marriage shall not be heard unless established by an official marriage document'. The potential non-recognition of such marriages held serious implications for the rights of both husband and wife.[24]

In recent years, *'urfi* marriage has become a phenomenon for several reasons. In some cases such a marriage takes place because of the elevated social status of the husband, particularly one who has been married before, who wants to be with a woman who in society's view is of a lesser social status; examples might be the marriage of a doctor to a nurse, a director to a secretary, a master to a servant. Other reasons include a husband who wants to take another wife but not leave his existing wife, thus protecting her and their children. Financial reasons may also encourage *'urfi* marriage, for example a woman who does not want to lose her entitlement to her former husband's pension, or a widow seeking to keep her son exempted from military service as her only son and sole provider.[25]

Although *'urfi* marriage is not acknowledged by the law, it is nevertheless valid in *shar`i* terms, so a wife in such a marriage is in the position of being married, and therefore not allowed to marry anyone else, but unable to get a divorce, should she wish to end the *'urfi* marriage. Imagine her husband has married another woman officially, but is refusing to divorce his wife in the *'urfi* marriage. By his possession of the customary document of the *'urfi* marriage, he effectively controls the future of this woman and any children she may have had by him, whom he may even be refusing to acknowledge. This is a classic example of a woman who may be 'suspended' for ever, neither married nor divorced.[26] To look ahead briefly here, the new personal status law (no. 1 of 2000) provided relief for these 'suspended women', adding to the above-cited clause of the 1931 law the proviso that 'none the less, claims for judicial divorce (*tatliq*) shall be accepted if the marriage is established by a document/in writing (*kitabatan*)'.

The marital home One of the reasons why the issue of child custody pre-occupies both the social and legal sectors is its connection with the matrimonial home. The abiding housing crisis in Egypt has problematized the provision of accommodation for custody and the extent of the entitlement of a divorced wife with custody to the matrimonial home after the marriage has ended.

Under Law no. 25 of 1920, the person responsible for maintaining the children was required to pay a sum of money to the mother or other custodian for her breastfeeding and caring for the children, including the cost of accommodation. In previous times, the divorced wife would generally go back to her birth family's home, or could easily rent a separate dwelling for herself and the children. These days, however, things are much more complicated in light of the housing crisis; the wife's birth family home might not be able to accommodate her and her children, and it is extremely difficult for the woman to get a separate dwelling because of the huge costs involved. Disputes and cases abounded between divorced couples over entitlement to the matrimonial home. Court rulings varied, with some giving the right to the husband and evicting the wife and children, leaving them to try to sort out a home for themselves; others allowed both the disputing parties to stay in the home, despite the serious social implications of this and the fact that it was in violation of *shar`i* rulings on irrevocable divorce; and yet others gave the right to the wife and children to stay in the home.

The conflicting rulings attracted the attention of legal experts, and in a report on Law no. 44 of 1979, the parliament's Joint Committee of the Legislative Committee and the Office of Social Affairs and *Awqaf* and Religious Affairs called for 'a speedy and decisive remedy'. The 1979 law responded by empowering the divorced mother to take over the matrimonial home independently, including the right to conclude a new contract with the landlord as long as she was in occupation of the place during the custody period; the husband had to move elsewhere. The exception this constituted to the normal principles of tenant–landlord contracts is indicative of the inter-relationship between the economic and the social. It was restricted to rented homes; in the case of a home either owned by the husband or assigned to him by his employment, the divorced wife did not have the entitlement. As it was, many men found ways to circumvent the law. By way of example, the Giza court of appeal for personal status ruled in favour of one man's right to the matrimonial flat after he had bought the building in which it was situated; the first instance court had given the right to his ex-wife who had custody, but the husband appealed after buying the property (Mansur n.d.: 45).

The need for new personal status legislation in Egypt The contradictions and discrimination described in this section attracted wide objections from intellectuals and human rights activists rejecting the injustice being done to the weaker sectors of society. For its part, the judicial system faced many problems in dealing with the accumulated numbers of disputes and cases arising from implementation of the law. The examination in this section of the legislative instruments regulating family relations in Egypt serves to contextualize the results of the field study set out in the following chapter.

THREE

Understanding the law: Egyptian family and social attitudes (results of the field study)

The study

§ THE field study was divided into two parts, the first related to the perception of marriage as a social process, involving not only the husband and wife but also other parties; and the second, building on the first, concerned with attitudes to the personal status law governing this social process. For the first part, certain straightforward and specific questions were put to the respondents, as follows:

1. What is the appropriate age for males and females to establish an independent and stable family unit?
2. What rights do women have in choosing their partners, and what criteria inform this choice?
3. What is the purpose of the financial elements, notably the dower (or dowry) and jewellery (*shabka*),[27] in so far as they may be factors affecting the success or failure of the marriage?
4. What is the sample's position on polygyny?
5. How are the roles and responsibilities of family members distributed?
6. What are the most common reasons for divorce and family breakdown?

The sample

The sample included 200 individuals chosen from four governorates (Cairo, Sharqia, Minya and Qena), using a predetermined restricted sample method. The sample included the following: eighty individuals from Cairo (40 per cent of the total number of the sample), forty from Sharqia (20 per cent); forty from Minya (20 per cent) and forty from Qena (20 per cent). Table 1.1 sets out the rural/urban variables, with 70 per cent of the sample from urban areas and 30 per cent from rural areas. All the participants from Cairo were from urban areas, owing to the lack of rural areas in the capital; in the other governorates the sample came in equal numbers from urban and rural areas. Table 1.2 shows the distribution of the sample according to gender. The inclusion of 60 per cent females compared to 40 per cent males in the sample was a deliberate choice, primarily because of the aim of exploring the position of Egyptian women towards the law. Table 1.3 shows respondents according to their educational level, with 57.7 per cent of the sample illiterate, 20 per cent having completed primary education, 14 per cent having completed secondary education, and only 8.5 per cent having completed higher education. Table 1.4 shows that 46 per cent of the total number of the sample are married, 19.5 per cent single but engaged and soon to be married, 18.5 per cent single, 11 per cent divorced and 5 per cent widowed. It is also worth noting here that more than 65 per cent of married women in the sample had not chosen their husbands, and the majority had married before they reached twenty years of age. Early marriage was one of the major reasons behind them having left school: 50 per cent were uneducated, 19 per cent had not completed their primary education, and 23.2 per cent had left school for marriage.

Table I.1 Distribution of sample according to geographical location

Governorates Variables	Total		Cairo		Sharqia		Minya		Qena	
	N	%	N	%	N	%	N	%	N	%
Rural	60	30	–	–	20	50	20	50	20	50
Urban	140	70	80	100	20	50	20	50	20	50
Total	200	100	80	100	40	100	40	100	40	100

Table I.2 Distribution of sample according to sex

Governorates Variables	Total		Cairo		Sharqia		Minya		Qena	
	N	%	N	%	N	%	N	%	N	%
Male	80	40	30	37.5	18	45	15	37.5	17	42.5
Female	120	60	50	63.5	22	55	25	63.5	23	57.5
Total	200	100	80	100	40	100	40	100	40	100

Table I.3 Distribution of sample according to standard of education

Education level	Total		Cairo		Sharqia		Minya		Qena	
	N	%	N	%	N	%	N	%	N	%
Primary	40	20	14	17.5	7	17.5	9	22.5	10	25
Secondary	28	14	9	11.25	7	17.5	5	12.5	7	17.5
Higher	17	8.5	9	11.25	3	7.5	3	7.5	2	5
Illiterate	115	57.5	48	60	23	57.5	23	57.5	21	52.5
Total	200	100	80	100	40	100	40	100	40	100

Table I.4 Distribution of individuals according to marital status

Marital status	Total		Cairo		Sharqia		Minya		Qena	
	N	%	N	%	N	%	N	%	N	%
Married	92	46	28	35	22	55	22	55	20	50
Engaged single	39	19.5	10	12.5	9	22.5	9	22.5	11	27.5
Unengaged single	37	18.5	26	32.5	3	7.5	4	10	4	10
Divorced	22	11	12	15	5	12.5	2	5	3	7.5
Widowed	10	5	4	5	1	2.5	3	7.5	2	5
Total	200	100	80	100	40	100	40	100	40	100

Ideal marriage age

The results showed a variation in the age of marriage perceived as ideal, between urban and rural areas and according to the educational level (Table 1.5). The majority of those in the rural areas still valued early marriage for women, whereas in urban areas, especially in Cairo, the percentage of those believing in early marriage was low. With regard to educational variables, the study reveals that sixteen of the males in the sample with basic (primary) education held that the ideal age of marriage for females was under sixteen (constituting 8 per cent of the sample as a whole), while none of the males with higher education agreed.

Among those who agreed with early marriage for females, the main motivating factors given were:

1. Religious/moral factors: a belief that early marriage precludes females from any 'wrongdoing'.

Table I.5 Ideal age for female marriage

Variables	Below 16		16–22		23–26		27–30		30–35		35–more	
	N	%	N	%	N	%	N	%	N	%	N	%
Primary												
Male	16	8	3	1.5	–	–	–	–	–	–	–	–
Female	18	9	3	1.5	–	–	–	–	–	–	–	–
Secondary												
Male	4	9	7	3.5	5	2.5	–	–	–	–	–	–
Female	1	0.5	7	3.5	4	2	–	–	–	–	–	–
High												
Male	–	–	10	5	2	1	–	–	–	–	–	–
Female	–	–	5	2.5	–	–	–	–	–	–	–	–
Illiterate												
Male	12	6	19	9.5	2	1	–	–	–	–	–	–
Female	31	15.5	49	24.5	2	1	–	–	–	–	–	–

2. Economic factors: in rural areas early marriage means the young woman's labour can be used in the service of her husband's family and in particular her mother-in-law, and of her husband in the house and the field. In some villages in the Delta, the wife can save her husband the costs of hiring a labourer.
3. Cultural factors: these are manifested in the two values of protecting the honour of the virgin girl, and avoiding spinsterhood.

Table 1.6 sets out the main reasons expressed in support of early marriage by males and females in the sample agreeing with the practice.

Table 1.6 Motivating factors for early marriage

Motive	Male			Female		
	Rural	Urban	Total	Rural	Urban	Total
Protection from 'wrongdoing'	9.5	2	11.5	18.5	4.5	23
Girl's labour in serving husband and in-laws	6.5	1.5	8	2.5	–	2.5
Getting used to husband	8.5	3	11	13.5	3	16.5
Protecting honour/avoiding spinsterhood	6	1	7	16	4	20

Table 1.6 shows a difference between the motivating factors for early marriage as expressed by men and women. While the order of motivations began for both sexes with early marriage as a 'protection against wrongdoing', for males the second reason cited was that the wife would get used to her husband from an early age, with economic factors third and the cultural values last on the list. For women, the cultural factors were second, with economic benefits to the groom's family last on this list.

The right of the young woman to choose her life partner

The field study showed that 56 per cent of the total sample agreed that a young woman had the right to choose her husband (Table 1.7), while 16 per cent agreed with this on condition that the final decision should be down to her parents. The percentage of those supporting this right was higher in urban areas (14 per cent of males, 32.5 per cent of females) than in rural areas. It was also higher among women than men.

Respondents gave the following reasons for their agreement to the principle of the woman's right to choose her partner, in order of significance: first, that since it is she who is going to live with her partner, she should have the right to choose him; second, she knows the person proposing to her better than anybody

Table I.7 Opinion on the young woman having the right to choose her life partner (% of sample)

Opinion	Male			Female		
	Rural	Urban	Total	Rural	Urban	Total
Agree	3.5	14	17.5	6	32.5	38.5
Disagree	6.5	6	12.5	5.5	5	10.5
Agree with condition	2	5	7	3	6	9
No details	2	1	3	1.5	0.5	2

else, so she is more capable of making the judgement; and third, religion gives her this right.

Respondents who did not agree that a young woman had the right to choose her own partner gave as reasons the following: that a young woman is immature and so her parents should manage this matter for her, since they are more able to judge by reason of age and experience and their knowledge of what is in her best interests; and that the decisions of young women are based on emotions rather than reason.

Marriage and marriage arrangements

The respondents ranked in Table 1.8 factors or personal characteristics that they had taken or would take into consideration when choosing their spouse:

Table I.8 Desired characteristics of life partner

Female respondents	Male respondents
Economic status	Being religious
Age	Family
Family	Appearance
Being religious	Economic status
Appearance	Age
Love	Level of education
Level of education	Love
Personality	Personality
Like-mindedness	Like-mindedness

For the purposes of this question, the concept of the partner 'being religious' was defined as having knowledge of the basic rules of Islam and being committed to regularly carrying out religious obligations, rather than a general faith un-accompanied by a commitment to practice and religious rules.

For women, the ranking of certain of the criteria differed according to the respondent's level of education. The importance of the husband's level of education increased with the level of education of the female respondent, followed for this group of respondents by the significance of similarity in age, a condition which was not significant for the illiterate women, especially in the rural areas.

Table I.9 Factors taken into consideration in choosing life partner

Data	Male			Female		
	Rural	Urban	Total	Rural	Urban	Total
Being religious	13	22.5	35.5	14	16.5	30.5
Family	12.5	20.5	34	12	22.5	34.5
Appearance	6	23	29	5.5	22.5	28
Economic status	5	15.5	20.5	14	37.5	51.5
Age	5.5	10.5	16	9.5	30.5	40
Educational level	1.5	11.5	13	4.5	16	20.5
Love	2.5	9	11.5	3	19	22
Personality	1.5	6.5	8	2.5	15.5	18
Like-mindedness	0.5	4	4.5	0.5	9	9.5

* Respondents were given more than one option, giving a total of over 100%.

It is also worth noting, in regard to the results set out in Table 1.9, that a large proportion of the male respondents who were either married or engaged stated that their parents had played a significant role in selecting their future wife, whether directly or indirectly. In most cases it was the mother who had played the leading role, either selecting the bride or proposing a particular bride from among a number of possibilities.

Factors affecting the level of dower

Table 1.10 shows the factors that male respondents considered when setting the level of dower, ranked as follows in order of importance: financial status of the groom, financial status of the bride's family, the bride's beauty, her educational level and her professional status. A higher value was placed by urban males on the last two factors as they affect the bride's potential participation in the financial responsibilities of her family.

The purpose of *shabka* and dower

Eighteen per cent of the male respondents said that the main purpose of the gold jewellery given to the bride, known customarily as the *shabka*, is to secure her financial rights, as it becomes her own property. However, 36 per cent said

Table I.10 Factors affecting level of dower (% of total) (males)

Factors	Rural	Urban	Total
Bride's beauty	7.5	16	23.5
Groom's financial status	11.5	22.5	34
Bride's family's financial status	9	18	27
Bride's educational level	1	6.5	7.5
Bride's professional status (i.e. whether or not she works)	1	5	6

*Respondents were given more than one option, giving a total of over 100 per cent.

that if she had a good relationship with her husband, the wife should give up the *shabka* in the event that the household or her husband fell upon hard financial times. Twenty-one per cent of males in the sample said that the *shabka* proved the seriousness of the groom and his affection for his bride; only 7 per cent of the male respondents said that *shabka* had a part to play in establishing the status of the wife among relatives and neighbours.

As for the female respondents, a large proportion (54.5 per cent) saw the *shabka* as a kind of savings to be used in setting up the house, for the children's needs, or for other household needs; 47 per cent said that it was to secure the wife's financial interests and 32 per cent that it played an important role in establishing her status. A slightly lesser number (30.5 per cent) held that it showed the seriousness of the groom and his affection for his bride.

Table I.11 Meanings given to the *shabka*

Female respondents	Male respondents
Value can be used in time of need	Value can be used in time of need
Guaranteeing her financial interests	Seriousness and affection of her groom
Establishing status	Guaranteeing her financial interests
Seriousness and affection of her groom	Establishing status

Table I.12 Purpose of the *shabka* (% of total)

Purpose	Male			Female		
	Rural	Urban	Total	Rural	Urban	Total
Secure bride's financial interests	5.5	12.5	18	11	36	47
Asset for future	14	22	36	14	40.5	54.5
Groom's seriousness	12	9	21	7.5	23	30.5
Establishing status	2	5	7	14	18	32

The different meanings given to the *shabka* by men and women are shown in Table 1.11, in order of significance to the respondents, while the detailed breakdown of responses is in Table 1.12.

As for the dower, the largest proportion of both male (40 per cent) and female (55 per cent) respondents held that the main purpose of the dower was as the husband's contribution to furnishing the marital home.

Table I.13 Purpose of dower (% of total)

Purpose	Male			Female		
	Rural	Urban	Total	Rural	Urban	Total
Secure bride's financial interests	2	10.5	12.5	7	4.5	11.5
Bridegroom's contribution in furnishing home	14	26	40	11	44	55

*Respondents were given more than one option, giving a total of over 100%.

The position on polygyny

The vast majority of male respondents in the sample stated that the husband had the right to marry another wife in a polygynous union if the wife was unable to have children, or if she had a long-term illness, on the pretext that 'the husband cannot take not being sexually satisfied for a long time, so he has to take another wife'. Table 1.14 shows the level of agreement on these and other justifications for polygyny among the male respondents.

Table I.14 Reasons for justifying polygyny (% of total) (males)

Reasons	Rural	Urban	Total
'Wife can't have kids'	12	9.5	21.5
Wife has chronic illness	8.5	5	13.5
Husband's high capabilities	5	2	7
'Religion allows it'	8	4.5	12.5
Wife is irritable and troublesome[28]	3.5	1.5	5

It is worth noting here that the religious justification for polygyny came towards the end of the list, after reasons that those who supported them saw as rational and practical. As for the relationship between the first and subsequent wives, a large proportion of the female respondents said that in most cases it was hostile.

The husband's responsibilities

Table 1.15 shows the functions identified by male and female respondents as the responsibilities of the husband.

Table I.15 Husband's responsibilities towards his family (% of total)

Responsibilities	Males			Females		
	Rural	Urban	Total	Rural	Urban	Total
Providing for needs of household	14	26	40	16	41.5	57.5
Fulfilling his (sexual) marital obligations	14	26	40	16	44	60
Sharing in raising the children	10.5	18.5	29	7.5	32.5	40
Protecting the members of his household	14	26	40	16	20	36

* Respondents were given more than one option, giving a total of over 100 per cent.

The wife's work outside the home

Table 1.17 sets out the level of agreement given by male and female respondents to conditions they considered to justify women going out to work (outside the marital home). In Table 1.16, the various conditions agreed to by the respondents are set out in order of how much agreement each condition attracted; the number in brackets shows the number of respondents who agreed with the particular condition, a number converted to a percentage in Table 1.17.

Table I.16 Reasons for allowing women to work

Female respondents	Male respondents
To meet financial needs (126)	Her husband allows it (73)
Does not clash with other duties (95)	Does not clash with other duties (25)
Her husband allows it (84)	In case of financial needs (49)
To realize her own aspirations (13)	To realize her own aspirations (4)

Table I.17 Women going out to work (% of total)

Reasons	Males			Females		
	Rural	Urban	Total	Rural	Urban	Total
Husband allows it	14	22.5	36.5	14	28	42
Work does not clash with her other duties	11	15	26	16	31.5	47.5
Financial need	4	2	6	22.5	40.5	63
Wife's aspirations	0.5	1.5	2	0.5	6	6.5

* Respondents were given more than one option, giving a total of over 100%.

Urban women in the field study were more aware of the importance of work to women in order to realize their own potential; almost 14 per cent of the urban female respondents held work important for this aspect, compared with just over 3 per cent of rural women.

Within the context of Egyptian society, it was reasonable to anticipate that only a low proportion of the male respondents would endorse women going out to work in order to realize their own aspirations. However, what is striking about the results of the field study here is the finding that this justification for women's work also came at the bottom of the list for women, suggesting that Egyptian women have been influenced by the male viewpoint that opposes the right of women to work.

As for the duties of a wife towards her husband in the event that she goes out to work, both the male and the female respondents gave first priority to her duty to contribute financially to the support of the family, and second priority to not allowing her outside work to affect her ability to maintain her 'natural functions' in looking after her children and her husband.

Difficult living conditions have clearly pushed widening sectors of society to accept women going out to work so that they can share in shouldering the family's financial burdens. It is for this reason that the respondents identified the duty to contribute to the financial support of the family as top of the duties of a woman working outside the home. Similarly, it was logical that the second most important duty of a working woman was held by the respondents to be that her work should not affect her care for the family; all are aware that there will necessarily be a certain impact, which they will have to accept for so long as circumstances oblige them to accept women entering the labour market. Many of the respondents stated in the in-depth interviews that a man who accepted his wife going out to work must necessarily accept that this would affect her role as a mother and a wife, but on condition that it did not lead to the break-up of the family or to a negative impact on the mother's child-rearing functions.

Table I.18 Duties of a working woman towards her husband and children (% of total)

Duties	Males			Females		
	Rural	Urban	Total	Rural	Urban	Total
Contributing to family support	2.5	24.5	27	4.5	41.5	46
Not affecting care of children and husband	8	14	22	15	28.5	43.5

*Respondents were given more than one option, giving a total of over 100%.

Physical punishment of the wife

When respondents were asked whether a man had the right to physically punish his wife, a large proportion of the sample agreed that he could if forced to do so; 43 per cent of the sample held that he could mete out severe physical punishment if his wife had done something wrong (23.5 per cent males and 19.5 per cent females), while a further 35.5 per cent held that a man could employ light physical punishment against his wife (12.5 per cent males and 23 per cent females). Thirteen per cent of the respondents said that the husband should only threaten to punish his wife (2 per cent males and 11 per cent females). Of the whole sample, only seventeen individuals (8.5 per cent of the sample, of which 2 per cent were males and 6.5 per cent females) held that a husband had no right to use physical punishment against his wife.

The results of the field study show that educational level had a positive impact on respondents' stance on the issue of physical punishment, as shown in Table 1.19. Of the twelve males who received higher education, only three of them (25 per cent of this group) accepted the idea of physical punishment, and five of them (41.7 per cent of this group) held either that a husband had no right to punish his wife physically or could only threaten its use. At the same time, all the illiterate males in the sample accepted the principle of some level of physical

Table I.19 Right of the husband to physically punish the wife (% of total)

Variables	Husband may physically punish wife		Light punishment		Threaten to punish		No right to physically punish	
	N	%	N	%	N	%	N	%
Primary school attended								
Male	13	6.5	6	3	–	–	–	–
Female	9	4.5	7	3.5	4	2	1	0.5
Secondary school attended								
Male	6	3	7	3.5	2	1	1	0.5
Female	2	1	5	2.5	2	1	3	1.5
Higher education								
Male	3	1.5	4	2	2	1	3	1.5
Female	–	–	2	1	1	0.5	2	1
Illiterate								
Male	25	12.5	8	4	–	–	–	–
Female	28	14	32	16	15	7.5	7	3.5
Total								
Male	47	23.5	25	12.5	4	2	4	2
Female	39	19.5	46	23	22	11	13	6.5
Overall	86	43	71	35.5	26	13	17	8.5

punishment against wives, with 75.8 per cent of this group accepting the idea of severe physical punishment.

The most critical finding of this part of the field study is that, in the sample, women themselves accepted the concept of physical punishment, as a kind of discipline affirmed by religion. Table 1.19 shows that 34.1 per cent of the illiterate female respondents accepted the idea of severe physical punishment, along with 16.7 per cent of women with secondary school education and 42 per cent of women with primary education. The impact of educational level is again clear here, with none of the women with higher education accepting this idea.

The field study also showed that many female respondents had been subjected to physical punishment by relatives during childhood (29.5 per cent of all female respondents); this was considered normal and routine, with the women harbouring no resentment but considering it an important tool for discipline in upbringing. Of the whole sample, 80 per cent said that they had been subjected to physical punishment, a larger proportion of these being among the men, and in inverse proportion to the socio-economic status of the family.

Reasons for divorce

The questions in the field study on the subject of divorce resulted in a number of observations based on the answers of the respondents. To start with the reasons for divorce, physical abuse came top of the list for the female group in the sample (60 per cent of the female respondents), followed by financial difficulties, and thirdly failure by the husband to fulfil his family responsibilities especially towards the children. No religious reason was given as a reason for divorce, and there were other factors that had no impact on the decision to divorce, notably marital betrayal (i.e. adultery). There was no case in the sample of adultery by the wife, and adultery by the husband was not mentioned, perhaps not being considered as an important reason for divorce in Egypt.

As for process, there were reports of the wife's family, her father and mother, participating in efforts to prevent divorce, while the participation of the husband's family was very limited. This is due to the fact that it is the wife's family that feels the embarrassment of their daughter's position in front of the society if she is divorced. In most cases where the wife's family intervened in this regard, it was the father who undertook the efforts at reconciliation or at pressurizing the husband. Furthermore, most of the cases of divorce in the sample had taken place at the wish of the husband, although there were a limited number of cases at the petition of the wife; in such cases the husband usually refused, so there was no way around going to court. Additionally, a large proportion of the sample held that divorce was void if uttered verbally in a moment of haste and anger (*iddtirab*).

Regarding the husband's responsibilities after divorce, the majority of the female respondents held them to be maintenance of the wife, maintenance of the children and playing a part in bringing up the children. Financial responsibilities (maintenance) were ranked highest in the answers of the majority of the sample (men and women) while the child-rearing and emotional responsibility were second in importance. In most of the divorce cases, the maintenance agreement that the parties had made was not kept and the two parties went to court for a ruling on the matter; however, a small proportion of the respondents reported that amicable informal sessions with the participation of relatives helped to solve the maintenance dispute. In most of the cases, the mother got custody of minor children from the marriage, with the father taking over in a small number of the cases. Where the father took over custody of his minor children, it was either the father or his sister who took care of them. Factors that were taken into consideration in deciding who would take custody of the children were, first, what the law said on child custody and, second, financial factors (the capabilities of the parties); the choices of the children played no role in identifying which of their parents would have custody.

Conclusion

In this chapter we have reviewed the results of the field study involving a sample of the public, in which we concentrated on marriage as a social process and the way the parties involved view marriage and their rights and responsibilities. These perceptions reflect substantively on the positions the public takes on the law, subjects dealt with in the following chapters.

FOUR

Law no. 1 of 2000: a new personal status law and a limited step on the path to reform

§ THIS chapter begins with a consideration of Law no. 1 of 2000, the most recent attempt to tackle the legislative gaps and violations of the wife's rights that characterized previous laws. This is followed by the positions taken on the law by respondents in the elite sample and another sample of the public.

The legislative process

The government's initiative in drafting a new personal status law could be attributed to a number of reasons. The existing law was a source of considerable embarrassment for the government on the international level, as opening up to the West economically had a social cost. Moreover, women within the Egyptian economic elite no longer accepted the status quo, and feminist pressure groups were formed for the amendment of the law. In addition, the huge number of personal status cases made amending the law a matter of pressing necessity.

A specialized committee of the National Democratic Party's women leaders was formed in 1998. This committee drafted a white paper and submitted it to the Minister of Justice, Counsellor Farouq Saif Al Nasser. The white paper contained six points for inclusion in personal status law, including the *khul'* procedure discussed below. The same year, the Ministry of Justice in collaboration with the National Council of Women presented a draft proposal for discussion before the People's Assembly; the amendments proposed in this document were not aimed at changing substance so much as at reducing the amount of time taken by litigation procedures, and at establishing family courts dedicated to personal status matters. In 1998, the draft law was discussed at the Shura Assembly (Senate); the government seemed comfortable with the idea and it was referred to the Council of State for review; it was approved. A copy of the draft was also sent to the Mufti of the Republic and the Shaykh of al-Azhar to confirm its compliance with the rulings of the Islamic *shari'a*.

The original draft of the law was to attract considerable criticism, some of which is outlined below, and a number of its provisions were to undergo changes before the law was finally passed in January 2000, as Law no. 1 of 2000 Concerning Certain Situations and Procedures of Litigation in Personal Status Matters. The most often discussed points in the draft included the wife's right to obtain from the court (if her husband refused to agree) a *khul'* divorce in return for waiving her financial rights from her husband; the wife's right to petition the court for the right to travel if her husband was refusing; the denial of legal validity (in terms of effects) to an out-of-court *talaq* not witnessed and formally registered with the relevant authorities; and the official recognition of divorce from an *'urfi* marriage.

Reaction of the *shar'i* establishment: scholars and religious tendencies

The Islamic authorities and institutions reacted with trepidation to the government's plans to issue a new personal status law, raising objections to a number of points that they considered contrary to the Islamic *shari'a*. There were, however, significant differences within and between the various bodies.

The Islamic Studies Academy (Majma' al-buhuth al-islamiyya) The Islamic Studies Academy was the first to express opposition, demanding changes and proposing amendments. In the session that approved the draft, fourteen of the members of the Academy were absent; fourteen members spoke and eight others stayed silent throughout the session.[29] Of the fourteen who spoke, according to the record of the meeting, five supported the law and eight objected. Over the course of four closed meetings, a committee of the Academy and certain professors of *shari'a* and of law drafted amendments to certain articles that they considered contrary to the *shari'a*, approved in their final form in the session of 11 February 1999, which in addition to Academy members was attended by the Minister of Awqaf Dr Hamdi Zaqzouq, the Mufti of the Republic, Dr Nasr Farid Wasel and the Dean of al-Azhar University, Dr Ahmed Umar Hashim.

Among the points which raised controversy in the committee was the reference to the dominant opinions of the Hanafi school in matters of personal status and of *waqf* not covered in the relevant legislative instruments. Some committee members held that since the law contained provisions taken from other schools of law (such as judicial divorce for harm, from Maliki rules, and some of the provisions on divorce), this provision should be amended; others argued that it was unnecessarily restrictive and rather out of touch with reality to have a text stipulating one jurisprudential school only. However, the idea of changing the text provoked considerable debate and in the end the committee members agreed to leave it as it was, in order that nobody should rely on unorthodox jurisprudential views such as those of the Shi'a.

On the question of the wife's right to *khul'*, the committee was split. The draft law contained a provision giving the wife the right to obtain a divorce from the court in exchange for waiving her financial rights, a procedure which some saw as acknowledging the wife's right to divorce whenever she wanted. Some committee members argued that this would open the door for women – particularly wealthy women – to flee their marital responsibilities and to break up their families. The other side argued that the Prophet himself had approved divorce by *khul'*, that a woman would go for a divorce only when she had real justification for such action, and that it was not in society's interests for a family to have to stay together when the wife had declared her hatred for her husband and her desire for a divorce. The committee finally agreed by majority vote that the wife should have the right to a *khul'* divorce in exchange for giving up all the property she had received from her husband, such as the dower and gifts, in addition to maintenance and the deferred dower. They also recommended that the court should do its utmost to effect reconciliation before issuing a ruling in such a case.

The committee was also split on the provision in the draft law that *talaq* would not be 'counted' (*i'tidad*) unless there were witnesses and it was documented. Some held that this provision, meaning that the incidence of the *talaq* would not be recognized unless there were two witnesses and it was documented with the notary, contradicted the *shar'i* rulings establishing that *talaq* can occur by mere pronouncement, without the need for documentation or registration. This group held that the provision should have added to it a phrase to the effect that *talaq* should occur 'religiously' – that is, between the worshipper and his lord – so that the woman accordingly becomes prohibited to him in terms of the *shari'a* even if the *talaq* had taken place without witnesses or documentation.

Other members believed that in order to guarantee the rights of the wife and protect her from a situation in which her husband engaged in marital relations with her when she was unaware that he had unilaterally divorced her, the article should remain. If the divorce had not been properly documented, the wife would retain all her rights under the law; this would oblige the husband to document the divorce properly. The committee agreed to recommend that it be taken into consideration that the terms of this provision did not affect the fact that a verbal *talaq* occurred religiously (*diyanatan*) even while not being 'counted' legally unless it was witnessed and documented.

'Urfi marriage was also a matter of wide debate among members of the committee. If they agreed that *'urfi* marriage should not be recognized, and that marriage should be officially documented, there remained the problem of wives in *'urfi* marriages who wished to obtain a divorce; as it stood, if such a woman married another man in an officially documented marriage, under criminal law she would be committing bigamy and would be liable to punishment. The committee accordingly added an amendment providing that claims for judicial divorce should be accepted if a wife in such a situation produced any material evidence for the establishment of the existing marital relationship, even if this were a letter from the husband to the wife. In such a case, they proposed, the woman could obtain a judicial divorce, although she would not be entitled to any other rights.

Another major amendment sought by the Academy on the basis of a consensus of its members was that a ruling of the court of appeal on judicial separation of a wife from her husband should be implemented only after the Court of Cassation had issued its ruling on the case, provided that the Court of Cassation should rule within a period not exceeding four months, unless the appeal period of two months had passed without the husband objecting, in which case the appeal court's decision should be implemented.[30]

Consensus was also forthcoming on the amendment of a draft text that stated that in the event of denial, claims of acknowledgement of paternity or of witnessing such acknowledgement would not be heard after the death of the testator unless there were official or written documents in the handwriting of the deceased and carrying his signature. In light of widespread illiteracy, Academy members felt that this would deprive many children of the opportunity to establish their lineage to their father, whereas the *shari'a* safeguards the establishment of paternity in order to protect the children from ruin. They therefore proposed that the text be amended to permit any other form of definite proof such as a blood test; the text of the law as finally passed allowed for such other forms of definite proof, without giving examples.[31]

With regard to other matters, Academy members also objected to the draft law failing to set out how the *'idda* (the waiting period after the end of a marriage, during which a woman may not remarry) was to be calculated, proposing that the law should stipulate the period according to particular standards: thus for a young woman still menstruating the *'idda* period should be sixty days, for an older woman ninety days, and for a pregnant woman until childbirth. They also recommended that in regard to the provision stipulating that the court would not hear claims by spouses where the wife was under sixteen or the husband under eighteen, an Explanatory Memorandum should note that this did not mean that their marriage was not *shar'i* and subsequently gave rise to *shar'i* rights.

Al-Azhar scholars The draft law provoked senior scholars at al-Azhar to issue a comprehensive statement setting out the points on which they disagreed. Another statement was issued by the al-Azhar Scholars' Front underlining their total rejection of the provision on *khul'*. A number of points were raised on *khul'* in the two statements, including the need for the husband's consent to *khul'*, how the divorce is to be effected, and whether it constitutes a final or revocable *talaq*, or indeed a dissolution of the contract (*faskh*), as well as the *'idda* of the wife. The statement by the senior al-Azhar scholars held that the *khul'* provision was an explicit violation of the rulings of the *shari'a*, and extremely dangerous for the integrity of the family. The first clause of the draft provision, stating that the spouses could agree together on *khul'*, was only part to conform to the *shari'a*; the rest of the clauses flouted the principle of mutual agreement, giving the decision to the judge and overriding the will of the husband, although as a party to the contract it should not be implemented without his approval, not to mention the right of *qiwama* which, the statement continued, was ignored in the provision. If the two spouses did not agree between themselves, the wife's unilateral claim for a divorce should not be heard; hatred and dislike were not objective grounds that could serve a *shar'i* ruling, and using them as grounds for divorce against the will of the husband was a serious matter that would throw a time-bomb into the Muslim household which the wife could detonate at any moment. The final clause of the draft, providing that the judge's ruling for divorce would be final and not open to appeal, was a disaster in the view of the scholars and 'raised doubts about this article'.

Progressive Islamists Progressive Islamists such as Hassan Duh and Gamal al-Bana believe that the most important issue is women's freedom. If we believe that women should enjoy freedom and the fulfilment of their personal potential, as men do, freedom being a gift from God rather than from the husband or the father, then issues like the *khul'* or women travelling abroad or other such matters would find a solution. If the issue of *khul'* is raised then *talaq* must also be considered; the man should not have the absolute right to divorce his wife unless the woman has the right to free herself from a husband she hates and with whom she can no longer live, so she should ransom herself and pay an exchange for her freedom.

On the issue of women travelling abroad without the husband's consent, Duh holds that the constraint on travel is to protect the wife from harm rather than that she should be deprived of travel. Accordingly, if the travel is safe and for a reason that realizes an interest for the wife and her family (such as for pilgrimage, studies or work) then the husband should support it rather than forbid her. If he acts arbitrarily then the court should pronounce with all speed in order that the woman not miss an opportunity she considers to be in her interest.

Some of those who had opposed the article on *khul'* cited a *hadith* which quoted the Prophet as saying that women who divorce by *khul'* were hypocrites. However, Shaykh Gamal Qutub, former head of the Fatwa Committee at al-Azhar and a prominent scholar, emphasized that the Prophet had never impugned anyone's faith nor insulted anyone, and that there was no proof that women divorcing by *khul'* were hypocrites. Furthermore, Shaykh Qutub held that the law oppressed women by requiring that they give up all their rights, as well as by providing that the court was to appoint two arbitrators to attempt reconciliation, delaying its decision more than once and for a period of up to six months during which the women would have to wait suspended.

Among other modern Egyptian jurists, the renowned scholar Shaykh Mohammed al-Ghazali had before his death called for the application of *khul'* provisions. While the court could postpone a woman's petition in the interests of the family and children, or in the hope of the families intervening to reconcile the spouses, 'if the wife refuses anything but divorce and gives back the property handed over to her, then she must be released and her feelings must be respected, it is not up to us to ask the hidden reasons for this wish of hers, to accept or reject it' (al-Ghazali 1994: 178). He also observed that men were not permitted to coerce their wives into requesting a *khul'*, making their lives so difficult that they would seek release at any price. Al-Ghazali quoted Shaykh Sayed Sabeq (*Sunni Fiqh*) to the effect that if a *khul'* was obtained by a man through harming the wife, the agreement is void; Imam Malik held in such cases that the *khul'* would be implemented as a divorce and the husband would have to return whatever he had taken as remuneration (in the *khul'*) from his wife (ibid., p. 180).

The parliamentary debate

The debate over the draft law went on for six sessions (morning and afternoon) with 111 MPs taking part. Some fifty-four members participated in the debate over the *khul'* article, and an unprecedented one-quarter of the membership joined in the discussions over the draft in general.

The biggest storm was caused by the draft article giving a wife the right to have recourse to the court to travel without the consent of her husband. The majority of the members of the Assembly opposed it, on the grounds that the *shari'a* did not give this authority to the judge, but rather ruled that the husband had the right to his wife's obedience, and she should not leave the matrimonial home without the permission of her husband, as proven by sound Prophetic *hadiths*. The wife could stipulate in her marriage contract her right to travel when necessary, and in this case the husband would be bound to comply. Some cited a Prophetic *hadith* to the effect that the believing woman may not undertake a journey of a day and a night without the presence of a *mahram*;[32] seeking permission was thus in accordance with the letter and the spirit of Islam and with the customs and traditions of the East.

Those approving the ruling said that some scholars, most notably Imam Shafi`i, considered women should be safe when travelling and permitted them to travel alone if the road was safe; indeed, that trustworthy women could take the place of a male *mahram*. The rejectionists objected that the law was not concerned with a woman's travel as a woman, but with the travel of a wife without her husband's permission; and this decision was the right of the husband alone. The rejectionists added that the Prophetic *sunna* explicitly established that the wife should not leave the matrimonial home without the permission of her husband: how could this be retained while the wife had the right to travel abroad without his consent? In the question of his wife leaving the house, the *sunna* did not have regard for whether the husband was being obdurate or arbitrary in his decision; had it made this a consideration, there would be room for an analogy with the matter of her right to travel, but this was not the case. Ultimately, the Assembly held for the striking of the article giving the judge emergency powers to approve the wife's travel without her husband's consent.

On the *khul'* provision, those objecting to it argued that it effectively took away the husband's authority and overruled his wishes, in violation of the Islamic *shari'a*. This was the position of many Assembly members, including prominent figures of the ruling NDP, who called for the text to be amended to comply with the juristic consensus requiring the husband's consent. They also argued that the text conflicted with the traditions and customs of Egyptian society by requiring the return of the dower, while in most marriages the full dower was not declared, which meant the husband stood to suffer a loss. The text should therefore be amended so that 'dower' became everything that the husband had paid. They also demanded that both parties to the dispute should have the right to appeal. On the other hand, those supporting the *khul'* provision held that the right of mutual consent was already established in the article, and in the event that they could not agree it was established jurisprudentially that recourse could be had to the courts where the judge could rule for *khul'*. In the end, the Assembly called for a new clause to be added to the provision on *khul'* requiring the court to appoint two arbitrators from the respective families to try to reconcile the spouses for three months before issuing a decision on divorce.[33]

On other matters, some Assembly members approved the idea in the draft law of reviewing prison sentences in personal status cases, on the grounds that modern legislation was always looking for an alternative to imprisonment because of the negative effects it had on human relationships and its fracturing of family structures, with no benefit to any party – what did it benefit a wife, for example, if the husband who was refusing to pay maintenance was put in prison? They agreed that there should be an optional alternative such as a fine. The Assembly therefore decided to strike Article 77 of the draft stipulating a three- to six-month prison sentence for a husband refusing to implement final court rulings for maintenances, fees and related matters, since there was a similar provision in criminal law. The issue of imprisonment of the husband was to return after the law was promulgated, as set out below.

There was a furious debate over what became Article 19 in the law as passed, regarding the appointment of arbitrators where this was required in cases of judicial divorce. The article stated that the court should charge the spouses, as far as possible, to name one arbitrator from the wife's family and one from the husband's in the following session, but if one of the spouses failed to do so or did not turn up, the court would appoint an arbitrator for him or her. The arbitrators had to appear at the session following their appointment to give their report, but if they differed or one of them did not come, the court would hear the statements of the two or of the one who came and might act on what they had concluded together, on what one had concluded, or on other material from the file of the case. Some demanded in this regard that the law should conform strictly with the Qur'anic text stipulating the choice of one arbitrator from the husband's and one from the wife's family to investigate reconciliation between the spouses.

Political parties and the law

The political parties that opposed the law appealed to arguments both old and new, for example that there should be harmony on these matters, that the timing was not right for certain of the provisions, that society was not yet ready to take up these *shar'i* principles, or that women were not yet mature enough to make good use of these rights, or were emotional and capricious by their nature and consequently would make poor use of the rights and destroy their families in the process.

The National Democratic Party The party's position on the law was at odds with that of its members in the People's Assembly. As a body, the party participated in preparing the law and announced its approval of it, while the parliamentary representatives had other calculations, most notably the upcoming parliamentary elections and the need to present to the electorate (the majority male voters) an image of being defenders of religion, filling for public opinion the space left by the absent 'Muslim Brothers'. During the debates this manifested itself in various ways, with some NDP representatives bringing in copies of the Qur'an to quote relevant passages in support of their argument. Some sought to have *khul'* left subject to the consent of the husband with the wife held 'disobedient' if she refused to return to her husband after he had announced his rejection of the *khul'*.[34] Parliamentary representatives were reported to have cheered and clapped when the government decided to cancel Article 26 of the draft relating to the travel of the wife without her husband's consent. The government also made amendments to certain articles such as Article 20 on *khul'*, to ensure that the seriousness of the wife's petition for divorce was confirmed. Observers attributed these last changes to election-related calculations, the government not wanting to embarrass its representatives before the voters, especially on such a sensitive matter. When a female NDP representative spoke against calls for women to return to the home, referring to the role of women in the time of the Prophet, it is reported that dozens of representatives shouted and banged their seats in protest, and one jumped up asking 'Are you like the women of the Prophet's time?' Another representative is reported to have become so angry he said that the law would encourage women to immorality when their business was to stay at home, and another to have stressed that the draft threatened the family's very being with destruction; with all due respect to his party obligations, his religious obligations came first.

The Tagammu' Party The Tagammu' Party declared its support for the law, its parliamentary representatives defended the draft in the Assembly and the party's newspaper emphasized its positive aspects. The party leader justified this position on the grounds that the draft had been fully discussed at the Islamic Research Academy, and that it included many positive matters and could be considered a legislative achievement – for example, for the poorest groups of women, it would result in reduced court fees and associated expenses. On the *khul'* provision, the party declared its acceptance on the basis of the opinion of the Islamic Research Academy that it was not against the Islamic *shari'a*, and considered that it would help to solve numerous problems and was in accordance with the logic and spirit of the age. As for the provision on the wife's travel, this also had its benefits as the draft was seeking to prevent arbitrariness by the husband in exercise of his rights.

The Ahrar Party The representative of the Ahrar Party was reported to have stressed the fact that his party respected all thinkers and trusted the government's representatives, the Shaykh of al-Azhar and the leader of the National Assembly, but that there were matters that could not be ignored. The party had reviewed the rulings of all the jurisprudential schools and had found no ruling permitting a women to travel without a *mahram*; so how could the law allow a wife to travel abroad without the permission of her husband, and tell the husband to go to the judge if he suffered as a result of his wife's travel, and put the judge instead of the husband in the position of authority on this matter? It was the Ahrar view that a woman was allowed to travel only in an emergency such as flight from the lands of unbelief. As for *khul'*, it was a classical Islamic principle with certain conditions, notably there had to be fear of not living within the limits of God.

The Wafd Party The deputy party leader and head of the Wafd's parliamentary group was reported to have said that the provision on *khul'* was designed to serve the daughters of the wealthy who would be able to pay what the *khul'* would require, but did not suit the daughters of the poor. The Wafd Party, which is supposed to represent Egyptian liberalism, withdrew from the debates and the vote in the People's Assembly. The deputy leader explained that nobody could say that *khul'* was against Islam, but there was a big difference between *khul'* as set out in the Qur'an, the *sunna* and the positions of the four Imams and the position in the law. There were parts of the law that required fundamental changes: would a woman be able to petition for *khul'* simply because she found her husband to be shorter or less handsome than his friends? The principle of *khul'* was the consent of the husband; this indeed was the import of the *hadith* about Thabit Ibn Qays (see further below), since the Prophet summoned the husband rather than divorcing the wife as soon as she complained and gave back the garden, and he divorced her with his consent. Under the terms of the new law, *khul'* would become a right for the wealthy wife only; what if Thabit's wife had sold the garden and spent the proceeds? The party's newspaper expressed the party's position using headlines such as 'Government wrests approval from People's Assembly's for personal status law amendments'.[35]

The Labour Party The Labour Party opposed the law vehemently; the sole

Labour Party representative in the parliament argued for the rejection of the 'poisonous draughts in the law that could destroy the family structure and the whole of society'. He questioned who would benefit from raising such controversial matters in Egypt, hinting at the influence of foreign powers. He objected to all the provisions in the law that represented in his view an explicit or implicit violation of the Islamic *shari'a*, specifying the articles related to *khul'*, the wife's travel, and divorce from *'urfi* marriage. Having only one representative in the People's Assembly, the party relied on its newspaper (*al-Sha'ab*) to attack the law and mobilize opposition to it, including charging those involved in drafting the law of having a Zionist conspiracy or other foreign parties behind them and implementing the resolutions of the Beijing World Conference on Women, aimed at destroying the Egyptian family. The newspaper ran headlines such as 'Revolt in the People's Assembly Against the Personal Status Law', and 'Revolution in Parliament Against the Draft', and 'Al-Azhar Woman Faqih Against the Law'. The Labour Party and its Muslim Brotherhood allies rejected the concept that a wife's hatred of her husband is reason enough for divorce, on the grounds that the Qur'an had repealed reliance on this alone as a basis for ending marriage – the reference here was to Surat al-Nisa, 19: 'if ye take a dislike to them it may be that ye dislike a thing, and God brings through it a great deal of good'. *Khul'* was permitted only in the case of fear of deviation, on the basis of Surat al-Baqara, 229: 'if ye do indeed fear that they would be unable to keep the limits ordained by God, there is no blame on either of them if she give something for her freedom'. Thus *khul'* is permitted only if it is established that the two together fear they will not abide by the limits of God. Party leaders affirmed that therefore the grounds for *khul'* had to be specified in the text to be not only on the sole basis of hatred, or else *khul'* should be left to mutual agreement between the spouses.

Female representatives in the People's Assembly and the Shura Assembly (Senate) Observers noted that only three out of fourteen female members of the Shura Assembly took part in the debate on the law. It appeared that female members of the Shura Assembly and the People's Assembly had liaised to minimize the number of female speakers, all of the females being from the NDP. Only one female representative attended the discussions on the draft in the Legislative Committee of the People's Assembly and it would seem that the NDP had instructed its female representatives to avoid public debate on the law.

Critical articles of Law no. 1 of 2000 as promulgated

Judicial *khul'* Article 20 of the law provides that if the spouses do not agree on *khul'* between themselves, the wife has the right to petition the court for a *khul'* in which she 'ransoms herself' by waiving all her *shar'i* financial rights and returns the dower. The wife does not have to establish grounds or prove injury or incompatibility; she must explicitly affirm that 'she detests her life with her husband, that there is no way their marital life can continue, and that she fears that she will fail to abide by the limits of God by reason of the hatred she has [for her marital life]'. The judge must appoint arbitrators to seek to reconcile the spouses for a period of not more than three months. Once issued, the *khul'* is not open to appeal.

This judicial *khul'* differs from an agreement between the spouses to end the marriage by mutual consent with a *talaq* with *ibra'*, the wife's waiving of any financial rights from her husband. Judicial *khul'* is also different to judicial separation for injury, which does not affect the wife's financial rights in the event the injury is established.

In justification of Article 20, a draft explanatory memorandum that was prepared to Law no. 1 of 2000 cited Surat al-Baqara, 229, and the Prophetic *hadith* related by Ibn Abbas of Jamila Bint Abdullah, wife of Thabit Ibn Qays, who came to the Prophet and said that although she could not reprove her husband morally or religiously, she detested him and feared matrimonial rights would not be fulfilled because of the extent of her aversion to him. The Prophet asked her if she would return the garden she had received from him as dower, and she said she would, so the Prophet told Thabit to accept the garden and divorce her.

Establishment of *talaq* Article 21 of the law provides that in the event of denial, *talaq* shall be established only by testimony and documentation; the notary, when asked to witness and document a divorce, must call both spouses and invite them to chose an arbitrator from each of their families, but if they insist on the incidence of the *talaq*, or the couple or the husband confirm it has occurred, then it must be documented immediately after the witnessing. The same applies to a wife seeking to exercise delegated divorce if she has stipulated that right in the marriage contract. The establishment of the *talaq* affects the rights of the other spouse if they were present at the procedures of documentation either in person or by appointed representative, or else from the date they are informed of it by official document. The draft explanatory memorandum noted that *talaq* occurs with regard to its legal effects only with witnessing and documentation, but that this does not take away from the fact that the *talaq* occurs religiously. It also observed that this provision on the need for witnessing and documentation would bring divorce into line with the position in Egyptian law on marriage since Law no. 78 of 1931.

This might have the effect of putting women in a very difficult situation, since a husband might divorce his wife orally, at home with no witnesses, and then not document the *talaq* with the *ma'dhun*; she cannot conclude another contract of marriage after the end of the *'idda* period, and indeed he might deny he has divorced her and call her to obedience. He might even divorce her three times without documenting it, so that she becomes irrevocably prohibited to him under the terms of the *shari'a*, while in official documents she is still married to him.

Mandatory reconciliation efforts in divorce cases Article 18 of the law provides that in cases of *talaq* and judicial divorce, the court is to attempt to reconcile the spouses before ruling on divorce; if they have children, the court is to offer reconciliation efforts on at least two occasions separated by at least thirty and not more than sixty days.

Establishment of revocation of *talaq* Article 22 of the law allows the wife to establish her husband's revocation of his *talaq* of her by all possible means. On the other hand, in the event of her denial of a revocation, the husband's claim to have revoked the *talaq* will be heard only if he had informed her by official document of the revocation within a period of sixty days for women who menstruate and ninety for those who count the *'idda* by month, starting from the date she was informed of the divorce.[36]

Divorce from *'urfi* marriage Article 17 of the law provides, in line with the previous (1931) law, that in the event of denial, claims arising from a contract of marriage will not be heard unless the marriage is established by official document, adding however that claims of divorce (*tatliq*) or dissolution (*faskh*) can be heard in the event that the marriage is established by any document. Other claims related to such marriages remain excluded; it is only the claims for divorce that are to be heard. Here, the legislator is seeking to provide young women who went into in *'urfi* marriages without realizing the risks involved and who want to get out with an opportunity to seek divorce from the court; this is in a way a recognition of *'urfi* marriage, although limited to a divorce ruling.

Consolidation of claims in one court Article 10 of the law authorizes the first instance court with local jurisdiction over *talaq* or judicial divorce to rule also in the first instance on related claims for maintenance or for fees – whether for the wife, children or relatives – and also on child custody, access, removal of the child (from the area), and the accommodation of the child's custodian. Other courts of first instance, or courts of summary justice, where claims are filed related to the parties involved in the divorce claim, must transfer them to the first instance court with jurisdiction over the divorce case. The draft explanatory memorandum pointed out that this would avoid having several courts involved, enabling the one court to rule on the different aspects of the dispute in a more speedy and equitable manner as it will have before it all the elements of the dispute. This provision was popular with members of the judiciary.[37] Also, where there is a dispute over the income of the person from whom maintenance or fees are claimed, the office of the public prosecutor is required under Article 23 to carry out an investigation to identify the level of income, submitting its conclusions in not more than thirty days from the date of receiving the court's request. While having regard specifically for the confidentiality of bank accounts,[38] the article requires any governmental or non-governmental party to provide any information they have identifying the income of the person from whom maintenance is required. The draft explanatory memorandum noted the 'practical reality' of the inaccuracy of pre-existing administrative inquiries and predicted that the instigation of this new judicial investigation would contribute to more equitable rulings on maintenance.

Non-payment of maintenance Law no. 1 of 2000 repealed, *inter alia*, the regulation on the organization of *shari'a* courts issued in accordance with Law Decree no. 78 of 1931 and with it Article 347 thereof, which set out the procedures for the imprisonment for up to thirty days of a man able but refusing to implement a court order against him for maintenance, fees for *hadana* or breastfeeding or accommodation. The article had been challenged as unconstitutional, but the Supreme Constitutional Court had held it constitutional on the basis of the opinion agreed upon among the Muslim Imams that a prosperous debtor able to pay his due may be imprisoned in order to force him to pay it.[39] Claims regarding maintenance debts were therefore subject to the Penal Code. Under the new law, maintenance became like any other financial obligation, so whether it be an order for maintenance for wives, divorcées, children or relatives, imprisonment does not arise but the provisions of civil law allow the attachment of part of the husband's salary or of his property in service of his debt. Law no. 1 of 2000 provided for the establishment of a system of family security to include guaranteeing the implementation of maintenance awards through their payment by the Nasser Social Bank, under regulations to be issued by the Minister of Justice.[40] On implementation, however, shortcomings in the text came to light. The bank was frequently unable to define the real income of the husband, particularly those not working in the governmental sector; it was reported that the source for funding for maintenance was not clear, nor whether monthly maintenance only should be paid out or also deferred maintenance. In view of these practical problems and faced with a need to close the legislative gap that they indicated, the People's Assembly reconsidered the matter and agreed on 15 May 2000 to amend the new law to allow the imprisonment of a man refusing to pay maintenance for up to thirty days.

The new marriage document

In accordance with Law no. 1 of 2000, a new marriage document was issued for the process of registration of the marriage. The standard form had been limited to details such as the names of the spouses, the agreed prompt and deferred dower and the witnesses to the conclusion of the contract. The new form allows inclusion of whatever conditions the two spouses wish to agree upon in the interests of ensuing the continuity of married life and the minimizing of disputes, whether during matrimony or even after its termination. These stipulations thus constitute a sort of special constitution for their relationship which binds both of them by its terms.[41] The basic principle is that the stipulations may not make what is prohibited lawful nor what is lawful prohibited. Thus the wife, for example, may not stipulate that her husband shall never divorce her for any reason whatsoever, nor may she stipulate that if he does divorce her, he may not revoke the divorce during the *'idda* period. For his part, the husband may not, for example, stipulate that his wife should not have children. However, the wife may, for example, stipulate that, upon divorce, all the marital moveable property be handed over to her as its owner.

Two issues that were the subject of much debate in the context of stipulations were the wife's stipulation that she had the right to divorce herself from her husband, and whether he had the right to forbid her from working. In-depth interviews with members of the judiciary in Egypt indicated that if the husband delegates his power of *talaq* to his wife,[42] and the wife elects to exercise it, her divorce of herself from him will be revocable in the same circumstances in which his would have been, and in theory the husband (but not the wife) could revoke the *talaq* during the *'idda*. If the delegation has been to divorce herself 'whenever and each time she wishes', then she will be empowered to divorce herself again from him if he revokes the first or second *talaq*s against her wishes. As for the husband, he may indeed stipulate that his wife may not go out to work, but jurisprudence of the Supreme Constitutional Court has held that if he has given his permission for her to work, then he may not subsequently forbid her unless there is evidence that she is abusing the reasonable limits of the right to work or is acting against the interests of her family.[43] Also on the marriage contract, the marriage notaries are instructed to verify the identification of the couple and to attach a photo of both husband and wife to the marriage document, with their thumbprints on their photographs accompanied by the signature of the *ma'dhun*. The couple must also confirm that they are free of any physical condition or disease that would lead to judicial divorce.

Loopholes in the law

The law has many positive aspects that we can consider steps forward. Nevertheless, it does have some gaps that might threaten its effectiveness on implementation. Among those noted by legal experts are the length of time it still takes for a woman to obtain a judicial divorce. It can take up to twelve years for a woman to obtain a final ruling, and although the new law requires the court to set a session to consider an appeal if lodged within sixty days of receiving the papers, it does not specify a time limit within which the court must pass its final ruling. Also, given the problems caused by the fact that the marriage contract is treated like ordinary civil and commercial cases and therefore divorce cases may go to three levels of litigation (including appeal and cassation), some experts propose that the law be amended so that the ruling of the first instance court is final in issues of both *talaq* and *khul'*.[44]

Results of the field survey: the opinions of the elite

Divorce from 'urfi marriage Table 1.20 shows that while the majority (69.2 per cent) of respondents approved of the part of Article 17 of the new law, a not insignificant minority of 30.8 per cent disapproved. The highest percentage of approval came from members of judicial circles (88 per cent), followed by lawyers (80 per cent). Journalists, party leaders and women activists gave broadly similar approval ratings (64.4, 68.7 and 66.8 per cent respectively). The lowest level of approval came from the NGOs activists (60 per cent).

The main reasons given for disapproval of the provision were that recognition of divorce in an 'urfi marriage would lead to moral and social disaster; men and women use the customary marriage regime to avoid the constraints of official marriage, and the law would encourage this type of secret marriage, giving rise to an increase in prohibited relationships and in adultery and fornication (*zina*). When previously a man and woman decided on an 'urfi marriage, they knew that it was not proper, and that it would be recognized only in claims of paternity. Now, however, by permitting divorce from this kind of marriage, the new law was officially recognizing it.

Those approving of the provision pointed out that the new law gave to young women who got involved in an 'urfi marriage without being aware of its serious consequences the opportunity of freeing themselves from the relationship, through seeking divorce at court, without recognizing any other claims related to the marriage.

Reconciliation in divorce cases This question related to Article 18 of the new law regarding the requirement that the court not rule on *talaq* or *tatliq* before attempting reconciliation between the spouses; and also to Article 19, which sets out procedures for the appointment of arbitrators where required in cases of judicial divorce, and allows the court to appoint an arbitrator for any parties refraining from appointing a family arbitrator or not attending the session. Table 1.21 shows a high approval rate from respondents (89.6 per cent), to the extent that none expressed outright rejection of it, while some (10.4 per cent) agreed with reservations, which were more in the vein of proposed alternative texts. Women leaders had the highest proportion of approval with reservations (33.3 per cent), as many of them had carefully examined the wording of the article, for fear that obscure phrasing might jeopardize women's rights or force concessions of which women were unaware. Some of those working in the law (lawyers at 20 per cent and members of the judiciary at 16 per cent) expressed reservations about the text by dint of their wide experience and knowledge of the problems that obscure wording can lead to in the consideration of cases of divorce and reconciliation.

The main reservations about the text were expressed as follows:

1. The law should have specified when reconciliation efforts were to be presented to the disputing parties, and what the procedures should be.

Table 1.20 Approval or disapproval of Article 17 regarding divorce from *'urfi* marriage

Respondents	Journalists		Judiciary		Lawyers		Party political officials		Civil society activists		Women leaders		Total	
	N	(%)	N	(%)	N	(%)	N	(%)	N	(%)	N	(%)	N	(%)
Agree	29	64.4	22	88	28	80	46	68.7	36	60	12	66.7	173	69.2
Disagree	16	35.6	3	12	7	20	21	31.3	24	40	6	33.3	77	30.8
No comment	–	–	–	–	–	–	–	–	–	–	–	–	–	–
Total	45	100	25	100	35	100	67	100	60	100	18	100	250	100

Table 1.21 Approval or disapproval of Article 18 on reconciliation efforts in cases of *talaq* and *tatliq*

Respondents	Journalists		Judiciary		Lawyers		Party political officials		Civil society activists		Women leaders		Total	
	N	(%)	N	(%)	N	(%)	N	(%)	N	(%)	N	(%)	N	(%)
Agree	42	93.3	21	84	28	80	61	91	58	96.7	14	77.8	224	89.6
Agree w/reservations	3	6.7	4	16	7	20	6	9	2	3.3	4	33.3	26	10.4
Disagree	–	–	–	–	–	–	–	–	–	–	–	–	–	–
No comment	–	–	–	–	–	–	–	–	–	–	–	–	–	–
Total	45	100	25	100	35	100	67	100	60	100	18	100	250	100

2. The text is not logical in considering a person who does not attend the reconciliation session despite being informed of it as rejecting the process.
3. The specification of a time period for reconciliation efforts of between sixty and ninety days is unjustifiably lengthy, and could be used by the husband to put pressure on his wife to accept reconciliation under conditions prejudicial to her interests.

Khul' An overall majority of 60 per cent of respondents agreed with the provision on *khul'*, leaving a substantial minority who disapproved. Table 1.22 shows that less than half of the political party functionaries in the sample (46.3 per cent) approved of the article, while approval ratings among the other groups of respondents fell in the same broad range: 62.2 per cent of the journalists, 68 per cent of the judiciary, 62.9 per cent of lawyers, and 66.7 per cent of the civil society activists and women leaders. The low level of approval among those working with political parties might be attributed to the imminent elections for the People's Assembly, as noted earlier in this section. Those disapproving of the provision gave the following reasons for their rejection:

1. The new law casts doubt on the concept of *qiwama* in the relationship between the man and the woman. The Qur'anic text states explicitly that men have *qiwama* over women and stands in no need of further interpretation or exegesis; this *qiwama*, conditioned as it may be by maintenance or other matters, is in any case not to be transferred to women. The new law, however, affirms the *qiwama* of women; she can divorce herself by *khul'* from her husband by a judge's decision, and this means the complete annulment of the man's *qiwama*.
2. *Talaq* is legislated as the man's right alone, and it may not be shared by anyone else.
3. The article on *khul'* is an explicit violation of the rulings of the *shari'a* and a serious danger to the cohesion of the family. It destroys the principle of mutual agreement, transferring the decision on acceptance and rejection to the judge and annulling the will of the husband, while he is a party to the contract which cannot be implemented without his consent. Claims for *khul'* should not be heard if there is no agreement between the spouses, but the law provides that they are to be heard and allows on the basis of her unilateral statement a forcible divorce from the husband. Unestablished hatred and dislike cannot serve as the basis for a *shar'i* ruling for a divorce against the husband's wishes. By incorporating this, the law throws into the Muslim household a time-bomb that the wife can set off at any moment: how are husbands to keep their households safe?
4. It is impossible to establish the real expenses incurred by the husband during the engagement, such as gifts for the fiancée and her family, the costs of going out and the value of the *shabka*.
5. There was only one case of *khul'* recorded during the time of the Prophet,

Table I.22 Approval or rejection of Article 20 on *khul'*

Respondents	Journalists		Judiciary		Lawyers		Party political officials		Civil society activists		Women leaders		Total	
	N	(%)	N	(%)	N	(%)	N	(%)	N	(%)	N	(%)	N	(%)
Agree	28	62.2	17	68	22	62.9	31	46.3	40	66.7	12	66.7	150	60
Disagree	17	37.8	8	32	13	37.1	36	53.7	20	33.3	6	33.3	100	40
No Comment	–	–	–	–	–	–	–	–	–	–	–	–	–	–
Total	45	100	25	100	35	100	67	100	60	100	18	100	250	100

Table I.23 Approval or disapproval of the clause denying appeal in *khul'* rulings

Respondents	Journalists		Judiciary		Lawyers		Party political officials		Civil society activists		Women leaders		Total	
	N	(%)	N	(%)	N	(%)	N	(%)	N	(%)	N	(%)	N	(%)
Agree	26	57.8	17	68	19	54.3	30	44.8	40	66.7	12	66.7	144	57.6
Disagree	19	42.2	8	32	16	45.7	37	55.2	20	33.3	6	33.3	106	42.4
No comment	–	–	–	–	–	–	–	–	–	–	–	–	–	–
Total	45	100	25	100	35	100	67	100	60	100	18	100	250	100

which means it is to be considered the exception to the rule. The exception cannot be used as a basis for analogy to open the door of *khul'*, destroying the family and giving scope for those who have money or those who come from outside the family to fund and pay for the *khul'* process.

6. Some questioned how a *khul'* could happen when many people agree to register a symbolic sum as dower in order to reduce the associated fees calculated as a proportion.

7. Some of those rejecting the provision used as a pretext a *hadith* to the effect that women who divorce by *khul'* are hypocrites.

8. When God put *talaq* in the hands of men, he did so knowing they had the ability to control their emotions and to be rational in difficult situations. God gave men the advantage of full reason and religion and gave them *qiwama* over women.

It should be noted that some of the respondents who accepted the article nevertheless suggested conditions by which the judge should abide. These included:

1. The judge should ascertain the reasons that led the woman to seek *khul'*.

2. The judge should have discretionary authority in assessing the seriousness of these reasons.

3. The judge should have the right to rule in favour of the husband after the *khul'* claim and leave the woman in the marriage with him.

4. The judge may make serious efforts to reconcile the woman who is seeking *khul'* and the husband divorced by *khul'*.

5. If the judge is unable to reconcile the couple and holds that the marriage cannot continue, he shall rule for *khul'*.

Lack of appeal in rulings for *khul'* The responses of the sample to this issue (see Table 1.23) followed those on the general principle of *khul'* set out above. The overall approval rate for the lack of appeal in *khul'* rulings was just over half (57.6 per cent); the rate of approval was highest among members of the judiciary (68 per cent), followed by civil society activists and women leaders (both at 66.7 per cent), then journalists (57.8 per cent) and lawyers (54.3 per cent). The lowest approval rate came from the political party functionaries, at 44.8 per cent. These answers were given without explanations for approval or rejection of the principle of no appeal.

Witnessing and documentation of divorce An overall majority of 72 per cent of the respondents agreed with the terms of Article 21 of the new law requiring that in the event of denial *talaq* has to be witnessed and documented to have legal validity (Table 1.24). The highest approval rate was among women activists (88.7 per cent), members of the judiciary (88 per cent), and lawyers (85.7 per cent). The lowest approval rate was registered among civil society activists

Table 1.24 Approval or disapproval of establishment of *talaq* by witnessing and documentation

Respondents	Journalists N	(%)	Judiciary N	(%)	Lawyers N	(%)	Party political officials N	(%)	Civil society activists N	(%)	Women leaders N	(%)	Total N	(%)
Agree	32	71.1	22	88	30	85.7	42	62.7	36	60	16	88.9	178	71.2
Disagree	10	22.2	3	12	5	14.3	23	34.3	23	38.3	2	11.1	66	26.4
No comment	3	6.7	–	–	–	–	2	3	1	1.7	–	–	6	2.4
Total	45	100	25	100	35	100	67	100	60	100	18	100	250	100

Table 1.25 Requirement of the husband's consent to the wife's travel

Respondents	Journalists N	(%)	Judiciary N	(%)	Lawyers N	(%)	Party political officials N	(%)	Civil society activists N	(%)	Women leaders N	(%)	Total N	(%)
Agree	33	73.3	22	88	31	88.6	55	82.1	24	40	6	33.3	171	68.4
Disagree	12	26.7	3	12	4	11.3	12	17.9	36	60	12	66.7	79	31.6
No comment	–	–	–	–	–	–	–	–	–	–	–	–	–	–
Total	45	100	25	100	35	100	67	100	60	100	18	100	250	100

(60 per cent). From the reasons for approval cited by members of the judicial institutions it is clear that they find in this article a way out of the predicaments faced by those working in personal status. As for women leaders, most of them welcomed this clause as a means to protect women, particularly among the popular classes, from their husbands' frivolous abuse of the oath of *talaq*.

Most respondents approving this article reasoned that it represents a guarantee of women's rights, protecting her against continued intimacy with a man who has divorced her without her knowledge. A *talaq* that is simply pronounced verbally and not witnessed or documented does not give rise to legal effects so in such circumstances the wife's rights would be preserved in full. This would oblige a man who has divorced his wife to document it, effectively ending *talaq* in the absence of the wife.

Those disapproving of the provision held that it had affirmed an extremely dangerous principle, not recognizing a *talaq* which occurs in religion. That is, if a man says to his wife 'you are divorced', in order to complete this process he has to go and document it officially, and this contradicts clear *sunna* from the Prophetic *hadith* on this matter. If the husband divorces his wife three times, thus divorcing her irrevocably, but does not have it witnessed or documented, he might continue to live and have marital relations with a woman who can no longer be his wife, a very dangerous situation for society. Furthermore, those rejecting this provision observed that the schools of law affirmed that *talaq* occurs in all circumstances.

Husband's consent to wife's travel The debate in the People's Assembly had resulted in the Shaykh of al-Azhar agreeing that the wife had to have her husband's permission before travelling; she is permitted to have recourse to the judge to complain if her husband forbids her. The original text, as noted in this study, had proposed that the judge be authorized to permit her travel instead of the husband, and had been removed from the draft law after much opposition and debate. The overall approval rate of respondents of the text as promulgated was 68.4 per cent (Table 1.25). The lowest rate of approval among respondents came from women leaders (33.3 per cent) followed by civil society activists (40 per cent). The lawyers gave it the highest rate of approval (88.6 per cent), followed by members of the judiciary (88 per cent), political party functionaries (82.1 per cent), and journalists (73.3 per cent).

The reasons cited by respondents for their approval of the position taken by the law were as follows:

1. The principle of *qiwama*, a right given to the husband by the Qur'an itself, implies also his right to decide in the case of the wife's travel.
2. The man is more capable of deciding what is to the advantage or disadvantage of the family or indeed the wife.
3. The law seeks to protect the interests of the family and thus stresses women's responsibilities in bringing up the children.

4. The Qur'an and *sunna* stipulate that the wife can only leave the house with her husband's consent. Travel by the wife must be considered one type of 'leaving the house.'

Those who disagreed gave the following reasons:

1. Article 31 of the Constitution provides that every citizen has the right of freedom of movement, and as citizens, women have full constitutional rights.
2. As passed, the law provides the husband with the possibility to arbitrarily dominate and suppress his wife.
3. It places obstacles to women's potential to develop their abilities by studying and working abroad.
4. It may constrain financial opportunities for the family.

Penalties for husbands refusing to pay maintenance In comparison with their answers on the previous positions taken in the law, there were wide differences between the respondents on this issue, with an overall majority disagreeing with the original position in the law ruling out imprisonment of a husband refusing to pay maintenance (see Table 1.26). The approval rate was 41.6 per cent, while 53.2 per cent disagreed. The highest rate of disapproval came from members of the judiciary at 92 per cent, followed by the lawyers at 82.9 per cent. This may be attributed to the fact that, more than the other groups of respondents, these two are involved in the implementation of the law in the courts, and are aware that the removal of the penalty of imprisonment would lead to husbands avoiding paying maintenance to their divorced wives and children, and other means would be of no avail in obliging them to do so.

Those who approved of the article reasoned as follows:

1. Some wives used to abuse the old provision allowing for imprisonment for refusal to pay delayed maintenance as an opportunity for revenge on their husbands.
2. Just as the forcible implementation of *ta'a* awards had been annulled, so the imprisonment provision had to be repealed, since some wives used to leave the maintenance to accumulate and then petition the court for their husbands either to pay up or go to prison.
3. A husband imprisoned for refusing to pay maintenance might be more hostile towards his wife and might take revenge on her.
4. Modern laws always seek alternative penalties to imprisonment because of its negative effects on family relationships; nobody gains from imprisonment, including the wife, and so it is better to have an alternative penalty such as a fine.

Reasons given for those disapproving of the provision were as follows:

1. The previous provision allowing for imprisonment was a deterrent for husbands, encouraging them to pay.
2. The Nasser Social Bank would not be able to determine the income of hus-

Table I.26 Opinion of the ruling out of imprisonment of husband refusing to pay maintenance

Respondents	Journalists		Judiciary		Lawyers		Party political officials		Civil society activists		Women leaders		Total	
	N	(%)	N	(%)	N	(%)	N	(%)	N	(%)	N	(%)	N	(%)
Agree	32	71.1	2	8	6	17.1	37	55.2	25	41.7	2	11.1	104	41.6
Disagree	10	22.2	23	92	29	82.9	26	38.8	32	53.3	13	72.2	133	53.2
No Comment	3	7.7	–	–	–	–	4	6	3	5	3	16.7	13	5.2
Total	45	100	25	100	35	100	67	100	60	100	18	100	250	100

bands refusing to payment maintenance if they were not employed in the governmental sector.

Comments A number of comments can be made on the findings of the opinion survey as carried out in its various stages. First, people were generally disconcerted about the new law and its effects when implemented. Many of the respondents expressed concern that it would have destabilizing effects on the Egyptian family, meaning that the status quo should be preserved even if this involved serious prejudice against women. Second, the groups of respondents most opposed to the law were the political party leaderships, whose objections arose from narrow interests related to upcoming elections. Third, some members of the judiciary opposed certain elements of the law on the basis of lack of clarity in method of application. Fourth, some members of the judiciary opposed the law on the basis of the views of certain scholars and their interpretations of the Islamic *shari'a*, while others were much more flexible in their understanding of the spirit of Islam. Finally, the presence of elements adhering to Islamic tendencies had an effect on the proportions of approval and disapproval of the provisions of the law. These elements were highly influenced by the views expressed by strict religious figures in the press. This was behind the low approval rates of certain groups of respondents such as civil society activists and women leaders, who might have been assumed to be the groups more likely to defend women's interests.

Results of the field study: the opinions of the general public

Knowledge of the law The field study of the opinions of the general public examined the extent of awareness among respondents of the new law and its various provisions during the People's Assembly debates and in the press. This study is by nature preliminary, since people's awareness of the law cannot be established until some time has passed after its promulgation. Nevertheless, the results give very significant indications of the extent to which the masses followed a law directly affecting their social lives. Respondents had followed discussions about the law in parliament and the press.

Among the respondents, an overall proportion of 45 per cent knew of the existence of the law (Table 1.27), of which 21 per cent were females and 24 per cent males. However, being aware that there is a new law does not necessarily imply a detailed knowledge of its contents; among the respondents, 22.5 per cent of males and only 12.5 per cent of females knew of the most significant provisions of the new law. It should be noted that there was a high rate of illiteracy among the female respondents, which meant that they did not have the opportunity to follow the law in the press; nor did their television viewing include what discussion programmes there were about the law. Their main source of information about the law was thus personal interaction, news they might hear from other women in the market or at the water tap. Men have greater scope for wider social

Table I.27 Distribution of sample according to knowledge of new law (% of total)

Variables			Most important clauses	General awareness	No knowledge	Total
Total	Male	N	18	30	32	80
		(%)	22.5	37.5	3.7	100
	Female	N	15	27	78	120
		(%)	12.5	22.5	65	100
Cairo	Male	N	8	10	12	30
		(%)	26.7	33.3	40	100
	Female	N	7	12	31	50
		(%)	14	24	62	100
Al-Sharqia	Male	N	3	7	8	18
		(%)	16.7	38.9	44.4	100
	Female	N	3	6	13	22
		(%)	13.6	27.3	59.1	100
Minya	Male	N	4	7	4	15
		(%)	26.7	46.7	26.7	100
	Female	N	3	7	15	25
		(%)	12	28	60	100
Qena	Male	N	3	6	8	17
		(%)	17.6	35.3	47.1	100
	Female	N	2	3	18	23
		(%)	8.7	13	78.3	100

interaction, including, for example, watching television news in the coffee houses, or reading the newspapers. Most of the respondents who knew about the new law stated that their knowledge came mostly from the press, followed by television and then personal conversations with friends. Many, however, did not have a clear idea of the law's contents, apart from the subject of *khul'*.

Of the respondents who knew of the law, 37.5 per cent of males and 22.5 per cent of females had a general awareness of it, while 32 per cent of males and 65 per cent of females did not know the law existed. The highest proportion of knowledge of the law was in Cairo, where 60 per cent of male respondents knew of the law – 26.7 per cent knowing the most significant provisions and 33.3 per cent having a general awareness of it. Besides this, educational level had a decisive impact (Table I.28) with 88.2 per cent of respondents with degrees and 28.8 per cent of those with secondary education having knowledge of the most significant articles of the law.

Opinion of the *khul'* provision Table I.29 shows that a majority of 48.5 per cent of respondents in the general public opinion survey disapproved of the *khul'* provision in the new law, with a minority of 40.5 per cent approving. There was

Table I.28 Knowledge of the new law by educational level (% of total)

Variables	Most important clauses		General awareness		No knowledge		Total	
	N	(%)	N	(%)	N	(%)	N	(%)
Primary								
Male	13	6.5	6	3	—	—	—	—
Female	9	4.5	7	3.5	4	2	1	0.5
Secondary								
Male	6	3	7	3.5	2	1	1	0.5
Female	2	1	5	2.5	2	1	3	1.5
Higher education								
Male	3	1.5	4	2	2	1	3	1.5
Female	—	—	2	1	1	0.5	2	1
Illiterate								
Male	25	12.5	8	4	—	—	—	—
Female	28	14	32	16	15	7.5	7	3.5
Total								
Male	47	23.5	25	12.5	4	2	4	2
Female	39	19.5	46	23	22	11	13	6.5
Overall	86	43	71	35.5	26	13	17	8.5

a noticeable male–female difference: fifty-two men (26 per cent of the total number of respondents, and 31.3 per cent of the total number of males in the sample) opposed the law, more than twice the number of males who approved (twenty-five males, 12.5 per cent of all respondents, and 31.3 per cent of male respondents). Among the female respondents, however, fifty-six women approved of the *khul'* provision (28 per cent of all respondents, and 46.7 per cent of the total number of female respondents). Nevertheless, the number of women was higher than might have been expected at forty-five female respondents (22.5 per cent of the total, and 37.5 per cent of the female respondents). It is also worth noting that more women than men declined to give their opinions on this question, not because they did not understand the *khul'* provision but rather because they were confused as to what position they should take or else refused to answer.

Table I.29 Opinion of the *khul'* position, by urban/rural residence (% of total)

Opinion	Male			Female		
	Rural	Urban	Total	Rural	Urban	Total
Agree	2.5	10	12.5	7.5	20.5	28
Disagree	10	16	26	5	17.5	22.5
No comment	1.5	—	1.5	3.5	6	9.5

Divorce from 'urfi marriage The results of the field study indicate (Table 1.30) that a high percentage of males in the sample opposed this article in the new law – a proportion of 28.5 per cent of the total number of respondents – with a proportion of only 8 per cent of the total sample being males approving it. Among women, the proportions were inverted, with female respondents agreeing reaching 30 per cent of the total sample and women disapproving representing 24 per cent. During interviews, female respondents showed more sympathy towards women involved in 'urfi marriages, considering that they had been tricked by men and the least that could be done to help them was to give them the right to get a registered divorce that would allow them to marry someone else.

Table I.30 Divorce from 'urfi marriage (% of total)

Opinion	Male			Female		
	Rural	Urban	Total	Rural	Urban	Total
Agree	2	6	8	6.5	23.5	30
Disagree	10.5	18	28.5	5.5	18.5	24
No comment	1.5	2	3.5	4	2	6

Witnessing and documentation requirements in talaq Here again the field survey showed a significant difference in the positions of women and men (see Table 1.31); males agreeing with the new law in this regard made up 17.5 per cent of the sample, those disagreeing 21.5 per cent, while females agreeing with the new position constituted 54.5 per cent of the sample and those disagreeing only 3.5 per cent.

Table I.31 Documented and witnessed divorce (% of total)

Opinion	Male			Female		
	Rural	Urban	Total	Rural	Urban	Total
Agree	3.5	14	17.5	12.5	42	54.5
Disagree	9.5	12	21.5	1.5	2	3.5
No comment	1	–	1	2	–	2

Wife's right to travel There was almost a consensus in the sample against the idea that a wife had the right to travel without her husband's permission; only 2 per cent of female respondents held for this right, all of them from urban areas and with higher education (see Table 1.32).

Table I.32 Wife's right to travel (% of total)

Opinion	Male			Female		
	Rural	Urban	Total	Rural	Urban	Total
Agree	–	–	–	–	2	2
Disagree	14	26	40	16	42	58
No comment	–	–	–	–	–	–

Imprisonment of husbands refusing to pay maintenance A male–female difference emerged again on the idea that husbands might be imprisoned for refusing to pay maintenance (see Table 1.33); a very small number of male respondents (1 per cent of the sample) agreed, while women agreeing with this position comprised 50 per cent of the sample. During the course of the interviews, many women expressed the view that without a severe penalty, no man could be obliged to pay his maintenance dues to his children or his former wife, and some held that even harsher penalties should be used to this purpose.

Table I.33 Imprisonment of a husband refusing to pay maintenance (% of total)

Opinion	Male			Female		
	Rural	Urban	Total	Rural	Urban	Total
Agree	–	1	1	11.5	38.5	50
Disagree	14	25	39	4.5	5.5	10
No comment	–	–	–	–	–	–

New marriage contract document Respondents were asked their view of the new marriage contract document and the special stipulations that they would insert in the document if given the opportunity. A large number of male respondents objected to the clause requiring the husband to disclose women to whom he is currently married, while all the women respondents approved of this clause. Most the female respondents also approved of the clause allowing the two parties to make special stipulations, while a limited number of males objected to it on the grounds that for a woman to insert stipulations would conflict with the principle of *qiwama* and with the *shari'a* 'which had set out the concept of marriage which might not therefore be modified'.

For the female respondents, possible stipulations were ranked as follows in order of importance:

1. delegated power of *talaq* (*al-'isma*)
2. the wife's right to work outside the house – that is, that the husband could not prevent her from working after marriage
3. the right to complete her education
4. the right to travel abroad for a legitimate reason
5. the right to divorce if her husband married another woman
6. that in the event of divorce the wife would be entitled to keep the matrimonial home and furniture
7. an independent dwelling
8. no physical or verbal violence
9. that there should be no interference in family affairs by the husband's mother or siblings

The choice of stipulations by female respondents differed according to their educational level and also according to whether they lived in urban or rural areas. For example, urban women stressed the importance of the stipulation on the right to work, to which none of the rural women referred. Rural women are of course already a significant factor in the agricultural workforce and associated labour such as the rearing of livestock and birds and the preparation of products for consumption by the family or for sale in the market. In the towns, however, the strict position being taken by the sons of the urban middle classes against women's work makes a stipulation on the right to work a priority for daughters of the same classes about to marry. It was this group of respondents also (urban middle-class women) who most cited the stipulation against the use of insults or physical punishment, which rural women did not bring up; this may be because physical punishment in rural areas takes on a legitimacy based on family and tribal relationships; the acceptance or refusal of certain forms of such punishment comes back to the wife's family and the expectations with which she has been brought up. It was similar with regard to the stipulation regarding an independent dwelling, although some of the female respondents from rural areas did refer to this. The fact that the extended family remains very much a fact in the Egyptian countryside makes the idea of an independent dwelling not acceptable, particularly as ownership is shared between members of the family and work on the home is carried out as a collective effort by its various members. In town, however, the wife's matrimonial home tends to be with her husband's family, opening the door to family fights and constant clashes, particularly between the wife and her husband's mother or sisters.

As for husbands, surprisingly enough, very few of them found stipulations they wanted to mention, perhaps because of not being used to the idea and not having thought about it. Stipulations mentioned by male respondents were thus limited to providing that the wife should look after the house, or should not go out to work without the husband's permission, or particular aspects of these such as that she should look after the children or clean the house.

FIVE
General conclusions

General

§ AS NOTED in the Introduction, through a focus on the social aspects of personal status law, this study sought to answer three basic questions: what sources of discrimination against women are still to be found in the law; whether it is sufficient to protect women's rights legislatively in order for them to be exercised in practice; and through what means women can be empowered to exercise their rights guaranteed under existing law.

Although this study has concentrated on personal status law, other areas of Egyptian law continue to discriminate between men and women in violation of international conventions on women's rights – provisions in the penal law concerning adultery, for example, and in the law of nationality on children born to Egyptian women married to non-Egyptians. As for the area of personal status, various aspects of Egyptian law appear to conflict with international human rights instruments. By way of example, Article 16(1)(a) and (b) of the Convention on the Elimination of All Forms of Discrimination Against Women provides for equality in the marriage contract in the freedom to choose the spouse. This right is guaranteed in theory in Egyptian law and the principles of the Islamic *shari'a*, with the wife's consent or a valid appointment of her father to act in her place being required for a valid marriage contract. In reality, however, this is often not the case as a result of social and economic considerations, including poverty, lack of education, and conservative customs and traditions that lead to girls being married off by their fathers without their consent, particularly to very wealthy, elderly and non-Egyptian husbands. Social traditions, moreover, view early marriage as a sort of guarantee and protection for young daughters, rather than education or work (Zulfikar 1995: 134). These articles of the Convention also raise the issue of polygyny, as a departure from the principle of equality in marriage. Egyptian personal status law addresses the issue only by requiring the husband to notify his existing and intended wives of his intention to marry polygynously. In the Islamic *shari'a*, polygyny is permitted only in exceptional cases, but in Egyptian law and practice there are no constraints on or scrutiny over the use of this theoretically restricted permission, with the result that in many cases it is exercised arbitrarily, with no reasonable justification, and with potentially very damaging effects on the feelings of self-worth and self-respect of the affected wife as well as on the interests of children.

As for other matters, the law gives the husband the right to stop paying his wife's maintenance if she withdraws obedience and leaves the matrimonial home without justification. In such circumstances he may call on her to return, through a registered letter identifying the dwelling known as the 'house of obedience'. The wife has the right to appeal against this for a period of thirty days, otherwise she loses her right to maintenance. The 'house of obedience' is in most cases the matrimonial home; it is supposed to be an appropriate and healthy residence for a family, appropriately and adequately equipped and furnished, and independent in the sense of not being shared with another family. The courts used to require that if rented, the dwelling be an unfurnished let, since furnished rents are usually temporary and less stable than an unfurnished let. However, in recent rulings, courts have started accepting furnished lets and also dwellings shared with other families, and have frequently compromised on the need for the 'house of obedience' to be adequately and appropriately equipped and furnished, requiring instead only the minimum necessities.

On the other hand, the study has identified obstacles posed by the judicial system (that is, before the promulgation of the new law, the effect of the latter not being clear at the time of writing) to the realization by women of social and legal rights. These included the lack of a court specializing in family affairs, and the dispersal of different claims relating to one issue between different courts, the lack of limits on time or deferrals, difficulties in establishing claims in regard to maintenance and *talaq*, an imbalance in the allocation of cases between the courts, a low number of cases reaching final settlement, and, even in those that do, discrepancies in the rulings issued by judges in different jurisdictions in similar cases. Delays in the system and mounting fees and associated expenses were factors that might oblige a woman to waive her rights rather than pursue her case through the courts.

Regarding the second question, it is clear from the study that legal reform alone does not suffice to guarantee women's rights, but rather, awareness of the law has to be raised. Many women, especially those from the poorest economic classes, are not aware of what rights the law does protect and have no possibility of putting its positive aspects to use. History and reality teach us of social groups dominated by a false ideological consciousness that comes out in defence of interests contradicting their own real interests; the study can be seen to confirm this in particular regard to the regulation of male–female relationships in the most critical and dangerous sphere of social interaction, i.e. that of the family, and in our focus on personal status law. By focusing not so much on legal analysis as on sociological and anthropological aspects of the conduct of different social actors in regard to this issue, and particularly in regard to awareness of the law, this study has sought to fill a gap in knowledge of this area and by so doing to offer practical tools for the reform process.

Proposals for development of the law

1. That the position on female judges be reviewed, with a particular need for them in personal status courts.
2. That *'urfi* marriage be reconsidered and the courts empowered to hear claims in such marriages, rather than only divorce claims from them.
3. That the law be amended to allow the adoption of views from all schools of law rather than only the Hanafi, so that it is possible to benefit from the opinions of progressive jurists whatever their school.
4. That the reconciliation procedures by the office of the district attorney be reviewed in order to reduce litigation procedures, since this will turn into a matter of routine and will not realize any real interests but rather lead to the unjustified prolongation of litigation.
5. That the text providing for judges to draw the attention of the female litigant to matters they consider relevant to the questions raised be reviewed, since this may challenge the impartiality of the judge.
6. That a family court be established to specialize in all matters related to the marital relationship, including divorce, maintenance, child custody and access etc., bringing them all in front of one court.

Administrative reforms proposed by members of the judiciary

Members of the judiciary with whom interviews were conducted agreed on a number of administrative proposals for change. These included the establishment of separate personal status courts dealing with all personal status cases, with jurisdiction based on claims of judicial divorce and objection to obedience rulings since these give rise to the other types of demands and claims; and departments dedicated on a permanent basis to personal status cases to the exclusion of other civil cases and criminal cases. This would mean the qualification and training of cadres of judges specialized in personal status law.

The recommendations also included the abrogation of objection to rulings issued *in absentia*, leaving appeal at the second stage where most rulings are reviewed whether issued *in absentia* or not; and finding a more positive role for the office of the state attorney for personal status, as a part of the court and a legal resource. Finally, the delay in resolving cases is sometimes due to the considerable burdens placed on judges who have three or sometimes four sessions per week, which could be eased by the reduction and simplification of procedures.

Recommendations made by civil society activists

1. The need for data to be provided on minor marriage and adolescent fertility rates in Egypt, particularly in rural and marginalized areas, to include details

of the impact of early marriage on the health and obstacles to the human development of both women and children.

2. The importance of sustaining and advancing an organized women's movement to take up women's issues and monitor the application of relevant laws.
3. The need for the work of local and non-governmental groups in raising awareness among women and creating networking tools for them, to draw up joint plans for the development of laws affecting them, combating illiteracy, examining the phenomenon of violence against women and supporting centres providing rehabilitation to victims of domestic violence.
4. The importance of encouraging individual women to report violations committed against them to the relevant authorities, and supporting them whether though media campaigns or legal aid.
5. The need to activate 'family guidance' centres attached to the Ministry of Social Affairs, supplying them with qualified experts to make citizens aware of the rights guaranteed in personal status law, and how they can claim these rights.
6. The need to increase efforts to raise awareness among women in popular and marginalized areas, especially in villages outside the capital, including by establishing fixed centres in poor areas for family guidance and legal assistance and working towards establishing a group of lawyers for the purpose.
7. That the time has come for the Egyptian government to withdraw its reservation to the article on equality in all matters to do with marriage and the family in the Convention on the Elimination of All Forms of Discrimination Against Women, which it ratified in 1981.
8. That civil society associations should have a basic role in implementing the new procedures, which enable the wife to present her claim to court through a form including all the relevant data, without fees and with no need for a lawyer to be appointed; civil society associations should be working to provide 'legal aid' to hundreds of thousands of women in this regard, and could also appoint lawyers to take up cases.
9. The minimum age of capacity for marriage should be increased to eighteen for females and twenty for males. Besides the immediate effect this would have on the population rate, it would also have a positive effect in reducing cases of divorce arising from early marriage, provided that suitable monitoring mechanisms were put in place to ensure the effectiveness of such an amendment; there is also a need for monitoring of medical examinations of couples intending to marry.
10. Personal status law should be amended to provide that women's custody rights extend to the age of twelve for boys and fifteen for girls and may be extended to fifteen for the boy and the age of marriage for the girl if the judge considers this to be in the best interests of the child. This would considerably reduce the number of child custody disputes before the courts.

Concluding comments

Perhaps more important and positive than the good clauses in the law itself is the fact that the new law was a product of battles and balances between dynamic groups in society. This was the first time that this principle became clear for all to see. Even after the law was confirmed in the People's Assembly, pressures continued from different parties for amendments to be made specifically to two articles. The first change resulted from pressure by men for amendment of the article on a woman's right to travel without the consent of her husband, and the second related to not imprisoning a husband for refusing to pay maintenance. Although one of these was against the interests of women, representing an attack on their freedom, nevertheless the widespread understanding, through direct experience, that it is possible to change the law through such pressure, and that the law itself is neither sacrosanct nor impossible to change opens the possibility for women to organize themselves for advocacy towards new gains.

APPENDIX
List of statutes

Law no. 25 of 1920 concerning maintenance and certain provisions of personal status, *Official Gazette*, no. 61 of 15 July 1920.

Law no. 25 of 1929 regarding certain provisions of personal status, *Official Gazette*, no. 27 of 25 March 1929.

Regulation concerning the organization of *shari'a* courts and related measures, issued in accordance with Law no. 78 of 1931, *Official Gazette*, extraordinary issue no. 53 of 30 May 1931.

Law no. 462 of 1951 abolishing *shari'a* courts and millet courts and transferring claims before them to the national courts, *Official Gazette*, no. 73 bis (b) of 24 September 1955.

Law no. 44 of 1979 amending certain provisions of personal status, *Official Gazette*, 21 June 1979.

Law no. 100 of 1985 amending certain rulings of the laws of personal status, *Official Gazette*, no. 27 of 3 July 1985.

Law no. 1 of 2000 regulating certain litigation procedures in personal status matters, *Official Gazette*, no. 4 of 22 January 2000.

Notes to Part I

1. The sample comprised fourteen from the Wafd Party, fourteen from the Arab Democratic Nasserite Party, fourteen from the National Progressive Tagammou Party, fourteen from the Labour Party, eight from the Al-Ahrar Party and twenty-three from Al Umaa Party.

2. The sample included five journalists from each of following newspapers: *al-Ahram*, *al-Akhbar*, *al-Jumhouria*, *al-Esboua'*, *al-Ahali*, *al-Sha'ab*, *al-Arabi*, *al- Ahrar*, and *al-Wafd*.

3. On women in the educational process, see the statistics in Siyam 1996.

4. The Egyptian government reported to the Committee on the Elimination of Dis-crimination Against Women (CEDAW) that the overall rate of female illiteracy in 1996 was 51 per cent (down from 57.41 per cent in 1992). (UN Doc. CEDAW/C/EGY/4–5).

5. In the above-cited CEDAW report, the Egyptian government reported that in 1997/98, the drop-out rate for compulsory (primary) education was 7 per cent among girls. (UN Doc. CEDAW/C/EGY/4–5).

6. See 'Awais 1977.

7. *Ila'* is a form of divorce effected when the husband takes and keeps an oath of abstinence from sexual relations with his wife for a period of four months, with expiation (*kaffara*) required if he does not keep the oath. *Zihar* is when the husband uses a phrase comparing his wife to the back of his mother (or another close female relative), which has the effect of prohibiting sexual relations until the husband has made expiation.

8. See Abu Zahra (1957: 352) on the problem of proliferation of the use of oaths of *talaq* followed by a return to married life in circumstances considered prohibited, and the approach taken in Law 25/1929 specifically to address this problem. Abu Zahra (ibid., p. 364) also notes that the law did not specify whether termination by *ila'* was to be considered irrevocable, as held by Abu Hanifa, or revocable, as held by Malik and Shafi'i; his opinion was that the law should be read as having taken the latter position.

9. *Shahadat al-tasnin*, showing a medical estimate of age based on physical character-istics.

10. *Talaq* and judicial divorce (*tatliq*).

11. See for example Ibn Kathir al-Dimashqi (n.d.: 741).

12. UN Doc. CEDAW/C/EGY/4–5, 30 March 2000.

13. Article 6 of Law 462/1055, referring to Article 280 of Law no. 78/1931.

14. Cited in al-Shabini (1995: 91); see also translation of Court of Cassation decision of 21 June 1934 in Qassem (2002: 31).

15. Law no. 147/1949, Articles 13 and 14; cited in Abdul Tawab (1980).

16. English translations of the legal provisions cited in the following paragraphs are taken from el-'Alami and Hinchcliffe (1996).

17. Decision no. 2445 of 1979; *Official Gazette*, 18 August 1979.

18. Article 11 bis of Law no. 25 of 1929 as amended by Law no. 100 of 1985.

19. Article 18 bis 3 of Law no. 25 of 1929, as amended by Law no. 100 of 1985.

20. Article 5 bis of Law no. 25 of 1929 as amended by Law no. 100 of 1985.

21. Article 1 of Law no. 25 of 1920 as amended by Law no. 100 of 1985.

22. Article 11 bis 2 of Law no. 25 of 1929, as amended by Law no. 100 of 1985.

23. Interview with advocate Fathi Kishk.

24. Interview with Counsellor Hosni Hamada, president of the Cairo Court of Appeal for personal status.

25. Judge Hamed Abdel Halim al-Sharif gives many examples of such *'urfi* marriages (al-Sharif 1987: 10).

26. Article 99(d) of Law no. 78 of 1931.

27. The *shabka* consists of gold and other jewellery customarily given by the husband to the wife on marriage.

28. *'nikdiyya'* and *'muz'iga'*.

29. The Islamic Studies Academy, minute of emergency session no. 12, general minute no. 278, 27 Muharram 1420 (13 May 1999).

30. A slightly amended provision is included in Law no. 1 of 2000 (Article 63), which requires the Court of Cassation, on receiving the appeal papers, immediately to set a date for the ruling to be considered within sixty days of it being filed.

31. Article 7 of Law no. 1 of 2000.

32. A relative within the degree of relationship that prohibits marriage between the *mahram* and the woman.

33. Included in Article 20 of the law as passed.

34. One Assembly member apparently said that a wife who seeks *khul'* against her husband's consent is disobedient and should be confined in the house until she dies; the leader of the Assembly had to ask the source of such a position.

35. *Al-Wafd*, 28 January 2000.

36. Unless the woman is pregnant or acknowledges that she was still in her *'idda* period when he informed her of the revocation.

37. Dr Bahaa Elddin Ibrahim, head of Cairo Appeal Court, interview.

38. Presidential Decision on Law no. 205 of 1990.

39. Counsellor Abdel Mun'im Ishaq Muhammad, deputy of the state judiciary body and head of the Supreme Constitutional Court section.

40. Articles 71 and 72 of Law no. 1 of 2000.

41. Counsellor Abdel Moneim Ishaq Mohammed, deputy director of the State Judicial Institution and head of the Supreme Constitutional Court section.

42. It should be noted there that the husband himself also retains the same power of divorce when he delegates the power to his wife.

43. Ruling of the Supreme Constitutional Court in case no. 18 of constitutional judicial year 14.

44. Dr Nabil Ahmad Hilmi, lecturer and dean of the college of law in Zaqaziq, *al-Ahram*, 19 January 2000.

Part II

Islamic Law and the Transition to Palestinian Statehood: Constraints and Opportunities for Legal Reform

Edited by Penny Johnson and Lynn Welchman

Introduction

§ THE main aim of the Palestinian case study is to assess the legislative and lobbying initiatives related to Islamic law (whether affirmation or reform) in the six years of a Palestinian interim authority (1994–2000) in the West Bank and Gaza, and to delineate the constraints and opportunities that will shape the struggle over legal reform and personal status law in the coming period of Palestinian statehood. The study considers a wide range of actors, including the Palestinian Authority/emerging state, women's movement and non-governmental organizations (NGOs), political parties and the Islamist movements, and legal and religious institutions. For comparative purposes, the report aims in particular to consider how processes of state-building and legitimation, both given the particular constraints and inequalities of this transitional period and in the context of the Arab world, incorporate, change or resist Islamic law, and how forces for change, particularly the women's movement and initiatives for gender equality, can work in this context.

Although existing personal status law was not substantively amended during this period, a series of critical events and debates occurred which revealed a number of major constraints and opportunities for the reform of existing law. Among these were the debates, both within the new Palestinian Legislative Council and in other fora, surrounding successive drafts of a Basic Law and a year-long 'model parliament', initiated by women's NGOs. The model parliament proposed wide-ranging legal reform on the basis of gender equity; its agenda erupted into public debate in the wake of a sharp attack from some leaders of Islamist movements. The attack brought political parties, the religious establishment and the Authority itself into the debate and the issue of legal reform and gender equity was to some extent subsumed by the issue of the nature of Palestinian democracy.

The research team from the Institute of Women's Studies at Birzeit University attempted to situate the issues in this debate into both the processes of state formation and social dynamics within Palestinian society. We thus analysed public opinion polls (including our own polling) as well as draft legislation and developments in the *shari'a* court system, in an attempt to understand how women and men articulate their own needs and interests. To strengthen this understanding, the team also interviewed the families of fourteen women workers who lost their lives in a factory fire in the town of Hebron in October 1999, in order to examine how poor families sought and received, or did not receive, public compensation, *diya* (the institution of financial reparation for death and bodily injury in Islamic law) and justice.

The full report is a lengthy document including two background appendices by Ala al-Bakri (on legal developments in the *shari'a* court system since 1994) and Jamil Hilal (on secularism in the Palestinian national movement), along with full polling results and the full report of the investigation into the Hebron factory fire by Fadwa al-Labadi, and is held on file at the Birzeit Institute of Women's Studies and at Emory School of Law with the Project Director, Abdullahi An-Na`im. As the team was preparing the full report for submission, in September 2000, the profound 'interim inequalities' of the transitional period, which the report briefly discusses, and the long delay in Palestinian independence erupted in Palestinian mass protest, Israeli excessive force, and bloodshed that at the time of preparing this edited version for publication, at the end of 2001, had claimed over a thousand lives, the majority Palestinian. The research team cannot submit this case study for publication without expressing its hopes that out of this tragedy, a new framework based on recognition of rights, equality between the parties and the implementation of international resolutions and international law will lead to a genuine and just peace and an independent and democratic sovereign Palestinian state capable of meeting the needs and fulfilling the rights of all of its citizens.

SIX

Legal context: *shari'a* courts and Muslim family law in the transitional period

Lynn Welchman

§ THE turbulent political history of Palestine (here the Palestinian West Bank, Gaza Strip and East Jerusalem) has produced a particular heterogeneity of laws and jurisdictions since the beginning of the twentieth century. During that time, laws were passed and courts established by the Ottoman Empire authorities, the British Mandate authorities, the Jordanian government (in the West Bank and East Jerusalem) and the Egyptian administration (in the Gaza Strip), the Israeli occupation authorities and, finally, the Palestinian Authority. The challenges of legal unification facing the last, the Palestinian Authority, are considerable.

Among these challenges is the fact that many areas of law differ in the West Bank and Gaza Strip. After the *Nakba* (catastrophe) of 1948 and the establishment of the Israeli state, the West Bank, including East Jerusalem, was annexed by Jordan, which embarked on a process of 'unifying' the laws on the East and West Banks. The Gaza Strip, on the other hand, was administered until the 1967 Israeli occupation by Egypt, which issued various laws through its Governor General[1] but unlike Jordan did not seek to annex the Strip or to integrate its laws and courts into Egypt's own national system. Different legal traditions also inform the two legal systems: Robinson (1997: 53) notes that the version of common law applied in Gaza (and Palestine as a whole) under the British Mandate was maintained by Egypt, while Jordan's annexation integrated the West Bank and East Jerusalem into the 'continental' code-based and more French-inspired tradition taken up in Jordan's legal system as well as in other neighbouring states.[2]

The matter of legal tradition *per se* is perhaps not so much of a problem for the area of law under consideration in this case study: family law for Muslims. To be sure, the Muslims of the West Bank and of the Gaza Strip are subject to different codifications of family law, and East Jerusalemites are also liable to be subject to sometimes conflicting rules from the Israeli domestic system as a result of the illegal annexation of the city by Israel. Under both Jordanian law and the Egyptian-issued law in the Gaza Strip, however, it is the system of *shari'a* courts that have exclusive jurisdiction, a jurisdiction they have retained from their wider residual authorities in earlier centuries.[3] Despite differences in the rules applying, which as described below are sometimes significant in particular in terms of women's rights, the legal tradition is perceived to be and presented as the same: codifications of rules selected for the most part from Hanafi *fiqh*, although with rules from other schools included in particular areas, applied in *shari'a* courts administered in a distinct framework from the regular (statute) court system and subject to distinct (*shar'i*) rules of procedure. Even so, suggestions that the basic approach in the unification of Muslim personal status law for the Palestinian areas of the West Bank and Gaza Strip should be to work from the starting point of the existing Jordanian law applying in the West Bank were not necessarily unanimously welcomed in Gaza.

Significantly for the opportunities and constraints for legal reform of family law in a period of consolidation of Palestinian identity through state formation, the system of *shari'a* courts and the laws they apply are also presented as rooted in the indigenous (pre-colonial) tradition and history of Palestine and indeed of Islam in Palestine. In this regard, George Bisharat (1989: 43) notes the 'greater moral legitimacy of the Islamic courts within the community and the greater familiarity and intelligibility of their laws and procedure' – that is, compared to the civil court system and the Israeli military tribunals in operation in the West Bank during the occupation.[4] In some of the recent and ongoing debates and discussions examined in this case study, the association of the *shar'i* system with an explicitly articulated national Palestinian identity and cultural heritage has been a feature of the claims for its place in the Palestinian state. In these claims, the 'rootedness' of the *shar'i* system both in terms of time and in terms of its presentation as 'indigenous' is implicitly held up for comparison with the statute court system and laws 'imported' from the West as of the nineteenth century.

Bisharat's perceptions of the relative 'familiarity' of the *shari'a* court system and laws to many Palestinians in the West Bank and Gaza Strip, and the claims to 'authenticity' and tradition made by those involved in the system, may be seen to be borne out, to a certain extent, by the findings of the poll carried out for the purposes of this case study in spring 2000. In her analysis of the results of the polling in Chapter 8 of this case study, Hammami finds the principle that *shari'a* should provide the general framework for personal status law to be a 'doxa' (following Bourdieu 1979); however, there is also significant support for reform within that framework, with particular reference to the extension of women's rights, notwithstanding a gender difference in this support manifesting between male and female respondents. On the other hand, her finding that only a minority of respondents believe that the *shar'i* establishment should have the sole power to decide on reform is indicative of a current of belief in democratic participation (so long denied to Palestinians) that may challenge the position of some members of the religious establishment on who is 'qualified' to participate in the family law reform process.

In order to set the context for the discussion and analysis in the following sections of legislative and advocacy initiatives related to personal status law in transitional Palestine, this chapter provides a brief overview of the current jurisdiction of and substantive laws applied by the *shari'a* courts in the West Bank and Gaza Strip. This is followed by a review of initiatives taken by members of the *shar'i* establishment during the transitional period to issues of reform of particular areas of the law, and the strategies of legal reform that these suggest. These initiatives were provoked in family law as elsewhere, as noted above, by the need to unify the different laws applying in the two areas,[5] and in the later examples by advocacy efforts from civil society, in particular the women's movement, described in Chapter 9.

Shari'a courts: jurisdiction and laws

Until the present, the *shari'a* courts of the Palestinian West Bank, and the Jordanian-administered *shari'a* court in East Jerusalem, are governed by Jordanian law, notably the Law of *Shar'i* Procedure 1959. Following the principles set out in the Jordanian Constitution 1952,[6] the law specifies *shari'a* court jurisdiction as including Islamic *waqf* (pious endowments), a range of family law and personal status matters,[7] and petitions for *diya* ('bloodwit', or material reparation for murder or physical injury) where the parties are Muslim or where a non-Muslim party agrees to *shar'i* jurisdiction.

In terms of substantive law, the West Bank courts apply the Jordanian Law of Personal Status (JLPS) of 1976, which replaced the 1951 Jordanian Law of Family Rights (JLFR). The fact that they apply legislation issued in Jordan after the 1967 Israeli occupation is an anomaly, since in all other areas the law was 'frozen' in its pre-occupation state, and Israeli military orders took the place of legislation. However, from the start of the occupation, the West Bank *shari'a* courts refused to have anything to do with the Israeli authorities, protesting at Israel's illegal annexation of East Jerusalem, the extension of Israeli municipal law to East Jerusalem and Israel's refusal to recognize the validity of rulings from the Jordanian-administered *shari'a* courts situated there, which comprised the first instance *shari'a* court for East Jerusalem and the *Shari'a* Court of Appeal. The latter reconvened under an initiative from the West Bank *shar'i* establishment after the occupation to hear appeals from all the West Bank courts and thus replacing, for West Bankers, recourse to the Amman-based *Shari'a* Court of Appeal which had been serving them under Jordanian rule (Welchman 2000: 51–76). In short, although the Israeli occupation authorities assumed all supervisory functions for the regular (statute) court system, the *shari'a* courts in the West Bank maintained a determined non-recognition of the occupation authorities throughout the period to 1994 and continued, in so far as practicalities would permit, to be administered by the Office of the Qadi al-Quda (Chief Islamic Justice) in Amman, through an Acting Qadi al-Quda in Jerusalem appointed by the Jordanian authorities.

By contrast, the *shari'a* courts in the Gaza Strip, which as noted above had not been integrated into the Egyptian system, were administered from 1967 to 1994 by the Israeli Military Governor of the Strip through the Officer for Religious Affairs (Abu Sardane n.d.: 247). In the Gaza Strip, the courts apply the Law of Family Rights (LFR) of 1954, issued by the then Egyptian Governor of the Strip.[8] The *shari'a* courts in Gaza do not apply post-1967 Egyptian law, so the personal status law promulgated in Cairo in 1979 and subsequently amended in 1985 and 2000 has not been applied; nor did the 1954 Law of Family Rights constitute a codification of the then existing Egyptian personal status legislation. The LFR bears a much closer resemblance to the Ottoman Law of Family Rights 1917, which was applied in Palestine but not in Egypt. Procedure in the Gazan *shari'a* courts is governed by the Law of *Shar'i* Procedure 1965,[9] which specifies juris-diction, although in abbreviated form, in the same areas as the Jordanian law, including personal status and family law matters, *waqf* and *diya*.

Both the Jordanian law applied in the West Bank and the Egyptian-issued law applied in the Gaza Strip purport to draw on rulings from other schools of law, although it is to the dominant opinions of the Hanafi schools that the judiciary is directed as residual reference in the absence of a particular provision in the codified law.[10] In their general sweep the West Bank and Gaza codes are as similar to each other as to those of other Arab states, and maintain certain gender specificities characteristic of 'classical' *fiqh*: it is indeed the pattern of these char-acteristics that is presented as the 'general framework' within which reform may be introduced.[11] Marriage is presented as a contract giving rise to rights and duties specific to each spouse; the husband must pay dower and maintenance to his wife, treat her well and provide a home for her; the wife is to obey her husband in lawful matters, including moving to live with him if he moves, while main-taining freedom of disposal over her private income and property. The marriage can be dissolved extra-judicially by the unilateral repudiation of the husband; by court decision on specific grounds presented by the wife[12] or if the marriage has been concluded irregularly; or by mutual consent involving a final *talaq* by the husband in exchange for a financial consideration by the wife (*khul'*).[13] Polygyny is permitted to a maximum of four wives. The mother is recognized as the natural custodian of her children until they reach specific ages, at which point, if their parents are separated, they are to return to their father, who is recognized as their natural guardian. Guardianship by the father (or other close male agnate) over females in marriage continues to be required in court if not unambiguously in law (Welchman 2000: 121–33). Succession is mostly governed by the classical Sunni rules, which recognize female as well as male heirs but generally give males double the share of females.

Beyond this general picture, the separate post-1948 legal histories have given rise to different rules in a number of specific areas, as summarized below.

Ages of marriage and custody

There are significant differences between Gaza and the West Bank in the rules governing both the minimum age of marriage and the maximum age of child custody. In the LFR 1954, rather than introducing the reforms they had codified in the 1920s in Egypt, the Egyptian authorities reproduced the provisions of the OLFR of 1917. The Ottoman law, in provisions that were innovative for their time, had set capacity for marriage at the ages of eighteen for the male and seventeen for the female, but allowed the judge to give permission for marriage below that age provided the applicant had reached puberty and in the case of the female her guardian gave permission for her marriage.[14] No marriage was allowed below the ages of twelve for the boy or nine for the girl. By the time these rules were reproduced in the law the Egyptians issued for Gaza, Jordanian law had already raised the minimum age to fifteen for both spouses, with the judge being allowed to authorize marriage from that age up to the ages of full capacity of eighteen for males and seventeen for females – again, provided the female had the consent of her guardian.[15] In 1976 this was amended to sixteen for the male, who no longer needs the judge's permission to marry once he has reached that age, while the female of fifteen has reached capacity for marriage but is still required to have either her guardian's or the court's consent until she reaches full capacity.[16] One final point that needs to be made here is that according to the explicit text of both the LFR and the JLPS, the ages are calculated according to the lunar year; so the minimum age of marriage for the female in the West Bank is around fourteen years and seven months by the solar calendar. The setting of a minimum age of capacity in marriage at the age of eighteen by the solar calendar has been identified as a lobbying priority by a number of initiatives in Palestine in the transitional period, and was endorsed by the model parliament outcomes discussed below in Chapter 9.

The Gaza law is also more conservative than the JLPS in its approach to female custody over children. Dominant Hanafi rules presume the mother to be the natural custodian of her minor children until the boy reaches the age of seven and the girl nine,[17] after which the children return to their father as the natural guardian (*wali*). In 1976 the Jordanians extended the custody of the mother 'who has devoted herself to the upbringing and custody of her children' to the age of puberty – that is, when the children physically reach puberty. The custody of a woman other than the mother was extended to the ages of nine for boys and eleven for girls.[18] In the Gaza Strip, on the other hand, the 'classical' Hanafi rules are maintained in the LFR 1954, allowing only the limited extension of the custody of the mother for a girl up to eleven years and a boy up to nine.[19]

Post-divorce maintenance

Another particularly significant difference is in the rules on post-divorce maintenance for a wife divorced 'arbitrarily', or without reasonable cause. The classical

Hanafi rules require a man who divorces his wife unilaterally by *talaq* to pay her maintenance during the *'idda*, the 'waiting period' after divorce during which the woman may not remarry, a standard period of three menstrual cycles or until childbirth if she is pregnant. He also has to pay her deferred dower. This is the end of his legally enforceable financial obligations towards her, unless she is undertaking custody of their children.[20] The question of post-*'idda* provision for divorcées was addressed by the Jordanians in the JLPS in a provision following a 1953 Syrian model, allowing a maximum of one year's maintenance to be awarded as compensation to a woman divorced arbitrarily and without good cause, payable in addition to her maintenance for the *'idda* period. Egypt, however, did not legislate on this matter until after the 1967 occupation, and the LFR has no equivalent provision. This means, in effect, that a husband unilaterally divorcing his wife in the West Bank, but not in the Gaza Strip, risks having his motivation scrutinized and a financial penalty imposed by way of compensation to the divorcée. This issue too is a matter of some focus for advocacy and lobbying initiatives aimed at reforming personal status law in Palestine today.

Judicial divorce

Divorce law in Gaza, on the other hand, provides a remedy for abused wives that is denied in the West Bank, by providing for 'injury' or prejudice as grounds on which the wife is entitled to petition the court for judicial divorce. This provision in the Gazan law, and its counterpart in the West Bank, is based on Maliki rules, but both provisions have adopted incomplete versions of the Maliki position. In the West Bank, the JLPS allows either spouse to apply for divorce on the grounds of 'discord and strife' (fundamental breakdown of the marriage), in line with the classical Maliki rules, while in the LFR in the Gaza Strip only the wife may apply on these grounds. On the other hand, the LFR takes another Maliki rule in allowing the wife to be granted a divorce by the court on establishing her husband's injury of her. It is only in the event of her failure to prove this injury that the case may be referred to arbitrators by the judge and proceed to a divorce on the grounds of strife or breakdown if the arbitrators are unable to reconcile the couple. In the West Bank, by contrast, if a woman successfully establishes her husband's injury of her, the judge is to 'warn the husband to improve his behaviour' and if he does not, then to transfer the matter to arbitrators. In both cases, if their attempts at reconciliation fail, the arbitrators are empowered to recommend that the judge divorce the couple, specifying the proportions of blame attached to each spouse so that the judge can order a proportionate financial settlement.

Here, the significance in the difference between the laws does not appear to extend substantially to practice. In an examination of the records of four *shari'a* courts in the West Bank for the years 1989 and 1992–94, claims for judicial divorce based on the grounds of 'discord and strife' accounted for 8 per cent of all claims for judicial divorce, behind the more common grounds of failure of the husband to maintain the wife and the injurious absence of the husband for over a year. On the other hand, the *shari'a* courts records in Gaza City and Rafah for the same four years failed to reveal a single claim for divorce submitted on the grounds of injury (Welchman 1999: 173). Nevertheless, the fact that divorce for injury is on the books in Gaza holds a certain protective potential; elsewhere in the region, it is a more common cause for divorce at the petition of the wife.[21]

The Oslo peace process: law and transition

In September 1993, the Declaration of Principles, signed by Israel and the Palestine Liberation Organization, formally kicked off the 'interim' or 'transitional' phase of the so-called Oslo peace process. In May 1994, the signing of the Israel–PLO Gaza–Jericho Agreement paved the way for Yasser Arafat's triumphal return to Gaza in July to head the Palestinian Authority, and for the incremental transfer from the Israeli occupation authorities to the Authority of a range of civil functions and responsibilities in Gaza and Jericho, including administration of the courts. With the signing of the 'Interim Agreement' the following year, the 'transitional' period became formally underway in the rest of the West Bank as well (although not, according to the texts, in occupied East Jerusalem). The transitional period was stipulated to come to an end five years after the signing of the Gaza–Jericho Agreement on 4 May 2000, when final status negotiations should be concluded.

The flaws in the agreements,[22] in particular the avoidance of the discourse of rights and the rule of international law, could not but have consequences both for people's lives and livelihoods in the transitional period and possibly the future, but also for the perception and potential of efforts at rights-based legal reform, as discussed in the following chapter. Chapter 7 also discusses the activity of the Palestinian Legislative Council, elected in 1996, and in particular the history of the draft Basic Law. The progression of the Basic Law's provisions on the place of *shari'a* (as a source of law) and of the function of the *shari'a* court courts is illustrative of differing aspirations and expectations on the part of drafters, legislators and different sectors of civil society. These points, and the advocacy efforts around personal status law launched by sections of the women's movement and NGOs, are considered later in this case study. The remainder of this chapter reviews actions and initiatives taken by leading members of the *shar'i* establishment during the same period.

Shar'i institutions in the transitional period[23]

Post-Oslo developments in the *shari'a* court system are distinguished by what appears to have been a markedly proactive approach by the members and leaders of that judiciary and in their serious take on the significance of 'institution-building' in the emerging state. On 20 May 1994, Yasser Arafat issued a decree

from Tunis ordering that 'all regular, *shari'a* and sectarian courts, at their respective levels, shall continue their functions in accordance with the laws and
regulations that are in force' and confirming existing judges in their positions.[24]
Also from Tunis, Arafat appointed Shaykh Muhammad Abu Sardane as Wakil
(junior minister, or under-secretary of state) to the Minister of Justice within the
Palestinian Authority for the affairs of the *shar'i* judiciary and *ifta* (the formalized
function of issuing *fatwas*).[25] Abu Sardane, recently retired from the *Shari'a* Court
of Appeal in Amman, had fled with his family to Gaza during the *Nakba*; the
local press reported that he had been among the original members of Fateh and
a member of the student division of the Muslim Brothers when he was in Egypt
(*Al-Quds*, 14 August 1994; Abu Sardane n.d.: 42).

Shaykh Abu Sardane immediately commenced his efforts to protect and promote the status of the *shari'a* court system and other 'Islamic agencies' of the
Palestinian state-to-be. He reports criticizing an early draft constitution for the
absence of reference to these institutions – the *shar'i* judiciary, *waqf* and *ifta*. In
relation to the first, he emphasized the fifteen-century history in Palestine of the
shar'i judiciary 'which was applying the principles of Islamic law long before
man-made laws were borrowed from the West' (Abu Sardane n.d.: 42–7). As is
noted in the following chapter, explicit provision for the establishment of *shari'a*
courts, with jurisdiction over matters of personal status, is included in Article 92
of the Basic Law. As for the function of *ifta*, when the Jordanian-appointed
incumbent died in 1994, Yasser Arafat appointed Shaykh Ikrameh Sabri as Mufti
of Jerusalem and the Palestinian lands,[26] and granted him the authority to appoint
muftis in the various districts of the Palestinian Authority territory (ibid., p. 52).
Shaykh Sabri heads up the Supreme El Fatwa Council, which has an office in
Ramallah. Muftis have been appointed for each town in the West Bank and
Gaza, drawing expenses but no salaries for their function, although in many
cases the individuals in question are already employed in other offices in the
shar'i (or wider Authority) system. The Council issues *fatwas* at the request of
private individuals as well as pronouncing on matters of public (and political)
interest. As discussed below in Chapter 9, certain differences have emerged
between the Mufti and Abu Sardane's successor, Shaykh Taysir Tamimi.

In the meantime, arriving in the Gaza Strip to take up his position, Shaykh
Abu Sardane was welcomed by the Justice Minister, Freih Abu Meddin, who
described the former's post as both important and sensitive (*Al Quds*, 9 August
1994). Once in place, Abu Sardane set about upgrading the *shari'a* court system,
according to his own claims doubling the number of employees in the first ten
months, introducing new training and qualification requirements, and overseeing
the production of standardized forms for use in the Palestinian Authority *shari'a*
courts of the West Bank and Gaza Strip (Abu Sardane n.d.: 247–8). At the same
time, he was dealing with the considerable complexities of the post-Oslo arrangements for the *shari'a* courts in East Jerusalem.

Relations between the Palestinian Authority and Jordan were increasingly strained by Jordan's insistence on its 'special role' in Islamic sites in Jerusalem, a role specifically singled out for Israel's 'respect' in the July 1994 Washington Declaration signed between King Hussein and Israeli Prime Minister Yitzhak Rabin.[27] Palestinian sensitivities over the status of Jerusalem were inflamed by the implication that Jordan might be involved at Israel's insistence in the 'final status negotiations' in regard to the future status of the city. East Jerusalem was excluded from Palestinian Authority jurisdiction under the Oslo Accords, and the fact that the *shari'a* courts there remained part of the Jordanian system was more than a symbolic institutional link. In September 1994, Jordan announced that it would be cutting administrative ties with the *shari'a* courts and the *Waqf* Department agencies in the West Bank as of 1 October, with the exception of those in East Jerusalem. The Palestinian Authority's Council of Ministers in turn announced that the Authority would take over responsibility for the employees of the *waqf* and the *shari'a* courts in the West Bank as of that date (Abu Sardane n.d.: 69).

There remained the question of the first instance *shari'a* court in East Jerusalem, and the *Shari'a* Appeal Court for the West Bank which, as noted above, had been convened in Jerusalem since the Israeli occupation. In memoranda forwarded on this matter, the Palestinians formally proposed that the existing connection be maintained, with the Jordanian government mandating the *Shari'a* Appeal Court in Jerusalem to work in the Palestinian *shar'i* system in the West Bank until the political future of Jerusalem was determined, and thus to hear appeals from the West Bank *shari'a* courts (Abu Sardane n.d.: 68). A petition from Palestinian *shar'i* judges to Yasser Arafat supported this position, and further sought the establishment of the post of Qadi al-Quda in the Palestinian Authority (*Al-Quds*, 4 October 1994). Abu Sardane's position was duly upgraded to Qadi al-Quda with the rank of minister, independent from the Palestinian Ministry of Justice and answering directly to the President of the Authority; this set him on the same governmental level as his Jordanian counterpart. The year closed with no response from the Jordanians regarding the arrangements for the *Shari'a* Court of Appeal proposed by the Palestinians.

In January 1995, with cases building up in the West Bank courts, Yasser Arafat established a *Shari'a* Court of Appeal in the Palestinian *shar'i* system; the court was to have its permanent seat in Jerusalem, while provision was made for it to convene elsewhere.[28] In practice, the Palestinian court sits in Nablus to hear appeals from all the West Bank first instance *shari'a* courts except Jerusalem. In Jerusalem, the first instance court hears cases and registers deeds from East Jerusalem, as before, while the *Shari'a* Court of Appeal still situated there hears appeals only from that one court, both still being administered by the office of the Jordanian Qadi al-Quda. The arrangements for execution of judgments reveal the continuing Palestinian claims over the *shari'a* court of first instance in Jerusalem. Appeal decisions from the Palestinian regular (non-*shari'a*) Court of Appeal (sitting in Ramallah) have held rulings from *shari'a* courts in Jordan and from the

Israeli-established and administered *shari'a* court of first instance in Jerusalem to be 'foreign judgments' coming under the terms of Law on the Execution of Foreign Judgments 1952, issued by the Jordanians and applied in the West Bank, which requires such rulings to be processed for implementation through the regular court system.[29] In the case of the Israeli-administered Jerusalem court, the Palestinian Court of Appeal has held that such rulings 'at the current stage fall outside the competence of the [Palestinian] Execution Department'.[30] In regard to Jordanian courts, the Court of Appeal has held that a decision issued by a *shari'a* court in Amman 'has been issued by a court outside the territorial jurisdiction of Palestinian land, and is consequently considered a foreign judgment' which was therefore outside the competence of the Palestinian Execution Department 'before the measures set out in the said law [of Foreign Judgments] have been followed'.[31] Thus, decisions from Jordan may be properly processed and implemented as foreign judgments, but those issued from the Israeli *shari'a* court in Jerusalem may not. By contrast, rulings of the Jordanian-administered *shari'a* court in Jerusalem are routinely executed by the Palestinian Authority's execution offices in the same manner as they execute rulings from the Palestinian administered *shari'a* courts (Bakri 2000: 37).

Shar'i establishment positioning on personal status law

At least two efforts to draft a Palestinian personal status code came from within the *shar'i* system during the transitional period. In 1995 Abu Sardane announced that he was establishing a committee made up of himself and the heads of the two *Shari'a* Appeal Courts in Gaza and the West Bank to unify application of Muslim personal status law in the two areas. Abu Sardane recognized that some existing provisions were no longer appropriate, and that the public interest should be realized by selecting from among the rules of 'the four well known *fiqh* schools or from other recognized schools'. Generally, however, he declared an inclination towards the Jordanian model applied in the West Bank, considering it better 'developed' than the Gazan law. He expected a draft to be swiftly completed and 'presented to President Arafat for constitutional approval to be given in accordance with the Proclamation and in light of the independence of the *shar'i* judiciary' (Abu Sardane n.d.: 180, 49–50). In terms of process, he was of course speaking before the election of the Legislative Council in 1996, but, at the same time, his action clearly asserted the right of the *shar'i* judiciary to be the prime resource in the drafting of any state-issued codification of *shari'a* law.

In the meantime, at the end of 1995, Abu Sardane himself proceeded to issue an administrative decision on a matter of substantive law – the minimum age of capacity for marriage in the Gaza Strip, setting the minimum ages of capacity at fifteen *hijri* for females and sixteen *hijri* for males, the ages applicable in the West Bank under the JLPS. After Abu Sardane returned to Jordan, his efforts were taken up by Deputy Qadi al-Quda Shaykh Taysir Tamimi. The latter was similarly vigilant of the status of the *shari'a* court system, notably when confronted in June 1998 with a draft of a Judicial Authority Law being considered by the Legislative Council's Legal Committee, which omitted any mention of the *shar'i* judiciary. A memorandum signed by Shaykh Tamimi and a number of other senior officials in the *shar'i* system recalled the presence of the *shar'i* judiciary in Palestine since the Islamic conquest, referred to Article 92 of the draft Basic Law, and called on the Legal Committee to draft a law for the *shar'i* judiciary (*Al-Quds*, 9 June 1998). In a meeting between members of the *shar'i* judiciary and members of the Legal Committee, the press reported that it was agreed that 'not mentioning the *shar'i* judiciary was an oversight'. For his part, Shaykh Tamimi reportedly declared that the draft Judicial Authority Law was unconstitutional as a result of the omission, and himself presented to the committee a draft Law of Establishment of *Shari'a* Courts in Palestine. He described 'the attempt to wipe out the *shari'a* courts' as 'aimed at dealing a blow to our national struggle and our historical battle with those who deny our rights' (*Al-Quds*, 10 June 1998). The link being made here between the *shari'a* court system and the national struggle is clear in its assertion of legitimacy.

Issues of substantive law similarly preoccupied Shaykh Tamimi in 1998, the year of the culmination of the efforts of the model parliament, discussed below. A newspaper interview with Shaykh Tamimi indicated some of his basic positions, including the title summary: 'Humans may not try to prohibit what Allah has permitted: the scholars of *shari'a* and the PLC members are the only party empowered to set the law of personal status' (*Al-Quds*, 8 March 1988). In the interview, Tamimi was reported as criticizing a number of particular points in the various proposals being discussed while conceding concerns on certain matters, including underage marriage of females and the exclusion of women from their lawful inheritance entitlements. In response to the discussions at the model parliament on matters of personal status, Shaykh Tamimi announced the establishment of a preparatory committee to work on the drafting of a personal status law. Shaykh Tamimi described the motivation as a need to unify the West Bank/Gaza laws 'as a basic step in establishing the state and establishing the principle of unified and inalienable Palestinian sovereignty'. The draft would be drawn from 'the Qur'an, the *Sunna*, and the recognized schools of *fiqh*' and would in time be presented to the Legislative Council's Legal Committee for discussion. The committee was of broader membership than that constituted by Abu Sardane, although confined to those with 'establishment' experience in *fiqh* and religious studies.[32]

A number of issues are referred to or involved in such reports. First it might be noted that Shaykh Tamimi continues to assert for the *shar'i* judiciary a certain measure of control (through claiming the right to the drafting function) over the content of the law they are to apply, subject to discussion and promulgation by the Palestinian Legislative Council. Second is the linkage between *shari'a*-related matters and the process of state-building and the principle of national unity: here, the appeal is to pre-occupation and pre-colonial history and the sense of continuity represented by the *shari'a* courts – a suggestion of 'authenticity' which is expressed directly in arguments about the nature of personal status law. At the same time, this appeal is based on a system that is premised upon the communal distinctions between Palestinians of different religions, and the 'unity' referred to in this framework can thus legally only really mean 'unifying' the laws in the West Bank and Gaza. Third, there is the insistence that persons working on drafting a personal status law are to be (suitably) 'qualified'. The clear implication is that they should be qualified in *fiqh* and 'religious studies'. The status of the *shari'a* as the sole source of legislation for personal status issues is not open to discussion.

That said, besides working on drafting a Palestinian personal status law in the above committee (reportedly complete in draft form by early 2002), Shaykh Tamimi has responded to certain practical concerns within the sphere of his current competence, through proceeding with the issue of a number of administrative directives to the *qadis* and other officials in the *shari'a* courts. These have included an attempt to tighten up registration procedures of marriage, with strict instructions regarding the functions and conduct of the official marriage notaries (*ma'dhuns*)[33] and regarding the procedure to be followed by the *qadis* in registering a deed of 'acknowledgement (*tasaduq*) of marriage'. The latter requires the detailed questioning of the parties regarding the circumstances and exact procedure (or ritual) of their out-of-court marriage, including their ages and anyone else involved in it, and the reasons why it had not been properly registered at court; all the information is to be passed to the Qadi al-Quda's office for verification.[34] Given the concern he had articulated about attempts to marry off underage females being discovered in the *shari'a* courts, it is likely that this was a major target of these instructions.

Another administrative directive requires mandatory blood tests for couples planning to marry (another concern raised during the debates on personal status)[35] and a fourth concerns the allocation by the *shari'a* courts of inheritance portions between the various heirs to an estate.[36] In the latter, the preamble notes representations made to the Qadi al-Quda's department regarding problematic circumstances in which some heirs get others to waive all or some of their portions, including through fraud (impersonation), ignorance and threats. The instructions set out the detailed information that has to be taken from the persons involved, including the personal representation of all those involved (or their guardians if they are minors or do not have legal capacity), to be verified by official identity documents and by persons qualified to identify them to the court. If real estate is involved, precise details of the property in question are to be registered and its monetary value included in the documentation taken down by the court. The final document is to be signed by all parties as well as the *qadi* and the court clerk, and the implications of the division to be explained to all those involved, including the monetary value of their portion 'especially if it involves real estate, a company, shares or such like'. Again, all the documentation is to be sent to the Qadi al-Quda's office for verification. Here the Deputy Qadi al-Quda is likely to be seeking to address, though a set of procedural safeguards, his publicly articulated concern over women not receiving their *shar'i* inheritance entitlements.

Conclusions

By the formal end of the transitional period in Palestine, the *shari'a* court system was established institutionally and constitutionally within the framework of governance of the emerging Palestinian state. Politically, leading members of the *shar'i* establishment have addressed both the President of the Palestinian Authority and the Palestinian Legislative Council on matters of both system and substance, and have sought to maintain a degree of authority over the process of unification of Muslim personal status laws through engaging in drafting processes, of which at least that overseen by Shaykh Tamimi, the Deputy Qadi al-Quda, appears to have produced a preliminary draft. There has also been a degree of engagement with, and regard for some of the concerns of, civil society actors, notably from the women's movement, on particular matters of personal status, which have drawn reform-minded responses within the framework of '*shari'a*'-based law justified on the legitimacy of interpretation and the public interest or the needs of society. Procedural measures have been used to address a number of such concerns in advance of any change to substantive law.

Positive engagement of this kind might in the future provide the Deputy Qadi al-Quda with differently located allies in civil society in the likely event of disagreement with his positions on certain points of law from others among the *'ulama*, already indicated on some points by the Mufti, Shaykh Sabri. Given Hammami's finding of a 'doxa' of the framework of *fiqh/shari'a* to govern Muslim personal status law in Palestine, along with general support for the idea of reform of the codified family law, such engagement might prove the focus of significant investment by elements of the women's movement, including those working for the equality paradigm, along with their continued engagement of the legislative and executive authorities.

SEVEN

Palestinian interim governance: state legitimation, legal reform and the *shari'a*

Penny Johnson

§ WHAT were the constraints and opportunities for legal reform of *shari'a*-based personal status law posed by the establishment of an interim Palestinian Authority (1994–2000)? At first glance, the establishment of the first democratically elected Palestinian government on Palestinian soil would seem to offer a critical 'political opportunity structure' (Randall 1998: 193) to develop laws that reflected the interests and requirements of Palestinian society. At the end of the twentieth century, a century during which Palestinians had largely been excluded from shaping the formal laws that governed them, an elected Palestinian Legislative Council convened its first session in early 1996. One of its first tasks was to promulgate a Basic Law where the constitutional principles guiding Palestinian legislation, as well as other fundamental matters, should be delineated.

An examination of the political dynamics of the interim period and the features of Palestinian rule are crucial to understanding why this law was not promulgated, despite many drafts and extensive efforts by the Legislative Council, until after the scheduled end of the interim period. They also provide a window into the complex links between state formation and legitimation, on the one hand, and the positioning of Islam, *shari'a*-based law and legal reform, on the other. While Palestinian governance under the Israeli–Palestinian interim agreements (the Oslo Accords) had limited and non-sovereign powers and even more limited territorial control, it is precisely these circumstances that produce a rich field of inquiry where processes of state formation, the legitimation of the state and the constitution of citizenship can be investigated, as it were, *in situ*. The way in which Islam as ideology, religiosity and *shari'a* as a legal system are positioned and promoted in relation to these processes is crucial to an understanding of the prospects of legal reform, particularly reform of family law for gender equality. As Kandiyoti (1991: 185) has observed: 'studies of women in Muslim society have not always acknowledged the extent to which aspects of state practice define and mediate the place of Islam itself'.

Such an examination of the Palestinian state-in-the-making is relevant to other state transitions, particularly given the fact that this emerging state is both authoritarian and weak, which is highly relevant in the Arab world context, and perhaps in other developing societies. Indeed, it may be the case that the limits on Palestinian sovereignty are 'exemplary of the limits to sovereignty that the new world order is able to impose on certain national collectivities' (Hammami and Johnson 1999: 317). The various actors shaping Palestinian political, social and economic development – among whom the Palestinian is routinely the weaker party, whether in relation to Israel or the international donor community – constitute a field of power where the emerging state is best conceptualized as a 'set of arenas, a collection of practices' (Curthoys 1993: 34).

Interim inequalities and features of the transition

This political opportunity structure is shaped by the contours of the interim agreements between Israel and the Palestinians and the conceptions of rights therein, as well as by the struggle over final status agreements. The Israeli–Palestinian agreements make no reference to the existing legal framework of international humanitarian law which regulates situations of occupation, *inter alia* prohibiting such structural measures as Israel's purported annexation of East Jerusalem and its settlement policy, as well as violations of the rights of civilians through collective punishment, torture, wilful killing and bodily harm, deportation and other prohibited measures. Nor do the agreements contain enforceable com- mitments to international human rights instruments. The fact that the interim agreements avoided the discourse of rights – and indeed that further arrangements may well do so – has a range of implications for rights-based legal reform. First, it weakens the legitimacy of the Authority and the upcoming state, and makes both the search for legitimacy paramount and an Islamist challenge based on assertion of rights (individual and national) credible. Second, the daily life of men and women has been deeply affected by a series of inequalities in mobility, resources and status. These dynamics of inequality without recourse weaken any social contract between state and citizen and erode the rule of law and the development of a public sphere of dialogue and advocacy. In an examination by Fadwa Labadi of the utilization of civil, *shari'a* and customary law by families seeking compensation and *diya* after a 1999 Hebron factory fire in which fourteen women workers lost their lives due to clear criminal negligence, described in the appendix to this case study, the weakness of both the rule of law and the public sphere is revealed, as families seek recourse in a heterogeneity of legal practices but find their greatest satisfaction in customary legal processes based on *shari'a* principles of *diya* but pursued outside the *shari'a* court system.

The denial of rights caused by Israel's continued role as an occupying power, its expansion of settlements during the transitional years and its repressive policies towards Palestinians, particularly in the extended closures of Palestinian areas, is easily traced in the eruption of the second intifada but was also a major influence on the transitional period as a whole. The almost seven years of interim rule by the Palestinian Authority were marked by contradictions between the Authority's perceived mission of state formation and the severe limits imposed upon it. Along with internal features of Palestinian rule, these features illuminate both the constraints of law-making and legal reform during this period, and, in the particular focus of this case study, the positioning of Islam and Islamic law.

State security, 're-masculinization' and civil society

A number of analysts have noted the dominance of security in the formulation of the Israeli–Palestinian agreements and their unpublished annexes (Shehadeh 1997; Jad et al. 2000) as well as in Israeli and US policies towards the nascent Palestinian Authority and in the Authority's own practice of governance. While Israel retained overall responsibility for security under the agreements and exercised it widely, the agreements also mandated the establishment of a 'strong Palestinian police force' to maintain internal order (and tactictly to control opposition) and to safeguard Israeli security. As a consequence, and given the Authority's own security concerns, over 50,000 Palestinian security, army and police personnel deployed in seven to nine security agencies consumed almost a third of the Authority's budget each year (Hilal et al. 2003). The dominance of security also reflected the militarized structure and ideology of the Palestine Liberation Organization returning from exile. Indeed, the PLO's 'statist character' in exile (Sayigh 1997: ix) strongly contributed to the Authority's inability to see civil society as separate from the state, conflating state and society into a 'unitary model' (Giacaman 1998: 8) that undermined democratic prospects and public debate.

In addition, the post-Oslo crisis in Palestinian nationalism and national ideology was brought about not only by the seeming abandonment of armed struggle, long 'the defining dynamic that drove the reconstitution and reorganization of Palestinian national politics' (Sayigh 1997: 23), but also by the deferral of the pressing national issues of refugees, settlements and Jerusalem to final status negotiations. This crisis seemed to have been partially 'solved' by the continued use of militarist symbols and to some extent the militarization of public life that led one early observer to declare that security services had a 'monopoly on public space' (Bishara 1998: 194). In this view, legal reform would seem to have to either attempt to fit into the narrow bounds of a monopolized public space and advocate change mostly within circles of the Authority, or become part of a wider struggle for democracy and human rights. In the history of the Basic Law, and in other efforts for legal reform, however, we find that both strategies tend to exist simultaneously.

Security-driven agreements and agendas contribute to a 're-masculinization of politics' (Craske 1998: 100) that has been noted in other contexts in states in transition, most notably in Latin America. Women's informal political activity – taking the form of social movements against dictatorship (Latin America) or occupation (Palestine) – is replaced by masculinized formal politics where political 'parties have returned to their pre-eminent position as the terrain of political action, displacing social movements' (ibid., p. 109). While the distinction between political parties and social movements is not entirely apt in the Palestinian context, an observation from Latin America that this move includes a 'reassertion of the public–private distinction' (ibid., p. 111) is important to consider in the context of Palestine and legal reform of *shari'a*-based family law. Family law has been characterized as the 'last bastion' of *shari'a* in contemporary Arab and Islamic states (Mir-Hosseini 1993: 12), where it remains the one general area of law where legislatures claim to maintain overall the sway of provisions drawn from *fiqh*. The distinction between private and public has a different history in the Arab context than in the West, and in Western liberal thought in particular, where the 'propensity to categorize entire spheres of life as either public or private' (Thorton 1995: xiii) is quite acute. However, in the perhaps more appropriate division of state, market and domestic spheres, the state's 'protection' and 'preservation' of the domestic sphere (and by extension women) as a repository of cultural and national authenticity in times of the assertion of (repressive) state power, rapid change and market penetration is a political act that strengthens state legitimation.

If we use 'public sphere' in a Habermasian sense as a realm where issues can be debated and discussed for public action, the activism of Palestinian women during occupation certainly enlarged the public sphere, sometimes by expanding their family roles into public resistance. The reassertion of a barrier between public and private could serve to place the domain of family law into a realm beyond the fora of public debate and 'public rights', as affirmed in the Palestinian Declaration of Independence discussed below.

Islamist opposition and *shari'a* 'red lines'

The fact that the primary opposition to the Palestinian Authority and the Oslo Accords has come from the Islamist opposition, particularly Hamas (an acronym for the Islamic Resistance Movement), is a crucial factor in the positioning of Islam within the discourse of the Palestinian Authority and in attitudes towards *shari'a* reform. Hamas has combined military action against Israel, and Israeli civilians, with social action inside the West Bank and Gaza, conducting both suicide attacks inside Israel, particularly in 1996 and the second intifada, and developing a strong political and social infrastructure in the West Bank and Gaza.

From the inception of the Palestinian Authority, Islamists employed on occasion a discourse of human rights against state interference in projects of legal reform. In an interview shortly after the establishment of the Authority, a leading spokesman of Hamas noted that reform of the *shari'a* is a 'matter for the Palestinian *'ulama*' and that state interference would be an 'infringement on our human rights as Muslims. We are not against innovation (*ijtihad*) but we cannot compromise on rights that are guaranteed in the *shari'a*' (Jarrar in Usher 1997: 336). By all accounts, Islamists have communicated their position throughout the transitional period that state-led reform of *shari'a* is a 'red line' that the Authority would do well not to cross (Jad et al. 2000: 150).

This is not to say that Islamists did not have their own project to enter the arena of state politics. Although they boycotted the January 1996 elections for the Palestinian Legislative Council, as these elections were tied to the Oslo Accords that they so deeply opposed, they readied themselves for municipal elections, which were never held, and may well enter into the national arena if new elections are ever on the agenda. As Hilal noted in a background paper to this study (Hilal 2000), the National Islamic Salvation Party, which is widely seen as the public party of Hamas, affirms Islamist principles but in the context of modern political institutions. Human rights are guaranteed 'regardless of race or religion' and the 'activation of public institutions, including the legislature and the judiciary' is an objective. While the affirmation of human rights is not unique among Islamist parties in the region, Hamas is also responding to a national liberation movement and struggle to which it is profoundly affiliated, if separate in organization, and which has asserted rights (individual and people's human rights) as an enduring basis of legitimacy for its claims for justice. This context is critical to an under-standing of how Islamist movements in the Palestinian context frame issues of *shari'a* and legal reform.

In the Salvation Party's programme, 'empowering women to realize their full rights' is situated within the context of the *shari'a*; indeed, the first articulated aim is 'the resumption of Islamic life and the implementation of *shari'a* in the various aspects of life'. The connotation that the Israeli military occupation disrupted 'Islamic life' which must be restored has a particular resonance in a population whose ordinary lives have been torn asunder by conflict, foreign rule and repression and where Islam, for the majority Muslim population, is a con-stituent of Arab, Palestinian national and local community identity.

Uneasy allies: the Authority, women's movement and donors

While the Palestinian Authority's support for the women's movement is influenced by its aim to contain Hamas, the Authority also hesitates to alienate conservative religious sentiments for fear of strengthening the Islamist opposition. At the same time, Hamas' opposition to the women's movement is aimed at striking a blow at the Authority. The Authority is thus an uneasy ally of the women's movement at important times in debates on legal reform (such as the model parliament des-cribed in Chapter 9), and the women's movement has generally been effective in using whatever political space that opens up with the Authority to lobby for such reform, although perhaps more persistently for women's political representation.

Advocacy and lobbying, whether for representation or reform, address a system of Palestinian governance where 'an ethic of familialism structures power' (Ham-mami and Johnson 1999: 324), most clearly seen in the power and patronage concentrated in the President, and in the manner in which this power is both exercised and accessed. Familialism has also included a reassertion of affiliations based on tribalism and kinship, including the establishment of a Department of Clan Affairs. As Labadi shows, this department played an important role in the utilization of *shari'a*-based but uncodified customary law in the aftermath of the Hebron factory fire. Familialism and formal law are in many ways antagonistic in operation and in competition, and the formal legal system was seriously undermined during years of direct Israeli occupation and has not, by all accounts, been able to redress all of its shortcomings in the post-Oslo period. As for the utilization of diverse systems to secure justice, as Botiveau (1999: 76) observes in relation to the relevance of social diversity to studies of the legal field: 'Competition is a reality. Any individual can, in certain circumstances, draw on more than one normative register.'

Finally, the Palestinian Authority is highly dependent for its very existence on the support of the international community, and in particular the donor community. Aside from state powers, particularly the United States, all the major international institutions have played major roles in the transitional period, with the World Bank the main coordinator of donor funding, along with the United Nations (Pederson and Hooper 1998: 14). While the World Bank and IMF showed scant interest in gender issues (Kuttab 1995; Taraki 1995), other donors, such as the United Nations and a number of European states, had gender agendas, which led them to support a variety of useful projects and initiatives, but also created severe imbalances in the resources and programmes of women's groups, as donor interest in training and workshops – often focused on topics of democracy and citizenship – were reflected in a superabundance of such activities, some productive and others activity for activity's sake, while other interests of women were relatively neglected (Jad et al. 2000: 141). Although overall donor support for activities for women and gender equality were quite minimal in terms of a proportion of the whole – the amount of donor aid directed at 'women' amounted to only 0.5 per cent of the $3.314 billion of donor disbursements in the period 1994–2000 (Hilal et al. 2003: 34) – it demonstrably increased the vulnerability of the women's movement to being attacked as 'Western'. Indeed, one prominent Islamist, attacking the model parliament initiative of the women's movement, focused on its foreign funding from the United Nations Development Programme.

Donors have also focused funding on strengthening the legal system and legislative capacity, legal reform and human rights, with a May 1999 report estimating that $100 million had been dispersed since Oslo (UNSCO 1999). This amount may seem large, but in fact it constitutes a very minor part of all donor disbursements. While this report led to government attacks on the NGO sector for what was seen as a disproportionate share of the funding, a more pertinent assessment would assess the activities in terms of their outcomes. Here, the record is mixed: while legal education has been strengthened and institutionalized, other activities – from technical assistance to the Legislative Council to support for

Ministry of Justice initiatives to harmonize the laws of the West Bank and Gaza – are obviously critical, but suffered from a perhaps common malady in donor-sponsored initiatives of addressing large-scale legal and political processes and problems through 'projects' and 'training'. As we will see in Chapter 9, this dynamic affected one of the most interesting and successful of these legal reform projects, the women's model parliament.

The Basic Law

The Basic Law was not only mandated in the interim agreements, but was clearly viewed by Palestinian leaders and legislators as a priority. Even before the election of the Legislative Council, a Palestinian legal expert, Dr Anis al-Qasem, was instructed by PLO Chairman Arafat to draw up a draft Basic Law (al-Qasem 1996). Al-Qasem's draft Basic Law made no reference to state religion or to *shari'a*, stating simply that 'the Palestinian people are the source of all authority'. In this, he was in the spirit of the secular and nationalist discourse historically used by the Palestine Liberation Organization. His fourth and final draft Basic Law, reflecting amendments after discussions with Palestinian women activists, was clear on gender equality, stating in Article 10: 'Women and men shall have equal fundamental rights and freedoms without any discrimination.'

From the first draft produced by the elected Palestinian Legislative Council, tensions in secular discourse and social vision were revealed. Almost immediately, the separate article on equal rights for women and men, cited above, disappeared and there remained only a general statement against discrimination on any grounds in Article 9: 'All Palestinians are equal before the law and the judiciary, without any discrimination between them in respect to rights and obligations on the grounds of race, ethnicity, sex, race, religion, political opinion or disability' (PLC 2000).

This provision also existed in al-Qasem's drafting of the Basic Law; the elimination of Article 10 was thus a conscious 'backgrounding' of gender equality. Indeed, council members opposed to the retention of Article 10 argued that there was no need for a special article on equality between women and men, adding, in a all-too-familiar simile, 'then why not a separate article for children or the disabled?' Only a handful of members, including several female PLC members and leftists, argued to keep the gender equality provision (interview with Dr Azmi Shuaibi, 2000).

The anti-discrimination article is similar to a provision in the Palestinian Declaration of Independence, proclaimed by the Palestinian National Council in November 1988, which affirmed that 'governance will be based on principles of social justice, equality and non-discrimination in public rights on the grounds of race, religion, colour, or sex' (Lockman and Beinin 1989: 389), but does not use the problematic notion of 'public rights', which might imply that rights within the family are excluded. The Basic Law's provision, however, does not refer to social justice. While both exclusions may not have been deliberate, we can conclude that the process of articulating equality and non-discrimination constitutionally is somewhat troubled in the Palestinian context – and almost certainly not complete.

Source of authority, *shari'a* and legitimacy

The Council does retain, in Article 2, the statement that 'the Palestinian people are the source of authority', and adds a fuller formulation: 'which is exercised through the legislative, executive and judicial powers on the basis of the principle of separation of powers'. Given our particular focus in this examination, it is important to start by confirming Hilal's point on the 'secular outlook' of most of the Basic Law (Hilal 2000). The separation of powers, as in Article 2, pluralism, a 'democratic parliamentary system' and individual human rights, are all-important concerns of the Council in successive drafts of the Basic Law.

Of importance for family law reform, however, is the Council's addition of clear provisions affirming Islam, *shari'a* and the role of religion in public life. Al-Qasem's draft had deliberately avoided any reference to this or other potentially 'divisive' issues, as he explains in a commentary:

> It has been the regular practice in the Arab states to declare that Islam is the religion of state and *shari'a* the main source or a source of its legislation. Within the Palestinian community, there are various trends on the subject: the secular, the modernist and the fundamentalist. It was thought that such an issue should be decided upon in an atmosphere of freedom when the time comes for the preparation of a permanent constitution. (al-Qasem 1992–94: 198)

By contrast, the Council's draft Basic Law affirms in Article 4 that:

1. Islam is the official religion of Palestine with respect accorded to the sanctity of all other religions.
2. The principles of the Islamic *shari'a* are a principal source of legislation.
3. The Arabic language is the official language. (PLC 2000)

The use of 'a source' rather than 'the source', and 'principles of Islamic *shari'a*' rather than 'the Islamic *shari'a*' are deliberate choices and reflect political compromises and debates, as noted below. The language as a whole reflects a pronounced tendency to adopt the language and practice of other Arab states, rather than to differentiate Palestine from them, as part of a project of legitimizing the emerging Palestinian state in the region and among Islamic states, as well as appealing to local constituencies. In an interview carried out in 2000 for the purposes of this study, Dr Azmi Shuaibi, a leading PLC member from a small progressive party, noted that Article 4 originally emerged when Palestinian legislators reviewed constitutions of Arab states and that it was primarily a matter of 'political justification and legitimation'.

While we would agree with Zubaida (1988: 154) that 'Islam, in this capacity, as a resource for official legitimation … has always constituted an important part of the political field', why this legitimation is required and how powerful it is are questions to explore in the Palestinian context, given the overtly secular history of the Palestine Liberation Organization. Hilal attributes this change first to 'a series of crises and blows' to the PLO in the 1980s and then to 'the establishment of the PNA', where 'political Islam and the Palestinian National Authority have both been manipulating popular religiosity and "traditional" solidarities and affiliations in a fight for hegemony over the public sphere' (Hilal 2000).

In describing 'state, power and politics in the modern Middle East', Roger Owen (1990: 40) broadly notes that: 'No regime felt able to abandon Islam entirely, for this would have been to cut the most important single ideological and cultural link between it and the bulk of the population'. In the Palestinian case, the single most important link historically has been Palestinian nationalism, identity and resistance as mediated between a movement of national liberation/ resistance and communities in exile and in Palestine, although the link with communities inside Israel proper has had a different character. This link is still present between the Authority and Palestinian society in the West Bank and Gaza, although greatly weakened with communities in exile. Even inside the territorial base of the Authority, however, it is eroded by the failures and contradictions of Oslo and the fears of greater concessions on fundamental rights in the final status agreements. The second intifada, launched on 29 September 2000, has, somewhat paradoxically, weakened both civil society and government at the same time. If the President and the Authority emerge from this crisis intact, the search for sources of legitimation is bound to intensify; the ability of civil society to articulate the needs and interests of the population will be critical to moving in a democratic direction. It is in this ideological context, as well as the cultural link to the population, that Islam as legitimation must be situated.

Social compromise and executive resistance This being said, however, the Council did not treat Article 4 in a pro-forma fashion, and it was the subject of a prolonged and sometimes heated debate inside the Council, so much so that, at one point, the Council postponed discussion of the first section of the Basic Law and went to the less controversial next section (interview with Shuaibi, 2000). The eighty-eight-member Council – with only five women members – has a small but activist pole that can be termed progressive and secular and another relatively small but also activist bloc that can be described as Islamist. In the centre are the bulk of the Council members who are predominantly loyal to the Authority, to its main political party (Fateh) and generally to President Arafat himself. Many members, however, are not active in engaging in parliamentary processes and not oriented to parliamentary skills. This centre largely conceives of Islam as an integral part of Palestinian culture, but is not highly ideological. It was thus the two blocs that largely contended over the text of Article 4: initially, the progressive bloc spearheaded the cancellation of the article and then the Islamic bloc led a successful initiative to reintroduce it. Gradually, a 'third way' emerged consisting of the series of compromises noted above where 'principles of *shari'a*' were used instead of '*shari'a*' and 'a source' instead of 'the source'. Whatever the failures in representation in the composition of the Council, this compromise can be viewed as a social consensus forged by a democratic process of national compromise that is important to take into account in any legal reform initiative.

Interestingly, a late addition to Article 4 by the progressive bloc added a reference to Palestine as the 'cradle of the three divine religions', which was subsequently removed due to lobbying and petition for amendment by the Islamist bloc and other parliamentarians. The proposed first point of Article 4 read: 'Palestine is the cradle of the three divine religions and Islam is the official religion of Palestine and all religions are given their due respect and sanctity.'

The formulation of Palestine as the cradle of the three monotheistic faiths is found in the 1988 Declaration of Independence and other Palestinian official documents. The first sentence of the Declaration, after evoking the name of God, begins: 'Palestine, the land of the three monotheistic faiths … ' This formulation draws from a broad vision of Palestinian heritage that included diverse civilizations and coexisting religions, thus constituting a foundation for the future. The Declaration goes on to state:

> Nourished by an unfolding series of civilizations and cultures, inspired by a heritage rich in variety and kind, the Palestinian Arab people added to its stature by consolidating a union between itself and the patrimonial land. The call went out from temple, church and mosque to praise the Creator and to celebrate compassion: peace was indeed the message of Palestine. (Lockman and Beinin 1989: 395)

The narrowing of this vision represented by the cancellation of the reference to Palestine as a 'cradle of three religions' in the Basic Law has a number of sources, including the Islamist visions of Palestine as an Islamic *waqf*, but it more strongly reflects localism. The drafters of the Declaration of Independence were cosmopolitan intellectuals in exile, particularly the poet Mahmoud Dawish and the well-known critic Edward Said, and the Palestine they evoked was a Palestine of memory, and perhaps of the future. The local legislators drew from the bitter and restricted experience of the present and a kind of provincialism born of this experience and the fragmented nature of Palestinian society in the West Bank and Gaza.

Another important article for legal reform, Article 92, seemingly passed without controversy. The relevant portion of the article reads: 'Matters of *shari'a* and personal status will be the responsibility of the *shari'a* and religious courts in accordance with the law.' Welchman describes in the preceding section how this article was relied upon by the *shar'i* establishment in challenging the omission of reference to the *shari'a* courts in the 1998 draft Law Regulating the Judicial Authority. The assigning by the Legislative Council of matters of personal status to the *shari'a* and religious courts 'in accordance with the law' represents what Hammami in the next section, following Bourdieu, calls a 'doxa', an unquestioned assumption or belief about the relationship between personal status and *shari'a*.

The Palestinian Legislative Council passed the final version of the Basic Law in a third reading and presented it to President Arafat at the end of 1996 and again, with some amendments in favour of executive powers and succession, meant as concessions to the President, on 2 October 1997, but it was not signed into effect by President Arafat by the end of the interim period. Indeed, this is the other history of the Basic Law – a long and sharp conflict between the legislature and President Arafat, which began with the President attempting to place the responsibility for drafting the Basic Law only with the Executive, to the extent that the Council's first draft received the reply that the Executive had no knowledge of such a law. In turn, the Council dismissed a draft submitted by the Ministry of Justice as 'not suitable'. The Executive's delay on the Basic Law most explicitly reflects a conflict over powers and responsibilities, compounded by a general and pervasive problem of the Executive's attitude towards the rule of law, which is also reflected the undermining of an independent judiciary. The last letter from the Speaker of the Council to the President requesting his signature on the Basic Law was dated 24 April 2000, shortly before the offficial end of the interim period, given in the interim agreements as 4 May 2000.[37]

Other legislation: the influence of public advocacy Among the mere twenty-four laws passed by the Legislative Council in the 1994–2000 period and signed into law by the President, there is none that explicitly contains *shari'a*-based provisions or refers to Islamic principles in general. The first law passed by the Palestinian Legislative Council regulated municipal and village council elections, which were supposed to take place soon after elections to the Council. These elections were postponed on a number of occasions and did not take place in the interim period. The official reason was the difficulties of holding village council elections, given that most villages are in Area B, under joint Palestinian-Israeli control with Israel having the upper hand in security matters, and some in Area C, under direct Israeli control. While there is a grain of truth in the official explanation, a major factor was the Authority's fear that Hamas would make a strong showing. While Hamas and other Islamists boycotted the national elections because of their connection to the Oslo Accords, they were fully prepared to enter into municipal elections. Other laws establish or regulate institutions (such as the Palestinian Monetary Authority) or professions. Two laws were essential requirements of donors, particularly the World Bank, these being the Law to Encourage Investment and the Law to Regulate Industrial Zones. Perhaps the two most interesting laws for this study are the NGO law and the civil status law, since both were strongly influenced by vigorous lobbying campaigns. After two years of debate, the Authority passed and signed into law a relatively liberal NGO law, which can perhaps stand as a 'larger symbol of what active and well-organized lobbies can accomplish within the constraints of PA rule' (Hammami 2000: 19), and thus is important to note for other prospects of legal reform. In the same vein, the civil status law (Law no. 1 of 1999) which regulates the registration of births, deaths, marriages and divorces, among other matters, permits, in Article 17, either parent to register his/her children, a change from prevailing Jordanian law that is the direct result of lobbying by the women's movement (PLC 2000: 220).

Draft Constitution and statehood after the second intifada The Authority may well transmute into the government of a state without new national elections. If so – or if elections basically confirm the present leadership and its political party – the main features of the state can be delineated which will have consequences for opportunities for legal reform. One predominant feature that the new state shares with other states in the region is its 'externality' – where the state is 'deriving powers and resources in good measure from sources external to the social formations which they govern' (Zuabaida 1988: 162). This is perhaps most clear in financial resources, which will probably continue to be mobilized from the international donor community for the first few years of statehood at least, as part of the price of peace. In the interim period, the majority of public revenue (aside from donor contributions) was generated by revenue clearances rather than direct taxation of the public (Diwan and Shaban 1999: 212–13), also weakening the link between government and governed, as well as public accountability.

In preparation for a possible unilateral declaration of a state in September 2000 (in the wake of the failure of the Camp David talks), a draft temporary Constitution was prepared by a legal expert mandated by President Arafat in his capacity as Chairman of the Palestine Liberation Organization – thus placing the draft Constitution outside the authority of the Legislative Council, although many provisions in the Basic Law are incorporated. At the time of writing, the status of this document is not known.[38] However, in its present version, it partially bypasses the process of debate and compromise in the Council and declares in its Article 5 that: 'The principles of the Islamic *shari'a* are *the* principal source for legislation and the religions of the book will organize their own personal status in harmony with constitutional rules and maintaining the unity, stability and development of the Palestinian people' [emphasis added].

This version of the Constitution may well stay on the shelf, but the process of drafting a constitution by executive order is a disturbing indication. The complex dynamics of the second Palestinian intifada will inevitably shape the coming constitutional debate in ways that are difficult to predict, although the populist religious cast of the intifada – and the even greater imperative of the political leadership to contain Islamist opposition to a political settlement – are obvious factors that will affect the positioning of *shari'a* and the possibilities of family law reform that address the needs and interests of Palestinian women, men and children. Despite the assertion of the draft Basic Law that the 'people' are the source of authority, the reliance of the Authority on the powers of both the USA and Israel may well be extended into the next phase, again weakening the development of constituency-based politics, but strengthening the impulse towards the new state gaining legitimacy from more ascriptive identities in general and in Islam in particular, especially if Islamists continue to challenge the prevailing political order.

However, as Hammami and Johnson (1999: 123) argue, there are 'multiple and contradictory faces' of the Authority, which, despite its status as a 'security regime' also 'continues to represent the national liberation movement from which it evolved and thus, despite its coercive function, it remains the political and institutional focus of the population's national aspirations'. The solution to these contradictions has tended to be a politics that could be termed 'authoritarian populism' which denies specific constitutencies and publics in favour of 'the people' (Johnson and Kuttab 2001) and also excludes those groups or individuals with dissenting voices as not of the people – sometimes citing their manipulation by or for foreign powers, Iran or various Arab states in the case of Hamas and the West and the donors in the case of human rights organizations (and occasionally women's organizations as well). Populism, or some form of mass politics, has tended to put Islam back on the agenda in other Arab and Middle Eastern countries, and may well do so in the Palestinian context. However, the contrary vein to authoritarian populism – of mobilizing active democratic publics – is also present in Palestine, most visibly in non-governmental organizations, but also in the presence and history of social movements, including an active and strategically minded women's movement, in the West Bank and Gaza. Their challenge as agents of reform in the complex situation outlined in this chapter is discussed in Chapter 9.

EIGHT

Attitudes towards legal reform of personal status law in Palestine

Rema Hammami

§ INASMUCH as state-sponsored reform of Islamic family law can be understood as part of nation- and state-building projects (Kandiyoti 1991), mobilizations by social groups for legal reform are also eminently political. Moves for legal reform by non-state actors always come up against competing interests and are ultimately resolved by relations and operations of power. In the process, however, mobilizational strategies involve attempts to define the interests and well-being of the collectivity in line with the particular vision of legal reform being put forth. In the process of asserting a particular vision of the 'common good', such movements thus imply or make overt claims about the nature of the society and its preferences that they are claiming to represent or address. And if, as Helie-Lucas (1994) asserts, Islamic family law has indeed become the preferential symbol for Islamic identity, then attempts to reform it immediately bring to bear fundamental issues of collective identity. Thus, specifically in relation to family law, political claims-making inevitably becomes an exercise in identity politics.

In the debates that have taken place over reform of Islamic family law in the West Bank and Gaza since the mid-1990s, such contending claims about the nature of Palestinian society – or the nature of Palestinian identity – clearly entered the political field. At the level of the public, powerful assertions were made by Islamist leaders about the Islamic nature of Palestinian society while counter-claims were put forth by secularist political factions about pluralism and democracy as core components of a collective identity that was pre-eminently nationalist (Hammami and Johnson 1999). As such, the debates broke open a long simmering conflict between a legacy of secular nationalism and a newer resistance identity that was nationalist but based in narrower ethnic and religious terms.

Within the particular reform strategies posed by different groups, identity claims-making was also apparent but often less consciously articulated. Underlying the varying positions were competing claims about the social attitudes towards *shari'a* based on radically different assessments of the nature of Palestinian society.[39]

Those representing Islamist visions tended to pose Palestinian society as unanimously committed to the current system of family law, and actually desiring the extension of *shari'a* into other areas of life. Within the women's movement there were two strands of argument. One attempted to pose secular national identity and universal human rights as prime values among Palestinians, and argued that these could be the basis for moving reform in the direction of civil law. Similar to the Islamists, the other strand within the women's movement (largely based in Gaza) posed the society as primarily religious but, importantly, claimed it is cognizant of injustices in the current system. Thus, widening women's rights within the current framework of *shari'a*-based family law was their proposed strategy. Ultimately, the various reform (or non-reform) strategies can be understood as political projects in which varying assumptions about the nature of the society become attempts at constructing an abstract 'social will' to which each party lays claim in an attempt to legitimize its particular vision.

This chapter attempts to assess critically these varying claims about Palestinian society's attitudes towards reform of family law by juxtaposing them with the analysis of various polling data produced on the population in the West Bank and Gaza since 1995. Due to the peculiarities of the 'peace process', Palestinians in the West Bank and Gaza have since the early 1990s become one of the most polled populations, if not in the world, certainly in the Middle East. While donor provision of resources for polling was linked to the political agenda of the Oslo Accords, the motivations and interests of Palestinian pollsters were (and are) much more varied. Thus, while the majority of polls have focused on measuring 'public mood' towards the peace process, changing political affiliations (in the narrow sense), or support for various types of political action, there has been a parallel but more covert interest by pollsters with the 'social'. This interest in the social comes from the opening up of a new political terrain engendered by the state formation process in which NGOs, the women's movement and to a lesser extent political organizations began to confront what seemed to be a post-conflict situation where social priorities and needs could finally take precedence over the exigencies of national liberation. Equally, the range and variety of issues addressed through polls had to do with a society which had been denied data on itself (by the Israeli occupation) finally having the freedom to produce and access such knowledge.

Public opinion polling is scarce in the Middle East, where autocratic regimes tend to view the public, as such, as threatening. In contrast, the Palestinian context has seen little direct intervention by the political authorities to limit or censor polling activities – probably because in the context of political negotiations with Israel they actually helped the Palestinian Authority assert that there is a Palestinian public with 'red lines' on certain issues of national rights, which the Authority cannot afford to be seen to be crossing. However, although outcomes of polls are regularly reported in the local media, a media discourse on the 'public' that deploys polling data in the creation of a 'public opinion' remains overshadowed by a nationalist rhetorical political tradition which continues to speak of the 'people' and the nation. Thus, although polling data are in the public domain, there remains a limited public for them – save among academics and think-tank analysts.

It is this surprisingly innocuous nature of polling in the West Bank and Gaza that, I will argue, allows us to use its findings, if not at face value, at least as a window into stated values, commonsense notions and dispositions of the various sectors of Palestinian society not yet self-conscious of themselves as a 'public'. Various positions have been put forth on the impact of the lack of free expression experienced under Israeli occupation on how the population responds to polls. At one extreme, Fouad Mughrabi (1996) suggests that continued fear and suspicion affects polling outcomes, while at the other, Nadir Izzat Said (1997) suggests that because of previous silencing, there is now a strong motivation to speak one's opinion. This debate is more related to questions about the political authority, security services and political opposition than to those that deal with social issues and religious belief.

In the context of analysing social movements, James Jasper (1997: 285–6) makes the following argument:

> Protestors' efforts to mobilize people and resources depend, naturally enough, on what cultural understandings are out there to appeal to. The beliefs, emotions and morals of individuals – misleadingly aggregated as 'public opinion' – continually interact with a variety of other formulations alongside those of protestors. Politicians, newspapers, reporters, and editors, school-teachers, preachers, police officials and many others, along with their institutions, are actively involved, often in conscious competition with the claims of protest groups. There are regular and frequent struggles over common sense, and without them we would have trouble perceiving the active construction of cultural meanings.

Public opinion, indeed, represents misleading aggregates of individuals' beliefs, emotions and morals. At the same time, public opinion data are one of the few means available to try and draw a larger picture of the varied cultural meanings held in a society. The ability to call on shared cultural meanings is what makes mobilizations for social or political change possible – and thus public opinion data can be a useful tool in the process of claims-making.

This chapter begins by assessing what various surveys suggest about the role of religion in social and political life in Palestine. This is followed by a review of attitudes towards the roles and rights of women in the society as expressed through various survey data. Finally, the findings of a poll on attitudes towards family law reform undertaken by the project team in Palestine in spring 2000 will be reviewed.[40]

Attitudes towards religion

In 1992, in the first comprehensive household survey of the population in the West Bank and Gaza, approximately 65 per cent of respondents were found to be religiously 'observant', another 15 per cent were found to be 'religious activists' and approximately 20 per cent were found to be 'secular' (Heiberg and Ovenson 1993: 260). These categorizations were based on how respondents scored in relation to a series of questions related to religious and political sentiments and actions. While 'measuring' religiosity through a standard survey format is, at best, highly proximate, the data did provide some indicators about the extent to which religious commitment and identification were features of Palestinian social and political life during that particular moment. By comparing these findings to subsequent surveys, the data show the extent to which various aspects of religiosity are fluid and, to some extent, are influenced by social and political events and processes even within limited time periods. Additionally, as the categorization of the 1992 data above attempts to show, religious beliefs and actions do not simply or automatically translate into politics: in other words, to be observant does not necessarily translate into support for Islamist movements. While this distinction should be obvious, in studies on political Islam there is often a tendency to conflate the two.

The 1992 survey found slightly higher religiosity in Gaza (78 per cent) than in the West Bank (74 per cent), although it found that religious activism was higher in the latter area – 19 per cent in the West Bank versus 16 per cent in Gaza (Heiberg 1993: 260). Three years later in 1995, the Center for Palestine Research and Studies (CPRS) attempted to measure some similar issues. Although they did not use the same questions, it is possible to make some overall comparisons. In 1995, the CPRS found that 43 per cent of the population unequivocally described themselves as religious; 47 per cent of Gazans compared to 40 per cent of West Bankers (Hammami 1997a). Although the absence of the category 'activist' makes comparisons about activist Islam impossible, the overall percentage claiming to be religious or 'somewhat' religious shows a decline from approximately 80 to 57 per cent within a period of only three years.[41] How can the drop be explained? The intervening three-year period between the two surveys saw dramatic changes in the everyday lives of Palestinians in the occupied territories. In 1992, the population was still experiencing the long, chaotic and debilitating breakdown of the first Palestinian intifada, and just coming out of the Gulf War. By 1995, a peace agreement had been signed between the PLO and Israel, and the populations of Gaza and Jericho were finally experiencing the first fruits of post-occupation normalcy with the Israeli occupation forces no longer a presence in their immediate communities. Clearly, while religious belief itself at the mass level is not so directly and immediately affected by political events and economic shocks, the weight given to religion within everyday life can be.

While the CPRS survey did not use the category 'religiously activist', its findings suggest the important distinction between religious piety on the one hand, and a commitment to political religion on the other. The 1995 survey further points to the fact that Islam as politics also needs to be differentiated, between abstract political values (an Islamic state) and concrete support for specific Islamist movements and ideologies. As Table II.1 suggests, in 1995, religion as a positive social value and as an abstract normative political ideal garnered great support. In contrast, actual Palestinian politico-religious groups and their leaders did not. The highest levels of religious feeling relate to it as a positive moral and ethical force in society – expressed in the high degree of respondents strongly agreeing on the need to promote God's word or viewing the parting from religion as a very important problem (approximately 75 per cent of respondents). The second role of religion, as an abstract normative political ideal, elicited slightly less support, although still quite high, as expressed in the number of respondents willing to sacrifice their lives for the Islamic Umma or those supporting the idea that 'Islam is the solution' (approximately 62 per cent of respondents).[42]

Table II.1 The role of religion in society versus politics (%)

	West Bank	Gaza	Total
The need to promote God's word (strongly agree)	77	85	80
Parting from religion (very important problem)	66	78	71
Willing to sacrifice highest price for Islamic Umma (always)	55	60	57
Islam is the solution (yes)	66	66	66
I support political Islamic parties (applies)	37	31	35
Role for religious men in politics (very important)	29	34	31
Candidate's religiosity is (very important) election qualification	37	41	38

Source: Hammami 1997a, based on 1995 CPRS poll

However, while respondents highly valued religion in ethical and abstract terms, there was much less support for political religious leaders and parties in the concrete with approximately only 34 per cent of respondents claiming to support them. Ultimately, the complexity and contradiction inherent in religious dispositions is also reflected in the fact that only 43 per cent of all respondents in the survey described themselves unequivocally as religious, but a full 80 per cent of them put a high priority on the need to promote God's word. This suggests the power of religion as part of a community's moral identity, but whose ideals individuals often feel unable to fulfil in their everyday lives.

Religious values and secular politics

The emotional commitment to Islam as a normative and abstract political frame-work can be clearly seen in the range of survey data undertaken since the early

1990s. For instance in the 1992 FAFO survey, 'Islam' was cited as the most important attribute the overwhelming majority (60 per cent) of respondents wanted to see in a future Palestinian state; 'democracy' came in a poor second at only 20 per cent of respondents claiming it as the main attribute they wanted to see in a Palestinian state (Heiberg 1993: 266). However, once again when issues are made more concrete, the outcome is not as clear. When respondents were asked for whom they would be willing to make the ultimate sacrifice, the Islamic Umma came third after the Palestinian people (see Table II.2).

Table II.2 For whom would you be willing to make the ultimate sacrifice? (% of total)

The family	45
The Palestinian people	33
The Islamic nation	17
The Arab nation	4

Source: Heiberg 1993: 272

Similarly, in 1995, the CPRS survey showed that while respondents might put a high priority on abstract religious values, these readily coexist with a high concern for more mundane and practical issues. Table II.3 shows how respondents ranked major priorities in Palestinian society. Although the need to raise God's word came number one, this was the only religious issue that ranked among the top ten.

Table II.3 Major priorities for Palestinian society

Critical social problem	West Bank	Gaza	Total (%)
The need to promote God's word	77	85	80
Employment/standard of living	65	75	69
Security and order	64	69	66
Equality before the law	63	73	67
Free higher education	61	69	64
Qualifications	61	67	63
Getting rid of *wasta**	57	70	61

* *wasta* is the popular referent for patronage. In action it means securing a position or accessing a privilege through personal connections
Source: Hammami 1996

As Table II.3 shows, issues of social and economic well-being also ranked very high. Additionally, what stands out from this table is the level of priority given to 'equality before the law' which here, given the context, seems to be predominantly about general social equality and rule of law, rather than necessarily being about the equality of men and women before the law.

Clearly, 'religiosity' in a society cannot be taken at face value, but needs to be understood as part of a complex array of beliefs and dispositions which are embedded in concrete but changing social, political and economic circumstances. Religious beliefs and attitudes coexist with a complex array of mundane needs and priorities, as well as other sets of non-religious ideas and commitments. Talal Asad's notion of Islam (or any religion) as a discursive tradition is useful in this context. He distinguishes between theological discourse (discourse about religion) and liturgical utterances, ways of speaking employed in prayer, sacrifices or preaching (Asad 1983: 243). While the latter induces religious dispositions in worshippers, the former attempts to put those dispositions in a larger intelligible framework about religion, society and politics. Liturgical utterance is the domain of dispositions (piety) that is much less changeable, while theological discourse is the domain of religion that is more public, where attempts to sanctify social or political practice as pious are carried out. Thus, on the one hand, the inner core of religious belief is often at odds or in tension with larger social and political discourses about religion, while, òn the other, theological discourse exists within a wider social world of secular thought and political ideology – and, in the Palestinian context, nationalism is a powerful discursive and practical field with which all other cultural meanings must interact.

Support for women's rights

The Palestinian context is unique in the Middle East as one in which women's activism has a long history which is both publicly recognized and perceived as socially legitimate up to the present. This is clearly a product of the intertwined histories of women's activism and national resistance; national crisis and resistance demanded new roles for men and women, and the national movement created frameworks in which these new roles could be articulated. In social and political life, we can see the translation of this in the almost symmetrical ratios of male and female at all levels of the education system, as well as in the range of public political positions held by women, and in, for instance, the strong turn-out for female candidates in the 1994 legislative assembly elections.[43] But attitudes towards women's rights vary according to the specific rights being addressed. In general, poll findings suggest that there are two main pendulums: on the one hand, support is higher when rights are abstract rather than concrete; on the other, support is higher for women's rights in the public sphere and narrows in the realm of marriage and the family. Thus, the 1995 CPRS poll showed that more than 90 per cent of men and women surveyed agreed that 'the relation between men and women should be based on equality in rights and responsibilities'. In the same poll more than 80 per cent of men and women asserted that 'women's oppression is an important issue'. However, high support for women's rights does not necessarily translate into support for concrete changes in gender relations in all spheres of life.

In specific, various polls tend to show that there is high support for women's political rights and a similar level of support for women's economic rights, but far less support for changes in property relations between men and women or in the redistribution of power within the family or marriage. As the data in Table II.4 suggest, support for an array of women's rights to political representation and to hold public office is very high – on average more than 70 per cent among men and 80 per cent among women.

Table II.4 Support for women's political rights (%)

Political rights	Men		Women	
Should women be represented in the PLC?* (CPRS 1995)	72		75	
Do you believe qualified women should have equal chances in public responsibilities? (JMCC 1995)	74		87	
Do women have the ability to lead? (CPRS 1995)	Yes	60	Yes	70
	Somewhat	23	Somewhat	20
Would you vote for a qualified woman? (JMCC 1995)	Yes	63	Yes	81
	Somewhat	16	Somewhat	10

* The Palestinian Legislative Council, the only popularly elected representative government body allowed for under the Oslo Accords.

Popular support for women's economic rights is also similarly high, but only in relation to women's access to wage work. In 1995, more than 70 per cent of men and almost 90 per cent of women believed that women have the right to work outside the home. In comparison, in 1992 the FAFO survey found a significantly lower percentage of men (56 per cent) and women (78 per cent) supporting women's right to work outside the home – attesting to the fact that economic crisis and political change can dramatically and quickly affect the way some aspects of women's rights are viewed. Specifically, the post-Oslo period witnessed a relative betterment in physical security simultaneous with a dramatic deterioration in the Palestinians' economic well-being. As such, women's contribution to family income became perceived as a practical need among men as well as women.

Along with high support for women's access to wage work, the 1995 survey found a similar level of support existed for women receiving equal opportunities and wages. However, in one of the few survey questions to attempt to assess women's access to property, only 28 per cent of men and a similarly low 38 per cent of women claimed that women would be able to manage their property on their own (PCBS 1999a). This indirect question indicates the strong social reservations towards women's independent property ownership, which in the concrete is exemplified by the low levels of women owning immoveable property (approximately 8 per cent of all women). Despite common knowledge of women's *shari'a*-based rights to property, it is clear that when practical interest contradicts religious prescription, the latter is easily superseded. This may be a negative example of where concrete interests supersede religious doctrine: in this case, the interest of men to continue the practice of withholding women's inheritance shares to immoveable property (Moors 1995). However, the contradiction between religious doctrine (or what is perceived to be religious doctrine) and concrete everyday interests can also work in favour of women, as will be shown later in this chapter.

While strong levels of support exist for women's political rights and rights to income through wage labour, these coexist with a much more limited level of support for women's rights within marriage and the family. As Table 11.5 shows, in contrast to rights in the public domain, within the confines of the private, and specifically in relation to marital relations, poll findings show a dramatic drop in support for women's rights. While the relatively low support for women's rights to divorce may reflect the deep social stigma attached to divorce as such, the significant gap (15 per cent) between men and women on this issue reflects the contradiction of interests between them. Both may be reticent about divorce, but women more readily perceive the practical need for women's right to divorce.

Table 11.5 Support for women's marital rights (%)

Marital rights	Men	Women
Women should have the right to divorce (CPRS 1995)	57	72
Husbands do not have the right to hit their wives (CPRS 1995)	53	61

Respondents' reactions to the question on domestic violence show a similar pattern; the fact that the right of husbands to strike their wives is regarded by many as religiously sanctioned probably makes it difficult to condemn. Simultaneously, women as potential or actual victims of domestic violence are more critical. The stark contrast between support for women's public versus private rights tends to support the contention of a number of feminist critics of the Palestinian national movement that it focused on the political mobilization of women but either neglected or actively avoided addressing power relations between men and women in the private domain. Clearly, nationalist movements, while creating new spaces and opportunities for women, tend like nation-states to construct citizenship rights only in the public domain, leaving the familial as a space in which males have rights and primary authority over females (Chatterjee 1993; Yuval-Davis 1997). At the same time, the basic acquisition of popular support for women's political rights represents the acquisition of major strategic assets for widening women's rights in other areas.

Attitudes towards *shari'a* law

Despite the very public debate that emerged over reform of *shari'a* law from the mid-1990s, surprisingly few surveys have been undertaken on the issue. Prior to the Institute of Women's Studies survey in spring 2000, commissioned by the research team for the purpose of this case study, the sole other such survey assessed only women's attitudes and showed that 85 per cent of women wanted personal status law to be based on *shari'a*.[44] The same respondents who overwhelmingly supported *shari'a* simultaneously claimed that that the current laws did not ensure equality between men and women (66 per cent) and assessed the current legal systems as negative (79 per cent). Bourdieu's notions of 'doxa' (what goes without saying) and orthodoxy (what cannot be said) are useful in explaining this apparent contradiction (Bourdieu 1979: 168–9). Doxa stands for aspects of tradition and culture which are so internalized that they exist as unquestionable commonsense beliefs and dispositions. Clearly, for many *shari'a* is a doxa – in this case assumed to be an unquestionable good that even the everyday negative experiences of the law and courts cannot undermine. In contrast, orthodoxy is when authority tries to reimpose the 'truth' of a doxa that has been brought into question, either because the reality on which the doxa rests has changed or because subaltern or oppositional voices emerge to question it. To quote Bourdieu (ibid., p. 169), orthodoxy 'is defined as a system of euphemisms, of acceptable ways of thinking and speaking the natural and social world, which rejects heretical remarks as blasphemies'. Attitudes in support of *shari'a* can thus also be explained with recourse to the notion of orthodoxy. While for some social groups the centrality of *shari'a* in regulating gender relations is taken for granted and beyond question, for others *shari'a* has become a central concept within a larger political project that attempts to replace the present set of social and political arrangements. The goal of this orthodoxy is an attempt to reassert *shari'a*'s central and 'natural' role in regulating all aspects of life. The suggestion here is that we need to differentiate between doxic attitudes in relation to *shari'a* as personal status law only; and newer orthodox attitudes which conceive of *shari'a* as carrying a much wider purpose and role beyond regulating gender relations. The doxa of *shari'a* in relation to personal status makes sense given that, as outlined in the previous section, it is the one general area of law in which *shari'a* has had a certain historical continuity to the present.

In terms of attitudes, doxa, in particular, represents an obstacle to uncovering more nuanced, complex and varied stances towards *shari'a* as a basis of family law. Thus, one way of circumventing this 'naturalized' nature of support for *shari'a* is to pose questions which actually move closer to the level of concrete need and practice and do not directly invoke the concept itself. Based on this understanding, the research team in Palestine undertook a survey in May 2000 designed in ways that may reflect more of the contradictory attitudes towards Islamic family law in order to find openings for change. The survey was a means to probe more deeply into the contradictions between abstract loyalties and commitments and the concrete problems and needs of men and women as they confront the law.

The *shari'a* family law survey

Methodology The survey was undertaken on 23 and 24 March 2000. A stratified random sample of 1,200 people over the age of eighteen was interviewed face-to-face throughout the West Bank and Gaza Strip. Fifty-nine sampling units in the two regions were selected, and from these researchers randomly selected households. Using Kish tables, interviewers then randomly selected individuals to be interviewed within the household. The outcome of the sample distribution is reflected in Table 11.6.

Table II.6 Sample distribution of *shari'a* family law survey (% of total)

Region	
West Bank	58
Gaza Strip	36
E. Jerusalem/Jerusalem	6
Residence	
Towns	44
Villages	39
Refugee camps	16
Gender	
Male	47
Female	54
Marital status	
Married	65
Single	29
Widowed	4
Divorced	1

The average age of the respondents was thirty-five and the survey has a margin of error of 3 per cent with a confidence level of 95.

Use of the courts According to the survey findings, only a small minority of the respondents used the courts within the year before the survey (18 per cent), and in the majority of cases this was for purposes of marriage (49 per cent), followed by inheritance. In both areas, marriage accounts for by far the greatest reason for using the courts (47 per cent of all court use in the West Bank and 73 per cent of all court use in Gaza). By law, all marriages should be registered with the courts, and the necessity of marriage records for other bureaucratic transactions (identity cards, passports etc.) ensures that most marriages get registered. Thus, marriage probably is the one time in most Palestinians' lives that they have to interact with the *shari'a* court system, through the marriage notary, the *ma'dhun*. In the West Bank, there was a much higher use of the courts for inheritance cases (almost twice as high as in Gaza). From the survey, it is unclear whether these were simply cases of registration of deeds, or whether they included cases of litigation over inheritance shares. The difference between the two regions in terms of number of inheritance cases suggests that both land scarcity and the predominance of a refugee population in Gaza may account for the lesser number of respondents claiming their use of the courts was for inheritance matters. While divorce ranks as third among West Bank and Gazans (14 per cent) as a reason for going to the courts (especially in cases of multiple court use), we find 'divorce' cited twice as much among Gazans. This is likely to be a statistical artefact given that the number of inheritance cases cited is so low in Gaza. Tellingly, cases covering dower claims, maintenance and separation combined accounted for less than 5 per cent of all court use. However, from surveys of court records, it is clear that a large proportion of cases of litigation in the courts (as opposed to simple bureaucratic registration) are over maintenance, though not over dower (Welchman 1999: 105). As such, the low number of respondents citing maintenance or dower as a reason for court use is the outcome of the overwhelming use of the court for simple registration as opposed to litigation.

Of those who used the courts, only 20 per cent expressed unequivocal dissatisfaction with them, although there was a clear gender gap (see Table 11.7). West Bank females who used the courts expressed, overall, the most displeasure at the courts, with 31 per cent of them unequivocally expressing their lack of agreement with the courts compared to only 18 per cent of men in the same region. Gazan females, while overall more positive about the courts than West Bank females, are also more negative towards the courts than their male counterparts, with 16 per cent more females who used the courts there dissatisfied than the men.

Table 11.7 Degree of satisfaction with courts based on use of the courts over the last year (%)

| | West Bank | | Gaza | | E. Jerusalem* | |
	Male	Female	Male	Female	Male	Female
Satisfied	65	44	74	71	100	33
Semi-satisfied	18	25	22	11	–	–
Not satisfied	18	31	4	18	–	67

*The East Jerusalem sample is so small as to be unrepresentative, and is cited here only for purposes of interest

The fact that such a small percentage of the surveyed population had used the courts in the last year, and that in most cases it was for the purpose of marriage, may explain the low level of dissatisfaction with the courts – i.e. in the majority of cases of court use, they are not making rulings on conflicting or sensitive issues. Additionally, given that the majority of court use was for registration of deeds and contracts rather than litigation, it could be argued that this low level of dissatisfaction is not based on a real test of the courts, in the sense of a test of the court's performance in dealing with a claim being made by the respondent.

All respondents were asked for their impressions of the courts regardless of whether they had actually used them or not. Three general questions were asked regarding whether respondents felt that the courts supported women's, men's and children's rights. While the majority of respondents claimed that they felt the courts did support women's rights, there is a clear gender gap on this issue, with 10 per cent more males (79 per cent) claiming that the courts support women, than women (70 per cent), themselves believe. Men equally believe that the courts support their rights (79 per cent), while women tend to see the courts more supportive of men's rights (83 per cent) than they see them supportive of women's rights (70 per cent). However, the question of rights is vague – in this context, the majority of respondents are probably conceiving of men's and women's rights within the context of the law. Despite this, women's awareness of bias shows up in their significantly higher assertion that the courts support men compared to women.

Marital age and freedom to choose a spouse Various surveys in the past have attempted to assess attitudes towards freedom to choose a marriage partner. In the past, however, it was generally assumed that this was an issue that was relevant only to young women. Although the CPRS survey in 1995 found a high level of support for women's right to choose their spouse (above 90 per cent for both sexes) the ambiguity of the question probably accounts for the outcome. The right to choose may simply mean for many people the right of women to refuse someone imposed on them by their parents. This interpretation is supported by the fact that in the FAFO study less than 10 per cent of men and women thought that choice of spouse should be the daughter's choice alone, while the majority asserted that a decision should be made collectively with the young woman's parents. On the other hand, the lack of freedom to choose a marriage partner is clearly not a problem only for women. A recent survey by the PCBS (1999b) found that while 43 per cent of women said they did not choose their spouse by themselves, a lower but significant percentage (28 per cent) of men also claimed they did not choose their spouse by themselves.

The 2000 survey tried to invoke indirectly the contradiction between the minimum legal marriage age and the decision-making power in the marriage process. In specific, did respondents feel that a person might be mature enough to get married but simultaneously not mature enough to decide on whom they married?

Table II.8 Are women under seventeen years of age and men under eighteen years of age mature enough to choose their spouse? (%)

| | West Bank | | Gaza | | Jerusalem | | Total | |
	Male	Female	Male	Female	Male	Female	Male	Female
Women under 17 'Yes'	12	8	10	6	12	7	11	7
Men under 18 'Yes'	13	11	19	15	21	6	15	12

Clearly, the findings in Table II.8 show the dominant trend in which choice of a marriage partner continues to be seen as an issue in which parents should be involved. When asked whether women under seventeen years of age and men under eighteen years were mature enough to choose their spouse, the survey found the following responses: 11 per cent of men and only 7 per cent of women felt that women under seventeen could be considered mature enough to choose their own spouse, and 15 per cent of men and 12 per cent of women felt that men under eighteen years could be considered mature enough to choose their own spouse. As such, the overwhelming stance is that neither men nor women are considered at these ages capable of making their own decisions regarding a marriage partner.

Congruent with this was the overwhelming support expressed by respondents for a minimum age of capacity for marriage of eighteen for both sexes (86 per cent of males support this compared to 90 per cent of females), as shown by the responses in Table II.9.

Table II.9 Should the age of marriage be raised for both males and females to eighteen? (%)

| | West Bank | | Gaza | | Jerusalem | | Total | |
	Male	Female	Male	Female	Male	Female	Male	Female
Yes	85	89	87	88	79	97	86	90
No	15	11	13	12	21	3	14	10

Divorce Earlier surveys have consistently found an overwhelmingly negative stance towards women's right to divorce. On closer scrutiny, however, it is not clear whether the findings are about women's rights to do so or represent a larger taboo towards divorce as such. The 2000 survey attempted to clarify the difference by asking under what specific circumstances women should have the right to request a divorce. Posed in this way, only 4 per cent of men and women came out against women's right to divorce under any circumstances (see Table 11.10).

Table II.10 Acceptable reasons for divorce

Acceptable reason for divorce	Women	Men	Total (% who answered 'Yes')
Husband is a collaborator	69.1	69.2	69.1
Husband is mentally ill	63.3	68.7	66.0
Husband physically abuses wife	57.8	52	54.7
Husband has abandoned family	58.8	50.7	53.1
Husband has a sexual disease	41.5	43.6	42.3
Husband physically abuses children	35.4	31.6	33.2
Husband marries a second wife	23.7	15.6	19.7
Women should not be allowed to divorce in any circumstances	4.0	4.5	4.2

Signficantly, in the Palestinian context, a 'nationalist' justification, a husband being a 'political collaborator' came out as the number one acceptable reason, supported by 69 per cent of respondents. Second was the husband's mental illness (66 per cent) and thirdly spousal physical abuse (55 per cent). Although only a minimal number of respondents (20 per cent) cited polygyny as a legitimate reason, it is significant that there is even this amount of support for divorce on grounds not recognized as such by prevailing personal staus law. Overall there was a consistent 5 per cent gender gap between men and women on all of the possible responses, with the latter slightly more responsive to women's need to divorce under the varying circumstances posed in the questions. However, in the case of polygyny there was the most dramatic gap between men and women's responses with 24 per cent of women and only 16 per cent of men citing this as a justifiable reason for women to divorce.

Reform of personal status law

In 1995 the CPRS survey found strong support for reform of existing law as long as it remained within the framework of *shari'a*. In that survey, 61 per cent of males and 57 per cent of females supported the statement that 'the existing Islamic laws (those that relate to social aspects) require reinterpretation in order to become more appropriate to contemporary life'. Between 1995 and 2000 there was a growth in support for this position with 84 per cent of males and 88 per cent of females responding positively to the statement that 'family law should respond to changes and new needs in Palestinian society' (see Table II.11). This suggests that the campaign undertaken post-1995 through the model parliament, discussed in the following chapter, had an important impact, not only by opening a public debate about the issue, but also in raising awareness about the need for reform.

Table II.11 Do you think family law should respond to changes and new needs in Palestinian society? (%)

| | West Bank | | Gaza | | Jerusalem | | Total | |
	Male	Female	Male	Female	Male	Female	Male	Female
Yes	81	90	88	86	89	84	84	88
No	19	10	12	14	11	16	16	12
Total	100	100	100	100	100	100	100	100

The 2000 survey was also able to assess what the preferred nature of reform should be: 41 per cent of males and 62 per cent of females supported change that gave women more rights within family law than presently existed (see Table II.12). This represents a significant gender gap of 20 per cent with a greater number of women desiring change that would provide them greater rights.

Table II.12 Do you favour more, fewer or the same level of rights given to women in the family law currently existing in your place of residence?

| | West Bank | | Gaza | | Jerusalem | | Total | |
	Male	Female	Male	Female	Male	Female	Male	Female
More	46	67	35	57	24	55	41	62
Less	6	2	11	5	6	2	8	3
Same	48	31	54	38	71	43	52	35
Total	100	100	100	100	100	100	100	100

Significantly, most of those who do not agree with expanding women's rights are not for further limiting them in the law, but are in favour of the status quo. Thus, 52 per cent of men and 35 per cent of women feel that the existent level of rights allowed to women should stay the same – and only 8 per cent of men and 3 per cent of women feel they should be more limited. Finally, it is clear that men hold much more contradictory stances towards the price of reform; the gap between the 52 per cent of men who want the status quo and the 84 per cent of men who earlier claimed to support reform (albeit indirectly) suggests that while supporting the abstract principle, the translation of this in ways that may potentially affect their practical interests is more problematic.

However, if reform is posed as moving in the direction of civil law, once again the doxa of *shari'a* comes to the fore. Thus, when asked in the current survey if they would support the right of individuals to marry under civil law if this did not affect the right of others to marry under *shari'a*, only 26 per cent of males and 21 per cent of females agreed. While this is a significant one-quarter of males and one-fifth of females surveyed, the overall impression from the responses is the profound commitment to *shari'a* as the basis for family law by both, but especially by women.

Reactions to Egyptian divorce reform: the case of *khul'* In terms of specifying proposed areas of change in the existing law, the survey asked respondents about their reactions to the recent law on divorce enacted in Egypt (see Table II.13).

Table II.13 Recently a law was passed in Egypt enabling women to ask for a divorce if they waive their financial rights. Would you like to see a similar law enacted in Palestine? (%)

| | West Bank | | Gaza | | Jerusalem | | Total | |
	Male	Female	Male	Female	Male	Female	Male	Female
Yes	34	41	25	30	50	48	32	37
No	66	59	75	70	50	52	68	63
Total	100	100	100	100	100	100	100	100

The question was not dependent on respondents' actual knowledge of the Egyptian reform, but asked whether they saw a law enabling women to divorce through waiving their financial rights as a positive innovation they would support

Table II.14 Why do you support or oppose a law enabling women to ask for a divorce if they waive their financial rights? (%)

	Females	Males
Positive support for women's divorce rights		
Support because allows women to divorce	27	33
Oppose because women should not lose property	44	28
Total	71	61
Negative support for women's divorce rights		
Support because divorced women should lose property	5	4
Oppose because women should not divorce	24	35
Total	29	39

in Palestine. Only one-third of respondents supported enactment of such a law, although a slightly higher percentage of women (37 per cent) than men (32 per cent) did. Lowest support for such a law was among Gazan males, while highest support was among Jerusalem females, followed by West Bank females. The survey went on to ask why respondents supported or opposed the enactment of such a law (see Table 11.14).

When one looks at the various positions above, clearly, the majority of men and women are responsive to the right of women to divorce, but they differ about the terms and importance of women's property in such circumstances. In particular, we can divide the respondents into those who, regardless of their stance towards the proposed reform, positively support women's right or ability to divorce versus those who, regardless of their stance towards the *khul'* law, are negative towards women's rights or ability to divorce. Seventy-one per cent of women support women's rights to divorce as such, but the majority of them (44 per cent) think that women should not lose their property rights in order to do so. Among males, a lesser 61 per cent support women's right to divorce as such, but only 28 per cent of those oppose women losing their property rights in order to do so.

In responding to this question, the majority of men and women reiterate their support for women's right to divorce. However, in comparison to the earlier question regarding under which specific circumstances women should be allowed the right to divorce, there is a dramatic drop in support. Once again, it is also clear from the above responses that women are more supportive of their right to divorce than are men, with an approximate 10 per cent gender gap.

Who should reform the law? One aspect of the political conflict that emerged in the model parliament campaign was over who had the right to propose reform of existing personal status laws, and who had the right actually to reform it, as discussed elsewhere in this case study. The 2000 survey sought to find out who was thought by respondents to be the legitimate body to decide on reform. The most support was expressed for the statement that 'the society should vote' at 33 per cent. This was followed by *shari'a* court judges only at 26 per cent; the Palestinian Legislative Council at 17 per cent; and the President at 12 per cent. As such, secular state institutions and democratic vote account for 59 per cent of the responses. If presidential decree is added to this, the result is that 72 per cent of respondents put the decision of reform of personal status law in the hands of secular authorities rather than the *shar'i* establishment. Throughout the myriad public opinion polls, Palestinians have consistently shown a strong identification with democratic institutions and forms of governance. The above assertion that the 'people should decide' suggests the degree to which democratic and inclusive decision-making is an orthodoxy within Palestinian society – one powerful enough to be invoked when addressing the doxa or orthodoxy of '*shari'a*'. It also attests to the degree to which personal status law is viewed as simultaneously of religion and about it, but is also seen as needing to function in relation to society, the state and political institutions. Such dispositions represent an opportunity for the development of a unified Palestinian personal status law through a process which is based on public debate and inclusion rather than one in which the law is marked off as an area for religious specialists with no accountability to members of the society whose lives it will frame.

Conclusions

In conclusion, the tentative picture we can draw from various survey data is that while there is a strong emotional commitment for *shari'a* to remain the framework for personal status law in Palestine, there is a lot of room for negotiating change within this. More specifically, there is a popular legitimacy for an extension of women's rights in family law, although there is clear male resistance in some areas, the most notable being the issue of property claims either in divorce or inheritance.

However, the specific principles of reform, while tending towards expanding women's entitlements, are also marked by a host of conflicting values and in-terests. For instance, commitments to social equality and justice (framed in the nationalist sentiment of equality and rights) coexist with strong impulses towards preservation of the family and masculine authority within it. Similarly, contra-dictory attitudes exist towards the issue of legal authority. On the one hand, support is professed for the expansion of religious authority into wider arenas of life, which coexists with the preference that 'the people' vote to decide on what the letter of religious law should be. The point here is that these contradictory values do not represent discrete contending social groups, but are multiple and contradictory stances within the same individuals and ultimately the population as a whole. As such, a successful legal reform strategy cannot base itself on only one underlying principle, such as equality, without addressing the other multiple and countervailing values with which it coexists.

NINE

Agents for reform: the women's movement, social politics and family law reform

Penny Johnson

§ THIS chapter examines the strategies of the Palestinian women's movement, particularly its equality strategy, in the post-Oslo period. The equality strategy has guided the movement's initiatives for gender-aware legal reform, including of *shari'a*-based family law. This strategy has been countered by other strategies, most sharply from Islamist currents, but also from the religious establishment and, to some extent, from within the women's movement itself. Debates erupted into the public arena during a year-long 'model parliament' organized by women's groups in 1998, and colour current efforts to influence the shaping of a new unified Palestinian family law. Women's movement initiatives in the interim period took place in a period marked by a general demobilization of the mass political activity that characterized Palestinian society in the era of Israeli military occupation, particularly from the late 1970s onwards when mass-based organizations of women, students and workers developed in the framework of the Palestinian national movement. The eruption of a new Palestinian intifada (uprising) in the autumn of 2000 occurred on radically different terrain, with civil society participation limited and its influence on strategy highly constrained. While the second intifada's aim of ending the occupation and achieving genuine Palestinian independence are common and deeply-held national goals, the intifada and its aftermath pose a set of challenges for civil society and 'agents for reform', such as the Palestinian women's movement under discussion here, to reformulate agendas to incorporate national and social goals that address wide sectors of society and the real needs, interests and rights of women and men in society.

Pre-Oslo agents of political mobilization

During the period of direct Israeli military occupation over the Palestinian population in the West Bank and Gaza (1967–93), Palestinian mass organizations were 'agents of political mobilization' (Taraki 1990: 62) that targeted specific social groups, primarily students, women and workers. Although the primary agenda was national resistance, the very fact that previously excluded social groups were propelled into nationalist politics gave these organizations the character of social movements. In addition, the organizations addressed social concerns – whether workers' rights, women's status or student issues – and also often provided social services, such as childcare and income-generating projects in the case of the women's movement.

In this context, a new generation of Palestinian women activists founded women's committees, linked to clandestine political parties. These activists had a strong commitment to the grassroots mobilization of women – usually cast as reaching women in villages and refugee camps, rather than the urban-based character of the established women's charitable societies – and an unwavering commitment to national liberation. From their inception, they also explicitly aimed to improve the status of women; agendas for this last goal developed slowly and unevenly in the context of national struggle.

Reform of prevailing Islamic family law was occasionally discussed among activists, but did not become an explicit part of any women's committees' platforms; the prevalence and repression of Israeli military law and the absence of any address for legal reform made family law reform a moot issue. The secularism of the political culture of the Palestine Liberation Organization, discussed by Hilal (2000), was reflected in the absence of religious references in women's committee literature, but this secularism did not generally offer any challenge to prevailing *shari'a*-based law or indeed to religiosity in the lives of the population. Both Muslim and Christian clergy were firmly part of the national movement in the framework of 'national unity', a key concept in Palestinian nationalism, although neither had a leadership role.

At the same time, this period witnessed aspects of a religious resurgence with a politicized cast. Funds from Gulf states assisted in the development of religious institutions, with the number of mosques in Gaza increasing from 200 to 600 in the 1967–87 period and from 400–750 in the West Bank (Sayigh 1997). In the wake of the 1979 Iranian revolution and the 1982 PLO defeat in Lebanon, Islamist groups, particularly the Muslim Brotherhood and its offshoots, were particularly successful in organizing Islamic blocs on university campuses and promoting Islamic dress among young women, particularly students. A new university, the Islamic University, established in Gaza in 1978, offered an Islamic alternative to the organization and curricula of the nationalist West Bank universities. Sharp clashes between nationalist and Islamist students occurred on several West Bank campuses in the mid-1980s. Although there were some attacks reported in Gaza on women wearing 'improper' clothing during this period, the women's movement in general was not involved in Islamist–nationalist confrontations and, interestingly, was not a particular target of Islamist anger.

Only in the wake of the most intense moment of nationalist resistance, the first Palestinian intifada (December 1987 to 1993) did explicitly feminist concerns and agendas begin to emerge, as women activists both sought to advance women's claims by virtue of their struggle and sacrifice, and also found this struggle relatively unacknowledged by their own political parties. At the peak of the intifada, in late 1988, the creation of a Higher Women's Committee provided a forum for discussion of social agendas where three out of four of the main women's committees advocated 'the replacement of *shari'a* … with civil legislation' (Giacaman and Johnson 1990: 168), reflecting the leftist background of these women activists and the secular outlook of their politics.

However, the intifada also saw the initial emergence of Hamas (Harakat al-Muqawama al-Islamiyya) the main Palestinian Islamist movement, from the more established Muslim Brotherhood. Women's increasing public visibility – with young women demonstrating and organizing in public space – met with a hostile response from Islamists and from conservative portions of the national movement (Hammami 1990); attacks on unveiled women in Gaza led to one of the first national conferences discussing social and gender issues, held in Jerusalem in December 1989 and entitled 'The Intifada and Some Social Issues' in which leading nationalist figures joined the women's movement to condemn coercion, a move that is echoed in the defence of the model parliament.

The Oslo transition: advocacy and protest

The profound political crisis of Palestinian nationalism after Oslo is the main contributor to the decline in mass political activity, as well as the transference from informal to formal politics that marks transitions to statehood. Interestingly, the women's movement has been the most successful of the social movements in the occupied territories in bridging the Oslo transition for a variety of reasons, including, paradoxically, women's marginalization from national leadership (Jad et al. 2000). This exclusion produced the ability to act more independently than other Palestinian social movements or mass organizations. At the same time, the mass activism that marked the women's movement's experience in the intifada has largely been replaced by an NGO model of lobbying, advocacy and workshop-style educational and developmental activities, although the movement's strategy and activities have included protests as well, such as demonstrations against Israeli closure of the West Bank and Gaza and for the release of prisoners.

This transformation has had contradictory effects on opportunities for legal reform. At the same time as it has given the women's movement tools and resources for legal reform initiatives, it has taken away some of its ability to mobilize – and to represent – women in various settings and strata of society and even its claims to nationalist 'authenticity'. Both the 'professionalization' of women's NGOs (Hammami 1995) and the nationalist and social history of the movement are important dynamics in considering the legal reform initiatives in the five years after Oslo and the constraints and opportunities in the coming period of Palestinian statehood.

The equality strategy

In this period, as noted by a number of analysts (Hammami and Johnson 1999; Jad et al. 2000), the women's movement has been guided by an equality strategy, which has been the driving force in such important initiatives as the creation of a Women's Charter (1994), the campaign for women candidates and platforms for the Palestinian Legislative Council (1995, with elections in January 1996 that yielded only five women members out of eighty-eight), reviews of existing legislation and campaigns against discriminatory legislation, the model parliament (1998), examined below, and other campaigns lobbying for equality provisions in the Basic Law or other legislation in the Palestinian Legislative Council.

The 1994 Women's Charter

The women's movement focused its activity at the beginning of the transitional period on an initiative for a Women's Charter, inspired by the South African model. Based on the equality provisions of the Palestinian Declaration of Independence and on other United Nations instruments, the Charter attributed existing 'discrimination and inequality against women' to the many colonialisms imposed on Palestine, ending with the Israeli occupation, reinforced by prejudicial 'customs and traditions'.

While the Charter went into some detail in regard to rights to political participation and particularly nationality, personal status issues were at the most general level, demanding 'the guarantee of women's full equality regarding issues of personal status'. In a message sent to the conference releasing the document in Jerusalem in August 1994, PLO Chairman Yasser Arafat endorsed the charter but added 'as long as there is no contradiction with *shari'a*'. As we will see below, this was to remain his position throughout the establishment of the Palestinian Authority in the transitional phase.

In the period following the Charter, personal status issues became central to a cumulative number of gender and law initiatives undertaken by the women's movement. The history of these initiatives shows both the strengths and problems of the equality approach which has dominated the strategic thinking of the Palestinian women's movement and suggests additional directions and strategies to explore when approaching the reform of *shari'a*-based family law in the Palestinian context.

The model parliament

From the outset of the interim period, women's groups and activists launched a series of activities reviewing existing legislation and proposing amended or new legislation on principles of equality between men and women, culminating in a year-long initiative for a model parliament in 1998, coordinated by a committee representing various women's institutions and powered by a specialized women's non-governmental organization, the Women's Committee for Legal Aid and Counselling (WCLAC).

The stated aim of the model parliament was to discuss, draft and have a symbolic vote on 'Palestinian legislation that ensures equality and women's human rights for Palestinian women, as well as their participation in building a civil society based on justice, equality, respect for human rights and rule of law' (Othman 1998: 63). While the real parliament was locked in conflict with the Executive over the Basic Law (see Chapter 7), in the regional workshops leading up to the model parliament, women and men – community activists as well as women's movement cadre – reviewed existing labour, social welfare and education, personal status, criminal and public law legislation, among others, and explicitly used the principle of equality to uncover and address gender inequities, as well as recommending special provisions for women's rights in such issues as maternity leave and violence against women. In general, regional groups working on 'benign' issues such as labour, social welfare or education were able easily to reach consensus over changes in line with the principle of equality (Hammami and Johnson 1999: 329).

Applying the principle of equality in personal status laws was more difficult, sharing with other attempts at reform in the Arab and Muslim world the problem of addressing the legally defined model of family and gender relations in *shari'a* based on complementarity between male and female roles, rather than equality. As Hammami and Johnson note: '[t]his "gender contract" – the exchange of male maintenance (*nafaqa*) for female obedience (*ta'a*) – is fundamental to women's status as "protected dependants" under Islamic law, and to a degree in social relations' (Hammami and Johnson 1999: 129, citing Moors 1996). For reformers, however, understanding the relation of this legal model with social practices and with a social gender contract that can vary in different societies according to their political, social and economic circumstances is key to identifying impulses and need for change. Thus, prior to examining the events of the model parliament and its conclusions, it is worth examining both how the model parliament attempted to reformulate this contract, and how gender interests and needs in Palestinian social life bear on such attempts to change the balance of gender rights and duties in *shari'a*-based law. Below we will briefly discuss maintenance and inheritance in this context.

Maintenance and inheritance: a conflict between rights and needs?

A 1994 conference sponsored by the human rights organization Al-Haq, entitled 'Women, Justice and the Law', at the very beginning of the interim period, was the first initiative to review existing legislation from a gender-aware perspective. Noting that both prevailing Jordanian law and the Gaza Law of Family Rights assessed the level of maintenance according to the circumstances of the husband, whatever the circumstances of the wife, a conference working group recommended that 'assessment of maintenance levels should also take into account the circumstances of the wife' (Welchman 1999: 103). This suggestion is very much in line with reform 'inside' the *shari'a* system that addresses needs and improves the position of women, basically replacing a minority Hanafi and Shafi'i view with a Hanbali and majority Hanafi view holding 'that the wife's maintenance is assessed in light of the circumstances of both spouses' (Welchman 1999: 102). It does not, however, attempt to change the terms of the gender contract, maintaining the husband's absolute financial responsibility for his wife.

In the 1998 model parliament, formulas for joint maintenance and responsibility for the family between husband and wife were considered. In her book that served as the sourcebook for the parliament, attorney Asma Khader (1998: 143) provided a somewhat complicated formulation: 'Maintenance of each human being is his or her responsibility, and the maintenance of the wife or husband who is not working is the responsibility of the other. The maintenance of the children is a joint responsibility between the partners according to their financial ability, during the marriage and after it is ended.'

In model parliament discussions, participants basically accepted this formula, but emphasized 'whenever possible'. This clause suggests a conflict between a strong impulse towards equality and equal citizenship in this critical period of state-building and awareness of the diverse social and economic circumstances of Palestinian women and the special conditions of Palestinian society faced with instability and serial crisis. In the Arab world, rising formal female labour force participation has fuelled legal reform, whether professional women demanding an end to restrictions on work and mobility or poor working women seeking to divorce non-contributing or otherwise burdensome husbands. Palestine's dependent and colonized economy and its highly restricted and gendered labour markets (particularly the Israeli labour market, which is almost entirely male) have provided very limited opportunities for women, with unusually low female labour force participation. In the interim period, labour surveys found only about 12 per cent of the female population over fifteen in the labour force, as opposed to over 70 per cent of men; female labour force averaged a higher 15 per cent in the West Bank and 8 per cent in Gaza (e.g. PCBS 1999a: 21). Coupled with a high burden of care in the household, given the absence of public social support and related persistent high fertility, with fertility in Gaza among the highest in the world, Palestinian women in many settings may well see male financial responsibility as a need more pressing than a new right for equality in family responsibility.

Indeed, analysts of *shari'a* court records note that maintenance claims 'appear to constitute over half the caseload of the *shari'a* courts in both the West Bank and Gaza Strip' with one study for the years 1992–94 finding such claims[45] at 68 per cent of all cases (Welchman 1999: 105), a majority for the wife's own person. This high proportion suggests that the right to maintenance remains a real issue for women, even given the small amounts allotted, underlining women's lack of access to other economic resources under the prevailing conditions in Palestine. Indeed, recent research by the Institute of Women's Studies has shown that half of all households receiving formal social welfare are de facto female-headed households, with widows and divorcées the overwhelming majority of these (National Commission for Poverty Eradication 1998).

The issue of maintenance illustrates the conflict between the equality of citizens and the different status of men and women in the system of family law, reflecting the contradiction between rights in civil/constitutional law (public rights) and rights in personal status law. But it also indicates some of the material and social reasons that make this conflict difficult to resolve solely by legal reform, without addressing the wider context and how women and men in various settings perceive and act on their interests and needs. In particular, women without access to the labour market or without adequate skills or education may have a different set of interests from working or professional women, whose voices were predominant in the model parliament. Diversity and difference among women's interests and needs is thus another challenge to the equality argument and its application in family law. In the aftermath of the parliament, the attention given by women activists to working with the religious establishment to establish a maintenance fund (*sanduq nafaqa*), at the same time as working separately to draft a family law, attests to a willingness to address this duality.

A more discussed and contested issue in the parliament and its aftermath is the issue of inheritance, in which women activists face both legal and societal hurdles. On the latter, a number of analysts of Palestinian society have noted the widespread phenomenon of women renouncing their share of inheritance in order to gain their brothers', sons' or other male relatives' putative social support and protection. These observations are confirmed by a recent survey by the Gender Unit of the Palestinian Central Bureau of Statistics which showed that only a quarter of Palestinian women report a right to any inheritance and of those a majority had not received their full share as defined by prevailing law. Statistics are not given for male entitlement so the low percentage of women reporting a 'right to inheritance or a portion of inheritance from the family or the husband' cannot be compared. However, the lower proportion of Gazan women reporting a right to inheritance (at only 16 per cent compared to 30 per cent of West Bank women) suggests that the absence of land among the largely refugee population of Gaza may mean that male entitlements are also low. Of those reporting a right to inheritance, 67 per cent of West Bankers and 48 per cent of Gazans did not actually obtain their share of inheritance (PCBS 1999a). Here once again, the absence of a state and public social provisions has probably prolonged and compounded a social practice that disallows women inheritance rights, however unequal, under prevailing Islamic inheritance principles. In the aftermath of the model parliament, approaches to inheritance became one of the sticking points within the women's movement itself.

Strategies in the model parliament[46]

In the main document prepared as a resource text for the parliament, 'The Law and the Future of Palestinian Women', attorney Asma Khader combined specific recommendations for amendments to existing *shari'a* law with a general recommendation for a unified family law to be applied in civil courts with a jurisdiction over the whole population. She argues that Islamic jurisprudence considers the marriage contract as a civil contract, rather than as a sacrament, and argues that men have monopolized the knowledge and interpretation of the *shari'a*. The law would treat all Palestinians as equal, respect the principles of religion and sources of Palestinian legislation (including *shari'a*) and make the civil authorities responsible for marriage contracts and other matters not requiring judicial intervention. Khader utilizes Palestinian national unity to show that the present situation of ecclesiastical and *shari'a* courts violates the principle of equality between citizens (Khader 1998: 112–17).

Within the various regional groups of the parliament, contesting approaches to *shari'a* quickly emerged. Where religious or socially conservative participants were generally not resistant to the principle of equality in other areas governed by civil authorities – with the important exception of provisions in criminal law governing penalties for adultery – the consensus was more difficult to reach when dealing with *shari'a*-governed personal status law. As noted in Chapter 8, several different approaches emerged to the question of reform of existing personal status law. A number of women activists consistently advocated applying the principles of gender equality in the Palestinian Declaration of Independence and United Nations resolutions and pushed for a civil family law applied in civil courts. They additionally invoked the PLO's signing of the 1979 CEDAW as a legal justification for this position (Othman 1998: 67). Others saw *shari'a* as already based on principles of Islamic justice and equality, and sought its true application. A third position essentially compromised between the two, by advocating reform within *shari'a* and affirming that Islamic law is responsive to change that reflects the needs of contemporary women and society.

Challenging the parliament's standing

The debate exploded in the wake of a sharp controversy that erupted during the model parliament's regional workshop in Nablus to discuss personal status law in March 1998. At that meeting, a prominent shaykh who heads the West Bank *shari'a* appeal court, Shaykh Bitawi, challenged the parliament's right to address personal status law at all, thus raising public questions about the right of individuals, especially secular women, to debate fundamental aspects of religion and law. His intervention, reported prominently in the local press, was the spark that touched off a larger Islamist attack on the model parliament and the women's movement. In contrast to his and other *shari'a* judges' tempered criticism and continued dialogue, the Islamist attack was vehemently of a different nature. In the aftermath of the parliament, the religious establishment was deeply concerned with affirming its own religious authority, but also was open to addressing problems in the fair implementation of *shari'a* law and considering the contours of a new unified Palestinian family law.

Islamist discourses

The Islamist discourse of the attack on the women's movement emerged from a larger Islamist literature, with particular features from Islamism in Palestine (Sh'hada 1999: 51) The main document of the movement spearheading the Islamist attack was a pamphlet entitled 'The Arab Woman and the Conspiracy of the Secular Women'. The booklet used the common formula of labelling the women's movement as an arm of the American and European conspiracy to destroy Islamic civilization. As Hammami and Johnson note, the women's movement, along with leftists and secularists in general, are termed dissemblers or hypocrites (*munafiquun*) – people who are most dangerous because they are seemingly part of the social fabric but are actually playing the role of destroying it from within. Palestine is seen as the target of many Western conspiracies, which it was able to withstand due to the strength of social and familial ties (al-Hoda in Hammami and Johnson 1999: 333). These ties are precisely what the women's movement are trying to destroy through the model parliament. The writers quote Khader's book extensively, as well as other published material by the parliament. The message of immorality and Western corruption was disseminated in Friday sermons by imams sympathetic to Hamas throughout the West Bank. In Gaza, the public campaign against the parliament was much more muted, reflecting the main division within the Hamas leadership, as well as the fact that mosques in Gaza are more closely controlled by the Palestinian Authority.

Human rights and Western agendas

The women's movement had assumed that the use of international frameworks of human rights and United Nations conventions as a source of argument would be acceptable in nationalist discourse, given the long history of Palestinian claims that are framed in its resolutions and language. However, the Islamists included a scathing critique of these international instruments as tools of the West for the exercise of power unequally under the cover of universal human rights. Thus, United Nations sanctions imposed on Iraq are compared to the lack of sanctions imposed on Israel. Universal human rights are masks hiding Western agendas to subjugate Muslims. The writers go on to assert that, given this unequal power, notions such as 'freedom of thought' will actually be used as a weapon against those who attempt to stop adultery within their own society – they will be accused of violating 'human rights' (al-Hoda in Hammami and Johnson 1999: 333).

In the booklet and subsequent public attacks, the main focus of the Islamists was not an issue in personal status law *per se*, but rather proposals regarding reform of the criminal code which touched on a set of issues concerning control of sexuality, morality and the family: the issue of *zina* (adultery). The parliament's recommendation that adultery not be considered a crime, but simply grounds for divorce, was presented by the Islamists as actively condoning immoral behaviour and the moral breakdown of society, a breakdown such as already exists in the West.

Islamist views on the parliament were not entirely uniform, in particular among the younger female constituency. For example, a leader of the Islamist Al-Khansa Society for Women made a relatively dissident statement in the local press (*Al-Ayyam*, 14 March 1998) stating that she was not against the parliament in principle, but resented the marginalization of Islamist women within it. Islamic women's organizations, which also were founded in the post-Oslo period as an alternative to the secular women's movement, took up the point of responding to the 'authentic' needs of society in an effective way.

Defending the model parliament: defending democracy or the state?

First among the defenders of the model parliament was the women's movement itself, although the attack was not anticipated and thus no response had been considered. This is perhaps telling in the sense that the model parliament was considered an NGO project that had little to do with the political dynamics, for example between nationalists and Islamists, that had been volatile on a number of occasions since the early 1980s. Although shaken by the public attack – some activists even initially recommended withdrawing Khader's book – the movement rallied around the parliament and used these political dynamics, and its own political experience and political capital, to defend it within political parties and with the public, facing Islamist spokesmen in television and public debates. New defenders of the parliament began to speak out in the press and media, and the parliament, almost despite itself, became a public space where visions of Palestinian society were articulated and underlying conflicts exposed. A strong sense that the parliament had posed a challenge to the Islamist social vision, which Palestinian nationalist factions had failed to mount, propelled a number of progressive activists into the arena.

From the standpoint of the Palestinian Authority, however, it was less the Islamist vision than their power and strategy that caused concern. In this view, the attack on the women's movement was a smokescreen attacking the Authority itself, via the women's movement, by associating it with the immorality of the West. In the closing model parliament session in the West Bank town of Ramallah, the assembly waited until the district governor arrived to open the session with a message from President Yasser Arafat. The governor gave a statement upholding freedom of thought and expression as crucial to Palestinian democracy and affirmed the President's support for women's rights and legal reform 'as long as they do not contradict *shari'a*', a direct reiteration of the ambiguous endorsement of the 1994 Women's Charter.

Final session: affirmation of democracy, gender agendas subsumed

In the final session of the model parliament in Gaza, the invited representatives of seven political parties (including a smaller Islamist group, the Islamic Jihad, but excluding Hamas) gave opening solidarity statements (Hammami and Johnson 1999: 335). The parliament thus assumed the stature of a nationalist event. Almost every speaker affirmed the important role of women in the national struggle, as well as the right of free speech as fundamental to the nationalist project. Typically, women's rights were linked to the modernist and nationalist project of state-building. Nationalism was also evoked as a justification for legal reform, including personal status laws: the laws in force were repeatedly described as 'foreign' and imposed by occupying powers. When it came to the specifics of reform, however, most of the political leaders were either vague or somewhat conservative in their focus and recommendations.

By contrast, in the deliberations of the parliament itself, the final session successfully addressed a range of personal status issues. One of the women's movement's consistent demands – raising the marriage age to eighteen for both men and women – passed easily, and, as the survey undertaken for this project shows, is a demand with popular support. Early marriage is increasingly seen as a problem in Palestinian society, with 25 per cent of females in a 1994 court record sample marrying at sixteen or under (Welchman 1999: 36). The prohibition on polygyny, on the other hand, passed by a narrow margin of forty-two for, thirty-two against, and five abstentions. A number of other useful recommendations, such as increasing women's rights in child custody and divorce and protecting her rights to dower and inheritance, were also offered in the Gaza session (*Al-Ayyam*, 28 April 1998; Welchman 2000: 365–7).

None of these achievements was noted in the final declaration of the parliament, which emphasizes the nationalist and democratic character of the forum it had created, terming it a 'democratic Palestinian platform' and going on simply to list the areas of legislation reviewed before quoting in full the equality provisions of the Palestinian Declaration of Independence. The Declaration ends with the slogans: 'We will continue our struggle for democracy. Yes to freedom of expression. No to the repression of thought. Our slogan is: Equality is our Path to Building and Progress.' The statement thus avoided the questions that the women's movement and other activists for legal reform would face in the next period: what is a viable platform for family law built on gender equality and what is the approach to, and role of, Islamic law in this initiative? Can gender equality be addressed, in President Arafat's words, 'without contradicting *shari'a*'?

And, crucially, does either state or society offer allies and opportunities to meet the needs, interests and rights of Palestinian men, women and children in a new Palestinian family law?

Towards a new family law: developments and strategies after the model parliament

Even before the closing session of the parliament, the Islamic religious establishment began to distance itself from the Islamist attack and formulate its own position, making public statements supporting *shari'a* reform as long as it was undertaken by the proper authorities (*Al-Ayyam*, 14 March 1998). The religious establishment formed its own committees to draft a Palestinian family law, one of at least three official committees approved by President Arafat. None to date has included women, although the Deputy Qadi al-Quda welcomed a 'women's subcommittee' in one of his public statements. However, this did not happen and, by late 2001, a unified family law had reportedly been drafted by the religious establishment but has not as yet been formally presented to government, legislature or to the public.

Another noticeable development has been the emergence of differences between different sectors of the *shar'i* establishment. As noted in Chapter 6, the Deputy Qadi al-Quda, Shaykh Taysir al-Tamimi, moved to address a number of particular issues raised during model parliament discussions and elsewhere through procedural intervention, issuing administrative instructions to the *shari'a* courts. On the other hand, the Supreme Fatwa Council, headed by Shaykh Ikrameh Sabri, has turned its attention to a number of family law matters addressed both during the course of the model parliament discussions and by interventions and opinions articulated by the Deputy Qadi al-Quda.[47]

The post-parliament *fatwa*s of the Council can be compared to those issued before the debate on family law became a matter of high public interest. Thus, in 1996, responding to a question as to the validity of a marriage not registered in the *shari'a* courts, the Council did not answer the question directly, but chose rather to emphasize the legitimacy of the requirement of registration, and to insist that registration was the best form of proof of a marriage and was necessary in order better to protect the rights of wives. The Council concluded by recommending that the criminal sanction for failure to register marriage should be increased. By contrast, in 2000, in a *fatwa* entitled 'early marriage', the Council responded to a question on the validity of early marriage, and whether a minimum age of capacity for marriage for females could be specified.[48] The *fatwa* mentions existing law only to quote the definition of marriage in the JLPS, and thereafter holds with the traditional doctrines of the majority of Sunni jurists, to the effect that minors of both sexes could indeed be married; it adds that consummation was not allowed if it would harm the female, even if she has reached puberty. This opinion stands in contrast to others already cited in this study: notably, the prompt action by Shaykh Abu Sardane, the Qadi al-Quda, in raising the age of marriage in Gaza by administrative decree, and the more recent efforts of his deputy in seeking to tighten up registration procedures and prevent underage marriage. It also ignores societal attitudes and concerns cited earlier in support of a higher age of capacity for marriage. In addition, in the earlier 1996 *fatwa*, the Council had argued for increased criminal sanctions for non-registration; yet under existing law, the marriage of a minor under the age of capacity for marriage is not allowed and could not be registered: thus a parent or other guardian wishing to marry off a minor would either have to do it without registration or submit false information, something that the Deputy Qadi al-Quda is specifically seeking to combat.

The public articulation of difference of views between these two branches of the *shar'i* establishment is a significant development in the ongoing debate around Palestinian family law, and illustrates yet another space in which these issues are in contention. In a 12 November 2001 seminar on reform of personal status law, held in Ramallah under the sponsorship of Al-Haq, a Palestinian human rights organization, the differences between the Deputy Qadi al-Quda Shaykh Taysir Tamimi and the Mufti of Jerusalem and Head of the Supreme Fatwa Council Shaykh Ikrameh Sabri were illustrative of these tensions in attitudes towards existing law and to reform of personal status law. On the first point, Shaykh Tamimi called on the Supreme Fatwa Council to respect existing law, implying that some of its *fatawa* were in contradiction to the law. In terms of reform, the sharpest conflict was expressed in positions on the age of marriage, with Shaykh Tamimi affirming that this was an issue on which legal jurists differed and thus interpretation was permitted; he advocated raising the age of marriage to the age of legal majority (*rushd*)[49] and also advocated raising the age of obligatory schooling. Shaykh Sabri took the position noted above that minors could be married at puberty. He was scornful of women's movement initiatives in the present and historically – singling out Egyptian feminist Hoda Sharawi's call to abolish polygyny in the 1920s, and affirming that women could be educated not to want to be second wives. In contrast, Shaykh Tamimi began his remarks by noting the need for legal reform, given the differences between laws in the West Bank and Gaza and the fact that these laws do not meet all the needs of society. While affirming that *shari'a* is the sole framework for reform, he positively noted the demands of the women's movement, political parties and religious scholars for legal reform. Tamimi had been instrumental in establishing a *sunduq nafaqa* and affirmed that *nafaqa* should not be restricted to one year after divorce but that women should be compensated according to the harm done them. Indeed, the two religious figures agreed on little but their support for the recent introduction of the requirement for medical examinations for thalassimia and HIV before marriage. The division between the two senior figures was echoed by other speakers from the religious establishment, pointing to two clear and opposing currents of thought and power that contest family law reform from within religious circles.

Divisions and compromises in the women's movement

The official initiatives spurred model parliament organizers to consider a process for drafting a unified Palestinian family law themselves, based on the painstaking process of applying the equality argument to existing legislation and the subsequent recommendations of the model parliament. Organizers recognized the possibility of new democratic allies, particularly from the political parties and human rights organizations, but also did not want to ignite another public debate before the initiative and the women's movement was fully prepared. The conditional support of the Authority was another factor to be taken into consideration.

A low-key strategy emerged to develop a declaration of principles and issues for discussion for a new Palestinian family law that would first be presented to allies in political parties, human rights organizations and other non-governmental organizations. The aim was the formation of a national committee for a new Palestinian family law to lobby the Palestinian Legislative Council and other relevant parties. A preparatory committee of women's organizations who participated in the model parliament began work on these documents in the summer of 1998 and almost immediately ran into problems both on the general approach and specific principles. There were a number of fissures between women's organizations, including differences between the West Bank and Gaza, but there were two main strategic divides. The first, between legal reform towards civil law and reform within *shari'a*, is familiar from other contexts. The second is more specific to the Palestinian context, but has resonance elsewhere: between an approach which can be crudely characterized as 'NGO', where legal reform is a project with a number of specific activities, and an alternative approach which can be equally crudely characterized as 'political', which sees legal reform as embedded in political (and social) processes.

The working out of the first division is embodied in a document prepared in February 2000, but not, at the time of this writing, presented as widely as had originally been planned, largely as a result of the circumstances of the new intifada which have both hampered physical movement for purposes of consultation, meetings etc., and directed intellectual and social energies towards other priorities. The document is an interesting compromise that contains elements of both approaches, well illustrated by its citation of principles of respect for human dignity and non-discrimination between the sexes as confirmed by 'divine scriptures and covenants and declarations of human rights'. During the attack on the model parliament, the women's movement's counter-defence to the Islamists had been to ground its equality argument in the language of nationalism and national resistance to occupation, state-building and democracy. This approach informs the introduction and conclusion of the draft document of principles which begins by citing the political conditions of the Palestinian people, characterized by the 'absence of sovereignty over land from the days of occupation until now', resulting in conflicting laws that do not meet the needs of Palestinian society.

In an interesting point, the document notes that family law is the most contro- versial of all the laws, given that it touches on family relations and is embedded in the culture of the society and therefore requires the 'efforts of the whole society to develop a Palestinian family law built on equality between the sexes'. The point that conflicts over family law mean that more, not less, democratic participation is required is a rather neat rejoinder to the religious establishment's appropriation of *shari'a* and family law as its sole province.

Democratic families, democratic society

There is a new stress on democratic family relations as the foundation of a democratic society, with the legal philosophy of a new family law proposed as 'democratic relations inside the family and the right of participation in decision- making for all individuals within it without discrimination as the foundation and safeguard of a democratic society'. Here, members of the family are cast as citizens, while the family itself is projected as a microcosm of society. This philosophy is followed by three basic principles which also address both family and societal imperatives: (1) equality and non-discrimination on the basis of sex, race, disability, religion or position (echoing the Basic Law); (2) the rule of law, the separation of powers and the independence of the judiciary; and (3) the full participation of husband and wife in family life.

Sources and issues for a new family law

Sources for the family law are headed by the Palestinian Declaration of Indepen- dence and the Basic Law. Third in line is a formulation that reads 'Goals (intentions) of Islamic *shari'a* and tolerance for the divine religions'. Here, the drafters amend the Basic Law formulation, replacing the word 'principles' (*mabadi'*) with the word 'goals' or 'intentions' (*maqasid*), probably in order to focus on the general intentions of *shari'a* to provide justice and equality for all humans.[50] A number of international covenants and declarations, including the Universal Declaration of Human Rights and CEDAW, are then cited.

The document also notes a number of key issues and principles, including women's rights as human rights, equality and democracy in the family and, interestingly, the consideration of 'domestic work as productive work'. Rationales for a new Palestinian family law include ending the separation between the West Bank and Gaza, the establishment of the Authority and the Palestinian Legislative Council and the 'historic role in the national struggle' of Palestinian women, including their sacrifice as martyrs, deportees and prisoners, which challenge the traditional and conservative view of the role of women.

Pluralistic elements of a new family law

A separate document addresses the proposed elements of a Palestinian family law and, here, differences arose over a number of issues, principally in formulations on polygyny and inheritance. Points where agreement was reached include the following, which are abbreviated from the text:

1. The full participation of husband and wife in the family as reflected in a marriage contract between two parties equal in rights and obligations.
2. The right of women inside the family to self-determination and to be their own guardian after legal majority, which occurs at eighteen years of age.
3. A minimum age of capacity for marriage for men and women at eighteen.
4. Divorce as a judicial proceeding only and in the presence of the two parties. and divorce to be initiated at the request of either party.
5. Establishing a maintenance fund (*sunduq nafaqa*) and alimony in the case of arbitrary divorce.
6. Guaranteeing equality between men and women when marriage ends, including in custody and guardianship of children and division of property and wealth from the period of married life on the consideration that women's work at home and in child-rearing is productive.
7. Joint responsibility in the maintenance of the family and children.

In the last point, the document gives a basis for a new gender contract, as it does in the first point where the actual marriage contract is seen as 'between two parties equal in rights and obligations'. The problem of addressing the material interests of women in specific situations, however, is raised in the point establishing a maintenance fund, which would potentially contradict the notion of joint maintenance if the fund were seen as available only to needy women, and not men. The document thus adopts a pluralistic approach, which needs more articulation to serve as an effective strategy.

A point calling for an end to the practice of polygyny because it diminishes the dignity of women and causes discord in the family proved controversial and required a note to the effect that committee members disagreed, with some advocating a total ban on polygyny and others supporting its restriction. The note also recorded disagreement on the principle of gender equality in inheritance entitlements.

The difficulties in reaching agreement on a text inside the preparatory committee, which was constituted from the women's movement itself, suggests the importance of exploring the second, more implicit, contradiction, between legal reform as a NGO project or as a political process. Here, the experience of the model parliament underlines that advocating gender-equitable family law reform in the Palestinian context – as is probably the case in the Arab and Muslim world in general – is far too complicated to be contained with a project framework carried out by one or more women's or other non-governmental organizations, and requires a wide process of democratic participation.

Conclusions: strategies and issues for action

The experience of the period of transition to statehood in Palestinian society has been both rich and complicated, and perhaps particularly so in the area that we have scrutinized here: agendas, constraints and opportunities for legal reform of *shari'a*-based family law. While no major reforms were enacted in this period, the contending and cooperating actors have developed strategies, built alliances and positioned themselves for the next phase of statehood. From one standpoint, the political field seems monopolized by an emerging state seeking legitimation within near crippling constraints and denial of basic rights, with its major internal challenge coming from a populist Islamist opposition. From another, social movements, including the women's movement, pose an alternative democratic challenge and both seek to advance Palestinian rights *vis-à-vis* the continuing Israeli occupation and denial of rights, and to advocate with the Palestinian Authority a 'set of arenas' for the rule of law, legal reform, and fair and effective social and economic policies, and to mobilize protest at abuses of power. In addition, the religious establishment has (partially) integrated itself with the emerging state, built new institutions and strengthened existing ones (the *shari'a* court system), as well as issuing some important new regulations.

Below, the researchers in this project have posed strategic questions and issues for discussion in an attempt to learn from this rich and complicated history, drawing in particular from the activism and ongoing strategic discussions and debates by the women's movement and its allies, rather than issuing recommendations. Indeed, the researchers – and the Institute of Women's Studies at Birzeit University – are positioned within the women's movement and within the Palestinian national context and share in the dilemmas and insights of both.

It is also true that the more profound the strategic issue identified, the more difficult the strategic response. We are in fact bringing to bear the specificity of the Palestinian context on a range of issues that have been (and are) present in the Arab women's movements throughout the twentieth century and into the twenty-first. The history and legacy of colonialism, the crises in the patriarchal order and gender roles, and the search for legitimation by weak, paternal and authoritarian states were enduring features of the landscape for much of the last century. As Thompson (2000: 4) notes in an important new study of gender and citizenship in Syria and Lebanon in the Mandate era, gender became a 'site of compromise and conflict' among male actors in the civic order, the stability of which was often ensured by 'gender bargains' or 'pacts' at the expense of women's rights.

We thus need to pay detailed attention to how these dynamics are constituted in the Palestinian case which offers particular constraints and opportunities, as a comparative perspective also shows that Islam and Islamic law are not ahistorical, but rather are shaped by specific political, social and economic circumstances. In our analysis of the recent transitional phase in Palestinian society, the authors jointly would like to draw attention to the following strategic issues for discussion:

1. The conditions of Palestinian state formation offer many constraints, but also some opportunities for gender-aware legal reform of family law. The multi-dimensional strategy pursued by social movements during the transitional phase – national resistance, government advocacy and mobilization for protest – is an important framework for maximizing opportunities in the next phase of state-building (where national resistance will remain in the search to advance national rights, for example of refugee populations and over land and water).

2. However, the weak and authoritarian nature of the emerging state and the clear search for legitimation through affirmation of its commitment to Islam and *shari'a*, among other factors, mean that a top-down strategy for legal reform (as originally in the case of Tunisia) is probably neither viable nor desirable. Instead, a wide democratic alliance is the most likely vehicle to ensure that gender agendas for reform are not isolated (and thus opposed as attacks on cultural identity) but instead positioned within citizens' rights a whole.

3. Countering claims of its inauthenticity, the women's movement should not only continue to press its national claims – based on women's participation and sacrifice in the national struggle – but actively develop a counter-authenticity of Palestinian identity rooted in commitment to the needs and interests of the marginalized groups, including poor women, whose needs may differ from those of professional and middle-class women who dominate the women's movement. We have noted, for example, the issue of maintenance, but there are a number of other issues (including nationalist issues such as prisoners, refugees and settlements) that differentially affect poor and middle-class women.

4. The latter point crucially addresses the opportunity to avoid a class–gender divide that has been an unfortunate feature in the history of Arab women's movements, where the women's movements, often despite themselves, have been isolated as elites, while the needs and interests of poor and working people have been taken as the ground for other movements, including Islamic populism. The past history of the Palestinian women's movement and its links to women in various settings give it an opportunity to avoid this divide. In the context of legal reform, this means vigorous campaigns not only to listen to women in various settings, but to incorporate their needs and social and economic interests into legal reform frameworks. In a small way, this study attempts to do just this, by incorporating a study of the Hebron factory fire into its research, with the aim of publishing the study locally for advocacy for safe working conditions, rights and protection, as well as adequate compensation within public and *shari'a*-based legal frameworks.

5. Recognizing the need for protection of Palestinian families in the specific context of the insecurity and conflict of the past fifty years and the absence of both physical and social protection is an important complement to the discourse of rights. Recognizing the importance families have played in national and individual survival also means developing legal reform in this context, perhaps with a dual emphasis on social protection through the institution of social security and strengthening democratic families.

6. The framework of the Palestinian national movement also offers greater opportunities for links between the women's movement and Islamic women's groups and dialogue between secular and religious women (which are two different but related activities) as well as between the women's movement and reform-minded elements of the religious establishment.

7. As the findings of various attitudinal surveys suggest, the majority of the population does support some type of legal reform, as long as it remains within the framework of *shari'a*. The meaning of this support requires much more discussion, and it is quite important to encourage a pluralism of views and defend the legitimacy of those who advocate legal reform towards civil law. However, given the radically different systems of family law that have developed under the rubric of *shari'a*, it is clearly useful to explore how to expand the principles of religious legal reasoning and legitimacy in the local context.

8. However, the specific principles of reform, while tending towards expanding women's entitlements, are also marked by a host of conflicting values and interests. For instance, commitments to social equality and justice (framed in the nationalist sentiment of equality and rights) coexist with strong impulses towards preservation of the family and masculine authority within it. Similarly, contradictory attitudes exist towards the issue of legal authority. On the one hand, support is professed for the expansion of religious authority into wider arenas of life, which coexists with the preference that 'the people' vote to decide on what the letter of religious law should be. The point here is that these contradictory values do not represent discrete contending social groups, but rather are multiple and contradictory stances held by the same individuals and ultimately the population as a whole. As such, a successful legal reform strategy cannot base itself on only one underlying principle (such as equality) without addressing the other multiple and countervailing values with which it coexists.

The issues and strategic directions outlined above may also resonate in comparative contexts, certainly across the Arab world, but perhaps in other states with systems presented as *shari'a*-based law. In the Palestinian context, they are offered as a partial analysis for action built very much on the wisdom and experience of social movements in the Palestinian context, and particularly the women's movement. In the next period of statehood, there will be the enactment of at least a temporary constitution, setting the broad framework for new legislation, and

almost certainly a state-directed initiative under the aegis of the religious establishment to unify personal status law between the West Bank and Gaza. The
women's movement and other social movements have developed strategies and
initiatives to influence this process, requiring a widening of alliances and building
and mobilizing constituencies. Contending voices within the religious establishment, as noted above, will be joined by a plurality of voices from women's
organizations, human rights and other non-government organizations, political
parties and government institutions. This is necessarily a political process, and
perhaps a lengthy one. However, without it, no series of projects, however useful,
will be able to engage positively with the new, sweeping developments, conflicts
and dynamics of Palestinian state and society for legal reform based both on
gender equality and on the real interests and needs of the majority of women, men
and families in Palestinian society.

APPENDIX

Case history: *Diya* between *shari'a* and customary law

Fadwa al-Labadi

§ ON 21 October 1999, a boy working in a factory producing cigarette lighters in the southern West Bank town of Hebron dropped a box of lighter fluid he was carrying to a second-storey workroom (*Al-Ayyam*, 23 October 1999). A fire flared in the room where female factory workers assembled lighters for wages of less than US$1 per hour. Most had been recently recruited from their villages in the Hebron district and worked without written contractual arrangements or accident or health insurance. There was no fire extinguisher or any immediate exit to the outside in the poorly ventilated room. The factory itself, in a densely populated neighbourhood, was licensed only to refrigerate vegetables, not to produce cigarette lighters (*Al-Ayyam*, 24 October 1999). In the conflagration, fourteen female workers were burned to death.

The scale of tragedy in Hebron mobilized the Palestinian public in demonstrations in a number of Palestinian cities; in Hebron itself, angry protestors attacked the Hebron municipality, considering the mayor in particular to have failed to oversee the factory's working conditions or force prominent local businessmen to adhere to health and safety regulations. It was perhaps the most widespread social and economic protest directed at government institutions in the Oslo period.

In the aftermath of this tragic event, bereaved families and local communities mobilized several legal systems and systems of rules to seek justice and compensation, utilizing both the public channels of law and government and the processes of customary law. In the latter (and to some extent in the former), principles of *diya* ('bloodwit' or reparation) were invoked and contested, although not through the institutional processes of the *shari'a* courts, which retain jurisdiction over *diya*. Instead, both officials of the court and of the Authority were brought into the customary law process.

Context

As set out in Chapter 6, above, *diya* comes under the jurisdiction of the *shari'a* courts in the West Bank by virtue of the Jordanian Law of *Shar'i* Procedure 1959

(Article 2/11), where the parties are Muslim or where a non-Muslim party agrees to *shari'a* court jurisdiction. Until their abolition in Jordan in 1976, tribal courts on the east bank (Jordan proper) also had jurisdiction over *diya* where the parties could establish that they followed customary law (Hardy 1963: 79; Welchman 2001: 252). Homicide and other criminal matters are in the exclusive jurisdiction of the regular (statute) court system.[51] Depending upon the affected community, it may in reality be customary law that provides the major regulatory process – and indeed the legal substance – resulting in a *diya* settlement. Where such a customary process is activated, the regular court system may well respond; Hardy (1963: 76) reported in the early 1960s that, in Jordan, courts might adjourn in a homicide case 'until they hear that the two parties have become reconciled through the traditional process', and that 'when the courts do proceed to try the case, evidence that the usual *diya* has been paid counts heavily as a mitigating factor'.

Of all the governorates in the Palestinian West Bank, Hebron has a particular reputation for traditionalism, and may be viewed in some ways as a stronghold of customary and clan-based law (*al-qada al-'asha'iri*), reaching out to the Bir As-Saba'a (Beersheva) tribal areas to its south in the Negev (Welchman 2000: 10). Traditionally, functionaries from Hebronite families also fill considerable numbers of posts in the *shar'i* system. Shaykh Taysir Tamimi, the current Deputy Qadi al-Quda, is himself a Hebronite; his father, Rajab Tamimi, was deported by the Israeli occupation authorities in the early years of the Israeli military occupation.

The Institute of Women's Studies decided to investigate the utilization of customary law processes and the institution of *diya* in the context of the Hebron factory fire to see how a pressing public issue was actually resolved through the interaction of different agents and systems during a period of legal transition. Using a wider notion of law and family relations, *diya* itself has deep roots in practices and ideologies of inter-family and clan relations. The concept of homicide or accidental homicide as an injury to family (legally as a civil injury or tort), as well as or perhaps even rather than a public crime, may persist in such practices. *Diya* is also particularly important as we consider legal reform for the contending evaluations in Islamic jurisprudence and court and customary practice in matters of *diya* of the relative worth assigned to men and women in compensatory judgments. In the case under consideration, emerging state authority, customary legal practices and institutionalized *shari'a* cooperated and contended on this and other matters, with the result to date of a devaluation of women's worth, despite views and judgments to the contrary. The heterogeneity of legal practices and the cooperating and conflicting systems of authority are thus highly pertinent to an understanding of the practical intersections of *shari'a* principles in the Palestinian context and to projecting both the need for and the problem of legal reform. They also point to the constraints on and opportunities facing the emerging state authority in its efforts to exert a more centralized authority over these cooperating and conflicting systems. Nor is this a new phenomenon for many of those in high positions in the Authority; Botiveau (1999: 79) refers to Julie Peteet's (1987) observations in Palestinian refugee camps in Lebanon to consider the centralizing tendency demonstrated by the PLO in the 'fragmented legal field'. The three cases considered include one of *diya*, where the PLO court allowed the customary processes to run their course but 'only after giving the protagonists the choice, and ruling accordingly'. In this and the other cases, Botiveau observes: 'The Palestinian authority of the camp had to secure a political consensus between the different political organizations represented and avoid upsetting notables favouring the application of Islamic or customary law, while at the same time seeking to impose a "national" solution, i.e. a solution in conformity with revolutionary goals, which included combating the feud-system and protecting women's rights.'

The conduct of the Palestinian Authority in the aftermath of the Hebron factory fire provides an illustration of how elements within it sought to handle a situation involving similarly different tendencies and aspirations, although this time in the context of emerging state authority and an active though constrained legislature.

The IWS investigation occurred about nine months after the incident, principally through interviews with victims' families and through secondary sources such as reports by local labour rights organizations and the press. These were followed in November 2001 with interviews with the Acting Qadi al-Quda in the West Bank, Shaykh Taysir Tamimi, and again with the families of the victims, as well as contacts with the public prosecutor in Hebron.

Limits of male maintenance: females as breadwinners

Before exploring the processes of compensation, a brief examination of the victims and their families allows a glimpse into the realities of family survival that legal reform should address. The fourteen young women lived in twelve households, mostly in the same neighbourhood in the village of Dura, with four women living in another village, Halhoul. Five belonged to the same family grouping (two were sisters), a fact which may have encouraged resort to customary law. Almost all were single and none had any previous skill or received any training qualifying them for the job. Most had been recruited in the previous two weeks by a factory representative knocking at the door looking for young women workers. Almost all were first-time workers and the first female member of the family to work outside the home. Most of the families were large and relatively poor, with nine of the households numbering more than ten members. In several cases, fathers were dead or elderly or disabled, although a number of families had brothers working as unskilled and irregular labour inside Israel. The young women's participation in family income generation is a reminder that 'male maintenance' cannot necessarily guarantee family survival in the difficult circumstances of contemporary Palestinian society – and that compensatory processes based on traditional views of males as breadwinners will not be responsive to these circumstances.

Government and public law

The Hebron factory fire perhaps first and foremost revealed a chain of failures in governmental responsibility, public law and most particularly in enforcement of existing law and regulations. The enforcement of existing labour law, including proper monitoring by the Ministry of Labour and municipal officials, as well as the enforcement of customs regulations and municipal regulations, would have addressed many of the violations that contributed to the factory fire tragedy. In the wake of the tragedy, the available legal mechanisms, whether provisions for criminal prosecution or for compensation under articles in the labour law, were not fully utilized. Instead, the factory was sealed (another branch was transferred to a village outside the city) and the factory owner was ordered to be detained for six months on administrative order, according to the Hebron public prosecutor, until the magistrates' court had completed its investigation. He was, however, released on bail after a month on condition that he sign in daily at a local police station; he later left for the United States.

The first response to the incident from the executive authority was an order by President Arafat that a ministerial committee be formed, with representatives from the Ministries of Industry, Labour, Local Government and Parliamentary Affairs. This decision infuriated the public, especially relatives of victims, who perceived the committee as an essentially unobjective group of people whose members shared institutional responsibility for the tragedy. Tellingly, President Arafat also issued a personal order for US$3,000 compensation to be paid to each one of the victims' families, in addition to another $1,000 per family to be paid by the *Awqaf*, the Islamic institution overseeing charitable trusts and religious institutions (*Al-Hayat*, 26 October 1999). Here the policy appears to have been based on a mixture of personal and religious authority, as well as compassion for the victims, rather than an activation of the rule of law.

The committee issued an initial report on 24 November 2000, which called for the inspection of all factories in the Hebron area. Several that were found to be in violation of safety laws were in fact closed down (Atawneh 1999), although inspections probably did not include the majority of small workshops (of five persons or under) which fall outside prevailing labour legislation. The committee's initial report encouraged President Arafat to appoint a slew of new officials, including the long-delayed Hebron Muncipal Council, a full-time judge for the Hebron municipality and another for solving labour disputes. He also ordered the immediate establishment of a civil defence headquarters, perhaps in response to the poor perfomance of the municipal fire department, in addition to facilitating necessary means for safety committees to enable them to exercise their responsibilities more efficiently (i.e. to monitor safety rules). President Arafat also called on the Palestinian Legislative Council (PLC) to issue new labour legislation. A new Palestinian labour law was approved by the Legislative Council after the third reading in March 2000, and signed by President Arafat. However, it then seemed to be shelved for many months – one could perhaps speculate that some among the powerful business community were less than enthusiastic about the labour rights protections contained in the text, another example of the pressures brought during the transitional period by different constituencies on the basis of what are perceived as conflicting interests in the matter of 'national' legislation. It was nevertheless finally published in the *Official Gazette* and the date of implementation announced as January 2002.

The preliminary report from the ministerial committee, however, placed blame only on the factory owner, and failed to delineate processes of just compensation, both of which were unsatisfactory to the victims' families. Nine months later, no final report had been issued. At the time of writing, over a year later, a report has allegedly been issued but is not available to the public or indeed to members of the Palestinian Legislative Council who have requested copies. Thus, while some positive public actions were taken, the full weight of the law was not brought to bear, either to punish the guilty, or to compensate the bereaved, or to respond to the public interest in the case.

Customary law: lives at half value?

Although customary law ended up providing a more active and effective process of reparation than did the public law, it nevertheless manifests many short-comings. Among these, there is the fact that it is common for clan relationships to be used to pressure the victim's family to make concessions to that of the wrongdoer, under the rubric of forgiveness and the inevitability of the loss – the allusion to 'fate'. In addition, tribal law is influenced by the relative social status of victim and wrongdoer (i.e. the more powerful one's family is, the more concessions may be gained from the other party). The factory victims are a case in point, both in the changes in the valuation of *diya* noted below and in the fact that notables overseeing the customary law process chose to overlook the fact that certain government-appointed officials in positions of formal responsibility were clearly and institutionally implicated in what had happened in their failure to enforce licensing and safety provisions in the existing law.

Clan-based politics and processes have in fact been officially encouraged by the Palestinian Authority; an early Presidential Decree (no. 161 for the year 1995) established a 'Clan Affairs' Department affiliated to the president's office (Jad et al. 2000: 51) leading to a resurgence in clan-based affiliations, such as the revival of *hamula* (clan) associations and their deployment in local and national politics. The effects of this type of action are apparent in the case of the Hebron factory fire.

In customary or clan-based law, there are immediate arrangements for a truce (suspending the possibility of blood revenge) and a peace offering which have to be put in place before any settlement can be made (*la tatyib qabl al-tatbib*).[52] Immediately after the fire at the factory, notables (*wujaha'*) from the Hebron area convened to negotiate these preliminary arrangements. Significantly, among these notables were officials of the Palestinian Authority and religious officials. The notables were charged under customary law with deciding upon the mechanism of peace between the families of the fourteeen victims and the 'guilty' party or parties, and on the amount of 'bloodwit' or compensation (*diya*) to be paid to the relatives of the victims, in addition to the length of the truce period, commonly known as *hudna* or *'atwa*.[53]

As a peace offering (*firash al-'atwa*), 2,500 Jordanian dinars (JDs) were paid to each of the victims' families and the period of truce between the wrongdoer and relatives of victims was set at one year. The amount of compensation money (here termed *al-diya al-mohammadiyya*) to be paid by the guilty to relatives of the victims was agreed upon by the two sides in the presence of the notables. According to relatives of victims, the amount agreed upon was given as a hundred female camels, forty of them pregnant, or 4.5 kg of gold, worth JD 35,000, for each victim. The figure of a hundred camels is the 'classical' *diya* for homicide.[54] This amount represents an equal valuation of a woman's life with that of a man, and was set by asking the opinion of local *'ulama*, notably the Deputy Qadi al Quda, Shaykh Taysir Tamimi. However, at the time and later, many contradictions arose as to whether or not a woman's *diya* should be of the same value as that of a man. Some held that a woman's *diya* should be half the amount of a man's, others held that it should be equal, while a third opinion held that specific circumstances should be taken into account and that in effect such decisions should be made on a case-by-case basis.

The notables constituting the *jaha* (i.e. those whose role it was to facilitate and oversee the arbitration and settlement process between the two parties, referred to in this case as the 'committee for clan reconciliation', *lajnat al-islah al-'asha'iri*) advised relatives of the victims to request the release of the factory owner from prison. The relatives took the advice and signed a petition stating that they had no objection if the owner were to be released while waiting for his court hearing, on condition that he paid 498,000 Israeli shekels (JD100,000) towards the compensation due the victims' families (as noted below, a slightly larger amount was finally paid when the owner was released from prison). The rest of the total compensation was to be payable at the end of the *hudna* period, a year from the date of the agreement. He was also asked to leave the country during the *hudna* period. Of special note here is the cooperation of the state court in the customary law processes. Indeed, the owner was not formally charged and his case was adjourned until April 2002, presumably after the resolution of the customary law process.

As noted above, as a first payment from the total amount of the *diya*, the sum of JD2,500 was paid to each family. If the factory owner were to prove unable

to fulfil his obligation, it would have been possible that the tribal system representatives (*wujaha'*) would intervene to pressure the victims' families to settle for
the amount they had received and to forfeit their rights to the sum outstanding.
In the event that the families refused to forfeit their rights, they would have been
able to resort to the judicial system to sue for what was owed them.

However, in the intervening period, the balance of power seems to have shifted
away from the victims' families. In particular, the 'classical' *diya* rule valuing a
woman's life at half of that of a man was reasserted and in the end only half the
full *diya* as originally agreed was held to be payable. This information, provided
by Shaykh Tamimi, was confirmed by the bereaved families in an interview with
an Institute fieldworker in November 2001. After the factory owner was released
from prison, he paid JD11,000 to each family, bringing to JD13,500 the total
amount paid by the owner per victim within the year of the *hudna* period. Another
meeting of the *jaha* was set for early 2002, at which time the factory owner was
due to pay the remainder of the half *diya*. As half *diya* is worth 2.25 kg gold or
JD17,500, the remaining sum due for each victim was JD4,000. However, the
families expressed concern that they might be pressured by the *jaha* to forfeit
their rights to even the remainder of the half *diya*. Further, more recent developments[55] include suggestions that the *jaha* may revise the valuation of 4.5 kg of
gold from JD35,000 to JD28,000, leaving the half *diya* at JD14,000; and that the
jaha has come under pressure to differentiate between married and single victims,
with a higher *diya* of JD12,000 for the former and a lower one of JD8,000 for the
latter. The lack of formal 'transparency' in this process, and the pressures apparently being brought to bear on members of the *jaha* in the interim are illustrations
of certain characteristics of the customary law process referred to above which
may combine to undermine the rights of the victims and their families.

Diya between *shari'a* and customary law

The *shari'a* courts did not act in this case, according to Shaykh Tamimi, because
the victims' families did not file a claim. *Diya* claims are processed at the *shari'a*
court only upon the filing of a claim by the victim or victim's family; the *shari'a*
court does not get involved in the process of appointing arbiters, but requires
prior proof of guilt before issuing a ruling for an amount of *diya*. The role of the
shari'a court ends after the ruling has been issued. After the *shari'a* court has
made its ruling for payment due, procedures are activated in the regular court
system (at the criminal court) for execution of the ruling. The offender must pay
within thirty days of the date of the judgment. The amount of *diya* that is
awarded by the *shari'a* courts in the West Bank for the victim is the same amount
for both female and male, according to Tamimi. This represents a positive development, mirrored elsewhere including, it appears, in some customary practices
in the region, from the 'classical' rules of *fiqh* which generally appear to have
held the *diya* for a woman to be half that of a man.[56]

The families of the victims of the Hebron factory fire, however, chose to implement principles of *diya* through customary law processes and did not file claim at the *shari'a* court. The Deputy Qadi al-Quda was consulted only about the amount of *diya* payable, his answer being, as noted above, that the full *diya* worth 4.5 kg gold was payable for each of the female victims. Given that the *jaha* subsequently decided that only half the full *diya* was payable, it is possible that had the victims had recourse to the *shari'a* court and a different process, they might have received a ruling for the full *diya* which would then theoretically be executable in the regular court system.

Was justice served?

Did the bereaved families receive satisfactory justice in this tragedy? The answer is mixed, but their own conclusions are that the processes, particularly the deliberations of the public committee, were unsatisfactory. The families were clearly motivated by a search for just compensation, rather than material greed, as shown by the fact that relatives agreed to establish a charitable fund in the victims' names and that in this spirit a mosque has been built in their neighbourhood in Dura. However, the resort to the framework of customary law rather than to the institutional framework of the *shari'a* courts seems to have worked against these poor families.

Did the public perceive that justice was done and public wrongs righted? Customary law processes are processes of community involvement, but limited in participation to the more powerful members of the community and also limited in objectives. The other public measures taken by the Authority were gestures and actions in the immediate aftermath of the tragedy, some of them useful, positive legislation, the implementation of which, however, was temporarily stalled, and a report that remains secret. The rule of law as a tool for public good does not seem to have been fully utilized. While customary law processes may for some community members feel more familiar and satisfy certain needs for community expression and involvement, a heterogeneity of legal practices can work for the public good only if legal frameworks of cooperation and implementation are institutionalized and accessible and the public interest is addressed. In this area of law, so tragically illustrated by the case of the victims of the Hebron factory fire, the emerging state authority in Palestine failed to represent this public interest institutionally.

The author wishes to thank Lynn Welchman and Penny Johnson for their contribution to this case history.

Notes to Part II

Raw polling data

Center for Palestine Research and Studies (CPRS): December 1995. Survey of Social and Political Attitudes. Jerusalem Center for Media and Communications (JMCC): 1995 on Attitudes Towards Legislative Council Elections. March 1999 (with WPPS) on attitudes towards gender equality.

Institute of Women's Studies, Birzeit University, Comparative Islamic Family Law Research Team: May 2000 Survey.

1. From 1962 this legislation was passed by a Legislative Council and approved by the Governor General, in accordance with a Basic Law issued for the Gaza Strip by the Egyptian Prime Minister (Shehadeh 1997: 77).

2. Robinson (1997: 54) considers 'the divergence in the legal codes and traditions of the West Bank and Gaza Strip' to be 'the single most important obstacle' to legal reform in Palestine. He discusses at some length the 'considerable rifts' that have arisen as a result of the 'politics of legal reform' between the legal communities in the West Bank and in Gaza.

3. See Welchman (2000: 30–45) on *shari'a* court jurisdiction under the Ottomans and the British.

4. Bisharat (1989: 121) further observes that the relatively more 'familial' ambiance of the *shari'a* court and the formal religious attire of the *qadi* 'associates the *qadi* with an indigenous rather than an alien tradition'.

5. The issue of the application of Israeli laws to the Muslim Palestinians of East Jerusalem is not considered in this review: see Welchman (2000: 56–67).

6. Articles 103 and 105 of the Jordanian Constitution specify as exclusive *shari'a* court jurisdiction over questions of personal status where the parties are Muslim, issues of *diya* where the parties are Muslim, or one is a non-Muslim but agrees to *shari'a* court jurisdiction, and matters relating to Islamic *waqf*.

7. These include marriage, divorce, dower, *jihaz*, maintenance, paternity, child custody, guardianship, and 'all that happens between two spouses the source of which is the contract of marriage', as well as matters such as the property of orphans and missing persons (Article 2).

8. Published in the *Palestine Official Gazette (Al-waqa'i' al-filastiniyya)* no. 35 6/15/54 as Order no. 303 of 1954.

9. Published in a special issue of the *Palestine Official Gazette* on 22/5/65.

10. Article 183 of the JLPS; Article 187 of the Egyptian-issued Law of *Shar'i* Procedure in the Gaza Strip.

11. The following overview of the substance of the two laws was first published in the *International Survey of Family Law* (2000 edn), and I am grateful to the editor, Dr Andrew Bainham, for permission to reproduce here, in amended form, the relevant extracts.

12. And in certain circumstances (e.g. breach of a stipulation in a marriage contract, or

a disease or physical condition preventing consummation of the marriage) by the husband.

13. Recent research (Welchman 1999: 136) indicates that this is the most common form of divorce registered in both the West Bank and Gaza Strip.

14. OLFR, Articles 4–7.

15. JLFR, Article 4.

16. JLPS, Articles 5 and 6.

17. Provided she meets certain conditions related to mental, physical and moral capacity to bring up children, and does not marry a man outside certain very close degrees of relationship to the child.

18. JLPS, Articles 161 and 162.

19. LFR, Article 118.

20. In which case he must pay for the children's maintenance and pay his ex-wife a fee or wage for her services in undertaking custody.

21. For example in Morocco: Mir-Hosseini (1993: 102).

22. The agreements include: the Declaration of Principles, 13 September 1993; the PLO–Israel Agreement on the Gaza Strip and Jericho (also known as Oslo I) of 4 May 1994, superseded by the Interim Agreement on the West Bank and Gaza Strip of 28 September 1995 (also known as Oslo II). See Shehadeh (1997) for a rigorous legal analysis of the agreements.

23. Some parts of the following section were first published in Welchman (2000); I am grateful to the publishers, Kluwer Law International, for permission to reproduce here, somewhat amended, the relevant extracts.

24. Published in *Al-Quds*, 24 May 1994, reproduced in *Palestine Yearbook of International Law*, 4 (1992).

25. Decision no. 17 of 6 May 1994 appointing Abu Sardane Wakil to the Ministry of Justice for *shari'a* courts (Abu Sardane n.d.: 93 and 42).

26. For a short while there were two muftis in East Jerusalem, the other appointed by the Jordanian authorities; see Welchman (2000: 81).

27. Reproduced in *Palestine Yearbook of International Law* (1994–1995), pp. 277–9.

28. Decision no. 6 of 2 January 1995.

29. Law no. 8 of 1952, Articles 3 and 4 (Bakri 2000: 37).

30. Appeal decision 521/1996 (Bakri 2000: 37).

31. Appeal decisions 451/1996 and 620/1996 (Bakri 2000: 37–8).

32. As reported in: *Al-Quds*, 2, 5 and 14 April 1998, and *Al-Hayat al-Jadida*, 1 May 1998.

33. Administrative directive no. 15/481 of 15 April 2000.

34. Or, if it had been registered at some point but the document was no longer available, the details of that contract. Administrative directive no. 15/1358 of 11 September 2000.

35. Administrative directive no. 15/711 of 11 May 2000.

36. Administrative directive no. 15/1366 of 12 September 1999.

37. Yasser Arafat signed the Basic Law at the end of May 2002, following a prolonged Israeli military offensive into the West Bank including the siege of his Ramallah headquarters.

38. A new draft constitution was published on 8 February 2003, prepared by a committee headed by Dr Nabil Shaath, apparently in consultation with a wide range of advisors. Its Article 7 returns to the 'principles of Islamic *shari'a*' as a main source of legislation, but otherwise adheres to the text of the earlier draft's Article 5.

39. For an extended discussion of the different positions see Hammami and Johnson (1999) and Othman (1998).

40. Due to lack of space, it is possible to make only a few general comments about the problems of polling data used in the following discussion. I have used the data very conservatively – this means both in assessing the sampling and in taking a critical eye to the ways in which questions were posed. I have omitted questions that were too leading. In addition, analysis of the data has been limited to disaggregating by sex and region (West Bank versus Gaza). These two variables, commonly the most significant when assessing differential social attitudes in Palestine, also allow for staying at a greater level of sample size.

41. Given the consistency of the socio-economic indicators between the CPRS and the FAFO surveys, the difference cannot be attributed to sampling error.

42. 'Islam is the solution' is a common rhetorical means of expressing a belief in and desire for an Islamic social system and political system. The specific constituents of such a socio-political order tend to remain vague unless elaborated or constructed by specific Islamist movements or states. As for 'making the highest sacrifice for the Islamic Umma', again this is a measure of commitment to political Islam in the abstract. It is a measure of abstract primary loyalties, since it is usually asked in relation to family, clan, and secular nation (i.e. the Palestinian people).

43. Voter exit polls showed that while a large percentage of men and women had voted for female candidates, the regional and first-past-the post electoral system was unfairly stacked against them.

44. This was a survey undertaken by JMCC on behalf of the Palestinian Working Women's Society (PWWS) in March 1999.

45. Note that our study of the use of *shari'a* courts in Chapter 8 included not only cases but also administrative transactions; thus the registration of marriage was the most common interaction with the courts.

46. The account of events of the parliament is mainly taken from Hammami and Johnson (1999). See also on this, and on other legal issues addressed in the various documents and in the plenary discussions, Welchman (2000: 360–73).

47. The following information and analysis of the *fatwa*s was contributed to this section by Lynn Welchman.

48. Supreme Fatwa Council, no. 66/2000/5 of 4 May 2000.

49. In the provisions of the JLFR 1951 and, for the female at least, in the JLPS 1976, legal majority (*rushd*) (and full competence to marry) is achieved at seventeen and eighteen years by the lunar calendar for females and males respectively. In the Jordanian Civil Code 1976 (Article 43/2), the age of legal majority is set at eighteen years by the solar calendar for both (Welchman 2001: 250).

50. The term has resonance with *fiqh* writings: for Muslim jurists such as Ghazali and Shatibi, the 'five *maqasid*' of the *shari'a* ('the five fundamental universals for the protection of which the *shari'a* was instated') are 'the principles of protecting life, private property, mind, religion and offspring' (Hallaq 1997: 112 and 166).

51. Except for those in the jurisdiction of special tribunals such as, these days in Jordan, the State Security Court.

52. Writing in the early twentieth century about customary law processes following a murder in the Hebron district, Haddad (1920/21: 105) observes that 'Peace cannot follow directly after hostility'.

53. Haddad (1920/21: 104) uses 'armistice' to translate *'atwa*, and identifies *'atwa* as an older word meaning *hudna* 'in modern Arabic'. Hardy (1963) refers to *'awta* as 'the truce'.

54. Awa (1982: 74) notes two *hadiths* of the Prophet setting a hundred camels as the *diya* for homicide, with forty of these pregnant in the case of the 'heavier' *diya*. Most schools accepted payment of the equivalent amount in gold or silver.

55. Information from an interview with Advocate Naser Amro, a member of the *jaha*.

56. Watt (1968: 7) notes that 'in Mohammad's time the blood-wit for an adult male was a hundred camels, and for a woman fifty'. Awa (1982: 76) states that 'among the points of universal agreement in Islamic law is that the blood money of a woman is half that of a man'. See also Anderson (1951: 815). On the other hand, Hardy (1963: 84) reports a tribal judge from central Jordan as stating that there was no difference between a man and a woman in this matter: 'A neck is a neck.'

Part III

No Altars: a Survey of Islamic Family Law in the United States

**Asifa Quraishi and
Najeeba Syeed-Miller**

Introduction

§ THE family unit has long served as an organizing system for both social and legal regimes. The mechanisms to contract a marriage, raise one's children, or dissolve a family are now basic elements of any well-developed legal framework. Central to the establishment of a family law system is the recognition that it will be invoked most often when a conflict occurs between those who are related to each other through the family unit. Indeed, those who focus on family law issues find that 'the legal system is perhaps the most obvious manifestation of the value which society places on institutionalized mechanisms for conflict resolution' (Kressel 1997: 48). Religion has also played a role in defining family interactions and their social consequences. In addition to preserving the future of a religious tradition, the concept of the family contributes to the development of religious law, because the complex financial, social and legal relationships in the family structure demand constant attention and regulation. Moreover, the intimate nature of family relations often triggers the desire for religious sanction of one's actions, and most religions have filled this need well. Islam is no exception. Muslim jurists' *fiqh* addresses critical aspects of family life in various detail, from the requirements of a valid marriage to mechanisms for divorce, and a variety of questions in between.

Muslims in the United States are in a complex position when it comes to applying family law, because they are governed by two sets of relevant rules, one religious and the other secular: Islamic law governs the family relations of those Muslims who want to validate before God their most intimate relations, while, simultaneously, United States law binds them through simple territorial sovereignty.[1] Considering their religious identities important enough not to sacrifice at any secular altar, many Muslim couples are asserting their Islamic legal rights in American family courts and, as a result, the law surrounding Muslim marriages is becoming an important and complicated part of the US legal landscape.

Part III surveys the application and perception of Islamic family law in the United States, and the impact of living in this intersection of legal authority on Muslim families and communities. In the first chapter, 'Islamic Family Law in American Muslim Hands', we address the intellectual and social discourse of US Muslims on Islamic family law topics, paying special attention to key issues of concern and debate and providing a brief overview of the sources of information available. In the following chapter, 'The Muslim Family in the USA: Law in Practice', we examine the practices of Muslims in conducting their marital lives in the USA, leading to a review in Chapter 12 of court cases involving Muslim marriage and divorce litigation in the United States, drawing general conclusions where possible with regard to the attitudes of US courts. The final chapter puts this study in broader context by addressing the theoretical roots of the current US Muslim experience. Special attention is given to uniquely US-based efforts to interpret and apply Islamic norms and values in everyday lives. Looking at both academic and grassroots work, this review also points the reader in the direction of future trends and goals, including potential community-based efforts to address Islamic family law issues not satisfactorily resolved in formal American court-rooms.

This section will stand out from the overall project (surveying global Islamic family law and directed by Abdullahi An-Na'im) of which it is a part, because it deals with Muslims as a minority population in a non-Muslim state, presenting findings about the use of Islamic family law in places where it is not officially enforced by the state. The reader should thus keep in mind that most family issues involving Islamic law in this minority population are handled informally through internal mechanisms (family, community leaders, close friends, etc.), because Islamic law *per se* is not enforceable by state authority in the USA. Some cases do rise to the level of formal litigation in US courts, as will be seen, but the cases discussed in Chapter 12 may be unrepresentative of all applications of Muslim family law even within the formal court system, and are most probably not representative of applications of Islamic family law in the country as a whole. Nevertheless, despite its limitations in terms of space and scope, this study aims to provide the reader with a basic overview of how Muslims in the USA discuss topics of Islamic family law, the way it impacts on their lives directly, how the judicial system addresses its Muslim minority in these most intimate family issues, and, ultimately, what might be expected in the future from this unique community.[2]

TEN
Islamic family law in American Muslim hands

Authority figures

§ TO understand the wide variety of applications of Islamic family law that we will encounter in this study, it is important first to realize that the Muslim population in the USA is made up of a complex and continuously changing demographic. Of the estimated 6 to 8 million Muslims in the United States, about half are immigrants from Asia, the Middle East, Africa, Europe – literally, all over the world.[3] The other half is indigenous – meaning not only African Americans and European Americans, but also Native Americans and Latinos, as well as second- and third-generation children of immigrant parents. Moreover, of all the above ethnicities, any number can be converts to Islam or raised in the faith from birth.

This wide range of backgrounds is fertile ground for the pluralism of Islamic law (its *ikhtilaf* structure of simultaneously valid differing opinions)[4] and results in a healthy diversity of ideological perspectives among Muslims in the USA. Thus, we find Muslims on all sides in debates around topics such as polygyny, gender roles and adoption, to name just a few.[5] In finding a legal opinion to apply in their own lives, individuals can choose between the guidance of local Muslim scholars, community leaders, activist organizations, or their own personal interpretive efforts on a given question. Obviously, this plurality of sources creates a wide variety of applications of marriage and divorce procedures in the Muslim community – applications surveyed in more detail below.

Another wrinkle in US Muslim family law practices stems from the structure of authority in Islamic jurisprudence. Because there has never been an official church certifying individuals to speak on behalf of the religion, the field is open for any dedicated Muslim to seek to act as imam and lead a community. In a large Muslim society, there are usually societal checks to help maintain a sufficiently qualified cadre of these spiritual leaders. Even further, in Muslim countries with a formal system of *shari'a*-based family law in place, as well as private pious and learned individuals available to guide the individual petitioner, there are likely to be state-recognized and sometimes state-appointed muftis to issue guidance on issues of law, and state-appointed judges to apply it. In the USA, however, where there are no such checks, the quality of imams tends to run the gamut, and many take their place with little or no training in critical leadership areas (such as

Islamic jurisprudence, relevant US law and the workings of the US legal system, or counselling and mediation skills).[6] The impact of this phenomenon on the application of Islamic family law in the United States is significant, because it is to these imams that many go for Islamic marriage and divorce proceedings – proceedings that end up having varying validity under both US and Islamic law, depending on the imam. For example, many imams will not officiate at an Islamic marriage ceremony unless the couple has a valid state marriage licence first, or the imams will themselves be qualified to officiate marriages under the laws of the state, thus ensuring the secular validity of the Muslim marriage, but not all imams concern themselves with secular law and procedure. New Jersey attorney Abed Awad (interviewed in 2000) reports that some mosques in New York and New Jersey officiate Muslim marriages without any civil marriage licence, and in some cases even issue divorce and alimony orders where, arguably, Islamic law would not justify it. Maryland attorney Naima Said reports the same phenomenon in the Washington DC area (Said 1998). Similarly, Cherrefe Kadri (interview, 2000), a lawyer based in Toledo, Ohio, comments on the sharp difference between family dispute resolution processes undertaken under the authority of an untrained imam and those, for example, of an imam not only knowledgeable about Islam but also with experience as a social worker in the West. In the former, disregard for US marriage and divorce certification often prevails, not to mention frequent gender bias cloaked under the name of Islam.

Looking more specifically at what happens in family disputes, we first see that, as is true worldwide, many cases are resolved outside any formal process, whether a court or an imam. In the USA as elsewhere, Muslims often prefer to keep family conflicts within the family, and will turn first to relatives as arbitrators and mediators. One Muslim marriage counsellor himself reports that he advises Muslim couples to go first to parents, uncles or aunts before approaching him (Chang 1990). It might be noted, however, that this is often more difficult for immigrants, whose extended family is most likely to be overseas. Alternatively, where there are Muslim attorneys or social workers, these professionals often act as informal mediators, drawing client confidence from their expertise in the Western legal system combined with an understanding of Muslim concerns and, sometimes, their bilingual language skills. For example, Los Angeles attorney Sermid al-Sarraf (interview, 2000) reports that, in family dispute cases, he often first describes to clients what is likely to happen in full litigation in an American family court (including the accompanying high cost), and then assists the parties to try to reach an amicable settlement that avoids this costly approach. Similarly, Toledo attorney Cherrefe Kadri (interview, 2000) notes that she uses her mediation and Arabic-language skills to assist trust-building with clients attempting to resolve disputes out of court. Al-Sarraf (interview, 2000) also notes that he has an arrangement with a local Muslim scholar for reference on Islamic legal issues if any arise. He states that he has seen Islamic law referred to occasionally by the parties during these negotiations (for example, one party asserting things such as 'under Islam, you would get nothing'), albeit sometimes inaccurately. Usually, however, his experience is that the reality of the US legal system is what drives the ultimate resolution of these cases.

Intellectual resources

Muslims in the USA have a plethora of sources from which to learn about Islamic law, and Islamic family law in particular. A remarkable number of English-language books, articles, magazines, scholars, conferences, and now websites on this topic are available. They range in accessibility from the most readily available mainstream bookstores and popular Muslim magazines to more obscure academic pieces in scholarly journals and research encyclopaedias. The information available in these sources covers not only expositions and translations of classical doctrine, but also reformist and practical guides for the lay Muslim.

Among the more readily available resources are books such as those by Esposito (1982), Doi (1984, 1989) 'Abd al-'Ati (1977) and al-Qaradawi (n.d.), which include fairly thorough summaries of classical Islamic jurisprudence relating to marriage and divorce. The first two also include examinations of the application of Islamic family law in certain modern Muslim states, which are of considerable interest; for Muslims in the United States, however, it is the classical jurisprudence that is of the most relevance, as they seek to abide by Islamic law in the absence of state enforcement.

Other resources on Islamic family law are books written as historical and sociological resources for a primarily academic audience. These books include works like Amira el-Azhary Sonbol's *Women, the Family and Divorce Laws in Islamic History* (1996), a collection largely made up of empirical studies giving a sense of family law issues as they played out in Muslim history, with some special focus on contradicting the claims that Muslim women were prisoners of Islamic family law. The academic works, whether monographs or articles in legal and professional journals, may be less accessible to the lay reader, and offer for example critiques of legal reasoning in a particular school of thought or a particular legal issue, or presenting the law in a social or historical context. An example of an academic work with particular relevance for the USA is Mohammad Fadel (1998), who undertakes a detailed legal analysis of the doctrine of the guardian in Maliki law, not only explaining the legal theory behind the rule allowing a minor to be contracted in marriage by his or her guardian, but also critiquing what he determines is a basic legal error in the Maliki doctrine of emancipation for girls. He also makes the innovative argument that a local Muslim community should play the role of legal guardian for Muslims living as a minority in a non-Muslim country such as the United States, enabling them to adjust for these sorts of discrepancies in classical doctrine. Other works investigate the parameters of the Hanafi doctrine permitting a woman to contract herself in marriage without a guardian (Siddiqui 2000; Ali 1996). Azizah al-Hibri (1997) has also taken up the question of the right of a Muslim woman to contract her own marriage, as well as questions of a wife's duty to obey her husband and to initiate divorce.

Another aspect of considerable scholarly study is the Muslim marriage contract and its various elements. Works here include Farah (1984), Rapoport (2000), Shaham (1999) and el-'Alami (1992). Azizah al-Hibri (1993) compares Muslim marriage contracts with prenuptial agreements in an inter-faith symposium article and Mohammed Tabiu (1990–91) addresses the implications of defects in Muslim marriage contracts.

Finally, the complicated area of dissolution of marriage is also a subject of considerable academic writing, such as by el-Arousi (1977), Carroll (1996) and Quick (1998). The latter addresses this subject in the particular context of Muslims in North America, and reviews the efforts and actions taken by Muslim organizations in the West to achieve dissolution of marriage by an Islamic authority.

For those seeking a more practical resource on Muslim marriage, there are works such as the pieces by Maqsood (1998) and al-Khateeb (1996) which take a conversational tone to offer guidance based on Islamic law and principles to Muslim married couples. Works like these are not legal references on Islamic family law, but rather are focused on translating the basic Islamic rules of marriage for the average Muslim in plain language. Maqsood, whose book offers frank advice on the emotional, spiritual and sexual aspects of married life, has been called 'the John Gray of the Muslim world'.[7] A similar book by Mildred M. el-Amin (1991) begins each chapter with 'Dear Couple' or 'Dear Sister/Brother'. Al-Khateeb's article includes a sample marriage contract, examples of stipulations, and a short list of Islamic legal rules affecting marriage (see 'Terms of the contract', in Chapter 11 for further discussion of the resurgence of interest in Muslim marriage contracts).

Resources on Islamic family law often overlap with literature on the continually popular topic of women and Islam, as is evident from the number of Muslim family law works including the word 'women' in their titles. Many of these authors seek to critique classical Islamic family law with an eye to a women's empowerment, sometimes urging new interpretations of old texts.[8] Specifically US examples of this are included among the essays in Webb's *Windows of Faith: Muslim Women Scholar-Activists in North America* (2000) by well-known American Muslim legal scholars Azizah al-Hibri and Maysam al-Faruqi. Al-Hibri's piece, 'An Introduction to Muslim Women's Rights', includes an overview of marriage relations in Islam (e.g. contractual terms, guardianship, maintenance, divorce procedures) emphasizing how Islamic principles promote women's liberty in a way contrary to how these principles were applied and interpreted in patriarchal Muslim societies, ultimately leading to biases in the law itself. Maysam al-Faruqi's chapter, 'Women's Self-Identity in the Qur'an and Islamic Law', focuses on particular Qur'anic verses often cited on the subject of women's rights (e.g. male superiority over female, obedience of wives, beating), providing a critical analysis of juristic interpretation of each. Articles and collections like these testify to the emergence of a new contribution to the field of women and Islamic family law: the contribution of a specific US Muslim scholarly literature written by women. Gisela Webb says in her introduction to *Windows of Faith* that such works are 'evidence of the lively, creative, critical, and self-critical discussions currently taking place in the academy and in Muslim communities and professional organizations in the United States, raising issues of religious pluralism, democracy, gender, and modernity as they relate to Islam and Muslim identity' (Webb 2000: xii). Khaled Abou el Fadl's *Speaking in God's Name: Islamic Law, Authority and Women* (2001) similarly takes up issues of Islamic family law in the context of his critical analysis of authority and authoritarianism in Islamic law and society.

Consistent with Webb's observation, Muslim organizations are also a rich source of information on Islamic law, and Muslim women's organizations are especially interested in disseminating information about family law, often with a progressive look at well-known issues. For example, the Muslim Women's League, 'a non-profit American Muslim organization working to implement the values of Islam and thereby reclaim the status of women as free, equal and vital contributors to society', includes among its many position papers those titled 'An Islamic Perspective on Sexuality' and 'An Islamic Perspective on Divorce'.[9] Another example is Karamah: Muslim Women Lawyers for Human Rights, an organization which defines its objectives as seeking to 'increase the familiarity of the Muslim community with Islamic, American, and International laws on the issues of human rights', and 'provide educational materials on legal and human rights issues to American Muslim women'.[10] Karamah's website lists publications for further study, including family law titles such as 'Family Planning and Islamic Jurisprudence', and 'Marriage and Divorce: Legal Foundations', both by Azizah al-Hibri, founder of Karamah.

Of course, not all Muslim organizations take a progressive, reformist attitude towards the subject of Islamic family law and women's rights. Many Muslims advocate more traditional interpretations such as encouraging wifely obedience (in all but directly anti-Islamic behaviour), the primacy of motherhood and discouraging public careers involving cross-gender interaction. Examples of this end of the ideological spectrum can be found on websites such as that of Alsala-fyoon, which posts pieces such as 'The Duty of a Woman to Serve her Husband',[11] and in books like Muhammad Abdul-Rauf's *Marriage in Islam* (1995), which, for instance, describes household management as the wife's primary responsibility, though acknowledging that individual couples may agree on other arrangements.

The final arena of readily accessible resources on Islamic family law is the internet. This modern technology has created several avenues for the dissemination and exchange of information on Islam, and Islamic family law is no exception. These fora range from discussion groups (e.g. members of the 'sisters' list moderated from Queens University in Canada[12] often discuss the legal and social parameters of Muslim marriage and divorce) to online universities (e.g. the College of Maqasid Shari'a[13] offers a twenty-credit 'Introduction to Family Law' course) and websites devoted to education of family law-related issues, such as <www.zawaj.com> which describes itself as 'a complete portal site for information and resources regarding Muslim marriage, weddings, family relationships, and parenting'. On its website are posted articles describing the proper relationship between spouses, raising Muslim children, sexuality and Muslim cases in the courts. There is even a list of recommended scholars to contact for *fatwas* (Islamic legal opinions), complete with their email addresses.[14] Another site, called 'Loving a Muslim', includes a summary of Islamic family law in its effort to address the 'non-Muslim woman in a loving relationship with a Muslim man'.[15] Finally, <beliefnet.com>, the popular inter-faith site on religion, includes several links to family law issues in its Islam section.

Reviewing all these sources in the context of current discourse in the United States, one aspect of Islamic family law stands out as being of particular interest: the concept of the Islamic marriage contract. This subject has attracted recent and continuing attention, stemming largely from the fact that the jurisprudential importance of marriage as a contract makes drafting a marriage contract an important tool to particularize individual marital relationships, and has in fact been used as such throughout Islamic history. As Sharifa al-Khateeb puts it in her 1996 article in a Muslim women's magazine: 'The Islamic marriage contract is meant to solidify the [purposes of an Islamic marriage] and specify stipulations important to the woman and man.'[16] Interest in the Islamic marriage contract is growing, prompting a full weekend conference at Harvard Law School,[17] a panel at the 2001 national conference of the Islamic Society of North America (see Lieblich 2001), numerous Muslim magazine articles, and website discussions, all of which have contributed to educating the public (both Muslim and non-Muslim) about this now underutilized *shari'a* tool (ibid., p. 1). These efforts highlight the fact that Muslim marriage contracts can contain a myriad of additional clauses, from a promise of monogamy and a wife's delegated right of unilateral divorce, to equal participation in household chores and the right to complete one's education.[18] Some note that Islamic schools of thought differ over the enforceability of these clauses, though these details are not always fully explained in the Islamic law summaries available for the layperson's practical use.[19] Finally, addressing the question of the Muslim marriage contract in the United States, the Karamah organization lists among its projects 'drafting a model Islamic marriage contract which meets the objections of those American courts that have found Islamic marriage contracts unenforceable'[20] – a project whose importance will become apparent in Chapter 12, summarizing the treatment of Muslim marriage contracts by US courts.

Islamic law on divorce is also a popular topic among American Muslims, as the divorce rate rises and Muslims seek to understand their marital status under both religious and secular law. The lay Muslim's knowledge about divorce generally includes awareness of *talaq*, the husband's unilateral right to divorce by oral declaration, but details on its practical application (terminology, revocability, voidability) are less well known. Alternative methods of divorce such as *khul'* (divorce for remuneration conducted through mutual consent) and *faskh* (judicial dissolution) are further from public consciousness, and the situation becomes more complicated when one adds in the potential for a wife to include a delegated *talaq* right in the marriage contract.[21] Besides analyses of divorce law in the literature mentioned elsewhere in this review, some contributions by Muslims and Muslim organizations in the USA go beyond the classical Islamic law on the subject, offering instead non-mainstream interpretations. For example, the Muslim Women's League position paper, 'An Islamic Perspective on Divorce', after explaining the basic elements and types of divorce in classical jurisprudence, goes on to comment: 'The controversy with divorce lies in the idea that men seem to have absolute power in divorce. The way the scholars in the past have interpreted this is that if the man initiates the divorce, then the reconciliation step for appointing an arbiter from both sides is omitted. This diverges from the Qur'anic injunction.'[22] With this argument, the Muslim Women's League critiques the established *fiqh* allowing unilateral husband-initiated divorce, by appealing to the Qur'anic verse stating 'if you fear a breach between them, then appoint two arbiters, one from his family and the other from hers; if they wish peace, God will cause their reconciliation' (Qur'an 4: 35).

Whether it is in the form of summaries of classical mainstream jurisprudence or progressive interpretations of original religious texts, there is significant information on Islamic family law for Muslims in the USA seeking to educate themselves, either in the basics or the more complicated nuances of Islamic jurisprudence. The average Muslim carries around some understanding of the basics and very little of the jurisprudential nuances, but how he or she applies these Islamic laws in the context of US society varies widely, due somewhat to the varying levels of individual knowledge, but also because of ideological differences and simple practicalities. This variety in the practical application of Islamic family law is the subject of the next chapter.

ELEVEN

The Muslim family in the USA: law in practice

Solemnizing the union

§ THE intersection of US and Islamic law becomes important right at the formation of the family unit – the creation of the marriage itself. Each state of the USA
requires a civil marriage licence for every marriage created within its borders.
Details on the specific requirements for these licences vary from state to state, but
generally they require an official signature of the person performing the wedding,
qualified by the state to do so, and those of witnesses to the ceremony. Islamic
wedding requirements, consisting of an offer and acceptance and witnesses to the
event, do not conflict with this if the person officiating the wedding is registered
with the state as having this authority. In the United States, many Muslim leaders
and lay individuals have this state authority, thus making the Muslim ceremony
over which they preside simultaneously legal under the laws of the state, provided
all necessary forms are filed. However, because not all Muslim marriage officiants
carry such qualifications, Muslim weddings in the USA take a variety of forms.
Many conduct one Muslim ceremony with a state-qualified imam, but many
others have two events: a Muslim ceremony as well as a civil ceremony through
state channels.[23] Still others have only a Muslim ceremony and never bother with
state registration requirements,[24] a risky practice under US law because, barring
a finding of common law or putative marriage, the parties and their children
have no state-enforceable legal rights upon each other, thus affecting inheritance,
health insurance, taxes and even immigration issues.

Terms of the contract

As for the contents of these Muslim marriage contracts, most Muslims in the
USA seem to consider only one thing really important that would not otherwise
be included in a standard civil marriage licence: a provision regarding the wife's
bridal gift or dower (*mahr/sadaq*). The majority of classical Muslim jurists hold
dower to be an automatic result of the marriage contract, to the effect that even
if no dower is stipulated, or it is stated that there will be no dower, the wife is
entitled to claim a 'proper dower', assessed by her peers and those of her individual
standing (Esposito 1982: 25; Welchman 2000: 135–6; Ali 1996: 159). Customarily

the dower is divided into one part payable immediately on the marriage (the 'prompt dower', sometimes only a token amount or symbol) and another part deferred to a later date, either specified or more usually payable on the termination of the marriage by death or divorce (Rapoport 2000; Welchman 2000: 144; Moors 1995: 106–13). Written documentation of Muslim marriages thus routinely includes mention of the dower arrangements, and in the USA, many mosques and imams include a fill-in-the-blank provision in standard marriage contracts (Kadri, interview, 2000). Case law of Muslim marriage litigation in the USA reveals that Muslims do generally include *mahr/sadaq* provisions in their contracts, their nature varying with the financial status and personal preferences and aspirations of the parties.[25] Some examples of actual *mahr/sadaq* clauses in the USA and Canada are: $35,000, a Qur'an and set of *hadith*, a new car and $20,000 (Canadian), a promise to teach the wife certain sections of the Qur'an, $1 prompt and $100,000 deferred, Arabic lessons, a computer and a home gym, a trip around the world including stops in Mecca, Medina and Jerusalem, a leather coat and a pager, a wedding ring as immediate *mahr* and one year's rent for deferred *mahr*, and eight volumes of *hadith* by the end of the first year of marriage and a prayer carpet by the end of five years of marriage (al-Khateeb 1996).[26]

One case vividly illustrates the significance vested by some Muslims in their dower agreements: in *Aghili v. Saadatnejadi* (1997), the husband threatened not to record the Muslim marriage contract with state authorities unless the wife first agreed to relinquish that contract and sign a new one. The original contract included a dower of Iranian gold coins to the value of $1,400 and a provision for a payment of $10,000 as damages for any breach of contract by the husband. The husband's threat suggests that he felt bound by the *mahr* terms of the initial contract. Also, Los Angeles attorney Sermid al-Sarraf comments that he has seen, in informal divorce negotiations, a husband's recognition of the *mahr* amount, prompting the parties to include in their settlement an offset of this amount with other property (interview, 2000). Other Muslims tend not to consider the dower important at all, and include a clause about it (often only a token dower) in their contracts only because the Muslim officiating the ceremony tells them it is required (Kadri, interview, 2000).[27]

Discussions among US Muslim women include debates over the importance of the *mahr/sadaq* in the first place – some rejecting it as putting a monetary value on the bride, others advocating it as a financial protection for women in the event of death or divorce and sometimes as a deterrent against divorce (especially powerful where there is a large deferred dower).[28] There is indeed a dilemma presented by the institution: setting the *mahr* very high may provide good financial security for the wife and (where deferred) a good deterrence against husband-initiated divorce, but on the other hand, it burdens wife-initiated *khul'* divorces, which are usually negotiated with an agreement by the wife to forfeit her *mahr*, with the significant financial cost of waiving the outstanding amount and returning whatever prompt dower has already been paid. Setting the *mahr* low, or as only a token gift, has the reverse double-edged sword effect. That is, there is not as much to be lost in returning the *mahr* if the wife wants to negotiate a *khul'* divorce, but she also loses the deterrent effect on *talaq* divorce by the husband which is accomplished by a high deferred dower. Where the divorce occurs not through extra-judicial *talaq* or *khul'*, but rather judicial dissolution by third-party arbiters, the impact on *mahr* payment does not follow an absolute rule. Rather, the arbiters assess blame and harm caused by the spouses and allocate costs accordingly. Where there is no harm by the wife, she generally keeps all of the *mahr* (el-Arousi 1977: 14; Quick 1998: 36–9; Ali 1996: 125).[29]

As elsewhere in the Muslim world, additional stipulations (e.g. stipulations of monogamy, delegated right to divorce, wife's right to work outside the home, etc.) further defining the marital relationship of the new couple seem to be much less utilized than dower provisions,[30] presumably because the dower is obligatory whereas additional stipulations are not only optional but also a subject of little public awareness, and some clauses are even controversial in classical jurisprudence and local community attitudes (Kadri, interview, 2000). Nevertheless, the idea of particularizing one's Islamic marriage contract is gaining attention among the US Muslim population. Encouraged by Muslim women's organizations and activists seeing the use of additional stipulations as a tool for women's empowerment, more and more US Muslims are educating themselves about how to use the Muslim marriage contract. Says Sharifa Al-Khateeb of the North American Council for Muslim Women: 'The contract is a tool to help men and women design their future life together so there are no surprises … and so women won't be saying "I can't do this because my husband won't let me"' (Lieblich 1997).

Far from considering it a new, reformist feminist tool, many see the proactive use of the Islamic marriage contract as a way of protecting their basic Islamic rights. It is for this reason that Karamah reports it is working on a model marriage contract, grounded in classical Islamic legal principles, to be used by Muslims worldwide. One visitor to the Karamah website praises a friend for drafting her marriage contract to include clauses on monogamy and equal right to divorce (among others) and comments that many Muslim men unfortunately have a negative attitude towards drafting a marriage contract, considering it an 'insult to their ability to behave as model Muslims' and that they 'forget that in times of imminent divorce, men and women do become irrational and make demands that are hard to agree upon'.[31]

The empowering potential for women in the Islamic marriage contract has also attracted scholarly interest among academics. According to John Esposito, Islamic marriage contracts were originally intended to raise the status of women because, being party to the agreement, women could add stipulations of their own (Lieblich 2001). Carol Weisbrod (1999) notes: '[t]here is considerable interest among Islamic women in the idea of using the contractual aspects of Islamic marriage to protect women's rights.' Of course, such use of the contract stipulations presumes that the woman has the awareness and education necessary to utilize it. This is often not the case and, as Lynn Welchman has pointed out, the Islamic marriage contract system leaves 'the protection – or clarification – of rights such as education and waged employment for women out of the law per se and subject to the knowledge, ability and initiative of the individual women not only to insist on the insertion of a stipulation but to phrase it in a manner that gives it legal value' (Welchman 2000: 180). On the other hand, the marriage contract remains a very valuable tool because its grounding in classical law gives a 'clear indication of the acceptability of the changing of the more traditional parameters of the marriage relationship' (ibid., p. 180). It is for this reason that many activists take the need for education on the topic of marriage contract law so seriously, and their efforts largely focus on simply making women aware of this tool.[32]

Women's empowerment is not the only motivation, however. Those advocating the use of additional contractual stipulations focus not only on their potential to equalize gender-based advantages, but also as a way for both spouses proactively to express partnership in their new, unique union. Ayesha Mustafaa of the Muslim American Society says: '[i]t forces conversation on important issues: where you are going to live, whether your wife is going to work, whether she accepts polygamy' (Lieblich 2001).[33] Similarly, Kareem Irfan, of the Council of Islamic Organizations of Greater Chicago, says: '[t]he contract forces the bride and groom to have a reality check before marriage' (ibid.). What form this reality check takes depends upon the ideologies of the individual couple. For some, it may mean a reaffirmation of traditional roles, such as that the wife won't go to college or work after the couple has children (ibid.). But for others, especially non-immigrant Muslims whose image of married life is very different from the traditional one, arrangements such as monogamy and equal access to divorce are more or less presumptions in the structure of marriage, and these men are not threatened by a woman's interest in including these (and other rights-specific terms) in the marriage contract. Indeed, in many cases it is the groom as well as the bride seeking to have such stipulations included.[34] The attitude of many of these couples is exhibited in the following statement of one Muslim bride: 'I love him ... and I can't see him [taking a second wife], ever. But we put it in the contract because you never know' (ibid.). These young Muslims tend to view the contract drafting process not only as an allocation of rights and duties, but also as an exercise in learning to express their new identity as a couple, and, even more importantly, as a way to open up discussion (and determine compatibility) on important family issues (career, children, finances, residence location, etc.) that might otherwise be postponed to more stressful times (Quraishi 1999).[35] In other words, among a growing proportion of the American Muslim population, there is an interest in drafting more detailed, personalized Muslim marriage contracts – documents that are not a generic stamp of mere legal status conferred by some external authority, but rather, full, detailed expressions of the way each couple defines itself.

For those who choose to include specific stipulations in their marriage contract there are many insightful ideas from which to choose. Islamic history attests to Muslim marriage contracts including stipulations in which the husband promises not to marry additional wives (usually with the remedy that the wife may obtain a divorce, or even force a divorce of the second wife, if this promise is breached), delegates his *talaq* right to the wife, agrees not to relocate the family without the wife's consent, agrees never to prevent her from visiting her relatives, and to provide her with servants for household work as is befitting her accustomed lifestyle, among many others (Rapoport 2000: 14; Fadel 1998: 24–6; al-Hibri 2000: 57). Muslims in the United States have already taken advantage of the creativity allowed in these provisions and have included stipulations limiting visits from in-laws, that the wife will not be expected to cook or clean, protecting the wife's overseas travel required by her profession, and custody of the children upon death of either spouse (Lieblich 2001, 1997).[36] Many clauses affecting the ongoing marital relationship (such as rearing the children as Muslims, providing household services, allowing a wife to attend school, and location of the home) are included despite a realization by the couple that a US court would probably not intervene to enforce such terms (discussed further below). Other terms, such as a promise not to marry additional wives, have little effect in the USA for a different reason: the action is already prohibited by US law. Nevertheless, these couples feel it important to include such terms for religious reasons (i.e. thus preventing even a non-civil but nevertheless Muslim marriage to an additional wife), as a protection in the event they relocate to a jurisdiction that does allow such activity, and also as a mutual expression of the nature of their partnership. Finally, some marriage contracts use stipulations to provide for remedies in the event of a breach of other contractual terms (e.g. a monetary value or a wife's right to immediate divorce upon occurrence, etc.).[37]

Within the marriage

So far we have predominantly discussed areas where Islamic and US law are different, but not directly conflicting. There are, however, other practices where some might regard the two laws as in direct opposition, and Muslims fall on both sides of the question of which law takes precedence. Polygyny is one of these areas. Because classical interpretations of Islamic law allow men to marry up to four wives, some Muslims believe that the US prohibition of polygamy directly violates their freedom of religion and, believing that Islam supersedes secular law, proceed to become part of a polygynous marriage. Thus, we see for example, in *N.Y. v. Benu*, a husband giving custody of his children to his wife after he married a second woman, and other reports of Muslim polygynous marriages (Little 1993; Taylor, interview, 2000). Aminah Beverly McCloud relates the dilemma faced by many US Muslim women whose husbands take a second wife – they feel religiously bound not to object to a practice God has permitted. She notes that even some

Muslim leaders engage in this practice, leading to 'marriages of years of devotion fall[ing] into chaos' (McCloud 2000: 141–2). Generally, the first wife in these marriages is recognized as legal under US law, but any subsequent wives and their children are not. These later wives are 'married' to the husband in Muslim ceremonies either in the USA by imams willing to do so, or in ceremonies overseas where polygyny is legal. Because of the religious dilemma, however, McCloud states that many of these women file charges not for bigamy but for some sort of fraud. She also states that 'all of the potential legal consequences of the practice of polygamy in the American context have not yet appeared, but ... are bound to find their way into the courts as more and more women seek alimony and child support' (ibid., p. 142).

Clearly, the majority of the population does not engage in polygynous marriages, but views on the practice differ, as can be seen in a book by Abu Ameenah Bilal Philips and Jameelah Jones entitled *Polygamy in Islam* (1985), providing a lengthy social and legal justification for the practice. Moreover, many Muslims themselves committed to monogamous marriages nevertheless recognize Muslim marriages involving more than one wife as Islamically valid. Thus, in an online Muslim advice column responding to a woman wondering how to marry a man already legally married in the USA, the columnist does not question the Islamic legalities of such a marriage, but nevertheless advises against it because of the woman's uneasy feelings and apparent lack of knowledge of the first wife (Hanifa 2000). Others, on the other hand, argue strongly against Muslims participating in such marriages in the United States, urging that the Qur'anic norm is monogamy and pointing to classical juristic arguments constraining the institution of polygyny (al-Hibri 1993: 66–7). For example, Azizah al-Hibri cites classical Islamic scholars stating that if marriage to a second wife causes the first wife harm, it is forbidden, and also notes Islamic schools of thought allowing the couple to include a clause in the marriage contract barring the husband from taking more wives. Similarly, Amina Wadud (1999), in addition to critiquing several traditional justifications for polygyny, undertakes her own textual interpretation of the relevant Qur'anic verses and sets forth an alternative reading of the permission for the practice, emphasizing its specific limitation to the just treatment of orphans. The Muslim Women's League makes the additional argument that because the subsequent wives are not legally recognized under the laws of the state, then by definition they cannot be treated equally, a requirement of Islamic law in polygynous marriages.[38] That is, subsequent wives in the United States not only do not have any rights to general spousal benefits (such as insurance benefits and inheritance) but they also necessarily lack any avenue of enforcing their spousal rights if a husband chooses to abuse or divorce them, since the marriage will have no validity in the US courts. There is also the possibility of a prosecution for bigamy if the authorities are so inclined. Another argument against American Muslim men marrying more than one wife relies on the simple Islamic jurisprudential principle that one must obey the laws of the land where one chooses to live, as long as they do not prevent one from performing one's religious obligations. Since polygyny is at most permitted in Islamic law, rather than being an obligation, it is held that US laws requiring monogamy should be respected.

Another area of potential conflict in types of allowable marriages lies in the question of inter-religious marriages. Classical Islamic law allows Muslim men but not women to marry non-Muslim monotheists, those who belong to religious communities recognized as 'people of the book', whereas US law puts no religious restrictions on spousal partners (Esposito 1982: 20; Doi 1984: 36). Given the melting-pot nature of life in the USA, many Muslims, both men and women, do indeed marry non-Muslims (Haddad and Lummis 1987: 148).[39] While those who criticize Muslim women marrying non-Muslim men find a basis in standard *fiqh* positions, some object also to Muslim men marrying non-Muslims, on the basis that this constitutes an unfair double standard or results in a reduced number of Muslim men whom Muslim women may marry (Haddad and Lummis 1987: 146; Marquand 1996).[40] Others argue that the allowance is limited to those living under Muslim rule and therefore does not apply in places like the United States.[41] Azizah al-Hibri makes a *shari'a*-based argument against both Muslim men and women marrying outside the faith, arguing that the original reason (*'illa*) for the Islamic prohibition of women marrying non-Muslim men has now changed in our context. That is, the reason classical Muslim jurists denied a woman the option of marrying a non-Muslim man was to protect her from the husband's potential denial of her free exercise of her religion (acknowledging the patriarchal nature of marriage, and the fact that Christianity and Judaism prohibited inter-faith marriages at the time). Al-Hibri concludes that this *'illa* still exists, but argues further that additional realities of the American Muslim context (i.e. the likelihood of a Muslim man losing custody of his children and/or being unable to fulfil the Islamic obligation to raise them as Muslims if divorce from his non-Muslim wife occurs) mean that Muslim men also deserve the protective attention thus far granted to Muslim women, and, thus, the prohibition of inter-faith marriage should be extended to them (al-Hibri 2000: 68–9). Nevertheless, marriages in which the husband is Muslim and the wife Jewish or Christian are generally accepted by most US Muslims. For women marrying non-Muslim men, on the other hand, there is usually a stigma, or worse. Many Muslims follow Islamic *fiqh*'s rejection of women marrying outside the faith, and most respected imams will not officiate at such ceremonies (Haddad and Lummis 1987: 145).[42] Muslim women's reactions range from disregard of the rule and consequent critical attitudes, to full support and justification of the *fiqh* position as beneficial to society and family. In between are many who reluctantly accept the rule, and perhaps seek alternative interpretations.[43]

Some inter-religious marriages involving Muslims are inter-cultural marriages between indigenous US citizens and immigrants. When the immigrant is the husband, mainstream US culture has developed the fear that the husband will ultimately abscond with his children (and perhaps the wife) to his country of origin, depriving the wife of all spousal rights recognized in the USA. The 1987 book and corresponding film titled *Not Without My Daughter*[44] arguably largely created and certainly entrenched this fear in the wider US public (Baker 2002), resulting in particular attention in the State Department information on 'International Parental Child Abduction'.[45] A piece featured on its travel website titled 'Islamic Family Law' is posted to 'make clear the basic rights and restrictions resulting from marriages sanctioned by Islamic law between Muslim and non-Muslim partners', noting that 'for Americans, the most troubling of these is the inability of wives to leave an Islamic country without permission of their husbands, the wives' inability to take children from these countries, and the fact that fathers have ultimate custody of the children'.[46] While it appears to be a sincere effort to summarize Islamic family law for those living in the United States, the State Department's narrow focus on only Muslim–non-Muslim marriages skews the tone of its report and the reality of these issues. Clearly, the problems addressed (inability to leave without permission of husbands, barriers to custody) are faced by all women living under Islamic law, whether Muslim or non-Muslim. The State Department's limited view perpetuates the *Not Without My Daughter* stereotype that Muslim men are a particular threat to non-Muslim American women. Moreover, stereotypes in the dominant US culture that portray Arabs and Muslims as violent fundamentalists oppressive to women further fuel distrust of inter-cultural Muslim marriages in the non-Muslim population.[47] As will be seen in the next chapter, this distrust sometimes extends to Muslims and Islamic law generally, and has a direct impact when Muslim marriages end up in divorce courts.[48]

Stereotypes also frequently confuse religion with culture, again leading to mistakes about what exactly is part of Islam and Islamic family law. For example, though arranged marriages (in various forms, ranging from complete parental control against the wishes of their children to family-arranged meetings of a potential couple) are found in many Muslim cultures (Haddad and Lummis 1987: 149–51), Islamic source texts do not require third-party intervention as a necessary or even preferred process of finding a spouse. Muslim scholars in the USA, such as the late Fazlur Rahman among others, point out that there is nothing in the Qur'an or *hadith* 'asking Muslims to have arranged marriages' (Iqbal 1987). This is true even in the face of much of classical Muslim jurisprudence requiring guardian involvement in marriage negotiations for minors and even for adult women, reasoning (among other things) that this is necessary for their protection. Some Muslim women activists emphasize the non-Qur'anic basis for these guardian rules in arguments for reform beyond patriarchal interpretations in Islamic law (al-Hibri 2000: 60; Fadel 1998). Similarly, wedding particulars, from clothing and food to where the bride and groom sit, all vary from culture to culture, none of which commands Islamic official sanction, but may often be confused as such (Chang 1990).[49] It is not just non-Muslims who confuse culture with religion. Some Muslims assume cultural practices that have been within their families for generations are actually required by Islamic law. Thus, many debates within US

Muslim families, whether they are inter-generational or inter-cultural, often superficially seem to be about religion, but are really based on a mixture of cultural and religious/legal norms. These debates include, for example, arguments over the level of parental involvement in choosing one's spouse (and participation in wedding formalities themselves), the amount of pre-marital contact future spouses may have, the nature and amount of dower, allocation of household responsibilities (financial and physical), and spousal activities and work outside the home, to name just a few. Many of these issues do appear in juristic discussions (both classical and modern), but usually in the context of what role custom plays in law-making, as these issues are not specifically addressed in the Qur'an and *hadith* (see 'Intellectual Resources' in Chapter 10). As the community evolves and migrates, discussions of these topics become complicated as the line between law and culture blur for the average Muslim.

Male superiority within the hierarchy of the family is one culturally validated but also often religiously justified ideology (Marquand 1996).[50] Many US Muslims believe in a patriarchal final authority over family matters, and look to Qur'anic verses in support of this belief. Others resist this notion as an antiquated cultural preference, and look instead to Qur'anic and Islamic concepts of partnership and equality of the sexes (Wadud 1999, 2000; al-Hibri 2000; al-Faruqi 2000; Barazangi 2000; Muslim Women's League, 'Gender Equality', n.d.). Both philosophies, and variations in between, can usually support harmonious and successful families. However, the idea of male superiority sometimes is used to justify physical and mental abuse of other family members, especially women and children, as a Muslim male's right, presented as somehow endorsed by the *shari'a* (Kadri, interview, 2000; Winton 1993).[51] In the words of Kamran Memon (1993), an attorney and one of the first in the US Muslim community to write publicly on the subject:

> Tragically, some Muslim men actually use Islam to 'justify' their abusive behavior ... considering themselves to be Islamically knowledgeable and disregarding the spirit of Islam, they wrongly use the Qur'anic verse that says men are the protectors and maintainers of women to demand total obedience and order their wives around ... These men misinterpret a Qur'anic verse that talks about how to treat a disobedient wife and use it as a license for abuse.[52]

Even worse, as Memon and other Muslims note, is when battered Muslim women accept these religious claims and suffer the abuse, believing it to be some sort of religious duty on their part, and are unfortunately supported in this belief by Muslim community members, even leaders (Kadri, interview, 2000).[53]

This attitude, of course, disrupts the family unit with its acceptance of violence and general instability, and even more seriously if it drives the wife to flee the household or causes social workers to remove children from a dangerous family setting. Recently, members of the Muslim community have begun to recognize the problem of domestic violence, publicly speak against it,[54] and take proactive steps inspired by Islamic principles to respond to the situation (Nadir 2001: 78; al-Khateeb 1998: 17; Syed 1996; Memon 1993). For example, the Peaceful Families Project, a programme funded with a $76,000 grant from the US State Department and spearheaded by Sharifa al-Khateeb, has held conferences in several major American cities dedicated to educating and advising the American Muslim public to combat domestic violence in Muslim families (Kondo 2001). Moreover, a number of Muslim organizations have been established specifically to assist battered Muslim women, or have developed programmes targeted at this objective, through education, creation of shelters and providing legal and counselling assistance.[55]

Dissolution of American Muslim marriages

Most Muslims pursuing divorce are careful to follow local state rules in order to ensure its recognition under US law. Sometimes Islamic family law does arise in these civil divorce proceedings, usually in the form of a claim for payment of the *mahr/sadaq* amount. Family law attorney Abed Awad reports, for example, that he sees a trend of husbands resisting dower payments, sometimes using the *shari'a*-based argument that wife-initiated divorces entail the wife's forfeiture of the *mahr* (interview, 2000). Another Muslim attorney, Sermid al-Sarraf, describes one case where the spouses turned to Islamic law to assist in determining the custody of their children, each consulting different Muslim legal scholars on the question. In the end, however, other issues, such as competency and capability of support, played a stronger role in the custody decision (interview, 2000). In general, US Muslims facing divorce disputes seem to seek advice and assistance on both their Islamic and secular legal rights; and as the number of Muslim legal professionals and legal organizations in the USA grows, more and more experts become available who can assist with both simultaneously.

In a minority of cases, Islamic divorces are conducted outside the American system altogether, either by a husband's private *talaq* declaration or through a third-party determination by local Muslim arbiters, and the parties fail to file any divorce documents under state rules.[56] Such divorces would lack validity under US law, and the parties may be faced with complications in any subsequent attempts to marry in the United States (Little 1993).[57] They would also present obstacles to either spouse attempting to enforce any terms of an Islamic divorce settlement, such as the distribution of property or custody of children, in the event that the other spouse breaches the deal. Some case law, discussed in the next chapter of this report, reflects efforts by the courts to deal with these extra-judicial divorces.

Deliberately opting out of US default rules

Some Muslims are proactively interested in ways to legitimately opt out of United States legal norms that potentially conflict with their Islamic preferences. For example, in community property states some Muslims are concerned that a community property distribution of half a wife's property to her husband infringes on the Muslim woman's right to full and exclusive ownership of her property.[58] Others believe that community property distributions should not be given to Muslim women in addition to their *mahr*, which they hold already to fulfil the need sought to be resolved by community property statutes.

But community property is not absolutely mandatory, even in community property states. One can opt out of community property by executing a valid pre-nuptial agreement to that effect, but few couples have the knowledge or foresight to arrange this.[59] A complicating concern is the possibility that the *mahr* agreement will be insufficient or not ultimately enforced, and therefore opting out of community property distribution will leave a Muslim woman with neither *shari'a*-based nor secular-based adequate support. Ironically, there are historically established financial compensation norms in Islamic law aimed at responding to the same problem to which community property laws are addressed. Azizah al-Hibri (2000: 57) points out in this respect that under classical Islamic law, wives who perform household chores are entitled to financial compensation from their husbands for this work or, where the woman is accustomed to it in her social circles, to have paid help to do it for them because such work is not a religious obligation. While some Muslim countries today are seeking to revive this principle in practical terms in financial distributions upon divorce,[60] the doctrine remains unknown among most lay Muslims, in the United States and worldwide. Of course, enforceability of this Islamic doctrine in the United States is dependent upon voluntary compliance by ex-spouses, as it is unlikely to be applied by United States courts without some compelling reason to do so.

TWELVE
Islamic family law in US courts

§ WE now turn to the question of how Muslim marriages have fared in the US courts.[61] There is fairly little awareness in the US Muslim community about this subject, and consequently many mistaken assumptions are made. Much confusion surrounds the question of the validity of the marriage contract itself, as many assume that the law of pre-nuptial agreements will safeguard the enforcement of Muslim marriage contract clauses.[62] As will be seen in this chapter, Muslims seeking to enforce their marriage contract as a pre-nuptial agreement have actually had varying success in the courtroom. One essential question that will be addressed is whether David Forte's prediction that there will be difficulty in 'pleading Islamic law in American courts' has been fulfilled (Forte 1983: 31). In this chapter, we will review the treatment of Muslim marriage in published US case law, and review the thoughts of Muslim attorneys working in this field.

The validity of Muslim marriages

The question begins at the beginning – whether a Muslim marriage will be recognized as valid under domestic US law in the first place. As mentioned in Chapter 11, this is only a real concern where the couple did not also follow secular state rules in registering their marriage. But even where there is only a Muslim marriage ceremony, the courts have not rejected such marriages outright, but rather undertake their own inquiry into whether the marriage was valid under the laws of the place in which it was conducted. For example, *Farah v. Farah* was a 1993 Virginia case involving the proxy marriage in England of two Pakistanis (with a subsequent wedding reception in Pakistan) who subsequently moved to the United States. Because the proxy marriage did not follow English requirements for a valid marriage, the Virginia court held that it could not recognize it as a valid marriage, stating that the fact that the proxy wedding complied with general Islamic family law rules (which would be relevant in Pakistan) was irrelevant. Conversely, in a more recent case, *Shike v. Shike* (2000), a couple married in a Muslim *nikah* (marriage) ceremony in Pakistan and subsequently documented it in Texas by having a Texas imam sign a standard Texas marriage licence. Though the couple initially believed their *nikah* to be only an engagement,[63] the court's inquiry revealed that the parties' public representations were that of a married couple and therefore the court found the marriage valid under Texas law, even though performed outside Texas. Finally, in *Aghili v. Saadatnejadi* (1997), the Tennessee Court of Appeals held that an Islamic marriage ceremony, followed by later compliance with state marriage licence law, qualified as a legal marriage, reversing the trial court's summary judgment that the Muslim marriage 'blessing' did not qualify as a solemnization ceremony.

When there is no documentation of a marriage at all, Muslim or secular, then the court is faced with the difficult question of determining whether there was a 'putative' marriage (or in some states, a 'common law' marriage). This is what happened in *Vryonis v. Vryonis*, a 1988 case in California in which a couple entered into a private *mut'a* marriage (a marriage for a temporary period of time recognized under Shi'i but not Sunni Islamic jurisprudence) with no written documentation or witnesses. The court of appeals rejected the trial court's inquiry into the wife's reasonable belief in the validity of her marriage under Islamic law, and instead inquired into whether she had a reasonable belief of a valid marriage under California law. In the end, with no evidence of public solemnization, no licence, and no public representations of the couple as a married unit, the court answered the question in the negative. In reading *Vryonis*, it is interesting to note two elements considered by the court as persuasive against the existence of a real marriage: that (1) the wife kept her own name and (2) maintained a separate bank account. Commenting on this case, Azizah al-Hibri points out that, among Muslims, these facts would carry no persuasive weight against the existence of a marriage because the changing of the wife's family name on marriage is not required by *fiqh*, and indeed has not been a characteristic of most Muslim communities. And second, Muslim women often keep separate bank accounts to protect their right under Islamic law to exclusive control over their personal property (Muslim Women's League and Karamah 1995).[64]

Finally, there have been some cases of marriages held invalid by the courts where the Muslim parties are found to have violated basic norms of justice as recognized in the USA. For example, where a Muslim parent forces a minor to marry against his or her will, the courts have brought criminal charges against the parent.[65] In such cases, parental cultural defences are unsuccessful and held simply to violate public policy and the constitutional rights of the minor.

The enforceability of specific marriage contract provisions

The question of judicial enforcement of the terms of marriage contracts is important to Muslims because, as a minority community in a secular legal system, the only authority with physical state power to which individual spouses can turn when their partner breaches a marital agreement is the domestic courts. While local Muslim authorities (scholars, imams, family elders) are widely used to assist conflicts internally, these authorities ultimately rely on voluntary compliance by the parties; they do not have the police power necessary to force compliance against a recalcitrant spouse. However, courts interpreting complex personalized Muslim marriage contracts face a dilemma because there is a judicial preference not to interfere in an ongoing marital relationship (Rasmusen and Stake 1998: 484).[66] Thus, clauses that demand compliance during the life of a marriage (such as a spouse's right to complete an education, a promise of monogamy, or the nature of raising the children), even if they do not offend public policy, are rarely the subject of judicial oversight. If the marriage is at the point of breakdown, however, the court may be willing to include breach of marital agreements in its calculation of damage remedies for the violated spouse. This is often frustrating for those who would have preferred to maintain the marital relationship as agreed, rather than receive damages for its dissolution. As American legal scholar Carol Weisbrod (1999: 51) puts it: 'In many family law cases, money is not an adequate remedy … [but] other more direct remedies may be barred because, for example, personal services contracts are not specifically enforceable and the United States Constitution guarantees the "free exercise of religion," with all the complexities of that idea.' As will be seen, this may have serious consequences for those relying on agreements regarding the religious upbringing of the children.

Provisions regarding the *mahr/sadaq* in a Muslim marriage contract are some-what easier for the courts to handle because they are usually already defined in terms of a monetary amount payable upon dissolution of the marriage – a secular concept understandable to US judges. In the most recent case to take up the question, *Odatalla v. Odatalla* (2002), a New Jersey court treated the Muslim marriage contract in question under standard contract law and ultimately upheld the $10,000 postponed *mahr* as binding in a US court. Said the New Jersey judge: '[W]hy should a contract for the promise to pay money be less of a contract just because it was entered into at the time of an Islamic marriage ceremony? … Clearly, this Court can enforce so much of a contract as is not in contravention of established law or public policy' (Odatalla 1995). What is unique about this case is that, contrary to the predominant approach of most US courts up to this point, it did not analyse the *mahr* as a pre-nuptial agreement, but rather under neutral principles of contract law.[67] Abed Awad, who litigated the case on behalf of the prevailing wife, insists that the misconstruction of *mahr* agreements as pre-nuptial agreements under US law has created a serious warping of American judicial understanding of Islamic law as well as a hindrance to providing justice to US Muslim litigants.[68] As urged by Awad in the *Odatalla* litigation, *mahr* is not consideration for the contract, but rather an effect of it – an automatic consequence whenever a Muslim couple marries (Awad 2002). This is borne out by classical jurisprudence on the subject and the fact that Muslim jurists would assign an equitable *mahr* to those wives whose contracts did not specify one (Welchman 2000: 136, 140; Rapoport 2000: 14).[69] Thus, enforcement of Muslim marriage contracts, says Awad, should be by simple contract law principles, and not by the more particularized rules of pre-nuptial agreements that vary from state to state and generally carry heightened scrutiny (Awad 2002).

The characterization of Muslim marriage contracts as pre-nuptial agreements is not exclusive to US judges. Many lay Muslims, unaware of the legal distinctions between pre-nuptial agreements and simple contracts, often refer to Muslim marriage contracts as pre-nuptial agreements, and moreover some actively advocate the employment of this legal tool by US Muslims.[70] Attorney Abed Awad points out that these Muslims are often unaware of the technical requirements attached to valid pre-nuptial agreement drafting, and also that such agreements are assumed to override all other standard laws regarding dissolution of marriage, such as inheritance, community property, alimony and so on (Awad, interview, 2001). In Islamic law, however, these are separate questions – a Muslim wife is entitled to both her *mahr* and her standard inheritance portion – and Awad points to this as another proof that the Muslim marriage contract should not be seen as a pre-nuptial agreement.

A California case illustrates what happens when pre-nuptial agreement analysis meets an incomplete understanding of Islamic law in a US court. In *Dajani v. Dajani* (1988), the California Court of Appeals interpreted the *mahr* in a Muslim marriage contracted in Jordan to be a pre-nuptial provision 'facilitating divorce' because the 5,000 Jordanian dinars became payable to the wife only upon dissolution of the marriage. In California, as in most states, a pre-marital agreement may not 'promote dissolution' and thus a promise of substantial payments upon divorce may be interpreted to invalidate that clause.[71] The court thus considered the *mahr* windfall to be potential 'profiteering by divorce' by the wife and against public policy, and held the provision unenforceable, causing Mrs Dajani to lose her expected *mahr*. Azizah al-Hibri has critiqued this court opinion, showing it to reflect a basic misunderstanding of Islamic law and the institution of deferred dower, particularly since deferred dower is also due upon the death of the husband (al-Hibri 1995: 16–17).[72] It might also be pointed out that, under Islamic law, if a woman initiates divorce extra-judicially through *khul'*, then she is likely to forfeit her *mahr*.[73] Thus, a *mahr* clause in this situation acts as a deterrent to (not a facilitator of) no-fault divorce by the wife – a result quite opposite from the 'profiteering' assumptions made by the California Court of Appeals.

The whole life of the *Dajani* case, from trial to appeal, illustrates mistakes that can be made when US judges attempt to adjudicate matters of Islamic law. At trial, for example, Muslim experts testified to the *Dajani* judge regarding the forfeiture of the dower upon divorce initiated by the wife, and, based on this testimony, the trial court concluded that the wife must forfeit her *mahr* because she initiated the divorce, an oversimplified understanding of Islamic law on the matter. (Unfortunately, the court did not undertake an analysis of *faskh* dissolution in Islamic law where an inquiry into harm is made, distinguishing it from extra-judicial *khul'*.) But when it got to the Court of Appeals, the inquiry into Islamic law was even more superficial: it went straight to rejecting all *mahr* provisions generally as 'facilitating divorce'.

Demographic distribution may play a role in the ability of US judges fully to understand minority religious practices affecting family law rights. For example, the *Odatalla* case originated in New Jersey, in an area with a significant Arab-American population. Similarly, New York family courts dealing with Muslim litigants have relied on their experience with the Jewish *ketuba*, a custom carrying many parallels with Muslim marriage contracting. Thus, in *Habibi-Fahnrich v. Fahnrich* (1995), the New York Supreme Court, though a bit confused in its usage of terms,[74] specifically stated: 'The *sadaq* is the Islamic marriage contract. It is a document which defines the precepts of the Moslem marriage by providing for financial compensation to a woman for the loss of her status and value in the community if the marriage ends in a divorce. This court has previously determined that *sadaq* may be enforceable in this court.' In this case, the court ultimately ruled the *sadaq* at issue to be unenforceable, but it did so in a way that is more instructive to Muslims. In *Fahnrich* (1995), the New York court had difficulty giving effect to the *sadaq* provision in the Muslim marriage contract simply because the terms were too vague under basic contract principles. The clause '[t]he *sadaq* being a ring advanced and half of husband's possessions postponed' left too many financial calculation questions unanswered (e.g. half of which possessions calculated at what point in the marriage? Postponed until when?). Thus, it was a violation of the Statute of Frauds, not public policy, which doomed this *mahr* provision. In fact, these same criticisms would be likely to be raised under an Islamic investigation of the terms of the contract (Rapoport 2000: 5–21). In both jurisdictions, Muslims would be wise to pay more attention to writing clear terms in their marriage contracts.[75]

The need for clarity arises in another clause often included as standard in Muslim marriage contracts, stating something to the effect that the marriage is governed by Islamic law. These sorts of clauses have been found by one court to be insufficiently clear to warrant court enforcement of its terms. In *Shaban v. Shaban* (2001), the California Court of Appeals rejected a husband's attempt to enforce the *mahr* (the equivalent of $30) listed in his Egyptian Muslim marriage contract, instead awarding the wife $1.5 million in community property. The marriage contract included a clause stating that the 'marriage [was] concluded in accordance with his Almighty God's Holy Book and the Rules of his Prophet', and the husband asserted that this meant that the dissolution should be governed by 'Islamic law'. The court flatly rejected this attempt to incorporate Islamic law by reference, stating that 'Islamic law' was such a broad, abstract concept that brought too much uncertainty into the terms of the contract. Pointing out the many manifestations (schools of thought, state legislation) of Islamic law, the court concluded: 'An agreement whose only substantive term … is that the marriage has been made in accordance with "Islamic law" is hopelessly uncertain as to its terms and conditions.'[76] Thus, the Statute of Frauds, requiring clear contract terms, prevented its enforcement. Interestingly, the court did not even get to the question of whether the *mahr* clause was against public policy (as they had in

Dajani, and as the trial court had done in this case). Said the court: 'It is enough to remark that the need for parole evidence to supply the material terms of the alleged agreement renders it impossible to discuss any public policy issues. After all, how can one say that an agreement offends public policy when it is not possible even to state its terms?'

The California court's attitude in *Shaban* is significantly different from the New York Supreme Court's treatment of a similar clause in *Aziz v. Aziz* (1985), in which it found a Muslim marriage contract, with its *mahr* provision of \$5,000 deferred and \$32 prompt, to be judicially enforceable despite its being part of a religious ceremony, because it conformed to the requirements of New York general contract law. This is true even though the contract apparently stated that it united the parties as husband and wife 'under Islamic law'. The concerns of 'Islamic law' by incorporation so central to the California *Shaban* court apparently did not bother the New York Supreme Court. In the words of the court: 'The document at issue conforms to the requirements of [state contract law] and its secular terms are enforceable as a contractual obligation, notwithstanding that it was entered into as part of a religious ceremony.'[77]

There are two interesting aspects of *Shaban* that are relevant for our study here. First, the court's rejection of the entire contract because of a clause stating it is governed by 'Islamic law' is important to Muslims because most, if not all, Muslim marriage contracts include this type of statement. This is true even of marriage contracts drafted in the United States. Since the court appeared particularly frustrated with the lack of any other substantive terms in the contract besides this one and the *mahr* provision, it may be that by individualizing and embellishing their marriage contracts with many substantive stipulations, Muslim couples may be able to avoid a result like the one in *Shaban*, but there is no guarantee. In addition, as will be seen in more detail later, other states have found their way to enforcing Muslim marriage contracts despite such references.

The other interesting thing about the California court's treatment of *Shaban* is its absolute lack of interest in investigating the permutations of Islamic law if it were to govern the agreement. They are justifiably concerned about the complexity and diversity of 'Islamic law' and their reluctance to engage it is understandable. Nevertheless, one is left with the impression that the court took for granted the husband's version of Islamic law – i.e. that the wife would be limited to \$30 *mahr* under Islamic law, and that the obviously fairer thing to award the ex-wife of a now-wealthy American doctor after twenty-seven years of marriage is her community property entitlement of \$1.5 million. But if the court had decided to make a deeper investigation of Islamic law in such a situation, they might have found that the stipulated *mahr* is not always the end of the story for a Muslim court – she might have been given an adjusted *mahr mithl* if the stipulated *mahr* was out of proportion to women of her peer group, and she might even have been awarded *muta* maintenance (equivalent to alimony) in an amount close to the community property award (Rapoport 2000). Further, Islamic legal precedent establishing that women have no obligation to do housework or even to nurse children (and thus should be compensated for it if they choose to do so),[78] points to an awareness of the very problem that community property laws in the modern West seek to remedy (al-Hibri 2000; Walter 1999). It is a mistake to assume that awards under Islamic law are necessarily going to be worse for the wife than under US law. In fact, it appears that most spouses attempting to enforce Muslim marriage contracts in US courts are wives (not husbands), attempting to enforce rather high *mahr* amounts.[79]

An interesting aspect of these cases is that they show, in general, that for those courts that do undertake the effort, they have been fairly good at understanding the relevant Islamic jurisprudence defining the nature of a Muslim marriage contract, in order to discern which elements it can enforce as a secular court. These judicial understandings are largely from their own research as well as Muslim expert witnesses presenting courtroom testimony. Though they often disagree with each other in a particular case and frequently leave out juris-prudential details, the outcome of the cases indicates that, by and large, these experts have served to give the judges a rather good idea of the important elements at work. In one case, an appellate court even corrected its trial court in under-standing the nature of Muslim wedding officiants. In *Aghili v. Saadatnejadi* (1997), the Tennessee Court of Appeals, citing expert testimony, explained:

> In contrast to Western religious teaching and practice (particularly in Chris-tianity, both Catholic and Protestant, but also to some extent Judaism) Islam from its inception to the present has consistently rejected the distinction be-tween clergy and laity. Islamic law stipulates quite precisely that anyone with the requisite knowledge of Islamic law is competent to perform religious ceremonies, including marriage. One is not required to have an official position in a religious institution such as a mosque (*masjid*) in order to be qualified to perform such ceremonies.

This understanding of Muslim wedding officials (and imams in general), though it overstates the facts in assuming there is a need for an officiant at all (Islamic law does not require one), is still instructive in accurately trying to appreciate the different structure of religious authority in Islamic law as compared to other religions, and does so in a respectful way. There is here an appreciation that a Muslim marriage does not have to look like a Christian one, and need not have an altar or a minister in order to be valid. In this case, the court's awareness resulted in its rejection of the husband's claim that his marriage was not valid because the officiant was not a real 'imam'. Said the court, his 'right to bear the title imam is irrelevant'. Of course, the education of judges is not uniform across the USA (as the *Dajani* case exemplifies), but this review of the case law indicates an overall positive picture, especially in those states that have more experience with minority religious legal traditions, such as New York.

The lesson for American Muslims from these cases is that, even though a

Muslim marriage contract serves a religious function, if its terms are clear, an American court might find a way to enforce those terms serving a 'secular' purpose, such as the financial *mahr/sadaq* awards due upon dissolution. But a final note on secular court understandings of *mahr/sadaq* clauses: it is worth noting that Muslim jurisprudence, classical and modern, identifies a number of functions fulfilled by the institution of *mahr*, whether in its status in the contract or more broadly in the social life of the wife in particular. A number of these functions have been identified by US courts in the cases described above.[80] These include: (1) it serves the purpose of financial security for the wife in the event of a divorce;[81] (2) it may serve as a deterrent to the husband declaring a unilateral *talaq* divorce;[82] (3) it constitutes a form of compensation to a woman unjustly divorced by the husband's unilateral *talaq*; (4) it is the husband's consideration for entering the marriage, under basic contract law principles; or, lastly, (5) it is simply a gift from the husband to the wife.[83] Each of these functions of *mahr* might prompt a different analysis by a secular court attempting to understand it in secular terms, and there is consequently the potential for inconsistencies between courts and frustration by Muslim litigants who may interpret the purpose of their *mahr* differently than that focused on by the court. For example, if the *mahr* is merely a gift, then why does Islamic law treat it as a debt owed by the husband if he chooses not to pay it? (Esposito 1982: 25; Rapoport 2000: 10). If it is compensation for unjustified unilateral divorce by the husband, then what if the divorce at issue was initiated by the wife instead? If it serves as financial support for the wife after divorce, then does the initiator of the divorce (i.e. whether it is *khul'* or *talaq*) really matter, and can secular alimony and child support payments be substituted instead? Rapoport's review of the evolution of the deferred *mahr* suggests that that institution did act as a substitute for alimony, but this does not speak to the rationale of the prompt *mahr* (Rapoport 2000). Further complicating all these analyses are the myriad variations on what *mahr* amount is payable up-front and what amount is deferred – i.e. if it is substituted for alimony, then should Muslim women start asking for a large amount up-front instead of a large deferred amount, to protect themselves against the possibility that a court will award them neither alimony nor their deferred *mahr*? And then there is the question of how to treat dowers that are not specified in monetary terms at all. All of these questions remain unanswered, and perhaps there is no uniform answer that applies to the situation of every woman (i.e. while one might need financial security, another might need deterrence against her husband's unilateral divorce). Nevertheless, as these cases demand more and more judicial attention, they will also draw the eye of Muslim legal experts in the USA to focus on basic Islamic jurisprudence on the subject, its appropriate interpretation in the context of modern-day USA, and then address how to present these conclusions to the judiciary.

At present, US Muslim attorneys differ over the viability of pursuing the enforcement of *mahr/sadaq* provisions in the courts. Some believe it to be generally a losing proposition, citing local cases they have seen where the *mahr* was denied (Kadri, interview, 2000). Others are optimistic about the future of *mahr* recognition in the United States and encourage those pursuing these cases (al-Sarraf, interview, 2001). Indeed, in the cases reviewed above, spouses asserting the enforceability of a Muslim marriage contract as a pre-nuptial agreement did not always succeed. In both California cases dealing with *mahr* claims as pre-nuptial agreements, *Dajani* and *Shaban*, the court ultimately refused to honour the contract. In New York and Florida, the parties fared a bit better: in *Aziz* (NY) and *Akileh* (FL) the Muslim dower provisions were upheld, though the language of the Florida court indicates that they perceived the *sadaq* to be the husband's consideration for entering into the contract, an analysis with which Awad would strongly disagree.

Reviewing the history of the subject in general, it appears that interest in enforcing *mahr* provisions in the courts has taken particular hold in the Muslim community over the past five years or so. In earlier years, Muslim couples apparently tended to opt for informal recognition, voluntarily enforced through internal channels. As more and more Muslims draft formal Muslim marriage contracts in the United States, the courts will presumably see more litigation of *mahr* clauses. It remains to be seen whether there will be consistent treatment of these cases by state family law courts, and whether that treatment will be to review these cases as pre-nuptial agreements, seek to reject them as contracts with uncertain terms due to their religious references, or analyse them under straight contract law.

As for the enforceability of contractual stipulations other than the dower, there is much less case law because, as noted earlier, these sorts of stipulations are less popular in Muslim marriage contracts, and have even less frequently become the subject of full litigation ending up in published case reports. One stipulation many Muslims wonder about is a clause regarding the religious upbringing of the children, a relatively popular clause in inter-religious marriages. Specifics vary from state to state but, generally, agreements that a child will be raised in a particular religion are not enforceable in a pre-nuptial agreement, but if included in a separation agreement (when the marriage is ending) are usually recognized. For example, in *Jabri v. Jabri* (1993), a New York court held: 'Agreements between divorcing spouses with respect to the religious upbringing of their children will be upheld by the courts only when incorporated into separation agreements, court orders, or signed stipulations … In the absence of a written agreement, the custodial parent … may determine the religious training of the child.' And in *Arain v. Arain* (1994), the New York Supreme Court rejected for lack of supporting evidence a custody-change request based on a claim that the wife had violated her agreement to 'raise the child pursuant to the Muslim faith'. Muslims will note that this is in contrast to standard Islamic law rules on custody, which would hold that a non-Muslim's wife failure to raise the children as Muslims would cause her custody of the child to lapse at least once age of discrimination is reached. This US judicial policy is based on several reasons, including the unconstitutional judicial promotion of a particular religion, and avoidance of judicial interference in an ongoing marriage (*Zummo v. Zummo*, 1990). As a result, Muslim marriage contracts including a religion-of-the-child clause are unlikely to be enforced because these contracts are usually likened to pre-nuptial agreements in order to be enforced. However, upon divorce, if such an agreement is possible (either through divorce mediation, or informally between themselves), the parties may be able to accomplish this goal, if the agreement is included in their documented separation agreement. In any case, religious upbringing of the children is a complicated and risky business, and (as discussed earlier) is one of the reasons some Muslims today warn against marriage to non-Muslims (al-Hibri 2000).

The validity of Muslim divorces

The basic rule governing the validity of divorces in US courts is *lex domicili*, that is, the validity of the divorce is dependent upon the law of the domicile of the parties (Reed 1996: 311). Thus, where it is sought to enforce Muslim divorces conducted outside the United States, the court will look to the law of the foreign state. For example, in a case as old as 1912, *Kapigian v. Minassian*, the Supreme Court of Massachusetts held as valid the Turkish law of the time which automatically nullified the marriage of a non-Muslim woman to a non-Muslim man upon the wife's conversion to Islam, and therefore upheld the divorce of a Turkish Muslim woman convert whose husband was then living (and remarried) in the United States.

Of further interest to the Muslim community is the treatment of domestic non-judicial divorces – those accomplished by verbal *talaq* or through formal approval by a local Muslim imam. These have not fared well. In *Shikoh v. Shikoh* (1958), the federal Court of Appeals for the Second Circuit held that a religious divorce granted by a local shaykh failed to constitute a 'judicial proceeding', which was required for all legitimate divorces under New York law, and held the divorce invalid. Said the court, *lex domicili* still applied: 'where the divorce is obtained within the jurisdiction of the state of New York, then it must be secured in accordance with the laws of that state'. And even where the domicile is a Muslim country, the US courts have demanded a judicial proceeding. Thus, in *Seth v. Seth* (1985), the Texas Court of Appeals refused to recognize a *talaq* divorce conducted in Kuwait as valid because there was 'no factual showing [that] any official state body in either India [where they were married] or Kuwait ... had actually executed or confirmed the divorce and marriage'.

Looking over these cases as a whole, we might notice that they reflect a basic Western assumption built into the judicial reasoning – i.e. that a divorce has to be somehow officially recognized by some official body, even in a Muslim country, in order to be legitimate. However, Islamic laws of divorce do not follow this same premise, as private declarations of divorce (*talaq*) or private mutually-consented divorce agreements (*khul'*) are nevertheless given legal validity in Islamic *fiqh*. Of course, modern Muslim countries, with variations on classical Islamic law as their legislated codes, often require something more for legal recognition of a divorce, even if only a registration of an extra-judicial divorce with the authorities. The question that has apparently not yet reached a US court is whether it would recognize an extra-judicial *talaq* or *khul'* divorce if it had been registered with the state as a divorce deed, and therefore perfectly valid as a divorce in that particular country (as is the case in Egypt or Pakistan, for example) but not the subject of a 'judicial proceeding' as required by this US case precedent. If the question is ever raised and the court is willing to undertake a study of Islamic law in order to answer it, the argument might be made that the rationale behind the 'judicial proceeding' requirement is the due process principle of notice and the right to be heard,[84] and therefore *khul'* divorces (obtained extra-judicially but with mutual consent of both parties) should be recognized but *talaq* divorces (whereby a husband merely declares the divorce with no necessary consent by or even notice to the wife) should not. This level of Islamic law awareness and analysis, however, can only be hoped for, as the cases summarized thus far illustrate the serious misunderstandings of Islamic law upon which some of these cases have been adjudicated.

The divorce cases requiring 'judicial proceedings' and other cases where Islamic legal norms are rejected for violation of public policy, tend to reflect the presumption that the secular rules which override religious laws are somehow better, fairer, and reflect more progressive views on women, children and human rights. Yet, US Muslim scholars might take issue with this presumption, pointing out that in some cases, Islamic law is more progressive and beneficial to women than its secular counterpart. For example, the institution of *khul'* divorces, allowing a woman to end a marriage (usually for the price of her *mahr*) without having to go through the long and often painful process of divorce litigation, might be seen as a very useful tool for women. Moreover, the right to a *mahr* is so central to Muslim consciousness that it is usually the only marital stipulation Muslim women are aware they must include in their marriage contracts. Many see the deferred *mahr* as meaningful deterrence against a hasty divorce by the husband, and the prompt *mahr* as a means of ensuring financial security and independence to women who may or may not have an outside income. When a US court strikes down a *mahr* provision (whether as too religious or against public policy), many Muslim women believe this is a step backwards, not forwards, for women. Many assert that some of these cases do a serious injustice to Muslim women and to the aspects of Islamic law that protect their interests (al-Hibri 1995). Other woman-affirming aspects of Islamic law as yet unaddressed by US courts include the recognition that a woman's household work is financially compensable, that her property is exclusively her own, and the ability personally to tailor a marriage contract. These are all illustrations of Islamic jurisprudential progressiveness, some of which have only recently been paralleled in the West. Comparing different legal systems, therefore, must be undertaken with care, and it is dangerous to assume that a comity-based recognition of an alternative norm is always a concession to the lesser law. Sometimes it may be a step forwards.

Child custody

As in every community, many Muslim divorce cases necessitate a custody determination. Islamic family law can arise in these cases when one party asserts classical *shari'a* custody rules based on the age and gender of the children (Doi 1989: 37).[85] Such claims may play a large role at the informal level (mediated divorce settlement agreements, for example) in the US Muslim community, but published case law focuses mainly on the validity of overseas custody decrees from Muslim countries. There is not a huge amount of published case law on this subject, although Henderson (1997–98: 423) notes a certain recent increase, with only three cases involving state court interpretation of custody decrees from Muslim countries being reported between 1945 and 1995, while a further three were reported in the year 1995–96 alone. These cases reveal differing treatment by states towards Islamic law's custody rules, sometimes showing deference to Muslim courts and sometimes not, but always within the context of the US standard of the 'best interests of the child'. For example, in *Malak v. Malak* (1986), the California Court of Appeals evaluated one Muslim custody decision from Abu Dhabi and one from Lebanon. The Abu Dhabi decision, awarding custody to the father because of its rule automatically granting custody to fathers when the child reaches a given age, was held inconsistent with best interest standards and was rejected. The Lebanese Muslim court decree, on the other hand, was found to comply with American courts' expectations of notice and also legitimately considered 'educational, social, psychologic[al], material, and moral factors, for the purpose of insuring the best interest of the two children and their present future and in the long run'.[86]

Some courts have recognized the child's religion as a legitimate factor to be considered in a 'best interest' analysis, for courts in a society where religion is centrally important. Thus, in *Hosain v. Malik* (1996), a Maryland court concluded that, in Pakistan, custody determination of the best interest of the child was appropriately determined according to the morals and customs of Pakistani society. Said the court:

> We believe it beyond cavil that a Pakistani court could only determine the best interest of a Pakistani child by an analysis utilizing the customs, culture, religion, and mores of the community and country of which the child and – in this case – her parents were a part, i.e., Pakistan … [B]earing in mind that in the Pakistani culture, the well being of the child and the child's proper development is thought to be facilitated by adherence to Islamic teachings,

one would expect that a Pakistani court would weigh heavily the removal of the child from that influence as detrimental.

Judicial consideration of the religion of the child in 'best interest' analyses is not limited to review of international decisions. Some courts have found it relevant as a positive factor in their own 'best interest' evaluation, for example, where religion has been an important part of the child's life until that point; but, again, the importance given to this criterion varies widely from state to state.[87]

Returning to *Hosain*, it is interesting to note that the court there viewed classical Islamic custody rules as not necessarily contrary to public policy. Said the court: 'We would be obliged to note that we are simply unprepared to hold that this longstanding doctrine [*hazanat* – i.e. custody] of one of the world's oldest and largest religions practiced by hundreds of millions of people around the world and in this country, as applied as one factor in the best interest of the child test, is repugnant to Maryland public policy.'

Not all American courts are so reluctant to condemn classical Islamic custody rules outright, however. In *Ali v. Ali* (1994), for example, a New Jersey court rejected a Palestinian custody decree as not in the 'best interests of the child', commenting on the law applied by Palestinian *shari'a* courts in Gaza that automatically entitles the father to gain custody of a son at age seven in the following terms: 'Such presumptions cannot be said by any stretch of the imagination to comport with the law of New Jersey whereby custody determinations are made based upon the "best interests" of the child and not some mechanical formula.' Incidentally, this attitude also finds an audience in legal academia; Henderson (1997–98), for example, devotes an entire article to warning judges to be 'circumspect of foreign custody decrees based on Islamic law' because it is 'mechanical, formulaic and should not be followed'.

One final note on American judicial treatment of Muslim marriage litigation as a whole: the fact that many of the cases reviewed in this section involve marriages either contracted or ended in a foreign country may at first seem not directly relevant to a study of Islamic family law in the United States. However, the complex international demographic of the Muslim population in the USA means that many do not live in the same place over their entire lifetime – they may, for example, emigrate to the USA early in life, move overseas later in life, or live a dual citizenship in more than one country. Or, perhaps, because they have overseas relatives, an individual Muslim may live in the United States full-time, but have his/her Muslim wedding ceremony overseas with extended family. Cases where the marriage is executed or dissolved overseas could all end up being litigated in the US courts. As the population of second-generation and native US Muslims grows and more Muslim marriages end up in US courts for litigation, we may see more cases where the full law-related gamut of marital life occurs here in the USA. In these cases, comity to other nations will not be at issue, and US judges will be faced with the question of how to treat Islamic family law in the context of litigants from one of their own domestic religious minorities.

THIRTEEN
Future trends and predictions

§ IN order fully to appreciate the current developments in the broader picture of Muslim family law in the USA, it is imperative to investigate the roots of current theories utilized by Muslim thinkers in North America. Over the past sixty years or so, Muslims in the USA, whether indigenous, immigrant or simply based in the USA for a variety of reasons, have developed a vibrant and dynamic discourse on issues of Islam and modernity. This intellectual tradition focuses on both the development of theoretical approaches to relevant problems and practical methods for resolution of those challenges.

The theoretical basis for creating a new legal methodology for Islamic family law finds its origin in the early efforts of Muslim thinkers within the Western academy. For example, scholars such as the late Ismail al-Faruqi called for the 'Islamization' process of all Western disciplines (al-Faruqi 1982). Some of the intellectual forebears of this movement include Muslim scholars such as Muhammad Abduh and Rashid Rida, from the end of the nineteenth and early twentieth centuries. Rida has been characterized by Wael Hallaq (1997: 216) as one who 'steered a middle course between the conservative forces advocating the traditional status quo of the *shari'a*, on the one hand, and the secularists who aimed to replace the religious law by non-religious state legislation on the other'.[88] This involved, first, the turning of the Muslim focus on to Western thought and creating an environment where Muslim scholars began to distinguish between a full-blown condemnation of all Western thought and the possibility of reconciling various forms of knowledge. Al-Faruqi's legacy is found in works that present an Islamic viewpoint on disciplines as diverse as linguistics and physics. The late Fazlur Rahman was another scholar who engaged with issues facing modern Muslims and proposed specific strategies for addressing them. One of Rahman's specific contributions was a focus on the ethics of revival and emphasizing the link between morality and legal thought (Rahman 1982). The works of these and other scholars have opened the door for many new generations of reformers and thinkers who are grounded firmly within the Muslim tradition but are able to employ also concepts from other sources. In the area of Islamic law, and specifically *usul al-fiqh* (jurisprudential theory), Muslim scholars in the USA have explored a rich variety of issues that face the local Muslim community. One scholar who focuses on applying classical *usuli* scholarship to questions of modern Islamic law in the

USA is Taha Jabir 'al-Alwani, who reviews historical perspectives on the evolution of juristic disagreement in Islam and offers a methodology of modern inclusive scholarship (al-'Alwani 1985).

Bridging the worlds of Islamic and US law, there are a number of Muslim law professors in the United States. Though few, these professors have left their mark in community building and Islamic legal education, as well as excellence in their chosen secular legal fields. For example, Cherif Bassiouni, Professor of Law at DePaul University College of Law for over thirty years, is an expert in international criminal law and human rights. His numerous publications in several languages include pieces on general criminal law and human rights as well as Islamic law on these issues (for example Bassiouni 1982, 1983, 1987) and he has been at the forefront of international and national debates on issues of human rights and Islam (including receiving a 1999 nomination for the Nobel Peace Prize), urging that human rights are not alien to Islam, and in fact are founded on Islamic principles. Similarly, Abdullahi An-Na'im, Professor at Emory University School of Law, is a significant contributor to the discussion on Islam and human rights. An-Na'im (1990, 1992) has highlighted the critical issues and areas that must be addressed by modern Muslim societies in order to form institutions that respect basic human rights and liberties.

Another Muslim law professor, Azizah al-Hibri, has contributed to the ongoing dialogue of women's rights and Islam, publishing extensively on Islamic law issues especially affecting women (al-Hibri 1993, 1997, 2000). Professor of Law at the University of Richmond School of Law, al-Hibri is also founder of Karamah: Muslim Women Lawyers for Human Rights, and frequently makes presentations in both domestic and international fora speaking on *shari'a*-based legal mechanisms to protect the human rights and welfare of Muslim women. Finally, there are diverse perspectives on the use of classical scholarship and its connection to modern interpretations. Khaled Abou el-Fadl, Professor of Law at the University of California at Los Angeles, has, among other things, examined the historical and cultural record of Muslim communities who lived in non-Muslim states and drawn upon these lessons to particularize his interpretation of Islamic law to the US Muslim environment (Abou el-Fadl 1994). Abou el-Fadl remains grounded in the classical traditions to the extent that he continues to inform his own work with discussions from classical Islamic scholarship (Abou el-Fadl 2001).

The precarious position of being a part of a minority Muslim population has informed not only Muslim legal scholars, but also another group of reformers who have focused on activism as a tool to introduce new positive and creative responses to some of the legal needs of the community. For example, the difficulties of explaining Islamic family law to domestic courts and institutions, as well as the desire to resolve intimate matters with those who share the same faith-based system of ethics and morals, has prompted some members of the Muslim community to examine the viability of establishing local faith-based tribunals. Similar efforts have been embarked upon in the United Kingdom with the establishment of Muslim Law Shariah Councils (MLSC) whose aim it is to 'keep the identity of our community, to keep its laws, to keep it whole, while at the same time not breaking the laws of the state, having our own private language, while speaking the common language' (Shah-Kazemi 2001: 10). Muslims in the United States have begun to discuss the possibility of establishing such tribunals.[89] One of the differences between the US and UK experiences is that Muslims in the USA have, at least at the theoretical level, been interested in a model of marriage dispute resolution that is more egalitarian in its approach. The English MLSCs, on the other hand, seem predicated on the role of the *qadi* as mediator or judge in the process of Muslim marriage dissolution (Shah-Kazemi 2001). An example of the American approach can be seen in the work of Amr Abdalla, who calls for an Islamic model of interpersonal intervention in conflict based on three principles: (1) restoring Islam to its message of justice, freedom and equality; (2) engaging the community in the intervention and resolution process; and (3) adjusting the intervention techniques according to the conflict situation (Abdalla 2000: 153).[90] As the idea of establishing US Muslim tribunals evolves, it will be important to examine whether they will mimic the role of a Muslim *qadi* who is the expert, or rather will be infused with the involvement of various other Muslim professionals and community members. The choice between these two approaches will have a significant influence on the ultimate nature of decisions emerging from these tribunals.

The attitude of the US courts to the rise of these tribunals is as yet unknown, but there are indications that some judges would welcome the existence of reliable arbiters of Islamic family law issues, and may even be undertaking their own consultation with Muslim authorities in the interim. For example, in a recent divorce case in Pomona, California, a complicated *mahr* question was ultimately resolved by referral of the parties to two Muslim imams (mutually agreed to by the parties) on the *mahr* question, which was then returned to the family judge who allocated the dissolution amount accordingly (Erickson, interview, 2001). This very innovative approach honoured the parties' allegiance to Islamic law while still maintaining state jurisdiction over the case.

Muslims in the USA have a helpful precedent for these efforts in the experience of the Jewish community, which has already established an alternative dispute-resolution faith-based system. The Jewish community's *beit din* institutions play the role of arbitrators or mediators in marriage dissolution processes (Greenberg-Kobrin 1999: 364). Further, many states have adopted laws that include clergy as potential mediators or counsellors for family disputes; some now make it mandatory for couples and families to consult with some type of mediator whenever any issue of dissolution or custody arises (Lyster 1996). Muslims may find that, in addition to their imams, they can use the services of Muslim lawyers or social workers. Panels similar to *beit din* within the Jewish community might function as faith-based tribunals for various family law issues. Muslims may explore the option of naming possible mediators or arbitrators in their marriage contracts or pre-nuptial agreements. The contract that one signs must conform to all of the standard hallmarks of contract law.[91] The idea of restoring Islamic values through creating an Islamic mediation model is echoed in other Muslim activist work asserting a restoration of Islam to its basic values of justice, freedom and equality. Many US Muslims see the message of reform as central to any action taken by a Muslim. They find the impetus to form social change movements inherent in the fact that they are Muslim, and hope to find a space that exists between the realm of an Islamic belief system and their US cultural milieu.[92]

This feeling of individual obligation has been manifested in the creation of various organizational structures seeking positive change in the form of activist, grassroots activities and education of the Muslim and non-Muslim public on issues of both Islamic and US law. One example is Karamah, noted earlier, an organization engaging both the Muslim and non-Muslim communities on the topic of human rights and women. Its activities include participation in the Fourth United Nations World Conference on Women, and inter-religious fora on women's rights issues,[93] as well as the model marriage contract project noted earlier. Through this work Karamah has provided a critique of mainstream secular and Islamic opinions on legal issues relevant to women.

Another organization of interest to our study and mentioned above is the National Association of Muslim Lawyers (NAML).[94] Initially established in 1995 as a web-based community forum for discussions and networking among Muslim lawyers, this organization has now evolved into a formal organization addressing the needs of the burgeoning Muslim legal community. Its annual conferences have covered topics of interest to those following the legal situation of Muslims in the USA, both in terms of Islamic and US law.[95] Moreover, the searchable online database of Muslim attorneys provided on NAML's website is a significant contribution to the Muslim community at large, providing a readily usable contact list of legal professionals who are also sensitive to Muslim family norms.

The increased use of web-based communication has greatly contributed to the formation and expansion of unprecedented and spontaneous debates on Muslim family law issues such as marriage, divorce and child custody. In addition to the domestic impact of discussion groups such as the NAML email list, the use of web-pages to disseminate various new doctrines and religious rulings has had a tremendous effect on the international discussion of Islamic family law. The active nature of the American Muslim community online has placed it in an influential position in these global discussions of Islam and Islamic law. For example, during the Bosnian war, a Muslim website based in the US, <islam.org>, posted two religious rulings on abortion. The website rulings had an impact on the question of abortion within an international context by providing differing perspectives from various sources (Watanabe 2000; <www.islam.org>). In countries where the government or a specific group of scholars control a religious hegemony and discourage divergent interpretations and views, these types of diverse perspectives accessible via the internet can revolutionize the way that individuals view a certain topic.

The US Muslim experience is contextualized in a democratic, secular society. Women have emerged as an integral part of the Muslim activist and intellectual movements, as noted earlier in this study, especially in the areas of issues involving domestic violence and abuse of women in general. Muslim women have not only served as activists and community organizers; they have also been able to offer their perspective on relevant legal issues. In the United States, scholars such as Amina Wadud are able to publish their interpretations of the Qur'an openly and share them with the wider Muslim community (Wadud 1999). Furthermore, American Muslim scholars such as Aminah Beverly McCloud present the reality of a dynamic and living form of Islam within the African-American Muslim community (McCloud 1991). With voices like these in the community, immigrant Muslims cannot limit their interpretations to those scholars who exclusively represent their country or their school of thought. A back-home focused approach is thus challenged by indigenous and second-generation communities that are already fully aware of and dealing with modern Western society.[96]

FOURTEEN
Conclusion

§ THIS survey has sought to catalogue and explain the nature and application of Islamic family law within the US Muslim community. The potential of this community is evident by the wide range and depth of its contributions in this area. This study has demonstrated that Islamic family law as manifested in the United States has been a subject of significant interest and considerable complexity, both in terms of US domestic and Islamic law, as well as their interaction. In the previous chapter, we have seen that within the United States are significant trends of reform and activism addressing Islamic family law. Yet it is important to keep in mind that these reform efforts also face several potential problems as they progress. For example, one of the main concerns that the Muslim community shares with other religious groups in the United States is the recognition that forward-thinking actions and scholarship that steer away from religious orthodoxy may lose acceptance by the mainstream faith-based system. In a parallel situation, the Jewish orthodox community has, at times, refused to accept terms that do not conform to a traditional understanding of religious rights when those rights were negotiated in a *ketubah*, or religious pre-nuptial agreement (Greenberg-Kobrin 1999: 397).

Another major potential problem lies in the need to differentiate between culture and religion. Enmeshed in this particular question is the role of cultural practice and interpretation. While a cultural practice may actually protect the family rights of an individual, when the family serves as a negotiating representative in marriages, it is possible that a cultural pattern of family interaction can be more limiting than the constraints actually set by religious law (Hashim, interview, 2000).[97] The Muslim community will have to sift through its multi-cultural history and traditions and decide which practices will be preserved and which will be discarded if they do not fit an appropriate religious and societal agenda. Creation of a unified agenda or perspective will remain a challenge for this community. At the heart of this issue is the fact that there remain on-going internal debates in the United States' Muslim community as to who should be in charge or involved in formulation of community-wide agendas. In some instances, gender has remained a barrier to the full involvement of Muslim women. Different cultural practices are reflected in women's space in a mosque. For instance, *The Mosque in America* report notes that there is an increasing practice of separating women in prayer from men by a hung cloth, or having them pray in another room (Bagby et al. 2001: 11).[98] While this is not definitive evidence that women are not a part of the general community space, it is interesting to note that there is an increasing trend towards gender segregation in the mosque environment. The study did not reach the conclusion that certain cultural groups had higher levels of segregation in their mosques. This would be a relevant topic to explore in future studies and would provide an analytical tool to differentiate between cultural variables that affect gender participation and religious interpretations that are used to justify segregation. Finally, the reality of class differences among Muslim Americans has been an ongoing divide. For instance, the actions of the immigrant Muslim community have included acknowledgement that they 'had been guilty of ignoring the persistent and social problems of the indigenous Muslims' (Dannin 2000: 26).

Another important challenge for the future of Islamic family law in the United States stems from the demographic of Muslims. This report, in talking about Islamic family law in the USA, has assumed a certain level of adherence and belief in Islam as a legitimate organizing system for one's life and society. We have mentioned the several varieties of interpretation of Islamic law among the diverse Muslims in the United States, but there is also significant variation in levels of adherence to Islam as a source for behaviour in the first place. As noted in both Haddad and Lummis and the Mosque project, Muslim practice ranges from those who are 'unmosqued' to those who attend holiday prayers, and those who are more involved in their particular communities (Lummis and Haddad 1987: 9; Bagby et al. 2001: 3). It will be a challenge for Muslim scholars and activists in America to bring together these different types of Muslims and develop a consensus, especially in the volatile area of family law that touches on intimate interpersonal relationships and deep moral values. This is the ultimate challenge for any minority faith: to adhere firmly to its values and traditions while also adapting to the social, legal and cultural contexts in which it exists.

APPENDIX
Table of cases

US Supreme Court cases

Bradwell v. Illinois, 83 US 130 (1873)

Federal Court cases

Shikoh v. Shikoh, 257 F.2d 306 (2d Cir. 1958)

State Court cases

Adra v. Clift, 195 F. Supp. 857 (D. Md. 1961)
Aghili v. Saadatnejadi, 958 S.W.2d 784 (Ct. App. Tenn. 1997)
Ahmed v. Ahmed, 689 N.Y.S.2d 357 (Sup. Ct. NY 1999)
Akileh v. Elchahal, 666 So.2d 246 (Fla Ct. App. 1996)
Ali v. Ali, 652 A.2d 253 (NJ Sup. Ct. 1994)
Arain v. Arain, 209 A.D.2d 406 (1994)
Aziz v. Aziz, 488 N.Y.S.2d 123 (NY Sup. Ct. 1985)
Dajani v. Dajani, 204 Cal. App. 3d 1387 (1988)
Farah v. Farah, 429 S.E.2d 626 (Ct. App. VA 1993)
Habibi-Fahnrich v. Fahnrich, WL 507388 (NY Sup. 1995)
Hosain v. Malik, 671 A.2d 988 (Ct. App. Md. 1996)
In Re Marriage of Murga, 103 Cal. App. 3d 498 (1980)
Jabri v. Jabri, 598 N.Y.S. 2d 535, 537 (1993)
Kapigian v. Der Minassian, 99 N.E. 264 (Mass. Sup. Ct. 1912)
Maklad v. Maklad, WL 51662 (Conn. Super. Jan. 3, 2001)
Malak v. Malak, 182 Cal. App. 3d 1018 (1986)
Mehtar v. Mehtar, 1997 Conn. Super. LEXIS 2400
NY v. Benu, 385 N.Y.S.2d (Crim. Ct. NY 1976)
Odatalla v. Odatalla, 810 A.2d 93 (NJ Super. 2002)
Ohio v. Awkal, 667 N.E.2d 960 (Sup. Ct. Ohio 1996)
Seth v. Seth, 694 S.W.2d 459 (Ct. App. TX 1985)
Shaban v. Shaban, 88 Cal. App. 4th 398 (2001)
Shike v. Shike, Tex. App. LEXIS 2733 (April 27, 2000)
Shikoh v. Shikoh, 257 F.2d 306 (2d Cir. 1958)
Tazziz v. Tazziz, 533 N.E.2d 202 (Mass. App. Ct. 1988)
Vryonis v. Vryonis, 202 Cal. App. 3d 712 (CA Ct. App. 1988)
Zummo v. Zummo, 574 A.2d 1130 (Pa. 1990)

Notes to Part III

Our sincere thanks to Steve Vieux and Abed Awad for their helpful research assistance, and to all those who shared their experiences and expertise in our interviews with them (see attached interview list).

1. Anglo-American family law itself has religious Christian origins, as acknowledged in *Bradwell v. Illinois*, 83 US 130 (1873), where the Supreme Court described the 'divine ordinance' of the 'constitution of the family organization' (ibid., 141; Mason 1994: 53); but this aspect of US law will not be elaborated here.

2. The research material for this study is comprised of: interviews with professionals who serve the US Muslim community, legal research of current United States federal and state case law, review of general literature (books, magazines, newspapers) addressing issues concerning Muslims in the United States, internet searches of Muslim-related sites, and the professional experiences of the authors. As the research time was constrained due to publication deadlines, the report is itself quite limited, and makes no claim to be exhaustive of all issues, resources, scholars and other elements potentially relevant to this topic. For surveys conducted by other sources, see Haddad and Lummis (1987). Haddad and Lummis studied eight mosques located in the Midwest, upstate New York and the East Coast over a period of two years. They focused on personal backgrounds and religious attitudes of the seventy to eighty participants in the study. Haddad and Lummis surveyed 346 Muslims, 64 per cent of whom were immigrants, and 16 per cent were children of immigrant parents. Thirty-four per cent of their sample were Lebanese American, 28 per cent were Pakistanis, with individuals from other Arab nations comprising the remainder of the sample. Another useful and more recent study is *The Mosque in America: A National Portrait* (Bagby et al. 2001), sponsored by a number of Muslim organizations and part of a larger study of American congregations coordinated by Hartford Seminary's Hartford Institute for Religious Research. The project included a random sampling from 1,209 mosques across the United States, based on responses from 416 mosque leaders. The new survey showed African Americans were the dominant ethnic group in 27 per cent of mosques, South Asians in 28 per cent and Arabs in 15 per cent, with the remaining mosques described as 'pluralistic' (ibid., p. 3). See <http://fact.hartsem.edu> for further information.

3. See American Muslim Council (1992). The number of Muslims in the USA continues to be an unsettled issue. Haddad and Lummis (1987: 3) noted that these might be between 2 and 3 million. The Mosque in America project findings reflect 2 million Muslims who attend or participate in mosques to a varying degree, with an overall estimate of 6–7 million Muslims present in the USA (Bagby et al. 2001: 3). One of the supreme challenges for counting the number of Muslims in the USA is the fact that there remains a large, as identified by Haddad and Lummis (1987: 9), 'unmosqued' proportion of the population who not have a direct and regular affiliation with a mosque.

4. See Quraishi (2001); Al-'Alwani (1993: chapter on *Ikhtilaf*); Abou el-Fadl (1997: 18) notes the belief that 'a major contributing factor to the diversity of Islamic theological and legal schools is the acceptance and reverence given to the idea of *ikhtilaf* (disagreement)'.

5. See Sciolino (1996) on different 'versions' of Islamic law regarding marriage.

6. See Haddad and Lummis (1987) for a discussion on imams in the United States.

7. Azam's 'The Muslim Marriage Guide', at <http://www.beliefnet.com/story/73/story_7319_1.html> (reviewing Maqsood 1998).

8. See for example the articles by Raga El Nimr and Najla Hamadeh in Yamani (1996).

9. See <http://www.mwlusa.org> The Muslim Women's League is based in Los Angeles, California. Other Muslim women's organizations interested in similar work include the DC-based Georgetown Muslim Women's Study Project (organized to review the UN Platform for Action prior to the 1995 Beijing Fourth UN World Conference on Women), and the North American Council for Muslim Women (NACMW), based in Virginia, which was launched in 1992 with a large national conference.

10. See <http://www.karamah.org>

11. See <http://www.alsalafyoon.com>

12. The fora email is sisters@post.queensu.ca

13. See <http://www.studyislam.com>

14. Similarly, the Canadian Society of Muslims includes on its website many sources of Islamic jurisprudence, as well as articles on 'Family Matters' addressing such topics as birth control and abortion, adoption, custody and guardianship, polygamy, arranged marriage, and women's rights in an 'Islamic prenuptial agreement'. See <http://www.canada-muslim.org>

15. See <http://www.domini.org/lam>

16. See al-Khateeb (1996: 15). Similarly, another source says: 'The Islamic marriage contract is meant to solidify bond and specify stipulations that are important to both parties. The contract is intended to safeguard present and future legal rights of both the husband and wife, should encourage marital harmony, and should keep the family within the boundaries of the Qur'an and Sunna for the pleasure of Allah.' See 'Cont ... The Marriage Contract' at <http://geocities.com/lailah2000/contract2.html>

17. 'A Conference on the Islamic Marriage Contract', Harvard Law School Islamic Legal Studies Program, 29–31 January 1999.

18. For popular dissemination of this information, see al-Khateeb (1996) for a list of sample stipulations and Mills for similar suggestions. For a more detailed, academic discussion of contract stipulations, including specific examples, see Welchman (2000: 35), Shaham (1995: 464) and Abou el-Fadl (1999).

19. Compare Mills who leaves out Islamic jurisprudential differences in a list of suggested stipulations in the marriage contract with Abou el-Fadl (1999) who explains general Hanbali allowances of contractual stipulations, compared with other schools' reluctance on the same, and their use of legal devices created to accomplish similar goals.

20. See <http://www.karamah.org/projects/index.php>

21. See al-Hibri (1997: 28) who notes differing validity depending on school of thought; Welchman (2000: 167); and Carroll (1982: 277).

22. See the article, 'An Islamic Perspective on Divorce', at <http://www.mwlusa.org/pub_divorce.html> Similarly, the Muslim Women's League points out that classical custody laws (deciding custody based on abstract rules of the age and gender of the child) are among those that must 'adapt to dynamic circumstances', commenting that there is 'no Qur'anic text to substantiate the arbitrary choosing of age as a determinant for custody'. The League urges similar flexibility in determining alimony awards as well.

23. See *Akileh v. Elchahal* (1996), a case involving two separate marriage contracts – an

Islamic *sadaq* and a civil ceremony the following day incorporating the *sadaq* document specifying the wife's dower; *Ahmed v. Ahmed* (1999), distinguishing religious ceremony from civil; *Ohio v. Awkal* (1996), describing two separate marriage ceremonies, civil and Islamic, on separate dates; *Dajani v. Dajani* (1988), involving a Jordanian couple married by proxy in Jordan, followed by a civil ceremony in the USA upon the wife's arrival; and the al-Sarraf interview (2000) in which the lawyer describes Muslim couples generally having a Muslim ceremony first, and then taking care of state requirements.

24. See *Tazziz v. Tazziz* (1988), a marriage ceremony in the United States, in accordance with Islamic law; *NY v. Benu* (1976), a marriage performed by a local New York City imam not authorized in a city clerk's office to perform marriages; the Awad interview (2000), in which the lawyer describes mosques in New York and New Jersey performing weddings with no state licensing; and McCloud (2000: 140) who urges Muslim women in the USA to get civil documents of both marriage and divorce. Some US Muslims, less concerned with Islamic law *per se*, may have only the civil ceremony, forgoing the Muslim one entirely, but these cases do not fall within the subject of this study.

25. See *Farah v. Farah* (1993) (deferred *mahr* of $20,000); *Akileh v. Elchahal* (1996) (immediate *sadaq* of $1 and deferred $50,000; noting that when he proposed, the husband 'recognized that wife had the right to a *sadaq*'); *NY v. Benu* (1976) (sewing machine as dower).

26. See also marriage contracts on file with author (Quraishi). Islamic history verifies the use of non-monetary *mahr*. For example, a *hadith* from the Prophet explicitly validates the teaching of sections of the Qur'an (Doi 1984: 163) and the *shahada* (declaration of Islamic faith) of the groom as dower; see Ibn Sa'd (1997: 279) describing Umm Sulaim's marriage to Abu Talha, and stating that 'her dower was the Islam of Abu Talha'.

27. Kadri comments (interview, 2000) on her experience with clients whose only interest in attempting to enforce a *mahr* provision is in unfriendly divorce proceedings, with the demand for a high *mahr* being used as an opportunity to punish the husband.

28. See listserve email discussions on 'Sistersnet' (sisters@post.queensu.ca) in 1996–98 (notes on file with author Quraishi).

29. Ali (1996) comments that when divorce litigation is bitterly contested by a Muslim husband, it is often not because he does not want a divorce, but rather because he does not want to pay the *mahr*.

30. Kadri comments (interview, 2000) that brides and grooms tend simply to fill in *mahr* provision in standard boilerplate contracts and rarely add specified provisions. Similarly in interviews with four Muslim family lawyers, none reported seeing any particularized contracts of this sort (Awad, interview, 2000; al-Sarraf, interview, 2000; and Kadri, interview, 2000).

31. Email message to Karamah responding to Marriage Contract Project announcement (on file with author Quraishi). Another visitor to the website expressed dismay at not having a formal marriage contract written at her wedding, and asked if it is possible to create one retroactively.

32. See <http://www.karamah.org>

33. This is also the position of Mona Zulfikar, who spearheaded the marriage contract legislative efforts in Egypt. She says one of the most important aspects is to 'encourage frankness, mutual understanding and dialogue between the spouses, reduce the need to have recourse to the courts in difficult and bitter litigation procedures' (Zulfikar and al-Sadda 1996: 251; and cited in Welchman 2000: 181).

34. This is indicated by four out of the nine couples for whom one author (Quraishi) provided marriage contract information.

35. One of the brides assisted by this author (Quraishi) writes: 'It wasn't always easy to discuss the topics of our contract but in the end the entire process has brought me and … my fiancé so much closer and we have grown stronger' (personal email on file with author).

36. Quoting Samia el-Moslimany saying: 'I put in that the burden of domestic chores was going to be shared by both of us … My father thought it was trivial, but I wanted it in the contract.'

37. See *Aghili v. Saadatnejadi* (1997) in which $10,000 damages was provided as a remedy to the wife if the husband breaches contract.

38. See the position paper, 'Marriage on Islam', at <http://www.mwlusa.org>

39. Noting that over a third of the respondents reported marriages of Muslim women to non-Muslim men in their families; and noting that the number of Muslim men marrying non-Muslim women is larger.

40. 'Some Muslim women whom we interviewed expressed the opinion that the man's freedom to marry outside the faith is neither fair nor conducive to preserving the Islamic faith in future generations born in America' (Haddad and Lummis 1987: 146). Marquand (1996) quotes a father saying: 'I will have a huge problem if my son marries a non-Muslim … and will do everything I can do to stop it.'

41. See the article, 'Why Muslim man should not marry a non-Muslim woman', at <http://www.soundvision.com/marriage/nonmuslimwoman>

42. In one extreme example, Marquand (1996) reports some members of one Muslim community sought to displace a leader whose daughters had married non-Muslims, arguing that such a failure should cause him to lose his status in the community.

43. For example, says one Muslim woman, 'I love the religion with all my heart, but I don't like that the women don't have choice' (Todd 1997).

44. Mahmoody (1993); *Not Without My Daughter*, MGM Studios, 1991. This movie depicts the true story of Betty Mahmoody's escape from Iran with her daughter after her Iranian husband attempted to turn a two-week vacation into a permanent relocation of the family.

45. See <http://www.travel.state.gov/abduct.html>

46. See <http://www.travel.state.gov./islamic_family_law.html>

47. For more information about such stereotyping, see for example Shaheen 1997. In addition, refer to the online sources of the Council of Islamic–American Relations at <http://www.cairnet.org> and the Anti-Arab Discrimination Committee which can be found at <http://www.adc.org>

48. Betty Mahmoody (see above note 44) has herself served as an expert witness in a few cases involving Muslim marriages (Gustafson 1991).

49. Describing a 'traditional Muslim wedding in Walnut', including many things not included in other Muslim ceremonies, such as dancing, singing, bride and groom sitting side by side, and the bride's head covered.

50. Marquand (1996) quotes one Muslim saying, 'Sometimes male domination is machismo, sometimes it is genuine faith'.

51. Winton (1993) reports the story of a severely injured Muslim woman stating that her husband believed Islam allowed him to beat her.

52. Memon (1993) provides a summary of Islamic texts (including Qur'an 4: 34) used to justify battery, showing the misinterpretations by those who do so, and urges the American Muslim community to recognize and fight against domestic violence in their community.

53. Kadri (interview, 2000) notes a conversation with a woman complaining of her son beating her but who would not complain of such actions by her husband because she believed it was his right to do so. Attorney Kamran Memon (1993) notes that some imams tell these women to be patient and pray for the abuse to end, urging them not to leave their husbands and break up the family, and not break family privacy by talking about it to others.

54. Also featured on <http://www.zawaj.com>

55. These include (as a very brief sampling) the National Islamic Society of Women in America (NISWA) <http://www.niswa.org>; Baitul Salaam (House of Peace) <http://alnisaa1.hypermart.net> PO Box 11041 Atlanta, GA 30310; Kamilat, <http://www.Kamilat.org>; Karamah: Muslim Women Lawyers for Human Rights <http://www.Karamah.org>; the Muslim Women's League (who co-sponsored the Los Angeles conference of the Peaceful Families Project) <http://www.mwlusa.org>; and Muslims Against Family Violence, a project of 'Stepping Together' <http://www.steppingtogether.org>

56. In *Seth v. Seth* (1985), a non-Muslim male had converted to Islam after a marriage contracted under US civil law and subsequently divorced this wife by *talaq* and married a Muslim woman in a Muslim ceremony. In *Shikoh v. Shikoh* (1958), the husband, an Indian national, declared divorce before a Brooklyn imam before witnesses, signed and sent a copy of the imam's documentation of the declaration, entitled 'certificate of divorce', to the wife who was in Pakistan.

57. Little reports family lawyer Ahmed A. Patel saying that he reminds his clients who perform *talaq* divorces that they cannot remarry under US law.

58. Community property states in the USA include: Arizona, California, Idaho, Louisiana, Nevada, New Mexico, Texas, Washington and Wisconsin; income and property earned or acquired during marriage is divided equally between the two spouses upon dissolution, even if one spouse was the predominant source of income. Allen (1992) quotes a Minneapolis imam stating that 'in Muslim marriages, there is no notion of community property; whatever a woman earns outside the home she may keep, but a man is obligated to support his family'.

59. One encouraging case exhibits respect by one court for a religiously-motivated provision opting out of community property laws. In *Mehtar v. Mehtar* (1997), a Connecticut court upheld a Muslim couple's pre-nuptial agreement opting out of South African community property laws (the marriage contract was executed in South Africa), stating that 'the purpose of the agreement was to comply with principles of Muslim law held by both parties' and holding that the requirement of financial disclosure usually required to validate such opt-out clauses in Connecticut 'would be unfair to apply ... to an agreement mutually sought to honour deeply held religious beliefs'.

60. Iran is a primary example. Ayatollah Mohsen Kadivar has been quoted as saying: 'a woman should be paid by her husband for working in the house, for cleaning, for breast-feeding. She can even say "I don't want to do this work, I need a servant," and her husband has to pay for this. This is in Islam, that he has to do this' (Walter 1999).

61. The vast majority of family law cases are never published, and therefore are largely unavailable as a subject of research. Thus, most of the cases discussed in the chapter are appellate court cases, which may or may not be representative of Muslim family litigation in the United States. Moreover, family law cases are almost always a matter of individual state jurisdiction and thus the case precedent of one state does not bind another. The review of the cases in this study does, however, provide a good idea of the established persuasive and precedential authority to which a judge might turn in evaluating future cases.

62. For example, without citation to case law, Amina Beverly McCloud (2000: 140)

states that marriages of Muslim immigrants to the United States 'have generally received the protection of the courts' because 'marriage contracts are understood as pre-nuptial or nuptial agreements'. Similarly, Imam Yusuf Ziya Kavakci, the imam of a Texas mosque, urges Muslims to get pre-nuptial agreements because they can be used to 'safeguard your Islamic rights within a marriage and, if necessary, in the case of a divorce'. See 'Why You Need a Prenuptial Agreement' at <http://www.soundvision.com/weddings/prenuptial>.

63.   This attitude is probably culturally-influenced. Under Islamic law, once the offer and acceptance have been made (both usually included in a *nikah* ceremony), the couple is legally married. Because many Muslim couples sign the contract (*kitab* or *nikah*) at one ceremony but do not begin to live together until some later date, however, many believe themselves to be only 'engaged' after the *nikah*.

64.   See <http://www.Karamah.org> (audiotape also on file with author Quraishi).

65.   See *NY v. Benu* (1976) in which the mother was charged for contributing to the delinquency of her minor daughters, who were placed in foster care with a Muslim family, and the men who 'married' the girls were charged with first degree sexual assault of a child.

66.   Rasmusen and Stake (1998) comment: 'even if it does not offend public policy, courts are reluctant to enforce such terms because of the costs to the courts, the difficulty of enforcement without invading the sanctity of the marital home, and the possibility that enforcement would increase conflict within the marriage'.

67.   The court elaborated: 'the Mahr Agreement in the case at bar is nothing more and nothing less than a simple contract between two consenting adults. It does not contravene any statute or interests of society. Rather, the Mahr Agreement continues a custom and tradition that is unique to a certain segment of our current society and is not at war with any public morals' (*Odatella* at 98).

68.   In the cases reviewed below, for example, spouses asserting the enforceability of a Muslim marriage contract as a pre-nuptial agreement did not always succeed. In both California cases dealing with *mahr* claims as pre-nuptial agreements, *Dajani* and *Shaban*, the court ultimately refused to honour the contract. In New York and Florida, the parties fared a bit better: in *Aziz* (NY) and *Akileh* (FL) the Muslim dower provisions were upheld, though the language of the Florida court indicates that they perceived the *sadaq* to be the husband's consideration for entering into the contract, an analysis with which Awad would strongly disagree.

69.   Welchman (2000: 140) comments that a majority of jurists consider *mahr* to be an 'effect of the contract'.

70.   For example, Al-Khateeb (1996) includes a form titled 'Islamic marriage contract/ pre-nuptial agreement'.

71.   Pre-nuptial agreements also generally may not include provisions relating to child custody and child support.

72.   Al-Hibri points out that one might just as well interpret *mahr* provisions as facilitating murder – a conclusion just as ludicrous as the *Dajani* court's conclusion regarding divorce.

73.   Of course, she may be able to keep it if she goes through judicial dissolution, in which case the question of harm will be assessed by the arbiter, but this process is generally much longer and entails a burden of proof upon her.

74.   The court refers to the entire marriage contract, rather than the dower provision only, as a *sadaq*.

75.   Incidentally, and unfortunately, the marriage contract at issue in this case is very similar to generic boilerplate contracts distributed and used by many American mosques (samples on file with author Quraishi).

76. The court went on to say: 'Had the trial judge allowed the expert to testify, the expert in effect would have written a contract for the parties.'

77. Later, the Florida Court of Appeals in *Akileh v. Elchahal* (1996), when first confronted with the question of enforceability of a Muslim marriage contract, cited *Aziz v. Aziz* (1985) favourably and upheld a Muslim dower provision because it found that Florida contract law applied to the secular terms of the Muslim contract. The Florida court found that, even though the husband and wife later disagreed over the meaning of the *sadaq* (the husband claimed that his understanding was that women always forfeited the *mahr* if they initiated the divorce), there was a clear agreement at the outset of the marriage that *sadaq* was to be paid if the parties divorced, and the court honoured that agreement.

For reference back to our earlier discussion of the treatment of these contracts as pre-nuptial agreements, in the reported opinion, the New York court does not refer to the contract in *Aziz* as a 'pre-nuptial agreement', but in *Akileh* (1996), the Florida court references *Aziz* as a case enforcing the *sadaq* as a pre-nuptial agreement.

78. Moreover, it might be argued that a rationale for the institution of the deferred *mahr* provision is the fact that most husbands will be better placed to pay high amounts later on in their careers, also part of the rationale for community property laws.

79. *Shaban* happened to involve a very low *mahr* amount and thus it was the husband who sought enforcement of the marriage contract. The court went so far as to say that the wife performed under the contract by entering into the marriage, and this constituted sufficient consideration on her part.

80. For a comparative view of the judicial treatment of *mahr* in Germany, see Jones-Pauly (1999). For analysis of Muslim marriage cases in the UK, see Freeland and Lau (forthcoming); and Pearl (1985–86, 1995).

81. See *Aghili v. Saadatnejadi* (1997), 786 (likening *sadaq* to maintenance); *Akileh v. Elchahal* (1996), 247 (*sadaq* is a postponed dower that protects the woman in the event of a divorce); *Dajani v. Dajani* (1988), 872 (commenting that one purpose of the dower is to provide security for the wife in the event of death or dissolution, but also can be an outright gift).

82. See *Aghili v. Saadatnejadi* (1997), 786 n. 1 (commenting that *sadaq* was meant to protect the wife from unwanted divorce); *Shaban* (2001), n. 6.

83. See *Dajani v. Dajani*, 872.

84. This assertion is supported by the court's reasoning in, for example, *Maklad v. Maklad* (2001), where the court declined to give comity to an Egyptian certificate of divorce because the wife was not present at the time the decree was issued, had no prior notice that the certificate was sought, and was given no opportunity to be heard prior to its issuance.

85. Clearly not all Muslims subscribe to this as the only legitimate means of determining custody, but classical Islamic jurists addressed custody in these terms as the safest way of determining that the child will be placed with the best custodian. Some American Muslims argue for a different rule, pointing out that this is a jurisprudential invention, not one directly dictated by the original texts (see Muslim Women's League, 'Divorce'). It is, however, the classical Islamic custody rules that are most well known and are what is at issue in these cases (though often in modified form through modern legislation in these Muslim countries).

86. See also *Adra v. Clift* (1961), where the court upheld a custody decree from Lebanon.

87. Conversely, religion has been counted as a negative influence if it harms the child; see *In Re Marriage of Murga* (1980).

88. For an extensive discussion on the precursors to modern Muslim discourse in the area of Islamic jurisprudence, see Hallaq (1997).

89. At the second 'Islam in America' conference, 9–11 March 2001, at Harvard University, one panel was titled 'Feasibility of Muslim Courts/Tribunals in the United States'. A mainstream US television network even recently presented a fictionalized version of what one of these tribunals might look like, in an episode of the television show *JAG* ('The Princess and the Petty Officer', 14 November 2000, written by Mark Saraceni).

90. Various Muslim organizations in the United States have explored conflict resolution issues within the realm of an Islamic framework, for example, the Islamic Society of North America has held annual training conferences on conflict resolution. The organization scheduled a conference titled, 'Muslim Peacebuilding after 9/11' in 2003. For more information on such efforts, see <www.isna.net>

91. In particular, when one waives the right of pursuing litigation in court, the contract must be an 'objective manifestation of a party's intent to be bound by the religious court's decree and the party knowingly and voluntarily waived his rights to pursue litigation in secular court without any religious group's interference' (Weisberg 1992: 995).

92. For example, see the website, 'American Muslims Intent on Learning and Activism', at <http://www.amila.org> for their mission statement which states 'AMILA was formed in October 1992 by Muslims of college age and above to meet the spiritual, educational, political, and social needs of Muslims in the San Francisco Bay Area. We are working towards building an active American Muslim community with a strong commitment to spiritual enrichment, intellectual freedom, and community service.' AMILA's lectures, projects and activities reflect a progressive attitude towards claiming Islam as a vibrant American identity.

93. For example, Karamah recently participated (15 October 1999) in a panel of women of faith entitled 'Religion and World Conflict'. The event was organized by the International Women's Forum. See 'news and events' section at <http://www.karamah.org/news/index.php>

94. See <http://www.namlnet.org> There are also a few local city-based Muslim bar associations with similar focus, for example in Chicago and the DC area.

95. See <http://www.namlnet.org>

96. 'On the other hand is the generation of children and grandchildren who have no emotional ties to the homeland of the fathers and find little of value in their customs which are seen as counterproductive and an impediment to the progress in the society in which they are born' (ISIM 1998: 5).

97. As a teacher in a Muslim school, Hashim notes that parents from a specific cultural background would not allow female children to spend the night even for activities such as prayer outside of the home due to their interpretation of proper cultural gender roles. Eventually, she states, when parents were able to see that 'the religious teachings, in fact, promoted the practice of seeking opportunities to worship God', they did decide to allow their daughters to pursue such activities.

98. They compared statistics from 1994 with 2001 responses, noting that the proportion of mosques with separation by curtain, barrier or another room had increased to 60–66 per cent of those surveyed in 2001.

Interviews

1. Sermid al-Sarraf, family and estate planning attorney, Los Angeles, California, 8 December 2000.

2. Abed Awad, family law attorney, Nutley, New Jersey, 14 November 2000.

3. Sydney Ericson, family law attorney, Brea, California, 1 October 2001.

4. Jinan Hashim, teacher in an Islamic elementary school, Chicago, Illinois, 7 December 2001.

5. Cherrefe Kadri, family law attorney, Toledo, Ohio, 5 December 2000.

6. Tayibba Taylor, editor, *Azizah* magazine, Atlanta, Georgia, 12 October 2000.

Part IV

Domestic Violence and *Shari'a*: a Comparative Study of Muslim Societies in the Middle East, Africa and Asia

Lisa Hajjar

Introduction

§ ON 12 March 2000, some 300,000 demonstrators took to the streets of Rabat, Morocco, expressing their support for a proposed new law that would expand women's rights, including their right to divorce. Simultaneously, a comparable number of demonstrators took to the streets of the nearby city of Casablanca to protest the law as a deviation from *shari'a* (Islamic law). While divorce is a permissible and established option in Islam, in many Muslim societies it tends to be treated as a male prerogative; women can easily *be* divorced, but not *seek* divorce.[1] The proposed new Moroccan law aimed to lessen this gender imbalance,[2] sparking the competing demonstrations that, together, offer anecdotal evidence of sharply divergent views on Muslim women's rights.

Opponents of the new law framed their position as a defence of religion and the family, claiming that the law conflicts with women's duties to their husbands, and contravenes their *shari'a*-based status. Supporters heralded the new law as an advance for women, not (necessarily) a repudiation of *shari'a*. Those who had been working for years to bring such a law into being were seeking to alter women's status as perennial subordinates in the context of the family. Indeed, the law's significance, recognized by opponents and supporters alike, was its potential for eroding masculine privilege, albeit slightly, by enhancing women's options to end a marriage. But the controversy marked by the huge demonstrations intimidated the government, and the law was withdrawn (Maghroui 2001: 16–17).

In Morocco, as elsewhere, one of the most common reasons women would seek to end a marriage is to extricate themselves from a harmful situation. Support and advocacy for women's right to divorce are connected to women's vulnerability to domestic violence.[3] Indeed, the Moroccan law had been drafted in response to a recently published report with alarming statistics about the status of women, including 28,000 reported acts of domestic violence between 1984 and 1998 (ibid., p. 16).

Domestic violence can be defined as 'violence that occurs within the private sphere, generally between individuals who are related through intimacy, blood or law … [It is] nearly always a gender-specific crime, perpetrated by men against women' (Coomaraswamy 1996). One of the strongest predictors of violence against women is the restriction on women's ability to leave the family setting (Levinson 1989).[4] But, as most women's rights activists would concede, divorce does not constitute an adequate form of protection, or even an option for many women. Myriad factors discourage, impede or prevent women from leaving a violent relationship, including a lack of resources or support to establish alternative domestic arrangements, and powerful social expectations and pressures to maintain family relations at any cost.

In this study, the central question concerns the relationship between domestic violence and *shari'a*. This relationship is of critical importance because *shari'a* provides both the legal framework for administering family relations and a religio-cultural framework for social norms and values in Muslim societies. As the example of demonstrations over the Moroccan law illustrates, there are strong interconnections between gender relations, religion and law. The example also illustrates the challenges to pursuing legal reforms to enhance women's rights, and the ability – indeed, the likelihood – that constituencies with different interests and perspectives will mobilize and compete for state support.

This study seeks to provide an analytical framework and a comparative assessment of domestic violence in Muslim societies in the Middle East, Africa and Asia. The approach is socio-legal, probing the functions and uses of religious and other bodies of law, and tracing struggles over the rights of women in the context of domestic relations. Given the importance and attention devoted to the relationship between women's rights and Islam, to date surprisingly little comparative analysis has been generated about the relationship between domestic violence and *shari'a*. This study is an effort to redress this lacuna.

FIFTEEN

Domestic violence and *shari'a*

Section 1. Gender (in)equality, women's rights and the problem of domestic violence

Inequalities between men and women are common the world over, albeit the forms and conditions vary and change. It is a nearly universal truism that gender *matters* in ways that make and keep women relatively less free, less independent, less empowered, less financially and physically secure than men.

The arena where gender inequalities are most entrenched, in the context of family relations, is also where they are most widely accepted and thus most difficult to alter. Sexual and other physical differences between men and women lend themselves to understandings of social inequalities as both derivative of and conforming to 'nature', especially in terms of family roles and relations. Such understandings prevail in many cultures. But the challenges of contesting and altering inequalities are compounded in societies where gender and family relations are governed by religious laws, because the resultant hierarchies can be defended as divinely sanctioned.

Debates over the legitimacy of gender equality have been especially vigorous in Muslim societies, and display some common patterns related to *shari'a*.[5] The Qur'an, which believers accept as the literal word of God and thus eternally applicable, contains many verses that would seem inescapably discriminatory towards women. So, too, do many of the *hadith* (sayings by and reports about the Prophet Muhammad). Yet there are also many Qur'anic verses and *hadith* establishing the equality of men and women. These seeming contradictions lend themselves to multiple readings, claims and counter-claims about what Islam prescribes for women.[6]

The use of *shari'a* to administer family relations[7] contributes to certain commonalities in gender relations across Muslim societies, notably the privileging and empowerment of men over women within the context of the family. However, it is important to note significant variations as well. In engaging a comparative analysis, the state is the most important variable for understanding variations across societies, since, in the modern era, the state is the primary arbiter of law. State power is deployed to regulate gender and family relations, as well as the role of religion in society. Across the three regions that are the focus of this study, the history and politics of the state – that is, the specific experiences and legacies of colonial rule, and the trajectories of national independence, integration and development – have given rise to vastly different state projects and agendas in regard to gender relations, law and religion, and the relationships between them. 'State formation affects the position of women in society in several ways. In particular, the state mediates gender relations through the law ... in its attempts to foster or inhibit social change, to maintain existing arrangements or to promote greater equality for women in the family and the society at large' (Charrad 1990: 20).

The role of the state is particularly important to any discussion of domestic violence because of its capacity and responsibility for regulating (i.e., prohibiting, punishing etc.) violence. For the purpose of this study, which focuses on (and is limited to) relations and practices governed by *shari'a*, the categories of domestic violence considered here include, *inter alia*, beatings, battery and murder; marital rape; and forced marriage.

When violence occurs within the context of the family, it raises questions about the laws and legal administration of family relations. Are violent practices among family members legally permitted or prohibited? In practice, is violence ignored, tolerated or penalized? Do perpetrators enjoy impunity (whether de jure or de facto) or do they stand to be punished? Are civil remedies available to victims (e.g. right to divorce, restraining orders)?

In the 1970s, women's rights activists in many Western societies began pursuing an agenda (generally successfully) of bringing criminal law to bear on intra-family violence.[8] One outcome was to open up the 'private sphere' of the family to increased state intervention, at least in principle, by establishing prohibitions and punishments for violence between family members. Criminalization undermines the ability of perpetrators to claim that what they do at home is a 'private' matter. The model of criminalizing domestic violence has become a popular goal in other parts of the world as well.[9]

> Advocates of the criminal justice approach point to the symbolic power of the law and argue that arrest, prosecution and conviction, with punishment, is a process that carries the clear condemnation of society for the conduct of the abuser and acknowledges his personal responsibility for the activity ... It is, however, critical that those involved in policy making in this area take into account the cultural, economic and political realities of their countries. (Coomaraswamy 2000: 11)

The prospect of prohibiting and punishing domestic violence depends, foremost, on the state's willingness and capacity to reform criminal and family laws. But the issue, and possibility, of state-sponsored reforms is strongly affected by social beliefs and ideologies about gender and family relations. 'Law reform strategies work best ... when the social value base is in concordance with the desired new norms. As long as the old regime of values is in effect, the tasks of making the new norms operative, or activating the educative function of law to change values, will be difficult and require action on many fronts' (Women, Law, and Development International 1996: 37).

When the administration of family relations is based upon or derived from religious texts and traditions, as is the case in Muslim societies where *shari'a* constitutes the framework for family law, the possibility for reform is contingent on a serious and respectful engagement with religious beliefs and practices. The challenges to reform law in order to promote and protect the rights of women are daunting; in many contexts, *shari'a* is interpreted to allow or tolerate certain forms of violence against women by male family members. This raises questions, and stimulates debates, about what religion 'says' (or is believed to say) about the rights of women. It also raises questions about the willingness or ability of the state to prevent and punish violence within families, especially when prevailing views or powerful constituencies regard curbs on male authority as a contravention of *shari'a*.

Section 2. A framework for comparative analysis

To establish a framework for comparative analysis of the relationship between domestic violence and *shari'a* in Muslim societies, three factors must be taken into consideration. One is the marked variation in the uses and interpretations of *shari'a*, which evince a lack of consensus among Muslims and should deter generalizing about Islam. Across and within these societies, there are differences in popular, scholarly and official understandings as to whether Islam sanctions forms of intra-family violence.[10]

A second factor is the relationship between religious law and state power. For comparative purposes, this relationship can be divided into three general categories (elaborated in greater detail below): in some countries, the state 'communalizes' religion by according its authorities and institutions semi-autonomy from the national legal regime, the latter under the direct control of the state; in other countries, the state 'nationalizes' religious law by utilizing and incorporating its principles into the national legal regime; and in a few countries, the state 'theocratizes' religion by basing its own authority on religious law and functioning as its enforcer.

A third factor to consider in assessing the relationship between domestic violence and *shari'a* is the influence of trans-national discourses and movements. Two in particular are worth noting because of their relevance to the subject of this study: Islamization and human rights. Since the 1970s, Islamist movements have mobilized in many countries across the Middle East, Africa and Asia to demand a (re)turn to Islam through the establishment of a system of government that adheres to and enforces *shari'a* (Beinin and Stork 1997). In some countries, Islamists represent an opposition movement, in others they represent an influential constituency, and in a few they have assumed control of the state. However, regardless of the relationship between Islamist movements and regimes, there is a generally shared commitment to the preservation of patriarchal family relations. Indeed, even in contexts where Islamists constitute a hostile opposition, states are often willing to accommodate their demands on matters of gender and family relations as a means of placating them (Halliday and Alavi 1988; Kandiyoti 1988).

Since the 1970s, there has also been a mobilization of movements to promote international human rights. Human rights organizations have been established in most countries, leading to greater awareness of the discourse and principles of international law, and, consequently, more visibility and critique of violations. The kinds of activities that comprise this trend include monitoring and reporting on rights violations, networking with activists from other countries and regions, and advocating that governments adopt, adhere to and enforce international legal standards locally.[11]

The issues of women's rights within the family and the role of *shari'a* have been central concerns to both of these movements, albeit in often contradictory and even adversarial ways. The critical question is whether Islam and human rights offer compatible worldviews, and, if not, which should prevail. This is not an abstract philosophical matter; it is a deeply charged political concern that informs the strategies that local actors pursue to institute their visions and goals, whether their priority is to promote women's rights in accordance with international law, to promote an 'authentically Islamic' social order (however that is interpreted), or to reconcile religious laws and beliefs with women's rights (Afkhami and Vazeri 1996).

Section 3. Aims and methods of this study

This thematic study on the relationship between domestic violence and *shari'a* is part of a larger project on Islamic family law.[12] This study was designed with three main aims: (1) to map the problem of domestic violence in Muslim societies in the Middle East, sub-Saharan Africa and Asia; (2) to analyse and compare how states deal with this problem; and (3) to analyse and compare variations in interpretations and applications of *shari'a* in regard to intra-family violence.

Domestic violence is an extremely difficult subject to study because of the dearth of reliable information. This is the case not only in Muslim societies but virtually everywhere. The reasons for this include: the inability or disinclination of victims to report violence; the refusal or failure of authorities to document reports and/or make reports publicly available; and official and/or social accept-ance of certain forms and degrees of intra-family violence. Hence, the quality and availability of information about domestic violence varies, from non-existent to partial at best.

In the societies that are the focus of this study, estimated rates of domestic violence tend to be high. However, the available information is extremely limited and uneven. Egypt and Palestine are the only countries in the three regions for which national studies which focus on or include domestic violence have been undertaken (el-Zanaty 1995; Yahia 1998). For some countries, there is virtually no statistical information whatsoever. Most information about domestic violence that does exist comes from local and international organizations, including women's and human rights organizations, and certain bodies of the United Nations with mandates that focus on or include women's rights.[13] The lack and unevenness of information is an important finding in its own right. But clearly, it makes the first aim of mapping domestic violence in Muslim societies all but impossible.

In regard to the second aim of analysing and comparing how states deal with domestic violence, the two most important issues are the administration and laws governing gender and family relations, and official commitment (or lack thereof) to women's rights. The kinds of questions that this research raises include the following: Has the state signed and ratified the Convention to Eliminate All Forms of Discrimination Against Women (CEDAW)? If so, has it registered any reservations on the grounds that CEDAW conflicts with *shari'a*? Is there a constitutional authority guaranteeing equal protection of the law for women and, if so, is this authority used effectively to prohibit and punish domestic violence? Is there national legislation and/or administrative sanctions prohibiting domestic violence? What measures, if any, has the state taken or authorized to deal with domestic violence and the protection of victims (e.g. provision of social services and health care, education campaigns)? Some information about the role and activities of the state, such as ratification and reservations to CEDAW, is publicly available. But information about the laws, policies and jurisprudence pertaining to domestic violence is far more difficult to gather. The best sources tend to be organizations that work on women's rights issues, and these vary from country to country.

In regard to the third aim of analysing and comparing interpretations and applications of *shari'a* as it impacts upon the issue of intra-family violence, this study makes no claim to provide an authoritative opinion on what Islam 'really' mandates. Rather, the issue is what authorities and members of society believe and accept, and how these beliefs are shaped, debated and transformed. Despite variations across societies, there are some commonalities, not least a general tendency to interpret *shari'a* as sanctioning gender inequality in family relations. Specifically, *shari'a* tends to be interpreted to give men authority over women family members. Thus, gender inequality is acknowledged, and justified in religious terms on the grounds that God made men and women 'essentially different'; that these differences contribute to different familial roles, rights and duties, which are complementary; and that this complementarity is crucial to the cohesion and stability of the family and society.

Domestic violence is strongly, and directly, related to inequality between men and women. But the contested legitimacy of gender equality in Muslim societies impedes or complicates efforts to deal with domestic violence as a social problem. There is strong opposition to the notion that men and women *should be equal* in the context of the family. The corollary is the belief that domestic relationships are legitimately (i.e. 'naturally' and/or 'divinely') hierarchical. This belief is both derived from and reinforced by dominant interpretations of *shari'a*. However, for analytical purposes, this study 'brackets' the question of whether *shari'a* lends itself to or opposes formal equality for men and women in order to foreground the issue of violence. Specifically, the question addressed here is whether *shari'a* is interpreted to construe violence against women as a *harm* or a *right*.

As a point of clarification, the 'bracketing' of gender inequality distinguishes the approach of this study from most mainstream feminist and human rights discourse, which tends to regard inequality as *causal* for domestic violence (Dobash and Dobash 1980, 1992). This inclines feminists and human rights activists to prioritize the struggle for gender equality as the *means* of combating domestic violence (Connors 1994; Coomaraswamy 1999). This is premised on the idea that if women were equal to men and had equal protection under the law, men would not be able to get away with perpetrating violence against them. While this is a valid assumption, it either fails to engage with or delegitimizes the beliefs and ideologies (in this case religious and cultural) that provide justification for in-equalities.

Indeed, gender inequality and domestic violence *are* integrally related, and this understanding informs the analysis here. But in this study, the primary emphasis is on *violence*, and the social and cultural context in which it occurs. This relates domestic violence to a lack of rights for women in order to probe the rationales and justifications for that lack. 'Defining violence in this way allows us to address the record of violence against women as one not composed of a series of instances of abuse ... but as one located in a broad social and political context in which not only men but women – and society as a whole – act to perpetuate systems which result in various forms of abuse' (Toubia 1994: 17).

Focusing critical attention on the rationales that people utilize to claim that men have the 'right' to perpetrate violence against women can alter gender inequalities in all social spheres. Establishing the illegitimacy of violence against women undermines a tangible and harmful manifestation of masculine privilege. But such an approach is less controversial, and hopefully more persuasive, because it targets violent practices rather than gender inequality. Moreover, it recognizes that the priority and interest of most victims of violence would be to end the abuse, not their domestic relations.

The comparative dimension of this study turns on the ways in which *shari'a* informs both official policies and, more broadly, popular attitudes about intra-family violence. Among Muslims, adherence to *shari'a* principles tends to be construed as a means of demonstrating a commitment (socio-cultural as well as religious) to Islam. Thus, this study strives to engage seriously with beliefs and practices that underlie this commitment. However, this does not translate into a cultural relativist sanctioning of violence against women (Mayer 1991). The assumption here is that domestic violence is a problem that demands recourse, and that such recourse is not inimical to Islam.

It is the hope of those involved in this study that this research will provide a resource for action and advocacy to combat the problem of domestic violence, and to enhance legal and other remedies available to victims. Although the problem of domestic violence and efforts to deter and combat it are global in scope, any possibility for success must involve strategies and analyses that resonate with local cultural and religious norms and values.

The remainder of this study is organized as follows: section 4 lays out a framework for analysing domestic violence as a legal and a social problem. Section 5 focuses on domestic violence and *shari'a* in general terms of the scriptural and interpretive stances that inform their relationship. Sections 6, 7 and 8 focus, respectively, on efforts to establish an international legal framework for combating domestic violence within a larger campaign for women's rights, culturalist resistance to women's rights, and manifestations of such resistance within Muslim societies that utilize adherence to *shari'a* as their basis. The final substantive section (9) presents a comparative analysis of domestic violence in Muslim societies, highlighting variations in the relationship between religion and the state as it impacts upon the issue of intra-family violence.

Section 4. The problem of domestic violence

Domestic violence is a global phenomenon. According to feminist geographer Joni Seager, it is reported as 'common' in almost all countries (1997: 26–7).[14] It affects millions of women annually. According to Human Rights Watch (1999a: 392), it 'has been one of the principal causes of female injury in almost every country in the world'.

But domestic violence is also a hidden problem. For many countries, there is little or no statistical information, indicating that it is 'a crime that is under-recorded and under-reported' (UNICEF 2000: 4). For countries where data are available, the rates vary.[15] For example, in the United States, an estimated 28 per cent of women have been victims of domestic violence at least once in their lives. In South Africa, the estimate is 48 per cent. In Pakistan, estimates range from 70 to 90 per cent (Seager 1997: 26–7).

The prevalence of domestic violence is a powerful indication of the inequality and vulnerability of women across cultures. Domestic violence is the most common form of gender violence, the latter encompassing all forms of violent practices perpetrated on females *because they are females*. 'Whether gender violence operates as direct physical violence, threat, or intimidation, the intent is to perpetuate and promote hierarchical gender relations. It is manifested in several forms, all serving the same end: the preservation of male control over resources and power' (Green 1999: 1–2).

What distinguishes domestic violence from other forms of gender violence is the context within which it occurs (the 'domestic' or 'private' sphere) and the nature of the relationship between perpetrators and victims (familial). Because domestic violence occurs within the 'private' sphere of the family, making it visible (as a first step to making it redressable) is exceedingly difficult. It is the very 'intimacy' of domestic space and relationships that makes such violence difficult to study and document. And it is the importance of the family in every society that makes the formulation of effective strategies to protect women from abuse so controversial.

> In the case of intimate violence, male supremacy, ideology and conditions ... confer upon men the sense of entitlement, if not the duty, to chastise their wives. Wife-beating is, therefore, not an individual, isolated, or aberrant act, but a social license, a duty or sign of masculinity, deeply ingrained in culture, widely practiced, denied and completely or largely immune from legal sanction. (Copelon 1994: 116)

Women who are subjected to or threatened with violence at home often are incapacitated by the violence itself from seeking protection. They may be paralysed by terror and the ever-present threat of attack. Victims are also often deterred from even imagining alternatives because of the importance of the family as a social institution. This vulnerability is compounded by economic dependence on male family members, and by the fact that many women's principal identity derives from their membership and role in the family. The problem of domestic violence is exacerbated by social and legal constructions of the family as 'private', and popular perceptions of male power (including domination and aggression against women) as normative.

Although domestic violence occurs within families and overwhelmingly targets women, it is neither a 'private' matter nor a 'women's' problem; it is a societal problem, implicating both the ruling state and the community within which families are socially situated. Yet there is great reluctance or resistance in societies around the world to recognize and deal with this problem because of an unwillingness to see such practices *as violence*. By imagining and referring to beatings, confinement, intimidation and insults as 'discipline' or 'punishment', rather than 'battery' or 'abuse', the nature of harm is obfuscated. Moreover, if prevailing social beliefs about family relations include the idea that men have a right or obligation to 'punish' and 'discipline' women family members, then the tactics used to do so can be seen, and even lauded, as necessary to maintain order both at home and in society at large. If, however, the safety and rights of women are, or can become, the priority, then the use of violence against them can be seen and criticized as illegitimate.

In contexts where intra-family violence is not explicitly prohibited by law (i.e. criminalized), perpetrators enjoy *legal impunity*. In contexts where it is prohibited but the laws are not enforced, perpetrators enjoy *social impunity*. In either situation, such impunity constitutes a failure on the part of the state to exercise its powers and prerogatives to deter, punish and prevent violence against its subjects. It is also a failure of society to reject and condemn the brutalization and intimidation of women at the hands of family members.

As those involved in efforts to eradicate violence from women's family lives attest, changing social attitudes and official policies that contribute to the problem are arduous tasks. Exposing and criticizing domestic violence calls into question the structures and discourses of familial authority. Seeking means of ameliorating the problem entails challenges and changes to the ways in which such authority is legitimated and enforced. It entails, in short, changes in *law* and *society*.

Even in societies with robust legal rights for women, domestic violence is both commonplace and hidden, signalling an enduring difficulty in activating a legal solution. In societies where women's rights are weak, their vulnerability to violence is compounded by a lack of options to seek protection from the law. And in societies where gender and family relations are derived from religious law, if jurists and officials interpret the law to sanction violence for specific purposes or under certain circumstances, demands for reform can be condemned as heresy or apostasy. In Muslim societies, where family relations are administered in accordance with *shari'a*, mobilizing support and instituting legal reforms to prohibit intra-family violence necessitate an engagement with religious discourse, beliefs and practices.

Section 5. *Shari'a* and domestic violence

In Muslim societies, *shari'a* may function both as the basis of specific legal rules for organizing social relations, and as a general religio-cultural framework for norms and values. In both senses, dominant interpretations of *shari'a* accord men the status of head of their families with guardianship over and responsibility for women.[16] The complement to this is the expectation that women have a duty to obey their 'guardians' (husbands, fathers or other male heads of family). This hierarchical and highly patriarchal relationship is based on dominant interpretations of *shari'a* principles of *qiwama* (authority, guardianship) and *ta'a* (obedience), from which gender-differentiated rights and duties are derived.

The primary source of the Qur'anic principles of *qiwama* and *ta'a* is Sura 4: 34. This same verse contains the most commonly cited reference used to assert men's right or option to beat disobedient women. This verse is translated, and interpreted,[17] in a variety of ways, but a standard English translation, which captures popular understandings about authority, (dis)obedience and punishment, states:

> Men have authority [*qiwama*] over women because Allah has made the one superior to the other, and because they [men] spend their wealth to maintain them [women]. Good women are obedient [*ta'a*]. They guard their unseen parts because Allah has guarded them. As for those [women] from whom you fear disobedience [*nushuz*], admonish them and send them to beds apart and beat them. Then if they obey you, take no further action against them. Allah is high, supreme.[18]

Asghar Ali Engineer (1992: 47) reports the historical origin of this verse as the case of a man (S'ad bin Rabi') who slapped his wife (Habiba bint Zaid) because she had disobeyed him. She complained to her father, who complained to the Prophet Muhammad. Sympathizing with the woman, the Prophet told her that she was allowed the right to *qisas* (a form of legal retribution). Men in the community protested that this would give women advantages over them. Fearing social unrest, the Prophet sought and received the revelation (4: 34) which effectively reversed his earlier ruling giving women the legal right to retaliate.

In drawing interpretative meaning from this verse, several factors are at issue. First, because this was a revelation, it lends itself to interpretation that God sanctions beating disobedient wives as a last option (after admonishing them and abandoning their beds). But because beating women was quite common in that place and time, it also lends itself to the interpretation that God intended to restrict the practice. Moreover, to the extent that *shari'a* functions as 'living law' adaptable to changing circumstances (e.g. through *ijtihad*), even the apparently explicit sanctioning of beating can be construed not as an ageless and divine right but as a circumscribed means to express anger and frustration, and one that gradually should be abolished. For example, Azizah al-Hibri (2001: 75–81) argues that the Qur'an imposed limits on the common practice of beating, and transformed it into a symbolic act. Hitting was not to be a normative standard of spousal relations but was to be used minimally if it could not be avoided entirely. Al-Hibri supports this reading by pointing to the Prophet's declaration to men: 'The best among you are those who are best toward their wives.' Indeed, on numerous occasions he told men not to beat their wives and condemned the practice.

Other Qur'anic verses and *hadith* condemn violence between spouses. For example, Sura 30: 21 describes marital relations as tranquil, merciful and affectionate, and the relationship itself as based on companionship, not service or tyranny. In this vein, Riffat Hassan (1995: 12) writes: 'God, who speaks through the Qur'an, is characterized by justice, and … can never be guilty of *zulm* (unfairness, tyranny, oppression or wrongdoing). Hence, the Qur'an, as God's word, cannot be made the source of human injustice.' Thus an argument can be made (and indeed is being made) that '*shari'a*' does not sanction any form of violence against women, and that interpretations and applications that sanction or tolerate violence derive from mistaken social perceptions and enduring customs that run counter to the fundamental injunctions of the *shari'a* of mutual kindness and respect (Svensson 2000: 73).

Islamic jurists and scholars have grappled with the question of whether hitting constitutes a de jure right under *shari'a*, or a de facto option (see Eissa 1999). Some jurists have proposed that while husbands are allowed to beat their wives, they should not do so hard enough to cause pain or leave a mark (Badawi 1995). Nevertheless, the lack of consensus on this issue makes it difficult to mount a campaign against beating as unjust in principle.

While authorities responsible for the administration of family relations are not categorically indifferent to the beating or brutalization of women, the violence usually has to be extreme to prompt intervention, if that is a possibility at all. In fact, most of what is known about wife beating emerges out of divorce cases in which women use violence as a cause for seeking divorce. Even then, however, because of the importance of family relations, saving the marriage often is prioritized over saving or protecting women from violence. In many contexts, for a woman to obtain a divorce from a *shari'a* court on the grounds of violence, the harm would have to be provable and so great that the judge would determine continued cohabitation to be impossible. Under *shari'a*, legally proving harm in the face of denial by the husband requires two witnesses, which often is difficult to provide because domestic violence happens in private. And proving the impossibility of cohabitation is difficult because women often have to remain in, or return to, their marital home for lack of alternatives.

The notion that the use of physical force constitutes a right available to husbands certainly contradicts the Qur'anic ideal of marital relations as companionable and mutually supportive. It also runs contrary to the Qur'anic right of both men and women to dissolve a failed marriage, which would seemingly override the notion that women have a duty or obligation to submit to violence. Yet because there *is* a mention of beating in the Qur'an, it has impeded efforts to prohibit and criminalize domestic violence, and contributes to social attitudes about beating as a legitimate reprisal for disobedience.

Marital rape is another form of domestic violence that has proven difficult to prohibit within the context of dominant interpretations of *shari'a*. Although rape is a punishable crime in every Muslim society, nowhere is the criminal sanction extended to rape within marriage, arguably at least in part due to the understanding of sexual consent implied in the marriage contract. (It should be noted that the recognition of 'marital rape' as a crime is a relatively recent development in the criminal laws of many non-Muslim societies.) Similarly, under *shari'a* rules, sexual intercourse (whether forced or consensual) outside the framework of a lawful marriage is prohibited. Thus, marital rape may be viewed as 'uncriminalizable' under dominant interpretations of *shari'a*. For example, Sura 2: 223 may be interpreted as a Qur'anic basis for men's unabridged sexual access to their wives. This verse stipulates that 'your wives are ploughing fields for you; go to your field when and as you like'. Although other Qur'anic verses and *hadith* instruct men not to force themselves sexually upon their wives, these may be superseded or overshadowed by the principle of female obedience.[19] Indeed, a wife's refusal to have sex with her husband can be conceived as a defiance of her duties, and can give rise to accusations of 'disobedience', thereby triggering legalistic justification for beating.

Forced marriage is a form of psychological and emotional violence (with physically violent possibilities). Although the Qur'an does not sanction this practice, the principles of male authority and female obedience create conditions in which women's subordination to their 'guardians' can enable men to impose their will on matters of marriage. While the Qur'an recognizes 'mature' (post-pubescent) women's right to enter freely into marriage, their status as legal 'minors' under the authority of male guardians undermines their freedom or ability to assert this right in the face of male opposition.

Within patriarchal societies in general, there is little normative acceptance of social, legal or sexual autonomy for women. On the contrary, women's options and behaviour tend to be heavily regulated and restricted. In contexts where gender and family relations are governed by *shari'a*, wives have a legal duty to concede to male authority, as long as this authority is exercised in a manner compatible with *shari'a*, and as long as the male fulfils his own obligations within the relationship. If women should act in a way deemed 'deviant' or 'disobedient', depending on the way in which *shari'a* is administered in a given context, punishment may be the prerogative of the state, or may be left to the discretion of members of the family or the community. In either circumstance, Muslim women's vulnerability to violence is related, *inter alia*, to jurisprudential traditions and social understandings of male authority and female obedience.

Of course, Muslim women are not uniquely vulnerable to domestic violence. Nor are social attitudes about female obedience and masculine prerogatives to 'discipline' and 'punish' women uniquely 'Islamic'. What is particular to the situation of Muslim women are rationalizations deriving from *shari'a*. Indeed, the problem of domestic violence in Muslim societies in many ways resembles its counterpart elsewhere, and so too do the difficulties in combating it, given the cultural and legal gender biases operative in all societies. These difficulties have given rise to efforts to develop an international legal framework for dealing with a problem that is global in scope and harmful to women everywhere.

Section 6. Internationalizing the struggle against domestic violence

In the 1980s, women's organizations around the world began campaigning for international recognition and prohibition of domestic violence as a human rights violation. In the 1990s, domestic violence became a major issue in a worldwide campaign to end violence against women, part of a larger on-going effort to promote women's rights as human rights.

While these initiatives are important and commendable, their timing raises some troubling questions. 'Human rights' were established in the aftermath of the Second World War through the promulgation of a new set of international laws 'universalizing' the rights of human beings everywhere.[20] Over the last five decades, there have been prodigious efforts to prohibit numerous forms of violence as human rights violations. What, then, explains the delay in recognizing and condemning domestic violence as a human rights violation? One key explanation derives from the vagueness and inconsistency of international law in regard to domestic relationships. There are three general factors at issue: (1) the state-centred nature of international law; (2) the enduring emphasis in human rights discourse and practice on civil and political rights (i.e. 'public' rights); and (3) deference to the family as a 'private' domain. The delay in recognizing domestic violence as a human rights violation can be explained by the difficulty of framing abuses suffered by women at home into the conventional framework of international law. 'The distinction between public and private life in international law is one of the principal theoretical barriers to this effort' (Sullivan 1995: 127).

Although the Universal Declaration of Human Rights (1948) and other human rights instruments that came into force in the 1960s and 1970s (e.g. the International Convenants on Civil and Political Rights, and Economic, Social and Cultural Rights) prohibit discrimination on the basis of sex, international law proved a weak resource for women. This weakness inspired women's rights activists to begin pressing to extend international law into the 'private sphere'.

A major breakthrough was the Convention on the Elimination of All Forms of Discrimination Against Women (CEDAW), which was adopted by the United Nations General Assembly in 1979 and came into force in 1981. CEDAW is often described as the international bill of rights for women.[21] It clearly establishes the 'indivisibility' of women's rights in public and private life (Fried 1994), and brings violations by individuals within the purview of international law, at least indirectly, by making states responsible for the actions of private parties (Article 2). Ratification or accession to CEDAW obligates states to abolish all forms of discrimination against women. While CEDAW recognizes the importance of culture and tradition in shaping gender roles and family relations, it imposes upon states the obligation to take 'all appropriate measures' to modify social and cultural patterns of conduct that are discriminatory or harmful towards women.

Despite the gains that CEDAW represents, it has some serious limitations. It does not *explicitly* identify violence against women as a human rights violation. And it has even less enforcement power than most other human rights treaties (Zorn 1999: 288–9). The UN committee that administers CEDAW is limited to taking reports from state parties about their efforts to implement its requirements, and issuing recommendations. But the most glaring limitations derive from the reservations that many states have attached to their ratification or accession to CEDAW. Although CEDAW is the second most widely ratified human rights treaty (after the Convention on the Rights of the Child), it is the one with the most reservations.

To redress the limitations of CEDAW on matters of violence against women, in the 1980s women's rights groups 'began a worldwide campaign to make freedom from domestic and other forms of violence a universally recognized human right' (ibid., p. 289). In 1985, the final document of the Third UN World Conference on Women (held in Nairobi, Kenya) affirmed the seriousness of violence against women and the need for international measures to combat it.

In 1992, the UN committee for CEDAW issued General Recommendation no. 19, which holds that gender-based violence is a form of discrimination that states must take measures to eradicate. In 1993, women's rights groups presented a petition with almost 500,000 signatures from 128 countries to delegates at the World Conference on Human Rights (Vienna, Austria), demanding the recognition of violence against women as a violation of their rights (ibid., p. 289). Also in 1993, the UN adopted the Declaration on the Elimination of Violence Against Women, defining it as 'any act of gender-based violence that results in, or is likely to result in, physical, sexual or mental harm or suffering to women, including threats of such acts, coercion or arbitrary deprivation of liberty, whether occurring in public or private life'. This Declaration explicitly includes violence occurring in the family, including wife battering and marital rape.

In 1994, the UN appointed Radhika Coomaraswamy to serve as the first Special Rapporteur on Violence Against Women. The Rapporteur's role is to build on and extend UN initiatives. This Special Rapporteur's mandate includes domestic violence and, more generally, promotion of adherence to all international instruments and treaties establishing women's rights as human rights.

In 1995, the Beijing Platform of Action (issued at the conclusion of the Fourth UN World Conference on Women) included an affirmation of the need to combat domestic violence.[22] More than any previous initiative, the Beijing Platform articulates a clear set of factors that perpetuate domestic violence,[23] all of which governments are expected to remedy.[24] It also identifies the lack of information and statistical data about domestic violence as an obstacle to combating it. This inspired the World Health Organization (WHO) to establish a database on violence against women and develop a questionnaire and guidelines for undertaking national surveys, although this process is still in its nascent stages (United Nations 2000: 157).[25]

In 1999, the UN adopted an Optional Protocol to CEDAW, which allows individual women or groups of women (from signatory states) who have exhausted domestic remedies to petition the committee for CEDAW about violations of the Convention by their governments. This Protocol also grants the committee the authority to conduct inquiries into grave or systematic abuses of women's human rights in states that are party to the Convention and the Protocol.[26]

Coomaraswamy has taken a leading role in formulating and promoting legal rationales to clarify states' responsibilities to prohibit and combat domestic violence in accordance with their international obligations (Coomaraswamy 2000). The two major legal doctrines identified for these purposes are:

1. *The doctrine of state responsibility and due diligence.* States have an internationally recognized responsibility and obligation to exercise 'due diligence' to prevent, investigate and punish acts by private actors that constitute violations of human rights. Moreover, where a state fails to assume this responsibility, it is complicit in the violations committed by private actors. Complicity includes pervasive non-action. State responsibility includes the institution of effective legal measures, including penal sanctions, civil remedies and compensatory provisions to protect

women from domestic violence; preventive measures, including public information and education programmes to change attitudes that contribute to the perpetuation of domestic violence; and protective measures to assist women who are victims or at risk of domestic violence.

2. *The doctrine of equal protection of the law.* International law imposes a duty on states not to discriminate on a number of specified grounds, including sex/gender. Failure to fulfil this duty constitutes a violation of international law by the state. This means that states must apply and enforce the same criminal sanctions and punishments in cases of domestic violence as are applied to any other types of inter-personal violence. Any pattern of non-enforcement amounts to unequal and discriminatory treatment on the basis of sex/gender.[27]

The emphasis of these two doctrines clearly links gender inequality and domestic violence, and the obligations of states to combat both. These linkages are based on the following assumptions and principles: (1) gender violence is a form of discrimination and, as such, violates international human rights standards which all states are obligated to adhere to in their own practices and to enforce within all relationships (public and private) within their jurisdiction; (2) women have a right to equality with men, and this encompasses all relationships, including those of the family; (3) local laws that sanction gender inequality must be reformed to provide equal protection for women and men, and enforcement must be non-discriminatory.

The development of an international legal framework for women's rights as human rights has contributed to the mobilization of an international struggle against domestic violence (Bunch and Reilly 1999; Fried 1994). Such efforts have heightened and focused international concern about the rights of women in their relations with family members. Making international standards of rights a reality for women around the world, though, is an on-going and difficult project. It entails bringing local legal regimes into conformity with international law. And it entails reform of social attitudes to recognize the legitimacy of women's rights and a need for laws and other measures to protect them from violence.

Section 7. Cultures of resistance, or saying 'No' to universalism

The successes in defining and promoting women's rights, including the prohibition of domestic violence as a human rights violation, have generated criticism and reprisals. Social conservatives around the world have responded negatively to efforts to empower women and endow them with enforceable rights within the family, charging that such initiatives constitute an assault on 'family values', traditions, national cultures, and so on. In many societies, official and popular aversion to enforcing international standards for domestic relationships is far more powerful and influential than the forces seeking to promote and protect the rights and well-being of women.

The promotion of women's rights as human rights, and the recent declarations and conventions to internationalize and standardize those rights have become imbricated in raging debates over the legitimacy of human rights in general. Indeed, the rights of women constitute the quintessential challenge to the 'universality' of human rights. These debates have been particularly vigorous in many developing countries. Critics and opponents argue that international legal standards contravene local customs and cultures and/or religious beliefs and practices, and that their promotion constitutes a form of 'imperialism'. Indeed, the emphasis on individuals as rights-bearing subjects, and the tendency to prioritize political and civil rights over social, economic and cultural rights lend weight to arguments that human rights are 'Western' and (thus) 'alien'.[28]

Resistance to international human rights cannot be understood merely as a regressive reaction to change. Rather, it must be understood as a relational response to historic conditions and globalization. The creation (and continuing expansion) of human rights is one manifestation of the globalization of distinctly modern legal norms and political relations. In broad terms, this process of globalization includes the establishment of modern (sovereign, bureaucratic) states, which had, by the latter decades of the twentieth century, become virtually universal, albeit continuously subject to local demographic and territorial shifts and challenges. Globalization also includes the articulation of increasingly detailed standards and norms of government that apply, at least in principle, to all states.

The internationalization of a common set of rights for all human beings has provoked a great deal of anxiety about cultural imperialism, especially in societies in the Middle East, Africa and Asia. To the extent that human rights are *perceived* as a Western construct, their legitimacy in non-Western societies is debatable. Moreover, the requirement to reform local laws and to transform local social and political relations to conform to international law is widely construed as a manifestation of enduring Western hegemony, a neo-imperial twist on a centuries-old global power dynamic in which values and norms are articulated and spread unidirectionally from the West to 'the rest'.[29]

Women's rights, and the issue of gender relations more generally, have become the primary redoubts of these anxieties about cultural and legal imperialism. While certain aspects of modernity, such as national security and bureaucratization, have been embraced by states everywhere, the politics of culture – specifically, cultural difference – have marked women as a terrain for preserving that which is (imagined to be) particular to a given society. In the colonial era, women were targeted for social reform by Western administrators and Christian missionaries (i.e. the 'civilizing mission'). Modernizing reformers from colonized societies also targeted women as objects for intervention and change, whether to accommodate the imperatives of colonial administrations or to justify demands for self-rule. According to Deniz Kandiyoti (1991: 7), these variants of 'colonial feminism' created a close association in the minds of many Muslims between the (changing) status of women and Western cultural imperialism, and sparked countervailing attempts to maintain and reinforce 'authentic' relations and roles for women as anti-imperial resistance. 'Islamic authenticity may therefore be evoked to articulate a wide array of worldly disaffections, from imperialist domination to class antagonisms. This opens up the possibility of expressing such antagonisms in moral and cultural terms, with images of women's purity exercising a powerful mobilising influence' (ibid., p. 8).

When women are treated as markers of cultural authenticity, and when cultural discourses posit that women's human rights are an alien concept, part of a cultural onslaught emanating from 'elsewhere', the disadvantages that women experience *as women* can be justified and defended, even glorified, as an aspect of that particular culture. Conversely, when the promotion of women's rights is read as a sign (and imperative) of modernization (by vesting women with individual and inalienable rights), and when this goal demands the revision or revocation of local laws and practices, then it often provokes countervailing efforts to resist globalization and foreign influence by defending that which is (deemed) authentic and particular to a given culture or society.[30]

Whether state agents are the authors of such resistance, or are pushed in these directions by powerful constituencies, it is the state, as both the arbiter of law and the representative of society in the international legal order, that bears primary responsibility for the provision and enforcement of rights for its subjects. The struggles over women's rights are, in many ways, contestations over legal jurisdiction and authority, namely whether international legal standards will prevail to guide state policy, or whether other bodies of law (constitutional, religious, customary) are accorded precedence when there is a contradiction.

Although resistance to women's rights is strong, it rarely manifests itself as an open *defence* of violence against women as a cultural value or end in its own right (possible exceptions being female genital cutting and *sati*).[31] More commonly, concern about the safety and well-being of women is subordinated to other values or ends, including social stability, male superiority and, in some contexts, adherence to religion and/or tradition. But if this serves to enable practices that constitute domestic violence, whether by tolerating or ignoring them, it literally sacrifices women to some other 'social good'. There is, or there should be, an understood difference between the perpetration of violence against women because of culture (i.e. for reasons related to cultural ideologies and relations) and the conflation of this violence with the culture itself. As Jean Zorn points out:

> If wife beating occurs in almost every society in the world, if it is almost universal, then can it be said to be part of any society's unique culture? It is certainly not what sets that society apart from all others, that which gives the society its special character. One could argue that, even if international law should recognize cultural differences, universally applicable rules of international law may govern any behavior that is itself all but universal. (Zorn 1999: 292–3)

In societies where resistance to women's rights is expressed as a defence of social traditions and/or religious laws and norms, women's rights activists have been challenged to cultivate a persuasive distinction between 'culture' and violence against women. Disrupting tacit tolerance for practices that constitute domestic violence requires efforts to make such practices visible *as violence*, to delegitimize justifications for the use of violence by bringing culturally relevant arguments to bear in the defence of women's safety and well-being, and to challenge laws, jurisprudence and ideologies that construe such practices as vital to the greater good of society.

Section 8. *Shari'a* and (versus?) women's rights

In many Muslim societies, the belief that international standards for women's rights conflict with *shari'a* is strong and pervasive. This extends to the idea that women's human rights, and efforts to promote them, are 'un-Islamic' or even 'anti-Islamic'. Thus, resistance (official and popular) to reform *shari'a*, whose sources are regarded as divine, in order to accommodate international legal standards can be mounted and justified as a refusal to sacrifice or subordinate the sacred to the secular.

What this reflects is not an unyielding or inflexible commitment to religion *per se*, but a *responsive* influence of conservative ideologies and interpretations of religious prescriptions about gender and family relations in the face of sweeping social transformations that characterize modernization. 'Although Islamic rules have been reinterpreted, modified, or simply treated as inapplicable when dealing with changing circumstances in such issues as slavery and modern commercial practices, no such flexibility has been shown with regard to women's rights. For women, the trend of interpretation has worked almost exclusively in the opposite direction' (Abdel Halim 1994: 28).

The trend towards more conservative positions on gender issues can be traced through Muslim governments' participation in the international process to develop a legal framework for women's rights. This process has highlighted and sharpened differences over women's right to rights. In recent years, Muslim governments have consolidated their commitment to *shari'a* in direct response to pressures to incorporate international legal standards locally. This history reveals the fluidity of ideologies about gender relations, rights and law.

In 1963, the countries that sponsored a resolution calling for the preparation of a Declaration on the Elimination of Discrimination Against Women (the precursor to CEDAW) included Afghanistan, Algeria, Indonesia, Morocco and Pakistan (Connors 1996: 353). The UN Secretary General, pursuing the resolution's request for comments and proposals about the contents of such a Declaration, received responses from Afghanistan, Egypt, Iraq, Morocco, Sudan, Syria and Turkey, all of which were supportive of the idea of women's rights. For example, Afghanistan recommended that 'intense educational efforts' be made to combat 'traditions, customs and usages which thwart the advancement of women' and Egypt's response called for educational campaigns to overcome discriminatory customs and traditions (ibid.).

During the process of drafting the Declaration, a controversy arose over whether it should call for the abolition or the modification of customs and laws that perpetuate discrimination. This presaged the kind of controversy that would arise around the drafting and passage of CEDAW. But because the Declaration was just that – a statement lacking contractual force – it was passed unanimously. The drafting of CEDAW was a more difficult process, with a full week spent debating Article 15, which gives women equal capacity before the law, and Article 16, which provides for equality under marriage and family law (ibid., p. 354). When the draft Convention was voted upon, most of the abstentions on these articles came from Muslim countries. In the final vote, the Convention passed 130 to 0, with 11 abstentions, including Bangladesh, Djibouti, Mauritania, Morocco and Saudi Arabia.

CEDAW was opened for signatures in 1980. Most of the countries with majority Muslim populations that *have* signed CEDAW have entered reservations.[32] And all of the reservations except those of Indonesia, Turkey and Yemen (former Democratic Republic of Yemen) relate to the preservation of *shari'a* in matters of personal status.[33] But the reservations themselves vary in scope, terms and specificity. For example, Libya proclaimed that its accession to CEDAW is subject to a sweeping general reservation of any provisions that conflict with personal status laws derived from *shari'a*. Bangladesh reserved on Article 2, the core of the treaty, on the grounds that it conflicts with *shari'a*. Egypt and Morocco entered reservations similar to Bangladesh, but couched in a different language, namely stating a willingness to comply with Article 2 as long as it does not conflict with *shari'a*.

> As a matter of explanation, Morocco add[ed] that 'certain of the provisions contained in the Moroccan Code of Personal Status according women rights that differ from the rights conferred on men may not be infringed upon or abrogated because they derive primarily from the Islamic *shari'a*, which strives, among its other objectives, to strike a balance between the spouses in order to preserve the coherence of family life.' (ibid., p. 356)

Most of the reservations by Muslim countries pertain to Articles 15 and 16. Article 16, along with Article 2, constitutes the crucial core of the Convention because it addresses relations and rights in the 'private sphere', which is 'the fundamental site of discrimination against women which, effectively, sets the framework and opportunity for discrimination in public life' (ibid., p. 358).[34] Bangladesh, Egypt, Iraq, Jordan, Morocco, Tunisia and Kuwait all entered reservations to Article 16. While some countries reserved without elaborating on their reasons, others offered explanations that women are 'advantaged' by the domestic legal regime, which is based on *shari'a* (e.g. through payment of a dower, and men's obligations to support their wives financially). For example, Egypt's explanation states that the basis of spousal relations under *shari'a* is 'equivalency of rights and duties so as to ensure complementarity which guarantees true equality between spouses, not quasi-equality that renders the marriage a burden on the wife' (ibid., p. 359).

The substance and scope of reservations by Muslim countries sparked a great deal of controversy. Some countries, notably Mexico, Germany and the Nordic states, protested that the reservations are incompatible with the principles and provisions of the Convention as a whole.[35] Sweden issued a statement that such reservations 'would render a basic international obligation of a contractual nature meaningless. Incompatible reservations … not only cast doubts on the commitments of the reserving States to the object and purpose of the Convention, but also contribute to undermine the basis of international contractual [i.e. treaty] law' (ibid., p. 360).

Such objections raised the issue of reservations for international discussion. This, in turn, generated counter-objections by reserving states that such discussion amounted to 'an attack by the West on, first, the Islamic world and, by extension, the whole of the Third World' (ibid., p. 361). These discussions about reservations continued in various sessions and committee meetings of the UN. Although Muslim governments were not the only ones to enter reservations, their reservations articulated a common theme about the precedence of *shari'a*, leading to a general sense that the controversy was a debate about Islam.

Following the submission of Bangladesh's first report to the UN Committee for CEDAW, and no doubt influenced by the contents of that report, the committee formulated General Recommendation no. 4 expressing concern about the significant number and potential incompatibility of reservations as they affect the object and purpose of the Convention. The committee also requested the UN 'to promote or undertake studies on the status and equality of women in the family … taking into consideration the principle of El Ijtihad [sic] in Islam' (CEDAW 1987: 583, cited in Connors 1996: 362). In response, Bangladesh as well as Egypt charged that this amounted to cultural imperialism and religious intolerance. Such a charge resonated with other Third World countries, not only those with majority Muslim populations. This led to the passage of a UN resolution squelching the committee's proposal for studies about women and Islam. According to Ann Mayer:

> The result was that, faced with appeals to cultural particularism, the UN tolerated a situation where some countries would be treated as parties to a convention whose substantive provisions they had professed their unwillingness to abide by. Implicitly, the UN acquiesced to the cultural relativist position on women's rights … allowing parties to CEDAW to invoke Islam and their culture as the defense for their noncompliance with the terms of the convention. This was paradoxical, since … CEDAW was premised on the notion that, where cultural constructs of gender were an obstacle to the achievement

of women's equality, it was culture that had to give way – not that women's rights should be sacrificed. (Mayer 1991: 179)

'Islamic resistance' to international human rights law coalesced around CEDAW in particular, and women's rights in general.[36] In 1990, the Organization of Islamic States, to which all Muslim countries belong, issued a collective rejoinder to international efforts to establish women's rights in the domestic sphere as human rights: the *Cairo Declaration on Human Rights in Islam* established that all rights were subject to Islamic law, and that where there was a contradiction between international law and *shari'a*, the latter would take precedence.

The assertion on the part of governments that religious beliefs and jurisprudence justify the disregard for international legal standards illustrates persisting and onerous obstacles to women's rights. On the one hand, under international law the sovereign prerogatives of states do provide for autonomy and independence on the legal character of rights within a country. On the other, the international nature of human rights standards and the jurisdiction of international law obligate states to conform under the doctrine of state responsibility. Indeed, the rights and responsibilities of states are legally subject to the requirements and restrictions enshrined in international law. Abdullahi An-Na'im (1994) argues that the most effective means of reconciling state sovereignty and local culture with international legal standards entails the cultivation of a broader and deeper 'overlapping consensus' on the universal cultural legitimacy of human rights, including women's rights.

In exercising their sovereign prerogatives, Muslim governments have sought to present themselves as defenders of 'Islam' by building a firewall around *shari'a*. On the international level, despite the controversy that this has provoked, it epitomizes the capacity of states to speak and act in the name of their societies. Indeed, such a conflation is characteristic of the state-centric international order. Moreover, criticisms of Muslim governments' policies by 'others', be they representatives of foreign governments or international organizations, can further entrench resistance to human rights within those societies.

But does such a stance actually represent a 'Muslim consensus'? There is a substantial, albeit still marginal, discourse *within* Muslim societies that questions the putative incompatibility of Islam and women's human rights, and, by extension, governmental positions that assume that they are irreconcilable. This alternative discourse includes efforts to reinterpret elements of *shari'a* to provide for more egalitarian gender relations, and the censure or prohibition of practices that harm or disadvantage women.

Yet the degree to which this discourse can get a public hearing or impact upon national policy is limited by governments themselves. Many governments have acted to repress scholars, activists and organizations advocating women's rights, even when such advocacy seeks to show their compatibility to Islam. Najla Hamadeh (1996: 346) describes this as 'the authoritarian discourse of silence', which produces a sterile 'juridical monologue'. The *effect* is to reify religion by conflating 'Islam' with government positions. The *means* entails the use of state power to stifle and preclude dissenting views or alternative interpretations of religion. But the problem of politically authoritarian states, which characterize the majority of regimes across the three regions, is perpetuated – even bolstered – by their capacity to use religion (albeit in varying ways, as elaborated in the following section) to justify the lack, restriction or even outright violation of the rights of women.

Section 9. *Shari'a*, the state and domestic violence

The propagation of a collective trans-national and official position on the in-compatibility of women's rights and Islam belies variations in the role and uses of *shari'a* within Muslim societies, as well as differences between the three regions. To understand these variations, the most crucial issue is the relationship between religion and the state. In any given country, this relationship is informed by the particular history of state formation and development, as well as the demographic composition of the population. In the Middle East, Muslims comprise a majority of the population in every country except Israel. Islam is the dominant religion across the region, and most Middle Eastern governments identify it as the official religion. In sub-Saharan Africa and Asia, Muslims comprise majorities in some countries, whereas in others Muslim populations coexist with populations of other religions.

One regional distinction worth noting is that all the sub-Saharan African countries that *have* signed CEDAW have done so without entering reservations. However, such willingness has not, generally, translated into a more activist stance by African governments on matters of women's rights. In Muslim societies in all three regions, family and social relations are patriarchal, and *shari'a* has tended to bolster these arrangements.

> It may well be that restrictions imposed by Islamic and other forms of custom-ary laws are reinforced and magnified by state structures that institutionalize both Western and indigenous elements of patriarchy. All these elements come together to disadvantage women *vis-à-vis* men. These disadvantages exist in all societies. The degree and type of disadvantage differs from culture to culture but the fact of disadvantage is universal and certainly not unique to Islamic societies. (Callaway and Creevey 1989: 8)

One way of engaging a comparative approach to the relationship between domestic violence and *shari'a* is to highlight variations in the relationship between religion and the state. This relationship can be divided into three broad cat-egories: (1) 'communalization': religious laws, institutions and authorities are accorded semi-autonomy from the state; (2) 'nationalization': religious laws and jurisprudence are incorporated into or are influential over the state's legal regime;

and (3) 'theocratization': the state bases its own authority upon religious law and jurisprudence.

Communalization In countries where separate systems of personal status laws are applied to members of different communities, there are 'two tiers' of law, one under the direct control of the state, and the other based on religion (and/ or custom) and semi-autonomous from the state's legal authority. In such contexts, laws and legal institutions governing family relations are not only legally separate from state law, but also are regarded *ideologically* as 'outside' the state's domain.

Israel, India and Nigeria represent examples of countries where personal status laws are communalized. In all three, the populations are religiously diverse, the national political systems are (ostensibly) 'non-religious', and each has a constitutionally-based legal system.[37] In Israel, communalization provides every religious group (Jews, Christians, Muslims, Druze) with its own personal status laws administered by religious authorities (Swirski 2000), whereas in India, communalization applies only to minorities, not the Hindu majority. In Nigeria, sectarian law is administered under the rubric of regional states rather than communalization on a national scale.

In Israel and India, this two-tiered system was instituted at the time of independence as part of a broader project of national integration to accommodate religious and social differences and encourage loyalty to, or dependency on, the state by religious authorities and constituencies; communal autonomy over domestic matters formed an element of the 'social contract' in these countries. In Nigeria, communalization, and more specifically Islamization, is connected to recent political transformations, namely the end of military rule under regimes dominated by Muslims, which led to an Islamist retrenchment in the twelve northern regional states of the country where Muslims comprise a majority. But in all three, communalization of personal status laws deprives women of equal citizenship rights. This extends to the issue of domestic violence by impeding or preventing victims from seeking protection from the state, since what occurs in the family is legally constructed as a 'communal' issue, not the state's concern.

In Israel, the characterization of the state as 'Jewish' enables and reinforces discrimination against all non-Jews, men as well as women. Non-Jewish Israelis cannot claim the state as 'theirs', despite their status as citizens. This exclusion reinforces the significance of communal relations and institutions as sources of solidarity and protection (Haj-Yahya 1995, 1996; Shalhoub-Kevorkian 1999). Because the Israeli state sponsors and sanctions discrimination against its Arab citizens (Muslims, Christians and Druze), there is little appeal to regard the state as a legitimate source of relief or protection from domestic violence (Shalhoub-Kevorkian 1999: 202). In Israel, Arab women's struggles for rights as women are inextricable from their struggles for rights as Arabs living in a Jewish state (Ibrahim 1998). Consequently, in Israel communalization is both a factor in women's vulnerability to domestic violence and a source of solidarity from a discriminatory state.

In India, communalism – and especially communal autonomy for Muslims – has been the subject of intense debate since independence, challenged by those who advocate a uniform civil code that would apply to all Indians regardless of religion (Engineer 1996). Under this communal arrangement, the administration of *shari'a* is overseen by the All India Muslim Personal Law Board. The debate about communalism for Muslims heated up in 1985 following the notorious Shah Bano case. The Indian Supreme Court ruled that Shah Bano, a divorced Muslim woman, had the right to receive maintenance from her husband under Section 125 of the Criminal Procedure Code of India. This provoked conservative Muslim religious leaders and the All India Muslim Personal Law Board to protest state interference in a 'communal' matter. The Indian government capitulated to the pressure and passed a new law (the Muslim Women [Protection of Rights in Divorce] Act) negating the court ruling and fortifying the authority of Islamic law and Muslim religious institutions (Kumar 1994; Pearl and Menski 1998: 209–21; Singh 1994).

In India (like other South Asian countries), estimated rates of domestic violence tend to be among the highest in the world. Experts and activists explain this by emphasizing the link between violence against women and low socio-economic status, which characterizes the situation for the vast majority. While poverty is not causal for violence against women, it can increase women's vulnerability. For example, one form of domestic violence that is pervasive in South Asia, but particular to that region, is 'bride burning'. This refers to the killing of women (often staged as a 'kitchen accident') for their failure or inability to provide additional dowry resources to the husband's family. Although this phenomenon originated among Hindu communities, it has spread to Muslim communities in India as well as Pakistan and Bangladesh. In India, the parliament passed a law criminalizing bride burning and other forms of dowry-related harassment in 1983 (supplementing a 1961 law). However, the communalization of *shari'a* has left Muslims beyond the reach of these state interventions, including criminal sanctions, for dowry-related violence and murder; the Dowry Prohibition Act (1986) exempts 'persons to whom Muslim Personal Law (Shariat) applies'. This exemption, like the state's response to the Shah Bano case, was instituted to placate leaders of the Muslim community and to deter sectarian violence.

Communal politics in India exacerbates the vulnerability of the Muslim minority on a national level, and this serves to entrench the power of a conservative religious leadership within the community. This communal vulnerability fosters a rigid refusal by the All India Muslim Personal Law Board to reform *shari'a* to improve and strengthen the rights of women (Engineer 1999), and excludes Muslim Indian women from the protections of national laws and institutions (Lateef 1998).

In Nigeria, communalization has undergone a dramatic transformation in recent years as a result of national political transition and Islamization in the northern states with large Muslim populations. The primary manifestation of this has been the enforcement of *shari'a*. In 1999, *shari'a* in the northern states was extended to the domain of criminal law, whereas previously it had been limited to family law.

On the national level, the Nigerian Constitution guarantees equal rights to all citizens, including clauses that bar discrimination on the basis of sex. Nigeria has ratified, without any reservations, CEDAW and other human rights instruments that guarantee women's rights. However, the government has not instituted laws explicitly prohibiting domestic violence. The Northern Nigerian Penal Code reinforces the permissibility of domestic violence and the legal impunity of perpetrators: Section 55 of the Penal Code provides that

> wife beating is permitted in so far as it does not amount to grievous injury ...
> Nothing is an offense which does not amount to the infliction of grievous hurt
> upon any person and which is done by a husband for the purpose of correcting
> his wife, such husband or wife being subject to any native law or custom in
> which such correction is recognized as lawful. (cited in Effah et al. 1995)

Likewise, under this penal code marital rape is effectively permissible because it is not recognized as a crime.[38]

In Nigeria, official tolerance of domestic violence is further reinforced by a lack of social services and assistance for victims. For example, in one study an official at the social welfare office described that institution's mandate as 'palliative and ameliorative rather than judgmental ... [O]fficials try to appease both parties'. He continued by reminding the interviewer that 'the culture allows men to beat women. [Social Welfare Office officers] ask [women who report violence] if they are submissive to their husbands, or if they think their husbands are in a position to reprove them. When answers to these questions are not straightforward or forthcoming, [the officers] ask the couple to settle their differences "in bed"' (Atinmo 1997).

Official and popular tolerance for domestic violence in Nigeria appears to have been bolstered by the 'Islamization' taking place in Muslim-majority states in the country. The use of regional governmental power to enforce *shari'a* in states where it has been instituted makes it more difficult for women's rights advocates to use national legislation as leverage; the very process of Islamization has been a rejoinder to a loss of power on a national level, and the enforcement of *shari'a* has been the primary manifestation to carve out a domain of control and autonomy for Muslims.

Nationalization Any state that defines the official religion as Islam and draws upon religious law and jurisprudence for its legislation and policies, but does not derive or base *its own* authority exclusively on *shari'a* would fall within this category in which religion is nationalized. This characterizes much of the Arab world and some countries in Africa and Asia with Muslim majorities.

Linking the power of the state to the application and enforcement of religious law blurs boundaries between religion and state power. This blurring has been pursued to consolidate a Muslim national community, and as a means for states to promote their own legitimacy among sectors of society which are inclined to see a commitment to Islam as a marker of 'good government' in the format of an 'Islamic social contract'. It leaves open some space for debate over the relationship between *shari'a* and other bodies of law. On matters of women's rights in general and domestic violence in particular, there is room for manoeuvre to seek state intervention and legal reform through reference to criminal and constitutional laws. However, there is also room for conservative constituencies to mobilize pressure on the state to enforce *shari'a* in a conservative manner. And when faced with critics pressing for liberal reforms, the state can resort to repression on the grounds that it has both the prerogative and the duty to 'defend' Islam as an integral part of the national character.

Egypt provides a good example of all of these aspects and dynamics. In principle, Egyptian law, including the Constitution, provides women with a right to equality. However, in 1981, under pressure from Islamists, the Egyptian Constitution was amended to position *shari'a* as the main source of legislation.[39] The Supreme Constitutional Court has been given the task of determining whether new legislation conforms to *shari'a* principles. In practice, given the conservative ways in which *shari'a* is interpreted and applied to maintain male authority and female obedience, women's rights continue to be lesser than those of men and their vulnerability to violence is implicitly sanctioned by the state.

The issue of divorce is particularly illuminating of Egyptian women's limited rights and their vulnerability to violence. Egyptian courts follow a number of principles that function like legally binding precedents, which restrict women's rights and limit available relief even in cases of violence. For example, according to Principle 22, 'a husband's inappropriate conduct is not considered [by itself] grounds for divorce' (Tadross 1998: 18). Principle 59 states that 'a wife's return back to the home after having been harmed means that life could continue between them, which does not constitute grounds for divorce later' (ibid.). Even if a woman is being beaten or hurt by her husband, she does not have a right to leave the home. Instead, her option is to seek relief from a judge. Moreover, even if she pursues such a course, in the interim she must not refuse to be obedient to her husband while she continues to cohabit the marital home. If the judge finds sufficient proof of harm, and if he is unable to reconcile the couple, he can grant a divorce (ibid., p. 57).

Aside from the difficulties in meeting burdens of proof and the general reluctance on the part of judges to grant women a divorce, other factors impede women from leaving a violent home and pursuing a divorce. Often, women's families would not support such a decision or take them in, and establishing separate homes for themselves is both socially unacceptable and economically unfeasible for the vast majority. Another significant deterrent is the likelihood that women who seek divorce will lose custody over their children.

In January 2000, a new law pertaining to personal status issues was passed in

Egypt, inspired by pressure from women's and human rights advocates. But the text that passed was a significantly watered-down version of the original proposed law. One of its provisions allows for 'judicial *khul*'', through which a woman could obtain a divorce without having to 'prove' anything if she refunds her dower to the husband and forfeits all financial rights and claims from the marriage. While this does, in principle, provide recourse for battered women who might not be able to obtain a divorce through litigious means, in practice the option is limited to women with the financial means to meet the repayment demands and renounce their financial claims.

The role of *shari'a* in Egypt's national legal regime perpetuates women's subordination to male family members, and reinforces the 'privacy' of family relations, thus exacerbating women's vulnerability to domestic violence. However, it is important to emphasize that *shari'a* is not a *cause* of violence; it is a contributing factor that hinges (and changes) on the politics of interpretation and enforcement. Moreover, attitudes about and practices of intra-family violence in Egypt vary by social location, as revealed by the Egypt Demographic and Health survey, which was conducted with a representative sample of Egypt's population by the National Population Council in 1995. According to this study, most women who were ever married agree that husbands are justified in beating their wives at least sometimes. 'Women are most likely to agree that men are justified in beating their wives if the wife refuses him sex or if the wife answers him back' (el-Zanaty 1995: 206). This finding indicates that there is a high degree of tolerance for domestic violence in Egyptian culture, even among women. However, when it comes to the reasons people use to justify or tolerate wife beating, there was less agreement among the sample. Factors such as older age, years of marriage, marriage to a relative, the woman's original free consent to marriage, living in urban areas, higher levels of education, and wage employment all reduced the probability that a woman would agree that a husband has the right to beat his wife under any circumstance. Among those factors, higher education and employment were the most statistically significant. Nevertheless, even among those women who were most educated, around 65 per cent agreed that a husband was justified in beating his wife at least sometimes. Similarly, around 69 per cent of women who brought income to their families justified wife beating at least sometimes (ibid., p. 206–7).

In terms of the practice of domestic violence, the survey reported that one out of every three 'ever-married Egyptian women has been beaten at least once since marriage' (ibid., p. 208). Of those women, 45 per cent were beaten at least once in the preceding year and 17 per cent were beaten three or more times in the same period. Like attitudes toward wife beating, frequency of beating also depended on the social, economic and regional locations of the woman. For example, the study found that wife beating was less frequent among women under the age of thirty, and much higher among women living in rural areas. Pregnancy does not seem to matter in deterring men from beating their wives. Overall, about one-third of the women who had ever been beaten had been beaten during pregnancy.[40]

The case of Egypt illustrates the ways in which *shari'a*-based rules may contribute to the vulnerability of women, not by mandating domestic violence, but by fostering conditions in which it can be perpetrated with relative impunity. Socio-political pressures on the state by conservative constituencies have created a legal environment that undermines women's ability to seek state protection or intervention if this could be construed as violating popular perceptions of Islamic principles. There is a strong tendency to construe these principles as authorizing female obedience, and disobedience tends to be construed to license violence. Although the possibilities for law reform exist, as evidenced by the 2000 law, activists are constrained by an atmosphere where conservative interpretations of *shari'a* prevail. In contestations over women's rights, the state tends to support and accommodate religious conservatives to bolster its own legitimacy and deter opposition by this powerful constituency.

Theocratization In countries where the state defines itself as 'Islamic' and bases its own authority on *shari'a*, religious law *is* the law of the state. In such contexts, defence of religion is conflated with defence of the state, and critiques or challenges can be regarded and treated as heresy, which the state authorizes itself to punish. Iran and Pakistan represent examples of theocratization.

Iran defines itself as an Islamic Republic. Its official religion is Shi'i Islam (of the twelver Ja'afari school). Its legislature is an Islamic Consultative Assembly. A Council of Guardians comprised of clerics is authorized to ensure that all national laws are based on or compatible with Islamic criteria. Iran's supreme leader is an *ayatollah* (religious authority), and its top legal authorities must be *mujtahids*.

The Islamic revolution in 1979 was inspired, in part, by opposition to the Shah's reform of family laws, and one of the new government's first acts was the cancellation of the 1967 Family Protection Law, along with the institution of an array of new laws and policies that served to constrict women's rights in accordance with a conservative interpretation of *shari'a*. However, over time, the Iranian government has found compelling reasons or needs to expand rights and protections for women, in part to support the claim that Islamic government is good for its citizens. To these ends, in 1992, a new set of Divorce Amendments restored many of the elements of the abrogated 1967 law.

In Iran, the process of building and legitimizing a modern statist approach to Islam has opened up debates over *shari'a*, including dissenting views of patriarchal interpretations from within the *'ulama*. This debate has taken a highly public form in the national media. In a study of this debate in the pages of a women's magazine, *Zanan*, Ziba Mir-Hosseini writes,

> [A] 'feminist' re-reading of the *shari'a* is possible – even becomes inevitable – when Islam is no longer part of the oppositional discourse in national politics.

This is so because once the custodians of the *shari'a* are in power, they have to deal with the contradictory aims set by their own agenda and discourse, which are to uphold the family and restore women to their 'true and high' status in Islam, and at the same time to uphold men's *shari'a* prerogatives. The resulting tension – which is an inherent element in the practice of *shari'a* itself, but is intensified by its identification with a modern state – opens room for novel interpretations of the *shari'a* rules on a scale that has no precedent in the history of Islamic law. (Mir-Hosseini 1996: 285–6)[41]

The articles and views published in *Zanan* have raised questions about some of the most fundamental aspects of *shari'a*, including the legal basis for the assumption that men have authority over their families, or the obligation of unwilling women to submit to sex with their husbands. Within the context of a broader discussion about spousal relations, rights and duties, *Zanan* has focused specifically on the issue of domestic violence. Issue no. 18 (1994) is titled 'Sir, Have You Ever Beaten Your Wife?', and issue no. 19 (1994) is titled, 'Wife-Beating: Another Consequence of Men's Headship' (Mir-Hosseini 1996: 310–31). Number 18 includes interviews with men, women and children about their personal experiences with domestic violence, and commentary by a female lawyer discussing the legal rights of a woman who is subjected to violence. Number 19 discusses the jurisprudential dimensions of domestic violence, including a reading of Sura 4: 34 that draws upon fifteen traditions of the Prophet and utilizes a variety of interpretative strategies to argue against the religious legitimacy of wife beating.

Reformist trends in Iran have been mounting in recent years, as is evident in the election victories by reform-minded candidates (Kian 1998). However, these trends have been resisted and countered by a conservative clergy that exercises a great deal of national power. Although tensions between conservatives and reformists dominate Iranian national politics, the popularity of reformists and their ability to command a majority in elections suggests a social openness to greater rights for women (Kian-Thiebaut 1999; Mir-Hosseini 2000).

To the extent that these rights claims are being articulated in terms of *shari'a* indicates the possibility that religious rationales can be deployed to prohibit violence against women. According to Homa Hoodfar:

> [A] considerable sector of women's activism in Iran employs not secular debates but female-centered interpretations of Islam and of the political concept of 'Islamic justice.' Through this strategy, women not only derail the claim that feminism and issues of legal equity are Western paradigms which aim to undermine the authenticity of Iranian society, but they also break the male monopoly on interpreting Islamic texts. (Hoodfar 1995: 3)

The kinds of liberalizing trends and female-centred interpretations of *shari'a* found in Iran are strikingly absent in Pakistan, where the trend has been towards more conservative interpretations of *shari'a*, to the detriment of women. Pakistani women are among the most vulnerable in the world to domestic violence, where estimated rates range from 70 per cent to upwards of 90 per cent.[42]

Pakistan was created to provide a separate state for Muslims in South Asia to avoid minority status and subjection to a Hindu majority in India. The constitutional debates following independence were dominated by arguments over the place of *shari'a* in the country's legal system. Although religious leaders demanded that the country be established as an Islamic state, they settled at the time for language that defined Pakistan as an 'Islamic republic'.

The Islamization of Pakistan's legal system began with Prime Minister Zulfikar Ali Bhutto in the mid-1970s, but was greatly expanded following the military coup that brought General Zia ul-Huq to power in 1979. Zia appealed to Islamic values to legitimize his regime and granted religious parties, which did not enjoy much popular support, a power they had not previously had and a role in revamping the legal system. The consequences were borne principally by women and minorities; in the first year of his rule, Zia reversed virtually all the reforms that had benefited women in the previous thirty years (Rouse 1998). He introduced the Hudood Ordinances, which changed the laws on rape and adultery and made fornication a crime, and the Law of Evidence, which renders the evidence of a woman equal to only half that of a man in some cases. He introduced *shari'a* benches in the High Courts, which became centralized as the Federal Shariat Court in 1980. This court was authorized to review all laws to ensure their conformity with *shari'a*.

These changes to the legal system have reinforced social attitudes about male superiority and domination over women.[43] In the 1990s, Pakistan's democratically elected governments were unable or unwilling to repeal any of the Islamization laws that had been enacted under Zia's martial law regime. In his second term (1997–99), Prime Minister Nawaz Sharif proposed an amendment to the Constitution that would replace the legal system with Islamic law. At the time of the coup that removed Sharif from power in October 1999, the bill remained stalled in parliament. According to Human Rights Watch,

> Nawaz Sharif's continuing Islamization efforts ... reinforced the legitimacy of Zia ul-Huq's discriminatory Islamic laws; they have in effect also bestowed greater discretion and authority on judges to give legal weight, by invoking Islamic precedents and references at random, to biased assumptions about women in a variety of civil and criminal cases. For example, since 1996 courts have admitted cases challenging an adult woman's right to marry of her own free will, ostensibly an established right under family laws. (HRW 1999b: 23– 4)

Extremely conservative Islamists are a powerful constituency in Pakistan, including in the military that currently rules the country. If anything, their power and influence have been heightened by the US war in Afghanistan, launched in reprisal for the 11 September 2001 attacks, and by the raging conflict with India in Kashmir. President/General Parvaz Musharraf seems inclined to grant Islamists considerable influence within the country to offset anger over Pakistan's cooperation with the US in its 'war on terror'. Thus, national and international politics are important considerations in comprehending women's vulnerability to domestic violence.

In Pakistan, violence against women is endemic in all social spheres (HRCP 1998: 130). Yet despite the high incidence of intra-family violence, it is widely perceived by the law-enforcement system and society at large as a private family matter. There is virtually no prosecution of crimes of assault and battery when perpetrated by male family members against women; even intra-family murder and attempted murder are rarely prosecuted.[44] Although Pakistan ratified CEDAW in 1996, it has done little to reform its laws and practices to comply with the Convention.

In 1997, the Human Rights Commission of Pakistan (HRCP), an independent human rights organization, reported that '[d]omestic violence remained a pervasive phenomenon. The supremacy of the male and subordination of the female assumed to be part of the culture and even to have sanction of religion made violence by one against the other in a variety of its forms an accepted and pervasive feature of domestic life' (HRCP 1997: 185). According to a United Nations report on domestic violence, the family structure in Pakistan 'is mirrored and confirmed in the structure of society, which condones the oppression of women and tolerates male violence as one of the instruments in the perpetuation of this power balance'.[45]

The Islamization of the judiciary in Pakistan has exacerbated the problem. Judges have broad discretion to use Islamic precedents and references in a variety of civil and criminal cases (HRW 1999b: 23). Yasmine Hassan (1995: 57, 60) reports that in the absence of explicit criminalization of domestic violence, police and judges have tended to treat it as a non-justiciable, private or family matter or, at best, an issue for civil, rather than criminal, courts. If a domestic violence case does come before a criminal court, it falls under the Qisas and Diyat Ordinance of 1990, a body of Islamic criminal laws dealing with murder, attempted murder, and the crime of causing bodily 'hurt' (both intentional and unintentional). The law awards punishment either by *qisas* (retribution) or *diyat* (restitution) for the benefit of the victim or his or her legal heirs.[46] In *qisas* and *diyat* crimes, the victim or heir has the right to determine whether to exact retribution or restitution, or to pardon the accused. If the victim or heir chooses to waive *qisas*, or *qisas* is judicially held to be inapplicable, an offender is subject to *tazir* or discretionary punishment in the form of imprisonment.[47] In effect, the *qisas* and *diyat* laws have converted serious crimes, including murder and assault, into crimes against the individual rather than the state. In addition, women who have suffered domestic violence come under pressure by relatives to waive *qisas* altogether (HRW 1999b: 41–2; Shaheed 1994: 217). *Qisas* may not even apply in cases of wife murder if the woman has any children, because under Section 306(c) of the

Penal Code, the child or heir of the victim would also be a direct descendant of the offender. In most cases of spousal murder, the offender enjoys total legal impunity.

Honour killings represent a particular manifestation of domestic violence in which women are killed because they are seen as the repositories of family honour (HRCP 1997: 187). Although such killings fall under the murder provisions of the *qisas* and *diyat* laws, the courts generally apply the English common law principle of 'grave and sudden provocation' and award little or no punishment. For example, a man was tried for killing his daughter and a young man when he found them in a 'compromising state'. The judge sentenced the father to life imprisonment and a fine of Rs. 20,000 (US$500). When the case came before the Lahore High Court, the sentence was reduced to five years' imprisonment and a fine of Rs. 10,000 ($250) on the grounds that the man's actions were justified because his victims were engaging in immoral behaviour that could not be tolerated in an Islamic state such as Pakistan (ibid.). Another court used its discretionary authority under Section 338-F of the amended Penal Code which expressly permits the court to assess culpability on the basis of the Qur'an and *hadith* to decide that the right of self-defence could be invoked by male defendants in honour killings because 'a man who kills another man for defiling the honour of his wife or daughter is protecting his property and acting in self-defence' (HRW 1999b: 44–5).

Domestic abuse in Pakistan takes many forms, including being burned, disfigured with acid, beaten, threatened and even killed. In its annual report for 1997, HRCP reported: 'The worst victims were women of the poor and middle classes. Their resourcelessness not only made them the primary target of the police and the criminals, it also rendered them more vulnerable to oppressive customs and mores inside homes and outside' (HRCP 1997: 184). According to HRCP:

> The extreme forms it took included driving a woman to suicide or engineering an 'accident' (frequently the bursting of a kitchen stove) to cause her death... usually ... when the husband, often in collaboration with his side of the family, felt that the dower or other gifts he had expected from his in-laws in consequence of the marriage were not forthcoming, or/and he wanted to marry again, or he expected an inheritance from the death of his wife. (HRCP 1998: 185)

The pervasiveness of domestic violence in Pakistan provides powerful evidence of the failure on the part of the Pakistani state to defend women from violence. 'Islamization' of the country's legal regime has increased their vulnerability, and to the extent that these changes are acceptable to powerful constituencies, it is difficult for recent governments to institute law reforms, even if they were so inclined, because of the inevitable protests that this would provoke by conservative Islamists. However, the particular ways in which *shari'a* is interpreted and enforced in Pakistan – 'innovating' to achieve the most conservative possible approach – is subject to criticism that the Qur'anic principles are being violated.

As the above examples demonstrate, the relationship between religion and the state is critical for understanding and comparison of the problem of domestic violence in Muslim societies. The examples also demonstrate variations in understanding and implementation of '*shari'a*-based' rules in different states. While the use of *shari'a* to govern family relations contributes to certain commonalities, the variations across societies and over time are significant.

Section 10. Conclusion

Ultimately, the state is responsible for the regulation, restriction and punishment of domestic violence. Even if states commit themselves to the principle of women's rights (e.g. non-discriminatory clauses in national civil legislation, accession to international conventions), if they do not commit their resources to protect women from violence at home, they fail *as states* in their responsibility to protect their subjects from violence.

The problem of domestic violence and the difficulties in combating it are connected to the authoritarian and unrepresentative nature of many states in the Middle East, Africa and Asia. Authoritarian and/or unrepresentative rule bolsters patriarchal family relations, and fosters conditions in which social and religious conservatism can thrive (Sharabi 1988). According to Deniz Kandiyoti:

> The failure of modern states to create and adequately redistribute resources intensified tensions and cleavages expressed in religious, ethnic and regional terms … As the state itself uses local patronage networks and sectional rivalries in its distributive system, citizens also turn to their primary solidarities both to protect themselves and to compensate for inefficient administration. This reinforces the stranglehold of communities over their women, whose roles as boundary markers become heightened. (Kandiyoti 1991: 13–14)

When the state is incapable or unwilling to represent the interests of members of society, the importance of family and kinship relations for social survival is inflated. Consequently, any challenges to patriarchal authority in the domestic sphere – including but not limited to challenges to the use of violence – can be construed as threats to the family as an institution. This, in turn, lends itself to the idea that empowering women would corrode and menace the family, and that efforts to do so are, therefore, both dangerous and 'alien'. Conservative interpretations of Islam enforced through *shari'a* provide a means of counteracting this perceived 'threat' to the family, which, as the irony comes full circle, the state is willing to champion as a means of shifting critical attention from its own failings on to the putative dangers posed by advocates of women's rights.

Although *shari'a* is administered, interpreted and used in a variety of ways across Muslim societies, in certain contexts it may be used to justify failures and refusals on the part of states to provide women with the rights and protections that they are due as humans, as citizens, as women and as Muslims. And to the extent that popular notions about *shari'a* may conceive of certain forms of violence against women as normative and/or legitimate, this undercuts the efforts of those who seek to press the state to assume and exercise its responsibility.

In conclusion, because of the importance of the state – and the failure of so many states to protect and ensure the rights of their citizens – struggles for women's rights can be seen as part of a broader struggle against authoritarianism and unrepresentative rule, not a rejection of religion or culture. Many rights activists throughout the three regions are striving to cultivate and clarify this distinction, and it is to them that this study is dedicated with the hope that it can contribute to their cause.

Notes to Part IV

1. In 1958, two years after Morocco gained its independence from France, the state established a Code of Personal Status (*Mudawwanat al-ahwal al-shakhsiyah*), which reiterated and codified the (Maliki) tradition of family law jurisprudence. Among the provisions of this code was the husband's right to dissolve the marriage at will by means of *talaq* (repudiation), stating, 'I divorce thee', up to three times, although the code instituted the requirement of registering the divorce in court. If the husband chose to divorce his wife, she had no legal recourse, while her right to divorce was restricted and subject to confirmation by a *shari'a* court.

2. The background to this new law includes prodigious advocacy efforts by women's rights activists, and the political transition on the death of King Hassan II, who was succeeded by his son, Muhammad. Morocco has a vibrant women's rights movement, although there are some notable differences in the interests and goals that various sectors pursue; some have taken the position that women's rights can be assured and protected only through the replacement of the *Mudawwana* with a secular code enshrining liberal values, including the enforcement of the equality provisions of Morocco's Constitution. Others have sought to expand women's rights through the reform of Islamic jurisprudence, and to these ends the country has been a centre of some innovative efforts to reinterpret Qur'anic verses and *hadith* in a manner that would enhance the rights and equality of women. As a result of activism in the early 1990s, some modest reforms of the *Mudawwana* were instituted in 1993. But the accession to the throne by Muhammad, who, by many accounts is committed to bolder legal reforms, set the stage for the promulgation of the new law.

3. The *Mudawwana* does allow for the possibility of divorce on the grounds of 'general harm', but rules of evidence that would enable women to prove such harm are extremely difficult to fulfil, and judges tend to be sceptical of such charges and inclined to advocate reconciliation of the couple rather than prioritize relief for the wife.

4. In a comparative study of gender violence in ninety societies, four socio-cultural factors, taken together, were shown to be a strong predictor of spousal abuse in seventy-five societies. These factors are: (1) sexual economic inequality; (2) a pattern of using violence for conflict resolution; (3) male authority and decision-making in the home; and (4) divorce restrictions for women. The study found that the more dependent women are on men, the more vulnerable they are to violence (Levinson 1989).

5. *Shari'a* encompasses the ordinances derived from the Qur'an and *hadith*, and any other laws that are deduced from these two sources by methods considered valid in Islamic jurisprudence (*fiqh*). The two main methods are *ijma'* (consensus among Muslim jurists) and *ijtihad* (interpretation based on accepted rules of logic and religious texts).

6. The literature on women and Islam is vast. See Engineer 1992; el-Solh and Mabro 1994; Mernissi 1991; Moghissi 1999; and Yamani 1996.

7. These family relations, also known as 'personal status' issues, include marriage, divorce, custody and inheritance.

8. In the USA, women's rights activists initially began addressing domestic violence by responding to the concrete, urgent needs of victims by mobilizing to set up shelters and other resources to protect and assist vulnerable women. Later, frustrated by the unresponsiveness of the judicial system to battered women's situation, they turned towards a structural approach to criminalize domestic violence (Women, Law, and Development International 1996: 10).

9. Even in countries where a criminal justice approach has been adopted, for example the United States, there are serious problems and limitations to relying so thoroughly on the state. If the state lacks legitimacy, as it does for communities and populations subject to discrimination, victims are unlikely to see the state as a source of relief and protection, and are disinclined to bring the police into their homes or turn in family members. See Bumiller 1988; Crenshaw 1995; and Mills 1999.

10. Domestic violence includes psychological as well as physical abuse. Psychological aspects of relevance here include behaviour intended to intimidate and persecute, such as threats of abandonment, divorce or abuse; confinement and surveillance; threats to take away custody of children; verbal aggression and humiliation.

11. For information about NGO activities and initiatives in the Arab world, see Abdel Hadi and Darwiche (n.d.).

12. See <http://www.law.emory.edu/IFL>

13. The research for this study draws upon secondary sources, including reports and studies by organizations, research institutions and scholars who work on domestic violence. Three researchers, each working on a specific region (Bashar Tarabieh for the Middle East, Ngone Tine for sub-Saharan Africa and Patty Gossman for Asia), have surveyed the existing resources, and their research is incorporated in this study.

14. The few countries where domestic violence is not reported as 'common' include Côte d'Ivoire, Djibouti, Laos, Madagascar and the Maldives.

15. 'Research on domestic violence is fairly new, and has been undertaken perhaps only in the last 25 years. An increasing number of studies are now being undertaken in the developing world' (Davies 1994: 2).

16. Specific legal rules that epitomize and maintain gender inequality may include men's right to marry up to four women while women are restricted to marriage to one man at a time; differences in right to divorce, custody and inheritance; and differences in legal competency. Nevertheless, women are not entirely disadvantaged by *shari'a* nor thoroughly unequal to men; women have legal and financial rights, including independence (at least in principle) to manage their own affairs. Women are recognized as equal to men before God, the critical issue being not gender but devotion and righteousness.

17. For a discussion of interpretations of Sura 4: 34 in medieval and modern Islamic thought, see Stowasser 1998.

18. This translation is from *The Koran*, trans. N.J. Dawood (NY: Penguin Books, 1974), p. 370. For significantly different translations of this verse, see Engineer 1992: 46; An-Na'im 1996: 97.

19. For a detailed discussion of these issues, see el-Alami 1992.

20. For a history of human rights, see Henkin 1991; Lauren 1998.

21. As of 1 April 2000, CEDAW had been ratified or acceded to by 165 states. Only seventeen states had not ratified or acceded to CEDAW but, of these, eleven have majority Muslim populations: Afghanistan, Bahrain, Iran, Mauritania, Oman, Qatar, Saudi Arabia, Somalia, Sudan, Syrian Arab Republic and the United Arab Emirates (UN 2000: 151–2). Since then, Saudi Arabia has signed.

22. For an example of the way the Beijing Platform has been utilized by activists who work on or in Muslim societies, see Afkhami et al. 1998.

23. The factors identified in the Beijing Platform of Action include: 'social pressures, notably the shame of denouncing certain acts that have been perpetrated against women; women's lack of access to legal information, aid or protection; the lack of laws that effectively prohibit violence against women; failure to reform existing laws; inadequate efforts on the part of authorities to promote awareness of and enforce existing laws; and the absence of educational and other means to address the causes and consequences of violence' (Section D, para. 118).

24. Measures identified in the Beijing Platform of Action for governments to institute include: 'condemn violence against women and refrain from invoking any custom, tradition or religious consideration to avoid their obligations … exercise due diligence to prevent, investigate and, in accordance with national legislation, punish acts of violence against women, whether these acts are perpetrated by the state or by private persons' (Section D, para. 124).

25. The internet address for the WHO database on violence against women is <http://www.who.int/violence_injury_prevention/>

26. As of April 2000, only three countries with predominantly Muslim populations have signed the Protocol: Ghana, Senegal and Indonesia.

27. A third doctrine equating domestic violence with torture and cruel, inhuman and degrading treatment is being promoted by some feminist legal and human rights experts (see Copelon 1994).

28. See Chatterjee 1995; Halliday 1995; Howard 1990; Panikkar 1982; and Tibi 1990, 1994.

29. For a discussion of the implications of this on women, see Mohanty 1991.

30. See Ahmed 1992; Jeffrey and Basu 1998.

31. See Mani 1989; Walley 1997.

32. This comparative discussion of reservations to CEDAW draws on Connors 1996.

33. The reservations of Indonesia and Yemen pertain to Article 29(1) which allows reference of any dispute over the Convention to the International Court of Justice. Turkey's reservations include Article 29(1) as well as various paragraphs of Articles 15 and 16 (Connors 1996: 354–5).

34. The provisions of Article 16 would equalize men's and women's rights on matters of entering into and dissolving marriages, custody, inheritance, right to work and control over family decisions and resources. This article also prohibits child marriage and requires states to establish and enforce a minimum age of marriage, and to make registration of marriage compulsory.

35. Note that the Convention on the Elimination of Racial Discrimination allows a vote (two-thirds) by other parties to declare a state's reservations incompatible with the object of the Convention. CEDAW has no such provision.

36. The committee for CEDAW has persisted in seeking to minimize the impact of reservations based on *shari'a*. In 1994, the committee revised its guidelines for the preparation of country reports, recommending that states that have entered reservations should explain why they consider such reservations necessary, how they impact upon national law and policy, and how reservations to this Convention compare to reservations (or lack thereof) to other human rights treaties that guarantee similar rights.

37. While India and Nigeria have a constitution, Israel does not. However, Israel has a set of 'Basic Laws' that provide a constitutional framework for government.

38. In Nigeria, the issue of domestic violence is bound up in cultural notions of masculine privilege, which conservative interpretations of *shari'a* reinforce (Bukurta 1998; Ezeah 1993; Olawale 1996). One study found that 31 per cent of women have been subjected to physical abuse at least once in their lives (Odujinrin 1993 cited in United Nations 2000: 154). A study surveying rates of domestic violence between 1982 and 1988 found an upsurge in the practice, with a total of 1,220 women reporting battery over this period (Omorodion 1995). But it is unclear whether this indicates an increase in incidents of violence or women's willingness to report them. A 1997 study found that domestic violence is common in all regions and spans all social classes and groups (Atinmo 1997).

39. For an example of a state's attack on domestic critics of *shari'a*, see the discussion of the Egyptian government's treatment of the Arab Women's Solidarity Association in Mayer 1991: 180–1.

40. 'Among women beaten during pregnancy, a little more than half (56 per cent) reported being beaten less frequently during pregnancy than otherwise. For the remaining women, pregnancy did not protect them from violence: they were beaten equally often or more often while they were pregnant compared with when they were not pregnant' (el-Zanaty 1995: 208).

41. See also Mir-Hosseini 2000.

42. Human Rights Commission of Pakistan (HRCP), as well as an informal study conducted by the Women's Ministry, concluded that at least 80 per cent of all women in Pakistan are subjected to domestic violence (HRCP 1997: 130; Women's Ministry [Pakistan] 1985). Amnesty International (1997) has reported that some 95 per cent of women are believed to be subjected to such violence. Amnesty International (1998) has also reported findings by women's groups in Pakistan that 70 per cent of women are subjected to violence in their homes.

43. Pakistan ranks near the bottom globally for almost every social indicator concerning the lives of women. Only 25 per cent of Pakistani women are literate, compared to 55 per cent of men. See Amnesty International 1998; World Bank, 'Genderstats' at <http://www.genderstats.worldbank.org>

44. See generally Amnesty International 1998.

45. *Report of the World Conference of the United Nations Decade for Women: Equality, Development and Peace*, Copenhagen, 14–30 July 1980 (UN Publication, Sales no. E.80.IV.3 and Corrigendum), p. 30, cited in Y. Hassan 1995: 6.

46. For a detailed discussion of the *qisas* and *diyat* laws, see Human Rights Watch 1999b; Gottesman 1992.

47. According to Gottesman (1992: 454), the Federal Shariat Court has indicated that only crimes against the rights of God should be subject to *tazir*, not crimes against the rights of man. Distinguishing between the two categories of crimes involves determining whether the offender poses a threat to society at large.

Contributors

Essam Fawzy graduated in sociology from Zaqaziq University and then completed a Diploma in African Anthropological Studies at Cairo University's Institute of African Studies. He worked as a researcher at the Arab Research Centre and the Cairo Centre for Development Studies before taking up his current research position at the Alternative Development Studies Centre in Cairo. He has published widely, in English, Arabic and German, on a broad range of issues of socio-economic and political interest in Egypt, including a study on popular attitudes towards women judges, and a situation analysis of the supreme councils and national committees for childhood and motherhood in the Arab region.

Lisa Hajjar, a sociologist, teaches in the Law and Society Program at the University of California at Santa Barbara. In addition to domestic violence, her work on human rights issues has focused on torture, international criminal prosecutions and the legal practice of political lawyers. Her book, *Courting Conflict, the Israeli Military Court System in the West Bank and Gaza*, is forthcoming from University of California Press.

Rema Hammami is an assistant professor at the Women's Studies Centre at Birzeit University and also lectures in the Department of Sociology and Anthropology. She directs the centre's Gender, Law, and Development master's programme. She received her PhD from Temple University in Cultural Anthropology with a thesis entitled *Between Heaven and Earth: Transformations in Religiosity and Labour Among Southern Palestinian Peasant and Refugee Women, 1920–1993*. For the past several years she has been working on gender issues in Palestinian political and economic life and has served as the centre's consultant to the Palestinian Central Bureau of Statistics and the Ministry of Labour. She was director of the Women's Affairs Centre in Gaza from 1991 to 1995 and currently serves on the board of the Jerusalem Centre for Human Rights.

Penny Johnson is an associate researcher at the Institute of Women's Studies at Birzeit University and chaired the university's Human Rights Committee (1983–2000). Her current research interests include gender, war and citizenship, social policy, particularly social support and poverty eradication, and gender, family relations and public discourse. In a 2001 publication with Eileen Kuttab, she examined 'Where Have All the Women (and Men) Gone?: Reflections on Gender and the Second Palestinian Intifada'. She has served as member of the National Poverty Commission, contributing to the writing of the first National Poverty Report, and was a staff writer for the Palestinian delegation to the Madrid Conference and the Bilateral Negotiations and a member of the delegation's Human Rights Committee.

Fadwa al-Labadi is Assistant Professor in Gender and Social Development at Al-Quds (Jerusalem) University and formerly lecturer in Women's Studies and activities coordinator in the Institute of Women's Studies at Birzeit University. She was one of the founders of the Women's Studies Centre in East Jerusalem and former editor of its magazines, *Al-Mara* (Woman) and *Kul al-Nisaa* (Every Woman). She received her PhD in Women's Studies from the University of Kent at Canterbury, writing her thesis on *Women and Citizenship in Post-Colonial Palestine*. She has recently completed an MA in International and Comparative Legal Studies at the School of Oriental and African Studies at London University. Prior to her postgraduate education, she served as a teacher of Arabic in the public school system in the years of Israeli military occupation and was harassed by the Israeli military authorities for her labour and women's movement activities.

Asifa Quraishi is a doctoral student at Harvard Law School, writing her SJD thesis in comparative Islamic and American legal theory. She holds an LLM from Columbia Law School (focusing on federal *habeas corpus* law), a JD from UC Davis and a BA from UC Berkeley. She has held federal clerkships in the Ninth Circuit United States Court of Appeals and has published articles in the fields of Islamic and comparative law, including gender issues. Ms Quraishi has served on the board of Karamah: Muslim Women Lawyers for Human Rights and the Muslim Women's League and is a founding board member of the National Association of Muslim Lawyers (NAML). As first a youth and now a mother invested in the furture of the American Muslim community, Asifa Quraishi continues to be involved in the various educational and acivist projects that have been part of her life for many years.

Najeeba Syeed-Miller is a professional mediator in the Los Angeles County area. She has attended over four hundred hours of conflict resolution training. Her trainers include H. Jamal Muhammad of Pensylvania State University. Most recently, she returned from a one-month training course held in The Hague by the International Institute for Mediation and Conflict Resolution and the University of Erasmus. In addition, she recently co-trained United Nations relief workers who will serve in the rehabilitation efforts in Afghanistan. In 2003–04 she will be implementing a fellowship focused on alternative dispute resolution and diversity, with a special emphasis on family development and international conflicts.

Ms Syeed-Miller has mediated a large number of cases, including youth-oriented disputes, inter-racial disputes and community-based conflicts. She has trained hundreds of people in mediation skills and conflict resolution issues. Her trainees range from prosecutors to community leaders. While at law school she was the coordinator of Student Mediation Services and was awarded the Oexmann Fellowship for her work in community conflict resolution. During college, she served as the coordinator for the Peace and Conflict Studies Department and was awarded the Hazel Steinfeldt Scholarship for excellence in community conflict resolution work. Ms Syeed-Miller is dedicated to the use of mediation as a grass-roots tool. In addition, she has made presentations at universities such as Harvard Divinity School, Georgetown Law School, Columbia Law School and other institutions in the area of conflict resolution and minority communities. Ms Syeed-Miller chairs the national 'Muslim Peacebuilding' conference, which has been held for the last three years. The 2003 theme was 'Muslim Rebuilding after 9/11'.

Lynn Welchman is director of the Centre of Islamic and Middle Eastern Law (CIMEL) at the School of Oriental and African Studies (SOAS), University of London, and a senior lecturer in the SOAS Law Department. Prior to taking up the post at SOAS, she worked with the Palestinian non-governmental human rights movement for many years, and has also undertaken human rights work with international NGOs. Her PhD thesis was on the implementation of Muslim family law in the Palestinian West Bank, where she has also worked with the Women's Centre for Legal Aid and Counselling and served as a visiting lecturer at the Institute of Women's Studies, Birzeit University.

Bibliography

'Abd al-'Ati, H. (1977) *The Family Structure in Islam*, Indianapolis, IN: American Trust Publications.

Abdalla, A. (2001) 'Principles of Islamic Interpersonal Conflict Intervention: A Search within Islam and Western Literature', *Journal of Law and Religion*, 15 (Fall).

Abdel Hadi, A. and N. Darwiche (n.d.) 'Strategies to Fight Domestic Violence Against Women in the Arab Countries' (draft), New York: UN Division on the Advancement of Women.

Abdel Halim, A. M. (1994) 'Tools of Suppression', in Center for Women's Global Leadership, *Gender Violence and Women's Human Rights in Africa*, New Brunswick, NJ: Center for Women's Global Leadership.

Abdul Fattah, A. F. (1991) *Al-talaq fi'l-mujtami' al-misri bayn al-namat al-mithali wa'l-namat al-waqa'i*, unpublished PhD thesis, 'Ain Shams University.

Abdul Rahman, A. et al. (1999) *Al-mar'a al-misriyya wa'l-i'lam fi'l-rif wa'l-hadar*, Cairo: al-'arabi li'l-nashr wa'l-tawzi'.

Abdul-Rauf, M. (1995) *Marriage in Islam*, Alexandria: Al-Saadawi Publications.

Abdul Tawab, M. (1980) *Al-wasit fi qanun al-ahwal al-shakhsiyya raqm 44 1979 wa'l- qararat al-wizariyya al-munaffadha lahu*, Tanta: al-maktaba al-qanuniyya al-haditha.

— (1990) *Mausu'at al-ahwal al-shakhsiyya*, Vol. I Mansoura: Dar al-wafa'.

— (1996) *Al-wad' al-mu'asir bayn al-shari'a al-islamiyya wa'l-qanun al-wad'i*, Cairo: Dar al-shuruq.

Abou el-Fadl, K. (1994) 'Islamic Law and Muslim Minorities: The Juristic Discourse on Muslim Minorities from the Second/Eighth to the Eleventh/Seventeenth Centuries', *Islamic Law and Society*, 1 (2).

— (1997) *The Authoritative and Authoritarian in Islamic Discourses: A Contemporary Case Study*, 2nd edn, Austin, TX: Dar Taiba.

— (1999) '*Shurut* in Islamic Marriage Contracts', in *The Islamic Marriage Contract: An International Conference*, 29–31 January, Harvard Law School Islamic Legal Studies Program (audiotape).

— (2001) *Speaking in God's Name: Islamic Law, Authority and Women*, Oxford: Oneworld Publications.

Abu Lughod, L. (1998) 'The Marriage of Feminism and Islamism in Egypt: Selective Repudiation as a Dynamic of Post-Colonial Politics', in L. Abu Lughod (ed.), *Remaking Women: Feminism and Modernity in the Middle East*, Princeton, NJ: Princeton University Press.

Abu Sardane, M. H. (n.d.) *Al-qada' ash-shar'i fi 'ahd as-sulta al-wataniyya al-filastiniyya* [The *Shar'i* Judiciary under the Palestinian Authority], Gaza: Sharakat al-Fanun.

Abu Zahra, M. (1957) *Al-ahwal al-shakhsiyya*, Cairo: Dar al-fikr al-'arabi.

Abu Zeid, N. H. (1999) *Dawa'ir al-khauf: qira'a fi khitab al-mar'a*, Beirut: Markaz al-thiqafi al-'arabi.

Afkhami, M. and H. Vazeri (1996) *Claiming Our Rights: A Manual for Women's Human Rights Education in Muslim Societies*, Bethesda, MD: Sisterhood is Global Institute.

Afkhami, M., G. H. Nemiroff and H. Vazeri (1998) *Safe and Secure: Eliminating Violence Against Women and Girls in Muslim Societies*, Bethesda, MD: Sisterhood is Global Institute.

Ahmed, L. (1992) *Women and Gender in Islam: Historical Roots of a Modern Debate*, New Haven, CT: Yale University Press.

el-'Alami, D. S. (1992) *The Marriage Contract in Islamic Law in the Shari'ah and Personal Status Laws of Egypt and Morocco*, London: Graham and Trotman.

el-'Alami, D. S. and D. Hinchcliffe (1996) *Islamic Marriage and Divorce Laws of the Arab World*, The Hague: Kluwer Law International.

Ali, S. S. (1996) 'Is an Adult Muslim Woman *Sui Juris*? Some Reflections on the Concept of "Consent in Marriage" without a *Wali* (with particular reference to the Saima Waheed Case')', *Yearbook of Islamic and Middle Eastern Law*, 3: 156–74.

Allen, M. S. (1992) 'Muslim Faith Part of Daily Life for Imam of Minneapolis Mosque', *Star Tribune* (Minneapolis), 8 August.

al-'Alwani, T. J. (1993) *The Ethics of Disagreement in Islam*, Herndon, VA: International Institute of Islamic Thought.

— (1985) *Ethics of Disagreement in Islam*, Herndon, VA: International Institute of Islamic Thought.

'Amara, M. (ed.) (1991) *Al-'amal al-kamila li'l-imam al-shaykh Muhammad 'Abdu*, Vol. II, Cairo: Dar al-shuruq.

American Muslim Council (1992) 'Muslim Census Inaugurated', *AMC Report*, 2 (1).

el-Amin, M. M. (1991) *Family Roots: the Qur'anic View of Family Life*, Chicago, IL: International Ummah Foundation.

Amnesty International (1997) 'Women's Human Rights Remain a Dead Letter', London: Amnesty International, ASA 33/07/97.

— (1998) 'Pakistan: No Progress on Women's Rights', London: Amnesty International, ASA 33/013/98.

Anderson, J. N. D. (1951) 'Homicide in Islamic Law', *Bulletin of the School of Oriental and African Studies*, 13 (4): 811–28.

An-Na'im, A. (1990) *Toward an Islamic Reformation: Civil Liberties, Human Rights, and International Law*, Syracuse, NY: Syracuse University Press.

— (ed.) (1992) *Human Rights in Cross-Cultural Perspectives: A Quest for Consensus*, Syracuse, NY: Syracuse University Press.

— (1994) 'State Responsibility under International Human Rights Law to Change Religious and Customary Laws', in R. Cook (ed.), *Human Rights of Women: National and International Perspectives*, Philadelphia, PA: University of Pennsylvania Press.

— (1996) 'Islam and Women's Rights: A Case Study', *Women Living Under Muslim Laws Dossier*, 14/15.

al-'Arabi, M. H. (1984) *Al-mabadi' al-qada'iyya li mahkamat al-isti'naf ash-shar'iyya* [Legal Principles of the *Shari'a* Court of Appeal], Vol. II (1973–83), Amman: Dar al-Furqan.

Arabi, O. (2001) *Studies in Modern Islamic Jurisprudence*, The Hague: Kluwer Law International.

el-Arousi, M. (1997) 'Judicial Dissolution of Marriage', *Journal of Islamic and Comparative Law*, 7 (13).

Asad, T. (1983) 'Anthropological Conceptions of Religion: Reflections on Geertz', *Man*, 18.

al-'Ashmawi, M. S. (1996) *Al-shari'a al-islamiyya wa'l-qanun al-misri*, Cairo: Maktaba madbuli.

Atawneh, F. (1999) *'Karithat masna' al-wala'at fi'l-khalil'* [The Hebron Lighter Factory Disaster], Archive of the Centre for Democracy and Workers' Rights, 27 October 1999.

Atinmo, M. (1997) 'Sociocultural Implications of Wife Beating in Nigeria', in *Men, Women and Violence*, CODESRIA Institute.

Awa, M. S. (1982) *Punishment in Islamic Law: A Comparative Study*, Indianapolis, IN: American Trust Publications.

Awad, A. (2002) 'Court Enforces Mahr Provision: Odatalla Recognizes the Secular Terms of a Religious Agreement', *New Jersey Law Journal*, 9 September 2002.

'Awais, S. (1977) *Hadith 'an al-mar'a al-misriyya: dirasa thiqafiyya ijtima'iyya*, Cairo: Matba'at Atlas.

Badawi, J. (1995) *Gender Equity in Islam: Basic Principles*, Plainfield, IN: American Trust Publications.

Badran, H. (1994) *'Nisa' mas'ulat 'an usra'*, Seminar at the National Centre for Statistics, Cairo.

Bagby, I., P. Perl and B. Froehle (2001) *The Mosque in America: National Portrait, A Report from the Mosque Study Project*, 26 April 2001. Available from:<http://www.cair-net.org/mosquereport.com>

Baker, A. L. (2002) 'Perceptions of Islam and Their Influence on American Legislative and Judicial Decisions Involving Child Custody', 5 July 2002. Available from: <http://www.ishipress.com/baker-re.htm>

Bakri, A. (2000) *'Al-ab'ad al-qanuniyya wa'l-idariyya wa'l taghyirat 'ala al-mahakim ash-shar'iyya fi filastin, 1995–2000'* [Legal and Administrative Measures and Changes in the *Shari'a* courts in Palestine], background paper for Birzeit University's Institute of Women's Studies Comparative Islamic Law Project.

Barazangi, N. H. (2000) 'Muslim Women's Islamic Higher Learning is a Human Right', in G. Webb (ed.), *Windows of Faith: Muslim Women Scholar-Activists in North America*, Syracuse, NY: Syracuse University Press.

Bassiouni, C. (ed.) (1982) *The Islamic Criminal Justice System*, Dobbs-Ferry, NY: Oceana Publications.

— (1983) *International Extradition: US Law and Practice*, Dobbs-Ferry, NY: Oceana Publications.

— (1987) 'A Search for Islamic Criminal Justice: An Emerging Trend in Muslim States', in B. Stowasser (ed.), *The Islamic Impulse*, Washington, DC: CCAS, Georgetown University.

Beinin, J. and J. Stork (eds) (1997) *Political Islam: Essays from Middle East Report*, London: I.B. Tauris.

Berger, M. (1999) 'The Shari'a and Legal Pluralism: The Case of Syria', in B. Dupret, M. Berger and L. al-Zwaini (eds), *Legal Pluralism in the Arab World*, The Hague: Kluwer Law International.

Bishara, A. (1998) 'Reflections on the Reality of the Oslo Process', in G. Giacaman and D. J. Lonning (eds), *After Oslo: New Realities, Old Problems*, London: Pluto Press, pp. 212–26.

Bisharat, G. E. (1989) *Palestinian Lawyers and Israeli Rule: Law and Disorder in the West Bank*, Austin, TX: University of Texas Press.

al-Bishri, T. (1996) *Al-wada' al-qanuni al-mu'asir bayn al-shari'a al-islamiyya wa'l-qanun al-wada'i*, Cairo: Dar al-shuruq.

Botiveau, B. (1999) 'Palestinian Law: Social Segmentation Versus Centralization', in B.

Dupret, M. Berger and L. al-Zwaini (eds), *Legal Pluralism in the Arab World*, The Hague: Kluwer Law International, pp. 73–95.

Bourdieu, P. (1979) *Outline of a Theory of Practice*, Cambridge: Cambridge University Press.

Bukurta, M. E. (1998) 'Pattern of Wife Abuse within Families in Yola Adamawa State Nsukka', MA thesis, Department of Vocational Teacher Education, University of Nigeria.

Bumiller, K. (1988) *The Civil Rights Society: The Social Construction of Victims*, Baltimore, MD: Johns Hopkins University Press.

Bunch, C. and N. Reilly (1999) *Demanding Accountability: The Global Campaign and Vienna Tribunal for Women's Human Rights*, New Brunswick, NJ: Center for Women's Global Leadership, Rutgers University, and United Nations Development Fund for Women.

al-Buti, M. S. R. (n.d.) *Ila kull fata tu'min bi-allah*, Cairo: Maktaba Zahran.

Callaway, B. and L. Creevey (1989) 'Women and the State in Islamic West Africa', in S. E. Charlton, J. Everett and K. Staudt (eds), *Women, the State and Development*, Albany, NY: State University of New York Press.

Carroll, L. (1982) '*Talaq-i-Tafwid* and Stipulations in a Muslim Marriage Contract: Important Means of Protecting the Position of the South Asian Muslim Wife', *Modern Asian Studies*, XVI.

— (1996) 'Qur'an 2: 229: "A Charter Granted to the Wife"? Judicial *Khul'* in Pakistan', *Islamic Law and Society*, 3 (1): 91.

CBNSS (Central Bureau for National Service and Statistics), *Census 1976–1986*, Cairo.

— (1998) *Taqrir al-hala al-ijtima'iyya fi misr*, Cairo.

CEDAW (1987) 'Report of the Committee on the Elimination of Discrimination Against Women', Sixth Session, 42 UNGAOR Supp (no. 38), UN Doc. A/42/38.

Chang, I. (1990) 'Muslim Matchmakers: Islamic Leaders Adhere to Strict Religious Traditions in Helping to Bring Together Couples Far from Home', *Los Angeles Times*, 23 May 1990, Part E.

Charrad, M. (1990) 'State and Gender in the Maghrib', *Middle East Report*, 163 (March–April).

Chatterjee, P. (1993) *The Nation and Its Fragments: Colonial and Postcolonial Histories*, Princeton, NJ: Princeton University Press.

— (1995) 'Religious Minorities and the Secular State: Reflections on an Indian Impasse', *Public Culture*, 8.

Chiba, M. (1986) 'Introduction', in M. Chiba (ed.), *Asian Indigenous Law in Interaction with Received Law*, London and New York: KPI, pp. 1–9.

Connors, J. (1994) 'Government Measures to Confront Violence Against Women', in M. Davies (ed.), *Women and Violence: Realities and Responses Worldwide*, London: Zed Books.

— (1996) 'The Women's Convention in the Muslim World', in M. Yamani (ed.), *Feminism and Islam: Legal and Literary Perspectives*, New York: New York University Press.

Coomaraswamy, R. (1996) 'Further Promotion and Encouragement of Human Rights and Fundamental Freedoms, Including the Question of the Programme and Methods of Work of the Commission: Alternative Approaches and Ways and Means within the United Nations System for Improving the Effective Enjoyment of Human Rights and Fundamental Freedoms', Report to the UN Commission on Human Rights, 6 February, E/CN.4/1996/53.

— (1999) 'Violence Against Women in the Family', Report to the UN Commission on Human Rights, 10 March, E/CN.4/1999/68.

— (2000) 'Combating Domestic Violence: Obligations of the State', in UNICEF (ed.), *Domestic Violence Against Women and Girls*, Florence, Italy: Innocenti Research Center, UNICEF.

Copelon, R. (1994) 'Intimate Terror: Understanding Domestic Violence as Torture', in R. Cook (ed.), *Human Rights of Women: National and International Perspectives*, Philadelphia, PA: University of Pennsylvania Press.

Craske, N. (1998) 'Remasculinization and the Neoliberal State in Latin America', in V. Randall and G. Waylan (eds), *Gender, Politics and the State,* London: Routledge, pp. 100–20.

Crenshaw, K. (1995) 'Mapping the Margins: Intersectionality, Identity Politics, and Violence Against Women of Color', in K. Crenshaw, N. Gotanda, G. Peller and K. Thomas (eds), *Critical Race Theory: The Key Writings that Formed the Movement*, New York: New York Press.

Curthoys, A. (1993) 'Gender, Citizenship and National Identity', *Feminist Review*, 44: 19–38.

Dannin, R. (2000) 'Understanding the Multi-Ethnic Dilemma of African American Muslims', in Y. Haddad and J. Esposito (eds), *Muslims on the Americanization Path?*, New York: Oxford University Press.

Davies, M. (ed.) (1994) *Women and Violence: Realities and Responses Worldwide*, London: Zed Books.

Diwan, I. and R. Shaban (1999) *Development Under Adversity: The Palestinian Economy in Transition*, Washington, DC: Palestine Economic Policy Research Institute (MAS) and World Bank.

Dobash, R. E. and R. P. Dobash (1980) *Violence Against Wives: A Case Study Against Patriarchy*, London: Open Books.

— (1992) *Women, Violence and Social Change*, London: Routledge.

Doi, A. R. (1984) *Shari'ah: The Islamic Law*, London: Ta-Ha Publishers.

— (1989) *Woman in Shari'ah*, London: Ta-Ha Publishers.

Dupret, B. (1999) 'Legal Pluralism, Normative Plurality and the Arab World', in B. Dupret, M. Berger and L. al-Zwaini (eds), *Legal Pluralism in the Arab World*, The Hague: Kluwer Law International.

— (2001) 'Sexual Morality at the Egyptian Bar: Female Circumcision, Sex Change Operations and Motives for Suing', *Islamic Law and Society*, 9 (1): 42–69.

Effah, J., D. Mbachu and S. Onyegbula (1995) *Unequal Rights: Discriminatory Laws and Practices Against Women in Nigeria,* Lagos: Constitutional Rights Project.

Eissa, D. (1999) *Constructing the Notion of Male Superiority over Women in Islam: The Influence of Sex and Gender Stereotyping in the Interpretation of the Qur'an and the Implications for a Modernist Exegesis of Rights*, Occasional Paper no. 11. Montpellier, France: Women Living under Muslim Laws.

Engineer, A. A. (1992) *The Rights of Women in Islam*, New York: St Martin's Press.

— (1996) *Communalism in India*, New Dehli: Vikas Publishers.

Esposito, J. (1982) *Women in Muslim Family Law*, Syracuse, NY: Syracuse University Press.

Ezeah, P. C. (1993) *Socialization, Social Class and Marital Violence: A Study of Wife Abuse in Nsukka Local Government Area, Enugu State Nsukka*, MA thesis, Department of Sociology/ Anthropology, University of Nigeria.

Fadel, M. (1998) 'Reinterpreting the Guardian's Role in the Islamic Contract of Marriage: The Case of the Maliki School', *Journal of Islamic Law*, 3 (1).

Farah, M. (1984) *Marriage and Sexuality in Islam: A Translation of al-Ghazali's Book on the Etiquette of Marriage from the Ihya'*, Salt Lake City, UT: University of Utah Press.

al-Faruqi, I. (1982) *Islamization of Knowledge: General Principles and Work Plan*, Herndon, VA: International Institute of Islamic Thought.

al-Faruqi, M. (2000) 'Women's Self-Identity in the Qur'an and Islamic Law', in G. Webb (ed.), *Windows of Faith: Muslim Women Scholar-Activists in North America*, Syracuse, NY: Syracuse University Press.

Forte, D. (1983) 'Islamic Law in American Courts', *Suffolk Transnational Law Journal*, 7 (1).

Freeland, R. and M. Lau (forthcoming) 'The Sharia and English Law: Identity and Justice for British Muslims', in A. Quraishi and F. Vogel (eds), *The Islamic Marriage Contract: Case Studies in Islamic Family Law*, Cambridge, MA: Harvard University Press.

Fried, S. (ed.) (1994) *The Indivisibility of Women's Human Rights: A Continuing Dialogue*, New Brunswick, NJ: Center for Women's Global Leadership.

Ghasoub, M. (1991) *Al-mar'a al-'arabiyya wa dhukuriyyat al-'asala*, London: Al Saqi.

al-Ghazali, M. (1993) *Huquq al-insan bayn ta'alim al-islam wa i'lan al-umum al-muttahida*, Alexandria: Dar al-da'wa.

— (1994) *Qadaya al-mar'a bayn al-rakida wa'l-wafida*, Cairo: Dar al-shuruq.

Giacaman, G. (1998) 'In the Throes of Oslo: Palestinian Society, Civil Society and the Future', in G. Giacaman and D. J. Lonning (eds), *After Oslo: New Realities, Old Problems*, London: Pluto Press, pp. 1–15.

Giacaman, R. and P. Johnson (1990) 'Building Barricades and Breaking Barriers', in Z. Lockman and J. Beinin (eds), *Intifada: The Palestinian Uprising Against Israeli Occupation*, London: I.B. Tauris, pp. 155–69.

al-Gindi, A. N. (1987) *Al-ahwal al-shakhsiyya, ta'liq 'ala nusus al-qanun*, Cairo: Al-qahira al-haditha li'l-taba'a.

Gottesman, E. (1992) 'The Reemergence of Qisas and Diyat in Pakistan', *Columbia Human Rights Law Review*, 23 (2): 433–61.

Green, D. (1999), *Gender Violence in Africa: African Women's Responses*, New York: St Martin's Press.

Greenberg-Kobrin, M. (1999) 'Civil Enforceablity of Religious Pre-Nuptial Agreements', *Columbia Journal of Law and Social Problems*, 397 (Summer).

Griffiths, J. (1999) 'Preface', in B. Dupret, M. Berger and L. al-Zwaini (eds), *Legal Pluralism in the Arab World*, The Hague: Kluwer Law International, pp. vii–ix.

Gustafson, P. (1991) 'Woman's Status as Expert Questioned', *Minneapolis-St. Paul Star Tribune*, 28 February 1991, Section 2B.

Haddad, E. N. (1920–1921) 'Blood Revenge Among the Arabs', *Journal of the Palestine Oriental Society*, 1: 103–12.

Haddad, Y. (2000) 'The Dynamics of Islamic Identity', in Y. Haddad and J. Esposito (eds), *Muslims on the Americanization Path?*, New York: Oxford University Press.

Haddad, Y. and A. T. Lummis (1987) *Islamic Values in the United States: A Comparative Study*, New York: Oxford University Press.

Haj-Yahya, M. (1995) 'Toward Culturally Sensitive Intervention within Arab Families in Israel', *Contemporary Family Therapy*, 17 (4): 429–47.

— (1996) 'Wife Abuse in the Arab Society in Israel: Some Challenges for Future Change', in J. L. Edleson and Z. C. Eisikovitz (eds), *Future Interventions with Battered Women and Their Families*, Thousand Oaks, CA: Sage Publications.

Hallaq, W. B. (1997) *A History of Islamic Legal Theories*, Cambridge: Cambridge University Press.

Halliday, F. (1995) 'Relativism and Universalism in Human Rights: The Case of the Islamic Middle East', *Political Studies*, 43.

Halliday, F. and H. Alavi (eds) (1988) *State and Ideology in the Middle East and Pakistan*, London: Macmillan.

Hamadeh, N. (1996) 'Islamic Family Legislation: The Authoritarian Discourse of Silence', in M. Yamani (ed.), *Feminism and Islam: Legal and Literary Perspectives*, New York: New York University Press.

Hammami, R. (1990) 'Women, the Hijab and the Intifada', *Middle East Report*, 20: 24–31.

— (1993) 'Women in Palestinian Society', in M. Heiberg and G. Ovensen (eds), *Palestinian Society in Gaza, West Bank, and Arab Jerusalem: A FAFO Survey of Living Conditions*, Oslo: Fagbevegelsens Senter for Forskning Utredning og Dokumentasjon, pp. 283–311.

— (1995) 'NGOs: The Professionalisation of Politics', *Race and Class*, 37: 51–64.

— (1996) 'Survey of Palestinian Opinion', Nablus: Centre for Palestinian Research and Studies.

— (1997a) 'The Legacy of the Intifada in the Politics of the Present', Nablus: CPRS.

— (1997b) 'The Heritage of the Intifada in the Politics of the Present', in N. Izzat Said and R. Hammami (eds), *Analytical Studies of Political and Social Attitudes in Palestine*, Nablus: CPRS (in Arabic), pp. 20–32.

— (2000) 'Palestinian NGOs since Oslo: from NGO Politics to Social Movements?', *Middle East Report*, 214: 16–19.

Hammami, R. and P. Johnson (1999) 'Equality with a Difference: Gender and Citizenship in Transitional Palestine', *Social Politics*: 315–43.

Hanifah, B. (2000) 'Ask Bilqis', *Zawaj.com* [Internet], 25 December 2000. Available from: <http://www.zawaj.com/bilqis/12–25–2000.html>

Hardy, M. J. L. (1963) *Blood Feuds and the Payment of Blood Money in the Middle East*, Beirut.

Hassan, R. (1995) *Women's Rights and Islam: From the I.C.P.D. to Beijing*, Louisville, KY: NISA Publications.

Hassan, Y. (1995) *The Haven Become Hell*, Lahore: Shirkat Gah.

Hatab, Z. (1976) *Tatawwur bani al-usra wa'l-judhur al-tarikhiyya wa'l-ijtima'iyya li qadayaha al-mu'sira*, Beirut: Ma'had al-inma' al-'arabi.

Heiberg, M. (1993) 'Opinions and Attidudes', in M. Heiberg and G. Ovensen (eds), *Palestinian Society in Gaza, West Bank, and Arab Jerusalem: A FAFO Survey of Living Conditions*, Oslo: Fagbevegelsens Senter for Forskning Utredning og Dokumentasjon, pp. 249–82.

Heiberg, M. and G. Ovensen (eds) (1993) *Palestinian Society in Gaza, West Bank and Arab Jerusalem: A FAFO Survey of Living Conditions*, Oslo: Fagbevegelsens Senter for Forskning Utredning og Dokumentasjon.

Helie-Lucas, M. (1994) 'The Preferential Symbol for Islamic Identity: Women in Personal Status Laws', in V. Moghadam (ed.), *Identity Politics and Women: Cultural Reassertion and Feminisms in International Perspective*, Boulder, CO: Westview Press, pp. 391–407.

Henderson, M. E. (1997–98) 'U.S. State Court Review of Islamic Law Custody Decrees – When are Islamic Custody Decrees in the Child's Best Interest?' *Brandeis Journal of Family Law* 36 (4): 423.

Henkin, L. (1991) *The Age of Right*, New York: Columbia University Press.

al-Hibri, A. (1993) 'Symposium on Religious Law: Roman Catholic, Islamic, and Jewish Treatment of Familial Issues, including Education, Abortion, in Vitro Fertilization, Prenuptial Agreements, Contraception, and Marital Fraud', *Loyola of Los Angeles International and Comparative Law Journal*, 16 (9).

— (1997) 'Islam, Law and Custom: Redefining Muslim Women's Rights', *American University Journal of International Law & Policy*, 12.

— (2000) 'An Introduction to Muslim Women's Rights', in G. Webb (ed.), *Windows of Faith: Muslim Women Scholar-Activists in North America*, Syracuse, NY: Syracuse University Press.

— (2001) 'Muslim Women's Rights in the Global Village: Challenges and Opportunities', *Journal of Law and Religion*, 15 (1 and 2): 37–66.

Hilal, J. (2000) 'Secularism in Palestinian Political Culture', background paper for Palestine Case Study, Comparative Islamic Family Law Project, Birzeit: Institute of Women's Studies.

Hilal, J., P. Johnson and R. Musa (2003) *In the Public Interest: Public Revenues, Social Allocations and Social Needs in Palestine*, Ramallah: Forum for Social and Economic Policy in Palestine.

al-Hoda Society (1998) 'Arab Women and the Conspiracy of Secular Women', Birzeit: Student Committee of the Islamic Bloc (in Arabic).

Hoodfar, H. (1995) *The Women's Movement in Iran: Women at the Crossroads of Secularization and Islamization*, Women's Movement Series, no. 1, Montpellier: Women Living under Muslim Laws.

— (1997) *Between Marriage and the Market: Intimate Politics and Survival in Cairo*, Berkeley, CA: University of California Press.

Howard, R. (1990) 'Group versus Individual Identity in the African Debate', in A. An-Na'im and F. Deng (eds), *Human Rights in Africa: Cross-Cultural Perspectives*, Washington, DC: Brookings Institution.

HRCP (Human Rights Commission of Pakistan) (1997) *State of Human Rights in 1996*, Lahore: HRCP.

— (1998) *State of Human Rights in 1997*, Lahore: HRCP.

HRW (Human Rights Watch) (1999a) *Human Rights Watch World Report 1998*, New York: HRW.

— (1999b) *Crime or Custom? Violence Against Women in Pakistan*, New York: HRW.

Ibn al-Gouzi, A. R. (n.d.) *Ahkam al-mar'a*, Cairo: Dar al-kitab al-muhammadi.

Ibn Kathir al-Dimashqi, E. (n.d.) *Tafsir al-qur'an al-'azim*, 2/V41.

Ibn Sa'd, M. (1997) *The Women of Madina*, trans. A. Bewley, London: Ta-Ha Publishers.

Ibrahim, I. (1998) 'The Status of Arab Women in Israel', *Critique*, 12: 107–20.

Imam, A. (1994) 'Politics, Islam, and Women in Kano', in V. Moghadem (ed.), *Identity Politics and Women: Cultural Reassertions and Feminisms in International Perspective*, Boulder, CO: Westview Press.

Iqbal, A. (1987) 'For Moslems, It's Not Love and Marriage', *Chicago Tribune*, 18 September 1987, Section Chicagoland.

ISIM (International Institute for the Study of Islam in the Modern World) (1998) 'Towards Carving the Islamic Space in the West', *International Institute for the Study of Islam in the Modern World Newsletter*, 5: 106–13.

Izzat Said, N. (1997) 'The Conceptual and Methodological Challenges in the Study of Palestinian Public Opinion', in N. Izzat Said and R. Hammami (eds), *Analytical Studies of Political and Social Attitudes in Palestine*, Nablus: CPRS (in Arabic), pp. 1–19.

Jad, I., P. Johnson and R. Giacaman (2000) 'Transit Citizens: Gender and Citizenship Under the Palestinian Authority', in S. Joseph (ed.), *Gender and Citizenship in the Middle East*, Syracuse, NY: Syracuse University Press, pp. 137–57.

Jasper, J. (1997) *The Art of Moral Protest: Culture, Biography and Creativity in Social Movements*, Chicago, IL: University of Chicago Press.

Jeffrey, P. and A. Basu (eds) (1998) *Appropriating Gender: Women's Activism and Politicized Religion in South Asia*, New York: Routledge.

Johnson, P. (1997) *Social Support: Gender and Social Policy in Palestine*, Birzeit: Institute of Women's Studies.

Johnson, P. and E. Kuttab (2001) 'Where Have All the Women (and Men) Gone?: Reflections on Gender and the Second Palestinian Intifada', *Feminist Review*, 69: 21–43.

Joint Committee of the Legislative Committee and the Office of Social Affairs and Awqaf and Religious Affairs in the People's Assembly, *Report on the Decision on Law no. 44 of 1979*, Cairo.

Jones-Pauly, C. (1999) 'Muslims in the Diaspora: The Recognition of Marriage Contracts in German Law', Diasporas and Minorities Panel, in *The Islamic Marriage Contract: An International Conference*, Harvard Law School Islamic Legal Studies Program, 29–31 January (audiotape).

Kandiyoti, D. (1991) 'Introduction', in D. Kandiyoti (ed.), *Women, Islam and the State*, Philadelphia, PA: Temple University Press, pp. 1–21.

— (1998) 'Bargaining with Patriarchy', *Gender and Society*, 2 (3): 274–90.

Khader, A. (1998) *Al-qanun wa mustaqbil al-mar'a al-filastiniyya* [Law and the Future of Palestinian Women], Jerusalem: Women's Centre for Legal Aid and Counselling.

al-Khateeb, S. (1996) 'The Marriage Contract', *Sisters!*, 14 (August/September).

— (1998) 'Ending Domestic Violence in Muslim Families', *Sisters!* 17.

Kian, A. (1998) 'Women and Politics in Post-Islamist Iran: The Gender-Conscious Drive to Change', *Women Living under Muslim Law Dossier*, 12: 75–96.

Kian-Thiebaut, A. (1999) 'Political and Social Transformations in Post-Islamist Iran', *Middle East Report*, 29 (3): 12–16.

Kondo, A. (2001) 'Muslim Domestic Abuse Examined', *Los Angeles Times*, 24 June 2001, Section B5.

Kressel, K. (1997) *The Process of Divorce*, Northvale, NJ: John Aronson.

Kumar, R. (1994) 'Identity Politics and the Contemporary Indian Feminist Movement', in V. Moghadem (ed.), *Identity Politics and Women: Cultural Reassertions and Feminisms in International Perspective*, Boulder, CO: Westview Press.

Kuttab, E. (1993) 'Palestinian Women in the Intifada: Fighting on Two Fronts', *Arab Studies Quarterly*, 15 (2): 69–85.

— (1995) 'Investing in Half the Population: The World Bank and Economic Policy', *Gender and Public Policy Working Paper*, no. 2, Birzeit: Women's Studies Program, pp. 19–35.

Labadi, F. (2000) 'Report on the Victims of the Hebron Factory Fire', background paper for Palestine Case Study, Comparative Islamic Family Law Project, Birzeit: Institute of Women's Studies.

Lateef, S. (1998) 'Muslim Women in India: A Minority within a Minority', in H. Bodman and N. Tohidi (eds), *Women in Muslim Societies: Diversity within Unity*, Boulder, CO: Lynne Rienner Publishers.

Lau, M. (1995) 'Opening Pandora's Box: The Impact of the Saima Waheed Case on the Legal Status of Women in Pakistan', *Yearbook of Islamic and Middle Eastern Law*, 3: 518.

Lauren, P. G. (1998) *The Evolution of International Human Rights: Visions Seen*, Philadelphia: University of Pennsylvania Press.

Levinson, D. (1989) *Domestic Violence in Cross-Cultural Perspective*, Newbury Park, CA: Sage Publications.

Lieblich, J. (1997) 'Prenuptials About More Than Money', *Houston Chronicle*, 26 April 1997, Section Religion.

— (2001) 'Muslim Leaders Back Marriage Contracts', *Chicago Tribune*, 31 August 2001, Section Metro.

Little, H. M. (1993) 'A World of Differences in Family Law', *Chicago Tribune*, 26 December 1993, Section Womanviews.

Lochack, D. (1993) 'Normalité', in A. J. Armand et al. (eds), *Dictionnaire encyclopédique de théorie et de sociologie du droit*, 2nd edn, Paris: LGDJ.

Lockman, Z. and J. Beinin (1989) *Intifada: The Palestinian Uprising Against Israeli Occupation*, Boston, MA: South End Press.

Lyster, M. (1996) *Child Custody: Building Parenting Agreements that Work*, Berkeley: Nolo Press.

McCloud, A. B. (2000) 'The Scholar and the Fatwa: Legal Issues Facing African American and Immigrant Muslim Communities in the United States', in G. Webb (ed.), *Windows of Faith: Muslim Women Scholar-Activists in the United States*, Syracuse, NY: Syracuse University Press, pp. 136–44.

McCloud, B. T. (1991) 'African-American Muslim Women', in Y. Haddad (ed.), *The Muslims of America*, Oxford: Oxford University Press.

McDonald, J. and G. Hardesty (2001) 'Ruling – Dowry in Prenuptial Agreement: Court Judges Say Islamic Marriage Law Doesn't Apply to California Divorce', *Orange County Region*, 12 April 2001.

el-Magd, A. (2000) 'When the Professor Can't Teach', *Al-Ahram Weekly*, 15–21 June 2000, p. 486.

Maghroui, A. (2001) 'Political Authority in Crisis: Mohammed VI's Morocco', *Middle East Report* 31 (1): 12–17.

Mahmoody, B. (1993) *Not Without My Daughter*, New York: St Martin's Press.

Mani, L. (1989) 'Contentious Traditions: The Debate on Sati in Colonial India', in K. Sangari and S. Vaid (eds), *Recasting Women: Essays in Colonial History*, New Delhi: Kali for Women.

Mansur, M. H. (n.d.) *Maskan al-zaujiyya bayn qanun ijar al-amakin wa qanun al-ahwal al-shakhsiyya*, Alexandria.

Maqsood, R. W. (1998) *The Muslim Marriage Guide*, New Delhi: Goodword Press.

Marquand, R. (1996) 'Islamic Family Values Simmer in a US Melting Pot', *Christian Science Monitor*, 29 January 1996, Section United States.

Mason, M. A. (1994) *From Father's Property to Children's Rights: The History of Child Custody in the United States*, New York: Columbia University Press.

al-Maududi, A. A. (n.d.) *Al-hijab*, Cairo: Dar al-turath al-'arabi.

Mayer, A. (1991) *Islam and Human Rights: Tradition and Politics*, Boulder, CO: Westview Press.

— (1995) 'Cultural Particularism as a Bar to Women's Rights: Reflections on the Middle Eastern Experience', in J. Peters and A. Wolper (eds), *Women's Rights, Human Rights: International Feminist Perspectives*, New York: Routledge.

Mediation and Minority Cultures Conference (2000) Harvard Law School Islamic Legal Studies Program, Program on Negotiation, and Harvard Mediation Program, 15 April 2000.

Memon, K. (1993) 'Wife Abuse in Muslim Community', *Islamic Horizons*, March–April.

Mernissi, F. (1991) *The Veil and the Male Elite: A Feminist Interpretation of Women's Rights in Islam*, Reading, MA: Addison-Wesley.

Mills, L. G. (1999) 'Killing Her Softly: Intimate Abuse and the Violence of State Intervention', *Harvard Law Review*, 113 (2).

Mills, R. (n.d.) 'Women's Rights in the Islamic Prenuptial Agreement: Use Them or Lose Them', *Canadian Society of Muslims* [Internet]. Available from <http://www.muslim-canada.org/prenuptial.htm>

Mir-Hosseini, Z. (1993) *Marriage on Trial: A Study of Islamic Family Law, Iran and Morocco Compared*, London: I.B. Tauris.

— (1996) 'Stretching the Limits: A Feminist Reading of the *Shari'a* in Post-Khomeini Iran', in M. Yamani (ed.), *Feminism and Islam*, New York: New York University Press.

— (2000) *Islam and Gender: The Religious Debate in Contemporary Islam*, Princeton, NJ: Princeton University Press.

Moghissi, H. (1999) *Feminism and Islamic Fundamentalism: The Limits of Postmodern Analysis*, London: Zed Books.

Mohanty, C. T. (1991) 'Under Western Eyes: Feminist Scholarship and Colonial Discourses', in C. T. Mohanty, A. Russo and L. Torres (eds), *Third World Women and the Politics of Feminism*, Bloomington: Indiana University Press.

Moors, A. (1995) *Women, Property and Islam: Palestinian Experiences 1920–1990*, Cambridge: Cambridge University Press.

— (1999) 'Debating Islamic Family Law: Legal Texts and Social Practices', in M. L. Meriwether and J. Tucker (eds), *A Social History of Women and Gender in the Modern Middle East*, Boulder, CO: Westview Press, pp. 141–75.

Mughrabi, F. (1996) 'Opinion Surveys in the Social Sciences', in N. Izzat Said (ed.), *Survey Research and Data Bases in Palestinian Society*, Nablus: Center for Policy Research and Studies (in Arabic), pp. 22–34.

Muslim Women's League (n.d.) 'Gender Equality in Islam' [Internet]. Available from http://www.mwlusa.org/pub_gender.html>

— (n.d.) 'An Islamic Perspective on Divorce' [Internet]. Available from <http://www.mwlusa.org/pub_divorce.html>

Muslim Women's League and Karamah: Muslim Women Lawyers for Human Rights, (1995) *Challenges and Opportunities Facing American Muslim Women* [Internet] United Nations Fourth World Conference on Women, September. Available from <http://www.mwl.usa.org>

Nadir, A. (2001) 'Guiding Toward Harmony: Imams Commit Themselves to Tackling Domestic Violence', *Islamic Horizons*, 78.

National Centre for Social and Criminal Studies (1985) *'Al-masah al-'ijtima'i al-shamil li'l-mujtami' al-misri 1952–1980 (al-'adala)*, Cairo.

National Commission for Poverty Eradication (1998) *Palestine Poverty Report 1998*, Ramallah: Palestinian National Authority.

el-Nimr, R. (1996) 'Women in Islamic Law', in M. Yamani (ed.), *Feminism and Islam: Legal and Literary Perspectives*, New York: New York University Press.

Odujinrin, O. (1993) 'Wife Battering in Nigeria', *Journal of Gynecology and Obstetrics*, 41.

Olawale, A. (1996) *Women and Violence in Kano, Nigeria*, Ibadan: Spectrum Books.

Omorodion, F. (1995) 'The Social Context of Wife Battering', in J. Effah, D. Mbachu and S. Onyegbula (eds), *Unequal Rights: Discriminatory Laws and Practices Against Women in Nigeria*, Lagos: Constitutional Rights Project.

Othman, Z. (1998) 'The Palestinian Model Parliament: Gender and Legislation: Between Renewal and Stereotype' (in Arabic), *Palestine Policy*, 19: 57–85.

Owen, R. (1990) *State, Power and Politics in the Making of the Modern Middle East*, London: Routledge.

Palestinian Legislative Council (2000) *Directory of Laws 1996–2000*, Ramallah: PLC (in Arabic).

Pannikar, R. (1982) 'Is the Notion of Human Rights a Western Concept?' *Diogenes*, 120 (Winter).

PCBS (Palestinian Central Bureau of Statistics) (1998) *Report on the 1997 Population and Housing Census*, Ramallah: PCBS.

— (1999a) *Ownership and Access to Resources Survey*, Ramallah: PCBS.

— (1999b) *Labour Force Survey: Main Findings (April–June 1999 Round, October 1999*, Ramallah: PCBS.

Pearl, D. (1985–86) 'Cross-Cultural Interaction Between Islamic Law and Other Legal Systems', *Cleveland State Law Review*, 34 (113).

— (1995) 'The Application of Islamic Law in the English Courts', *Yearbook of Islamic and Middle Eastern Law*, 2 (3).

Pearl, D. and W. Menski (1998) *Muslim Family Law*, 3rd edn, London: Sweet and Maxwell.

Pederson, J. and R. Hooper (1998) *Development Assistance in the West Bank and Gaza*, Oslo: Fagbevegelsens Senter for Forskning Utredning og Dokumentasjon.

Peteet, J. (1987) 'La Justice au Quotidien dans les Camps Palestiniennes au Liban', *Revue d'Etudes Palestiniennes*, 24: 25–39.

Peters, R. (1990) 'Murder on the Nile: Homicide Trials in 19th Century Egypt', *Die Welt des Islams*, 30: 98–116.

Philips, A. A. B. and J. Jones (1985) *Polygamy in Islaam*, Riyadh: International Islamic Publishing House.

al-Qaradawi, Y. (n.d.) *The Lawful and the Prohibited in Islam: al-haram wal-haram fil islam*, trans. K. El-Helbawy, M. M. Siddiqui and S. Shukry, Indianapolis, IN: American Trust Publications.

al-Qasem, A. (1996) 'Introduction to the Palestinian Authority Basic Law', *Palestine Report* 16.

— (1992–94) 'Commentary on the Draft Basic Law for the Palestinian National Authority in the Transitional Period' *Palestine Yearbook of International Law*, 7: 189–203.

Qassem, Y. (2002) 'Law of the Family (Personal Status Law)', in N. Bernard-Maugiron and B. Dupret (eds), *Egypt and Its Laws*, The Hague: Kluwer Law International, pp. 19–36.

Quick, A. H. (1998) '*Al-Mu'allaqa*: The Muslim Woman Between Divorce and Real Mar riage', *Journal of Islamic Law*, 3 (1): 27.

Quraishi, A. (1999) 'The Islamic Marriage Contract: Diasporas and Minorities', in *The Islamic Marriage Contract: An International Conference*, Harvard Law School Islamic Legal Studies Program, 29–31 January (audiotape).

— (2001) 'The Plurality of Islamic Law', *Azizah Magazine*, Summer: 20.

Rahman, F. (1982) *Islam and Modernity: Transformation of an Intellectual Tradition*, Chicago, IL: University of Chicago Press.

Ramsis, Nadia (supervisor) (1991) *Hayat al-mar'a wa sahhituha*, Cairo: Sina' li'l-nashr.

Randall, V. (1998) 'Gender and Power: Women Engage the State', in V. Randall and G. Waylen (eds), *Gender Politics and the State*, London: Routledge, pp. 185–205.

Randall, V. and G. Waylen (1998) *Gender, Politics and the State*, London: Routledge.

Rapoport, Y. (2000) 'Matrimonial Gifts in Early Islamic Egypt', *Islamic Law and Society*, 7 (1).

Rasmusen, E. and J. E. Stake (1998) 'Law and the New American Family: Lifting the Veil of Ignorance: Personalizing the Marriage Contract', *Indiana Law Journal*, 7 (2).

Reed, A. (1996) 'Transnational Non-judicial Divorces', *Loyola of Los Angeles International and Comparative Law Journal*, 18: 311, n.1.

Robinson, G. (1997) 'The Politics of Legal Reform in Palestine', *Journal of Palestine Studies*, 27 (105): 51–61.

Rouse, S. (1998) 'The Outsider(s) Within: Sovereignty and Citizenship in Pakistan', in P.

Jeffrey and A. Basu (eds), *Appropriating Gender: Women's Activism and Politicized Religion in South Asia*, New York: Routledge.

al-Sadlaan, S. G. (1999) *The Fiqh of Marriage in the Light of the Quran and Sunnah*, trans. J. M. Zarabozo, Boulder, CO: Al-Basheer Company for Publications and Translations.

Said, N. (1998) 'Muslim Professional Women: Some Perspectives on Perceptions', *Islamic Legal Studies Program Panel*, Harvard Law School Worldwide Alumni Congress, 12 June 1998, Islamic Legal Studies Program, Rome, Italy.

Sayigh, Y. (1997) *Armed Struggle and the Search for a State: The Palestinian National Movement 1949–1993*, Oxford: Oxford University Press.

Sciolino, E. (1996) 'The Many Faces of Islamic Law', *New York Times*, 13 October 1996, Section 4.

Seager, J. (1997) *The State of Women in the World Atlas*, London: Penguin Books.

al-Shabini, A. A. (1995) 'Al-mar'a al-misriyya wa'l-ahwal al-shakhsiyya', in Marlene Tadros et al. (eds), *Al-muwatina al-manqusa: tahmish al-mar'a fi misr*, Cairo: Markaz al-dirasat wa'l-ma'lumat al-qanuniyya, pp. 136–99.

Shaham, R. (1995) 'Custom, Islamic Law and Statutory Legislation: Marriage Registration and Minimum Age at Marriage in the Egyptian Shari'a Courts', *Islamic Law and Society*, 2 (3): 258–81.

— (1999) 'State, Feminists and Islamists – the Debate over Stipulations in Marriage Contracts in Egypt', *Bulletin of the School of Oriental and African Studies*, 62: 462–83.

Shaheed, F. (1994) 'The Experience in Pakistan', in M. Davies (ed.), *Women and Violence: Realities and Responses Worldwide*, London: Zed Books.

Shaheen, J. (1997) *Arab and Muslim Stereotyping*, Washington, DC: Georgetown University Center for Muslim and Christian Understanding.

Shah-Kazemi, S. N. (2001) *Untying the Knot, Muslim Women, Divorce and Shariah*, Oxford: Nuffield Foundation.

Shalhoub-Kevorkian, N. (1999) 'Law, Politics, and Violence Against Women: A Case Study of Palestinians in Israel', *Law and Policy*, 21 (2): 189–211.

Shaltut, M. (n.d.) *Al-islam 'aqida wa shari'a*, Cairo: Dar al-shuruq.

Sharabi, H. (1988) *Neopatriarchy: A Theory of Distorted Change in Arab Society*, New York: Oxford University Press.

al-Sharif, H. A. H. (1987) *Al-zawaj al-'urfi fi nahiyat al-shar'iyya wa'l-qanuniyya wa'l-ijtima'iyya*, Cairo: Al-maktaba al-qanuniyya.

Shehadeh, R. (1980) *The West Bank and the Rule of Law*, Geneva: International Commission of Jurists.

— (1988) *Occupier's Law: Israel and the West Bank*, 2nd edn, Washington, DC: Institute for Palestine Studies.

— (1997) *From Occupation to Interim Accords: Israel and the Palestinian Territories*, The Hague: Kluwer Law International.

Sh'hada, N. (1999) *Gender and Politics in Palestine: Discourse Analysis of the Palestinian Authority and Islamists*, Working Paper Series 307, The Hague: Institute of Social Studies.

Shmais, A. (1994) *Al-mar'a wa'l-talaq*, Cairo.

Shukri, A. et al (1995) *Al-hayat al-yaumiyya li-fuqara' al-madina*, Alexandria: Dar al-ma'rifa al-jami'iyya.

Siddiqui, M. (2000) 'The Concept of *Wilaya* in Hanafi Law: Authority Versus Consent in al-Fatawa al-'Alamgiri', *Yearbook of Islamic and Middle Eastern Law*, 5: 71.

Singh, K. (1994) 'Obstacles to Women's Rights in India', in R. Cook (ed.), *Human Rights of Women: National and International Perspectives*, Philadelphia: University of Pennsylvania Press.

Siyam, E. (1996) 'Ummiyat al-anath wa mumarisat al-tamyiz didd al-mar'a', in Hassan Abu Bakr (ed.), *Al-awda' wa'l-mushkilat al-qanuniyya li'l-nisa' fi'l-rif wa'l-hadar*, Cairo: Amideast.

el-Solh, C. F. and Mabro, J. (eds) (1994) *Muslim Women's Choices: Religious Belief and Social Reality*, Oxford: Berg Publishers.

Sonbol, A. El-Azhary (1996) *Women, the Family and Divorce Laws in Islamic History*, Syracuse, NY: Syracuse University Press.

Spectorsky, S. (1993) *Chapters on Marriage and Divorce: Responses of Ibn Hanbal and Ibn Raywayh*. Austin: University of Texas Press.

Sreberny-Mohammadi, A. (1991) 'The Global and the Local in International Communications', in J. Curran and M. Gurevitch (eds), *Mass Media and Society*, London: Edward Arnold, pp. 118–38.

Stowasser, B. (1998) 'Gender Issues and Contemporary Quran Interpretation', in Y. Y. Haddad and J. Esposito (eds), *Islam, Gender, and Social Change*, Oxford: Oxford University Press, pp. 30–45.

Sullivan, D. (1995) 'The Public/Private Distinction in International Human Rights Law', in J. Peters and A. Wolper (eds), *Women's Rights, Human Rights: International Feminist Perspectives*, New York: Routledge.

Svensson, J. (2000) *Women's Human Rights and Islam: A Study of Three Attempts at Accommodation*, Lund, Norway: Lund Studies in History of Religions, Vol. 12.

Swirski, B. (2000) 'The Citizenship of Jewish and Palestinian Women in Israel', in S. Joseph (ed.), *Gender and Citizenship in the Middle East*, Syracuse, NY: Syracuse University Press.

Syed, I. N. (1996) 'Domestic Violence: Destruction of the Family', *al-Talib*, University of California Los Angeles (February).

Tabiu, M. (1990–91) 'Nature and Effects of Unlawful Marriages in Maliki Law', *Islamic and Comparative Law Quarterly*, 10–11: 77.

Tadross, M. (1995) 'Women Between Reality and Law', in A. Al-Shabiti and A. Abdulhakim (eds), *Partial Citizenship: The Marginalization of Women in Egypt*, Cairo: Legal Research and Resource Center for Human Rights (in Arabic).

— (1998) *Rightless Women, Heartless Men: Egyptian Women and Domestic Violence*, Cairo: Legal Research and Resource Center for Human Rights.

Taraki, L. (1990) 'The Development of Political Consciousness among Palestinians in the Occupied Territories, 1967–1987', in J. Nassar and R. Heacock (eds), *Intifada: Palestine at the Crossroads*, New York: Praeger, pp. 53–71.

— (1995) 'Society and Gender in Palestine: International Agencies', *Gender and Public Policy*, *Working Paper*, no. 2, Birzeit: Women's Studies Program, pp. 37–66.

Thompson, E. (2000) *Colonial Citizens*, New York: Columbia University Press.

Thorton, M. (1995) *Public and Private: Feminist Legal Debates*, Oxford: Oxford University Press.

Tibi, B. (1990) 'The European Tradition of Human Rights and the Culture of Islam', in A. An-Na'im and F. Deng (eds), *Human Rights in Africa: Cross-Cultural Perspectives*, Washington, DC: Brookings Institute.

— (1994) 'Islamic Law/*Shari'a*, Human Rights, Universal Morality and International Relations', *Human Rights Quarterly*, 16.

Todd, D. (1997) 'Love, Marriage and Islam: Strict Religious Rules on Marriage Torment Some Muslim Women in Canada', *Toronto Star*, 30 October 1997, Section Life.

Toubia, N. (1994) 'Women's Reproductive and Sexual Rights', in Center for Women's Global Leadership, *Gender Violence and Women's Human Rights in Africa*, New Brunswick, NJ: Center for Women's Global Leadership.

Toubia, N. et al. (1994) *Al-mar'a al-'arabiyya: lamha 'an al-tanawwu' wa'l-taghyhir*, Cairo: The Population Council.

UN (2000) *The World's Women 2000: Trends and Statistics*, New York: United Nations.

UNICEF (2000) *Domestic Violence Against Women and Girls*, Florence, Italy: Innocenti Research Centre.

UNSCO (Office of the United Nations Special Coordinator in the Occupied Territories) (1999) *Rule of Law Development in the West Bank and Gaza Strip*, Gaza: UNSCO.

Usher, G. (1997) 'The Islamist Movement and the Palestinian Authority: An Interview with Bassam Jarrar', in J. Beinin and J. Stork (eds), *Political Islam: Essays from Middle East Report*, London: I.B. Tauris, pp. 335–8.

Wadud, A. (1999) *Quran and Woman*, 2nd edn, Oxford: Oxford University Press.

— (2000) 'Alternative Qur'anic Interpretation and the Status of Muslim Women', in G. Webb (ed.), *Windows of Faith: Muslim Women Scholar-Activists in North America*, Syracuse, NY: Syracuse University Press.

Walley, C. (1997) 'Searching for Strategies: Feminism, Anthropology and the Global Debate over Female Genital Operations,' *Cultural Anthropology* 12 (3).

Walter, N. (1999) 'The Mullah Who Made Me Change My Views on Islam', *The Independent* (London), 7 May 1999.

Watanabe, T. (2000) 'US Freedoms Give American Muslims Influence Beyond Their Numbers', *Los Angeles Times*, 29 December 2000.

Watt, W. M. (1968) *Islamic Political Thought*, Edinburgh: Edinburgh University Press.

Webb, G. (ed.) (2000) *Windows of Faith: Muslim Women Scholar-Activists in North America*, Syracuse, NY: Syracuse University Press.

Weisberg, M. (1992) 'Balancing Cultural Identity Against Individual Liberty: Civil Court Review of Ecclesiastical Judgments', *University of Michigan Journal of Law Reform*, 995.

Weisbrod, C. (1999) 'Gender-Based Analysis of World Religions and the Law: Universals and Particulars: A Comment on Women's Human Rights and Religious Marriage Contracts', *Southern California Review of Law and Women's Studies*, 9 (77).

Welchman, L. (1988) 'The Development of Islamic Family Law in the Legal System of Jordan', *International and Comparative Law Quarterly*, 37 (4): 868–86.

— (1999) *Islamic Family Law: Text and Practice in Palestine*, Jerusalem: Women's Centre for Legal Aid and Counselling.

— (2000) *Beyond the Code: Muslim Family Law and the Shar'i Judiciary in the Palestinian West Bank*, The Hague: Kluwer Law International.

— (2001) 'Jordan: Capacity, Consent and Under-age Marriage in Muslim Family Law', *International Survey of Family Law*: 243–65.

Winton, B. (1993) 'Domestic Violence: Beatings, Bullets', *Phoenix Gazette*, 5 October 1993, Section Front.

Woodman, G. R. (1993), 'The Idea of Legal Pluralism', in B. Dupret, M. Berger and L. al-Zwaini (eds), *Legal Pluralism in the Arab World*, The Hague: Kluwer Law International, pp. 3–19.

Women, Law, and Development International (1996) *State Responses to Domestic Violence: Current Status and Needed Improvements*, Washington, DC: Women, Law and Development International.

Women's Centre for Legal Aid and Counselling (1997) *Nahu al-musawa: al-qanun wa'l-mar'a al-filastiniyya* [Towards Equality: The Law and Palestinian Women], Jerusalem: WCLAC.

— (1998) 'Declaration of the Final Session of the Model Parliament in Gaza', unpublished document (in Arabic).

Women's Rights Ministry [Pakistan] (1985) *Battered Housewives in Pakistan*, Islamabad: Women's Ministry.

Yahia, M. M. (1998) 'The Incidence of Wife Abuse and Battering and Some Socio-demographic Correlates as Revealed in Two National Surveys in Palestinian Society', Ramallah: Palestinian Authority, Besan Center for Research and Development.

Yamani, M. (ed.) (1996) *Feminism and Islam: Legal and Literary Perspectives*, New York: New York University Press.

Yassin, E. S. (1986) 'Development of Plural Structure of Law in Egypt, a Sunni-Islamic Society', in M. Chiba (ed.), *Asian Indigenous Law in Interaction with Received Law*, London and New York: KPI, pp. 13–80.

Yuval-Davis, N. (1997) *Gender and Nation*, London: Sage Publications.

el-Zanaty, F. (1995) *Egypt Demographic and Health Survey 1995*, Cairo: National Population Council.

— (1999) Seminar on 'Marriage Patterns in Egypt', International Population Council in collaboration with the US AID Project on Population Policies, Cairo.

Zorn, J. (1999) 'Women's Rights are Human Rights: International Law and the Culture of Domestic Violence', in D. A. Counts, J. Brown and J. Campbell (eds), *To Have and to Hit: Cultural Perspectives on Wife Beating*, 2nd edn, Urbana and Chicago: University of Illinois Press.

Zubaida, S. (1988) *Islam, People and the State*, London: I.B. Tauris.

Zulfikar, M. (1995) 'Wad'a al-mar'a al-misriyya fi dau' al-ittifaqiyya li'l-qada' 'ala kafat ashkal al-tamyiz didd al-mar'a', in A. Abdullah (ed.), *Al-waqi' al-qanuni li'l-mar'a al-misriyya*, Cairo: Amideast, pp. 118–48.

Zulfikar, M. and H. al-Sadda (1996) 'Haul mashru' tatawwir namudhij 'aqd al-zawaj', *Hagar*, 3–4: 251–60.

Index

Zed's titles on women's rights

A.A. An-Na'im, *Cultural Transformation and Human Rights in Africa*

A.A. An-Na'im, *Islamic Family Law in a Changing World*

Wolfgang Benedek, Esther M. Kisaakye and Gerd Oberleitner, *The Human Rights of Women*

Kum-Kum Bhavnani, John Foran and Priya Kurian, *Feminist Futures: Re-imagining Women, Culture and Development*

I. Bibars, *Victims and Heroines: Women, Welfare and the Egyptian State*

Gabriele Griffin and Rosi Braidotti, *Thinking Differently: A Reader in European Women's Studies*

M. Gutierrez, *Macro-Economics: Making Gender Matter*

H. Moghissi, *Feminism and Islamic Fundamentalism: The Limits of Post-modern Analysis*

Ranjani K Murthy and Lakshmi Sankaran, *Denial and Distress: Gender, Poverty and Human Rights in Asia*

R.P Petchesky, *Global Prescriptions: Gendering Health and Human Rights*

M. Poya, *Women, Work and Islamism: Ideology and Resistance in Iran*